Grade K

Addison-Wesley Mathematics

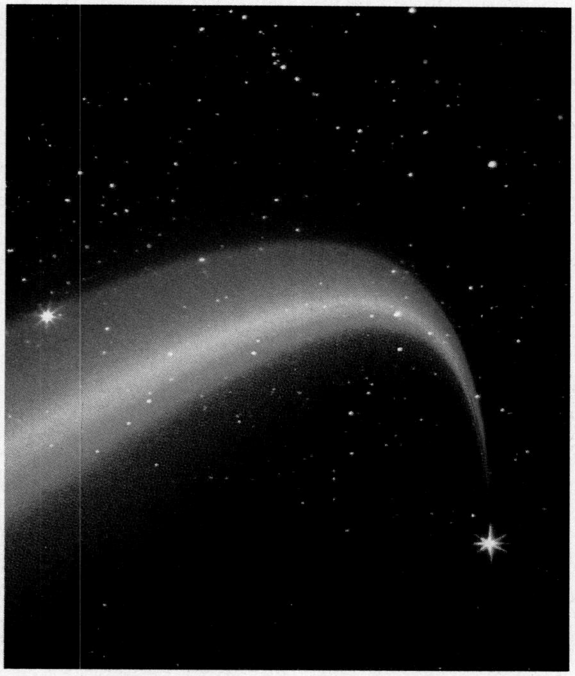

Robert E. Eicholz
Sharon L. Young
Phares G. O'Daffer
Carne S. Barnett
Randall I. Charles

Stanley R. Clemens
Freddie L. Renfro
Gloria F. Gilmer
Mary M. Thompson
Andy Reeves
Carol A. Thornton

Addison-Wesley Publishing Company

Menlo Park, California ■ Reading, Massachusetts ■ New York
Don Mills, Ontario ■ Wokingham, England ■ Amsterdam ■ Bonn
Sydney ■ Singapore ■ Tokyo ■ Madrid ■ San Juan ■ Paris
Seoul ■ Milan ■ Mexico City ■ Taipei

Program Advisors

John A. Dossey Professor of Mathematics
Illinois State University, Normal, Illinois

Bonnie Armbruster Associate Professor, Center for the Study of Reading
University of Illinois, Champaign, Illinois

Karen L. Ostlund Associate Professor of Science Education
Southwest Texas State University, San Marcos, Texas

Betty C. Lee Assistant Principal
Ferry Elementary School, Detroit, Michigan

William J. Driscoll Chairman, Department of Mathematical Sciences
Central Connecticut State University, New Britain, Connecticut

David C. Brummett Educational Consultant
Palo Alto, California

Multicultural Advisors

Ann Armand-Miller
Bill Bray
Valerna Carter
Moyra Contreras
Gloria Dobbins
Paula Duckett
Barbara Fong
Jeanette Haseyama
James Hopkins
Carol Artiga MacKenzie
Gloria Maldonado
Mattie McCloud
Dolores Mena
Irene Miura
Marsha Muhammad
A. Barretto Ogilvie
Margarita Perez
May-Blossom Wilkinson
Glenna Yee

Contributing Writers

Betsy Franco
Mary Heinrich
Penny Holland
Marilyn Jacobson
Ann Muench
Gini Shimabukuro
Marny Sorgen
Connie Thorpe
Sandra Ward
Judith K. Wells

Executive Editor

Diane H. Fernández

Cover Photo Credit: Don Carroll/The Image Bank

ISBN: 0-201-86500-9

17 18 19 20 –VO64- 10 09 08

Text printed on recycled paper.

Contents

Chapter 8 Numbers to 12

Chapter 9 Measuring

Chapter 10 Time and Money

Chapter 11 Putting Together

Chapter 12 Taking Away

Chapter 13 Sharing

Chapter 14 Numbers to 31

Chapter 15 Counting Patterns

I
Sorting and Classifying

Workmat

Theme: Autumn

Name ______________________________

I can sort animals.
I can show what does not belong.

Name ______________________________

I can sort the leaves by color.

I can tell which leaf does not belong.

Name ______________________________

I can sort hats in many ways.

I can sort balloons in many ways.

Name ______________________________

I can show what goes on each shelf.

I can tell what does not belong in each box.

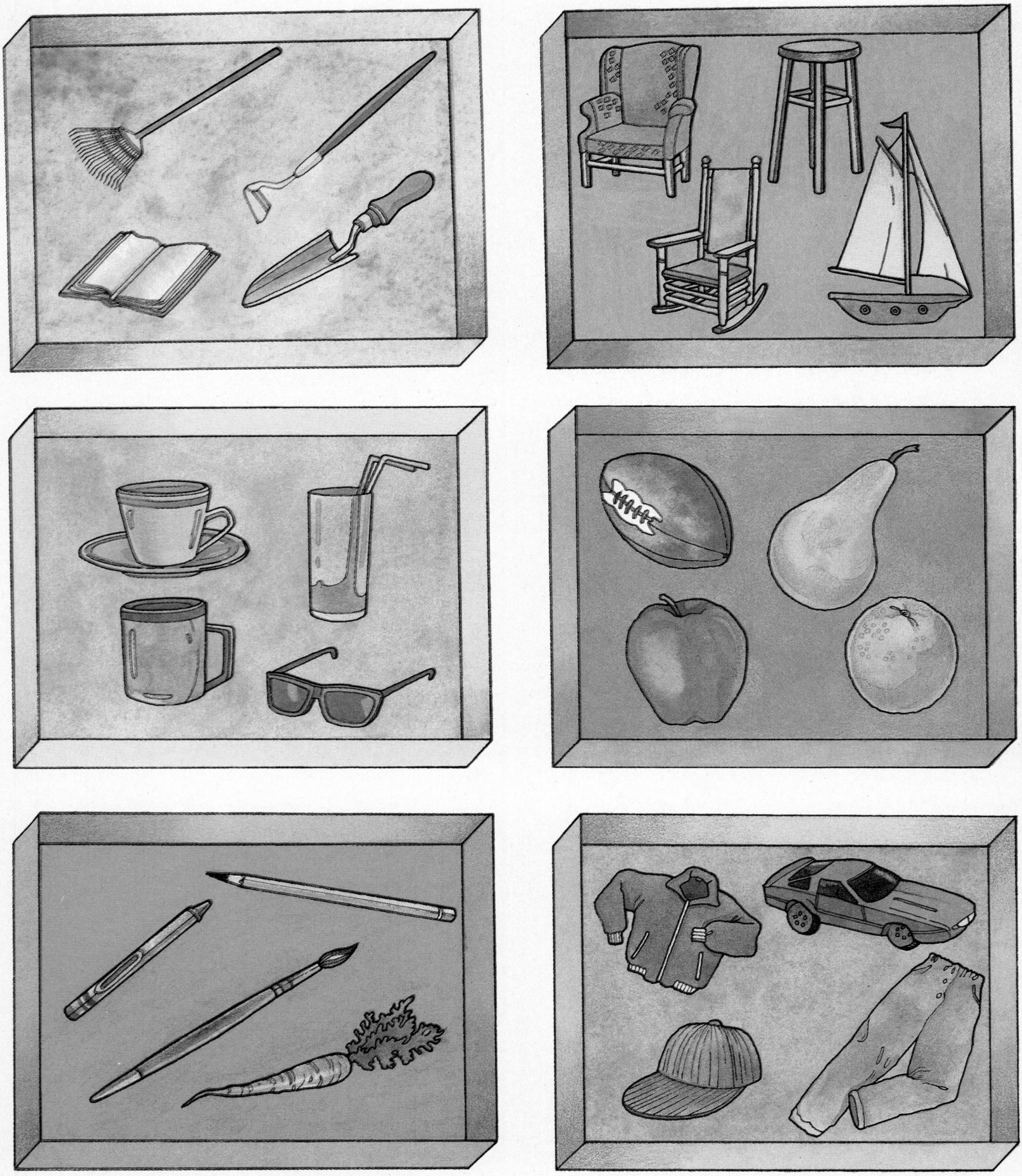

Name ________________________________

I can tell what belongs inside and outside.

I can show where each animal belongs.

Name ____________________

UNDERSTAND
FIND DATA
PLAN
ESTIMATE
SOLVE
CHECK

I can listen for clues in a story.

I can listen for clues in a riddle.

UNDERSTAND
FIND DATA
PLAN
ESTIMATE
SOLVE
CHECK

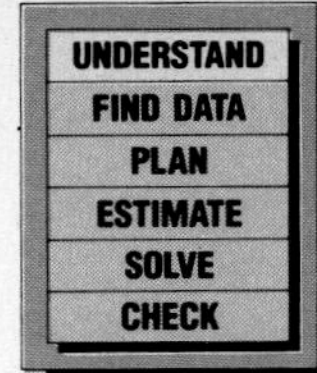

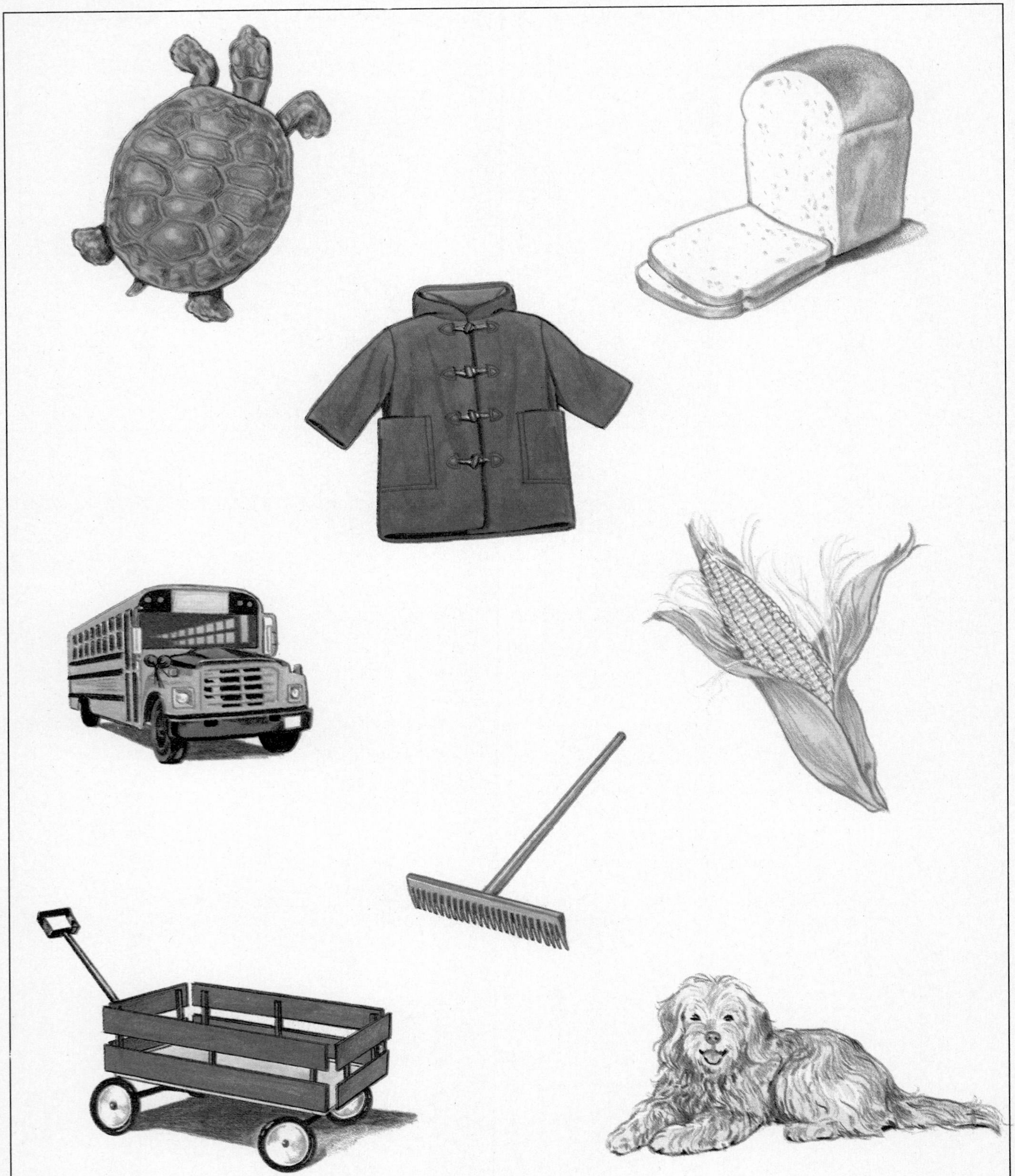

Name ______________________________

I can sort by color and shape.
I can show what goes in each box.

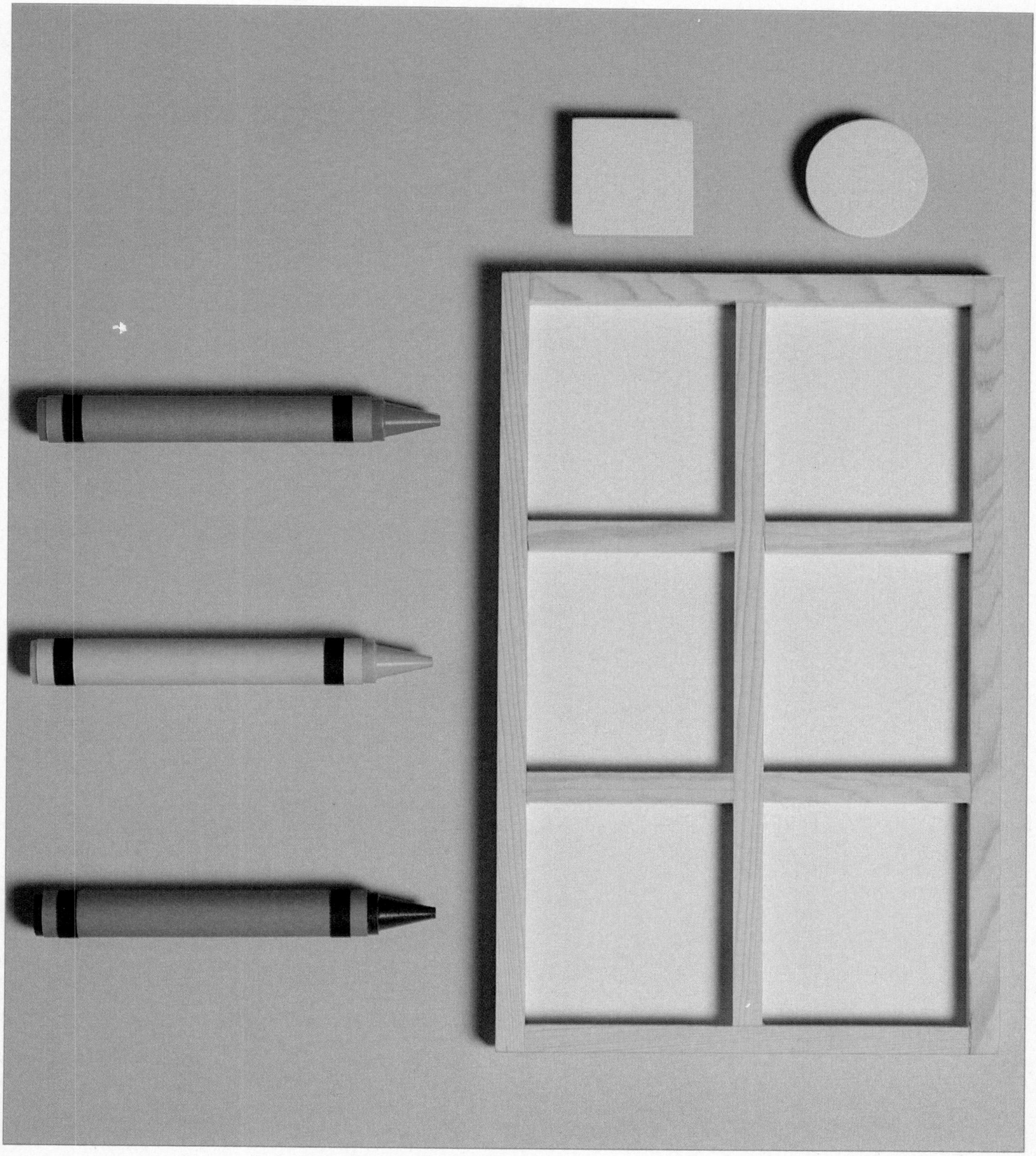

I can show what goes in each box.

Name ______________________________

Name ________________________________

I can put the pumpkins where they belong.

2

Working with Shapes

Workmat

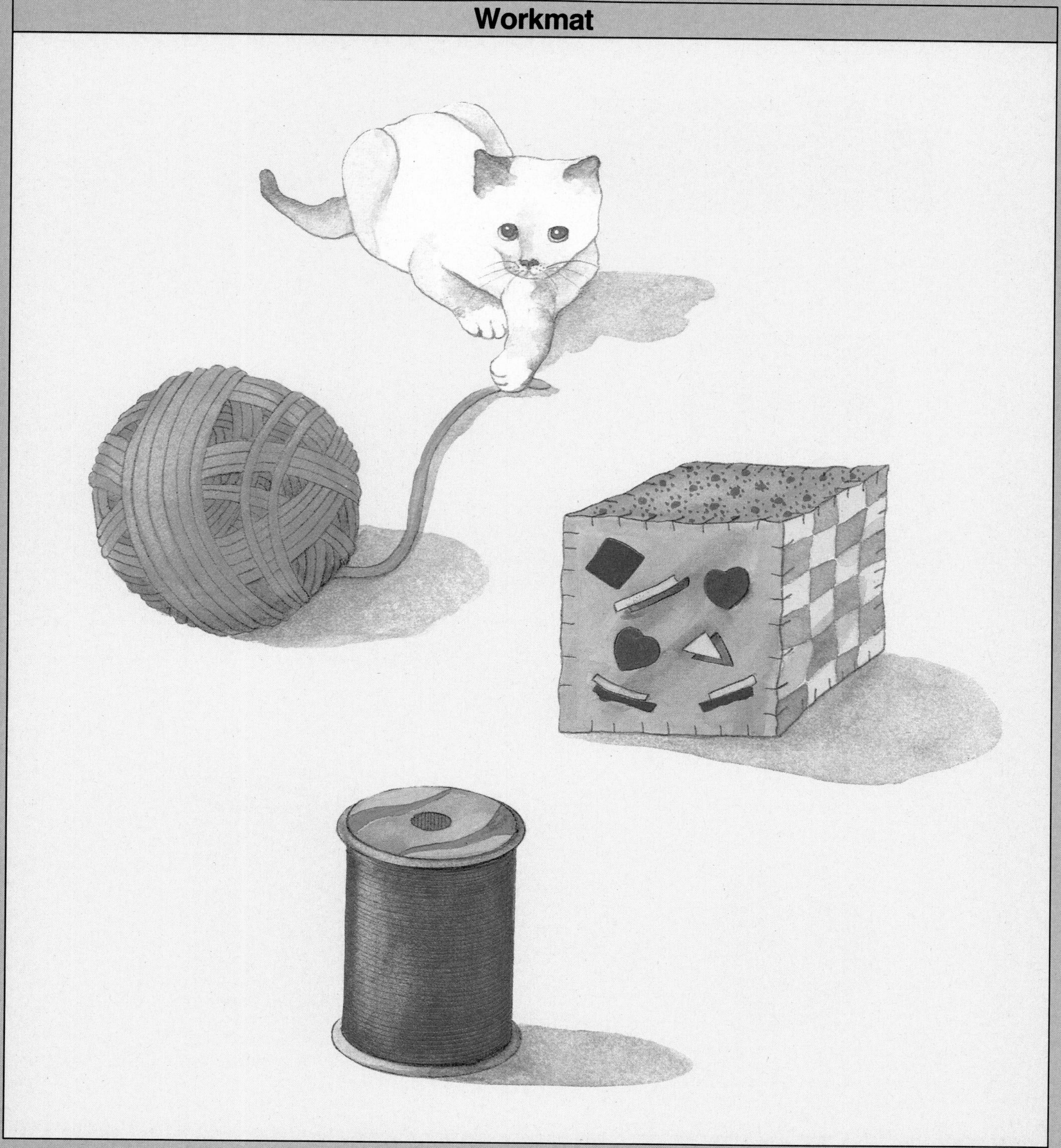

Theme: Things to Play With

Name ____________________

I can explore solid shapes.
I can tell which shapes will roll.

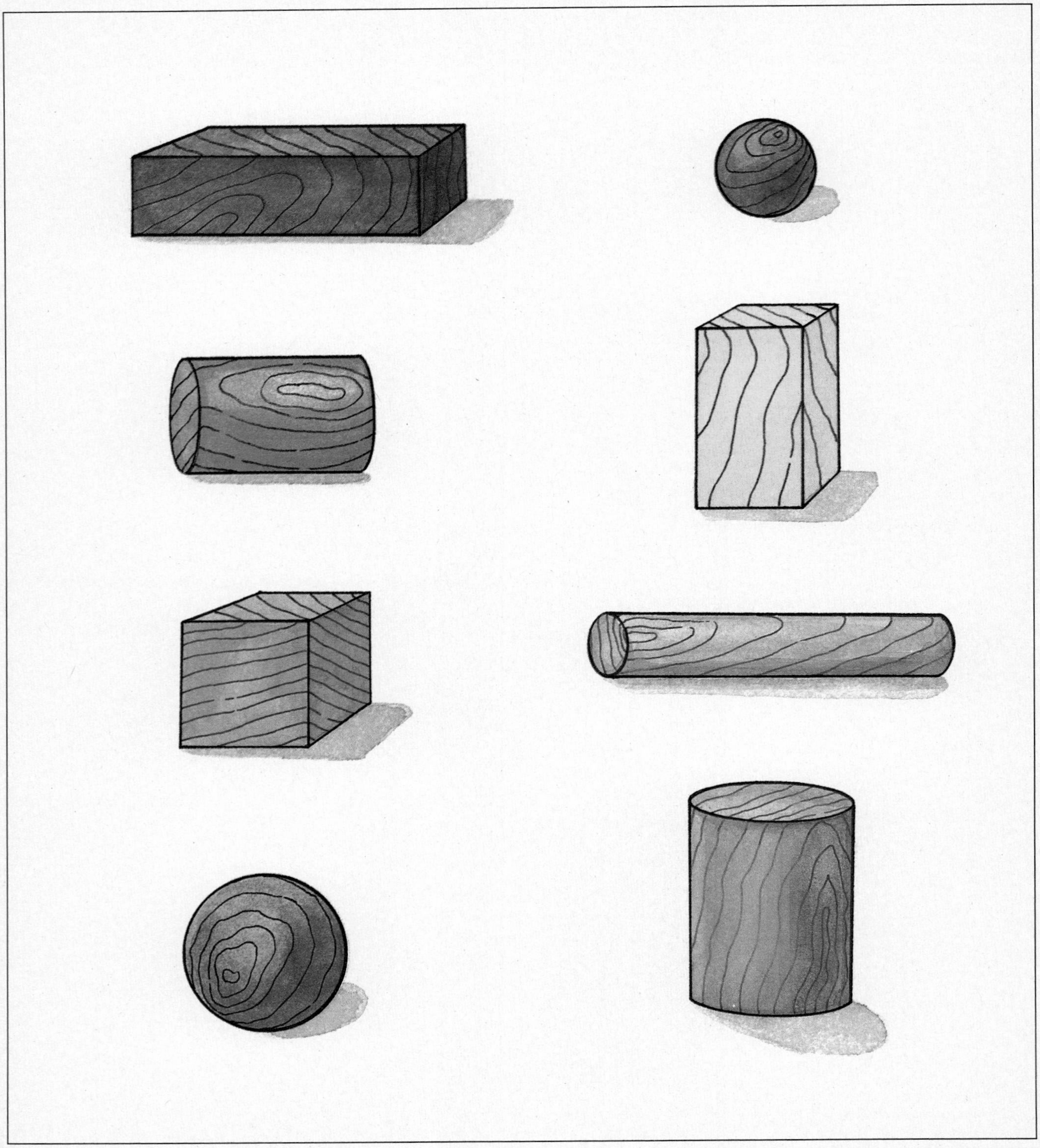

Name ______________________________

I can sort ball, box, and can shapes.

I can find objects with the same shape.

 ball	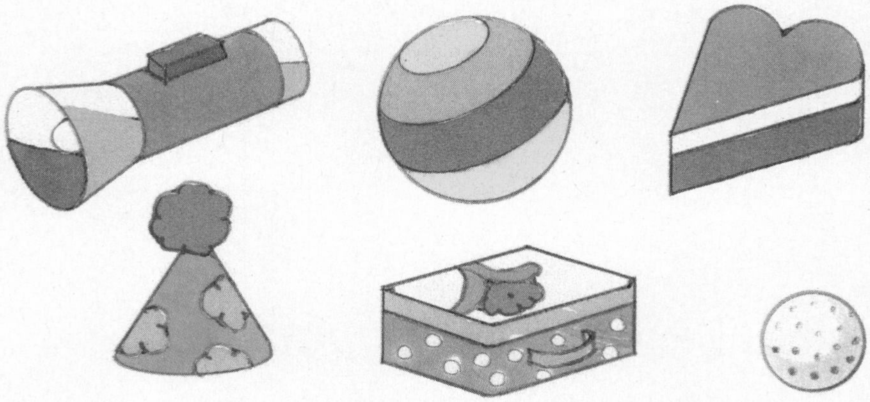
 box	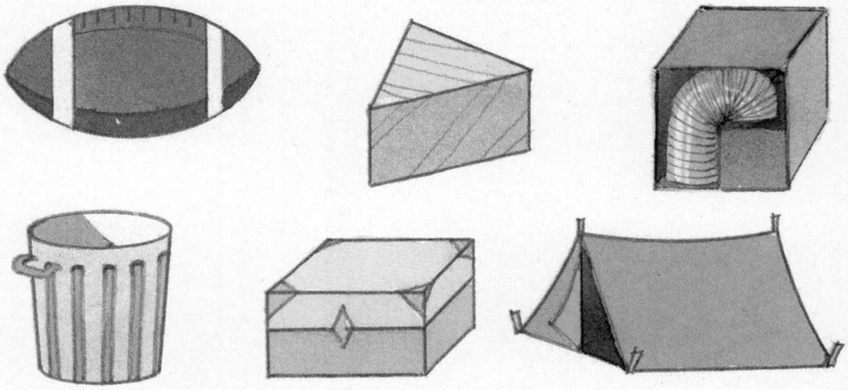
 can	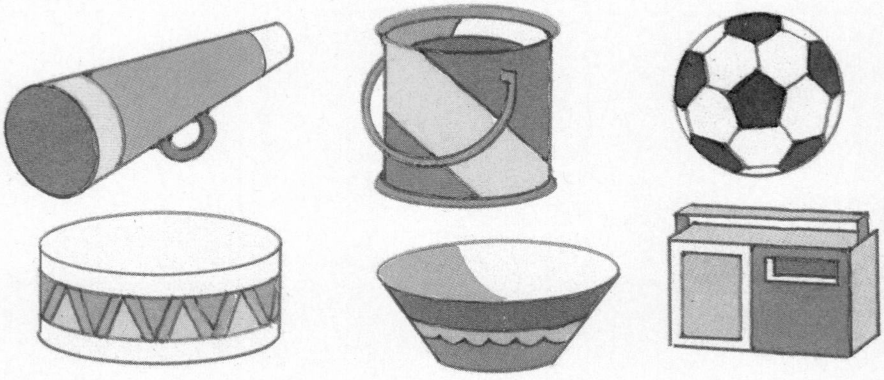

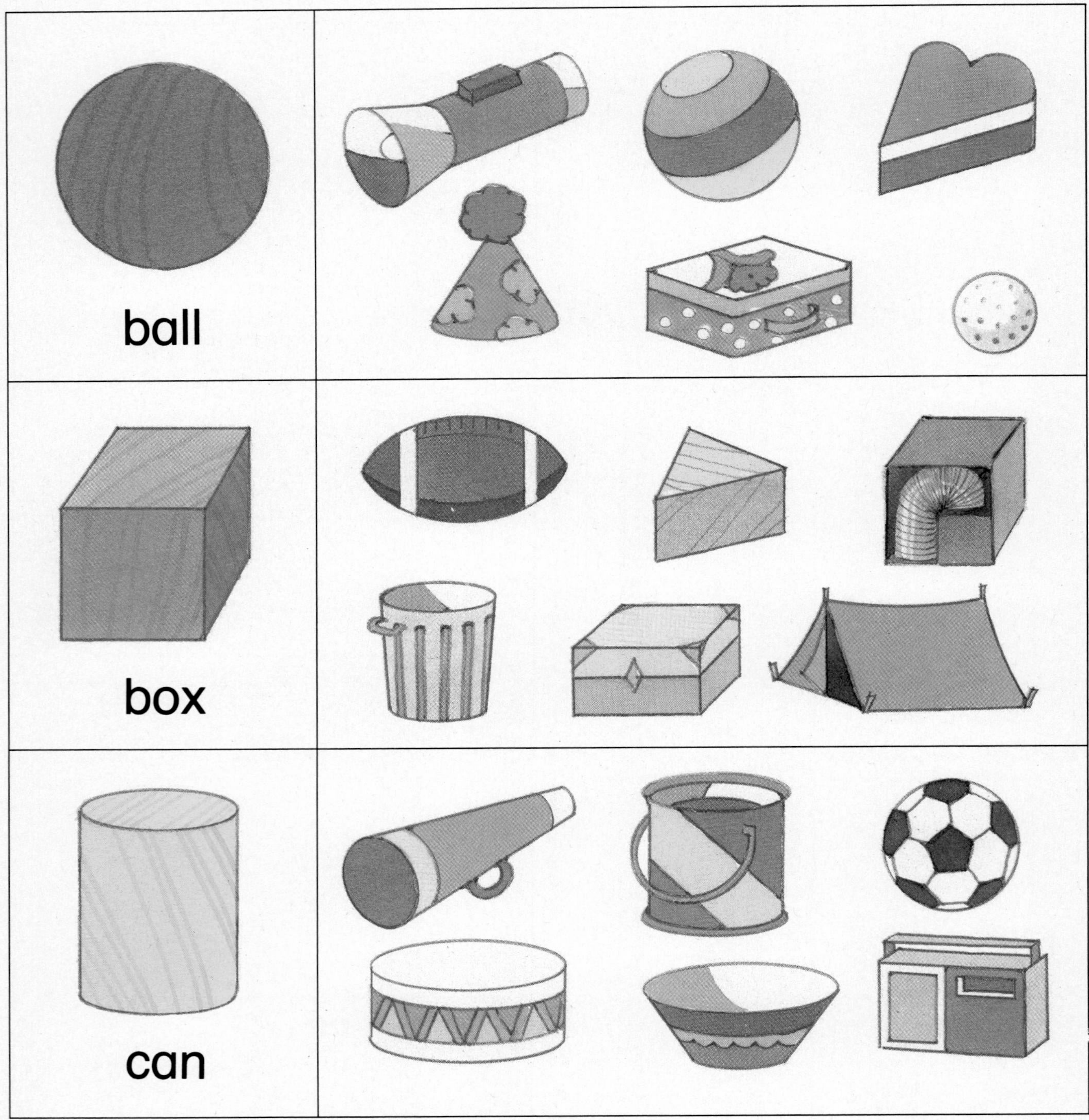

Name ______________________________

I can find circles, squares, and triangles in solid shapes.

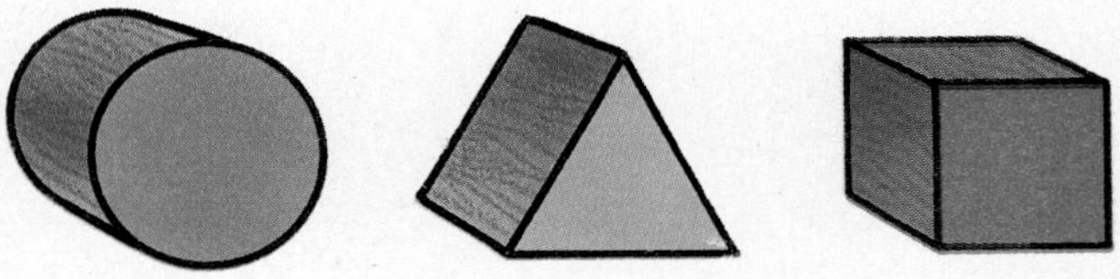

I can find matching shapes.

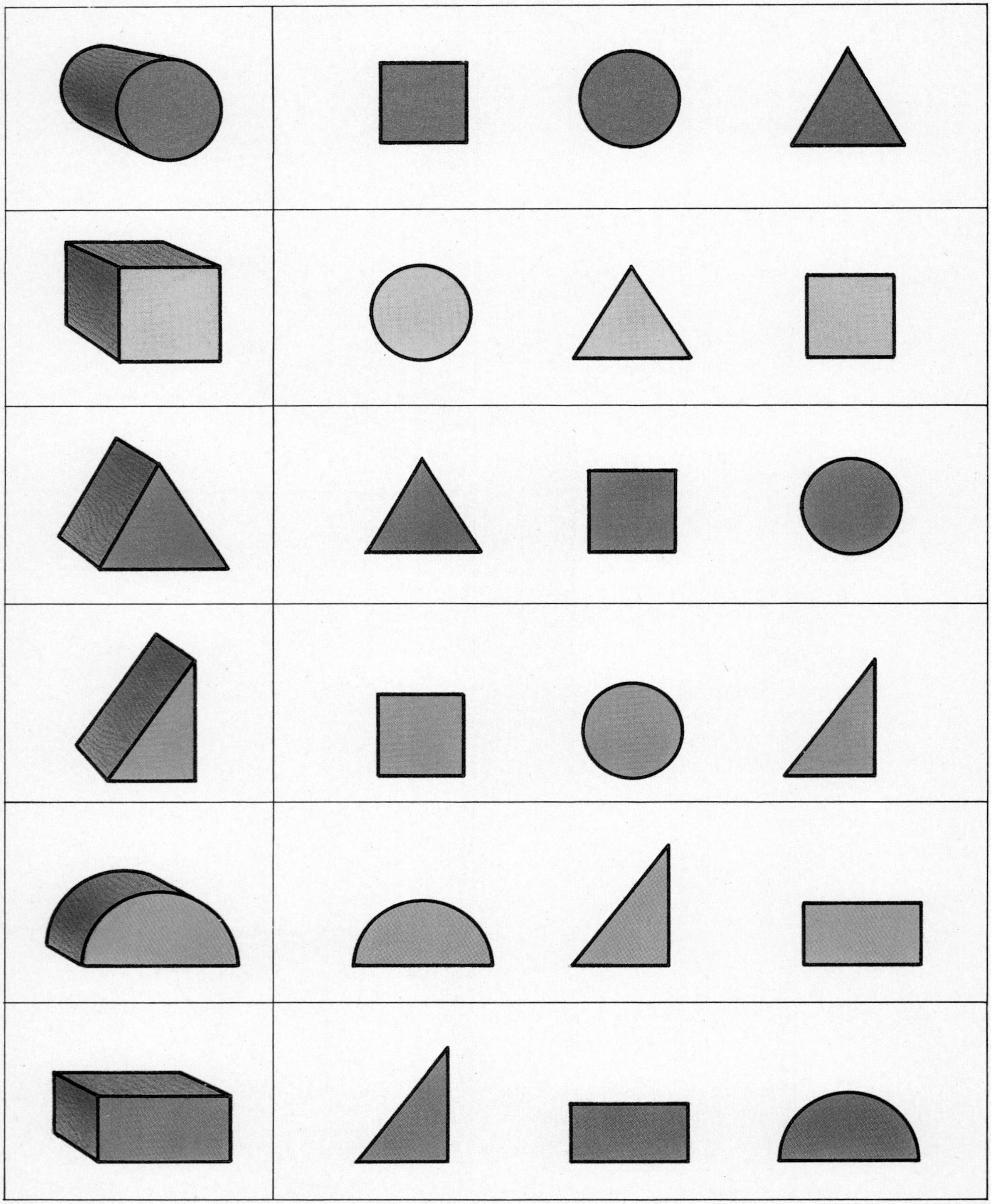

Name ____

I can sort shapes.

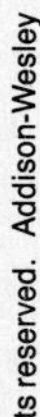

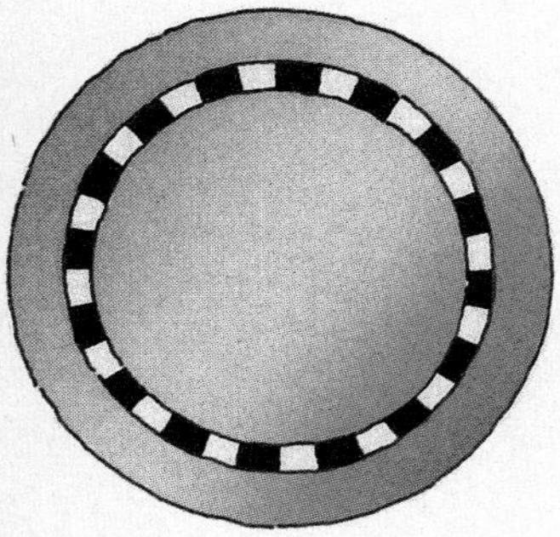

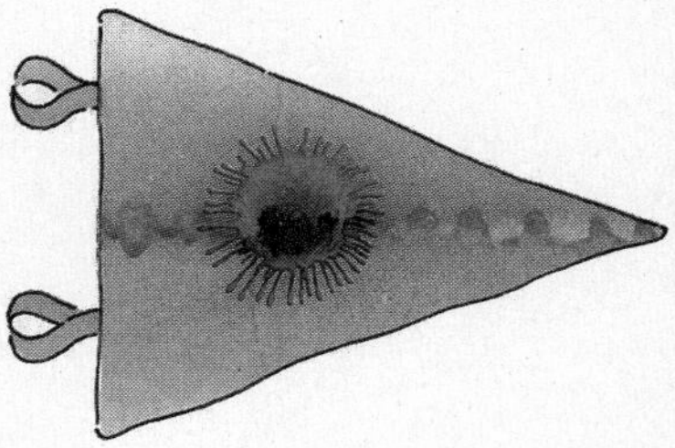

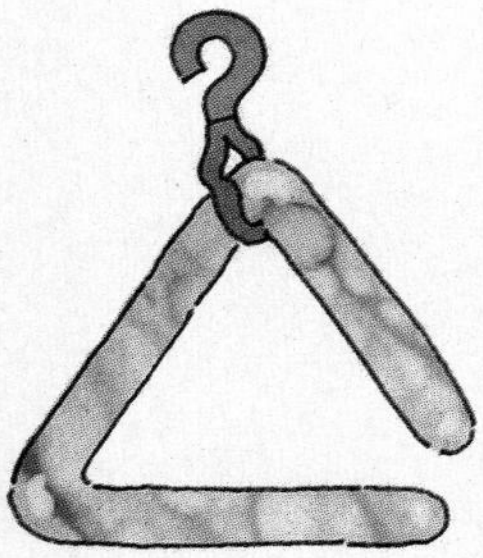

I can sort shapes.

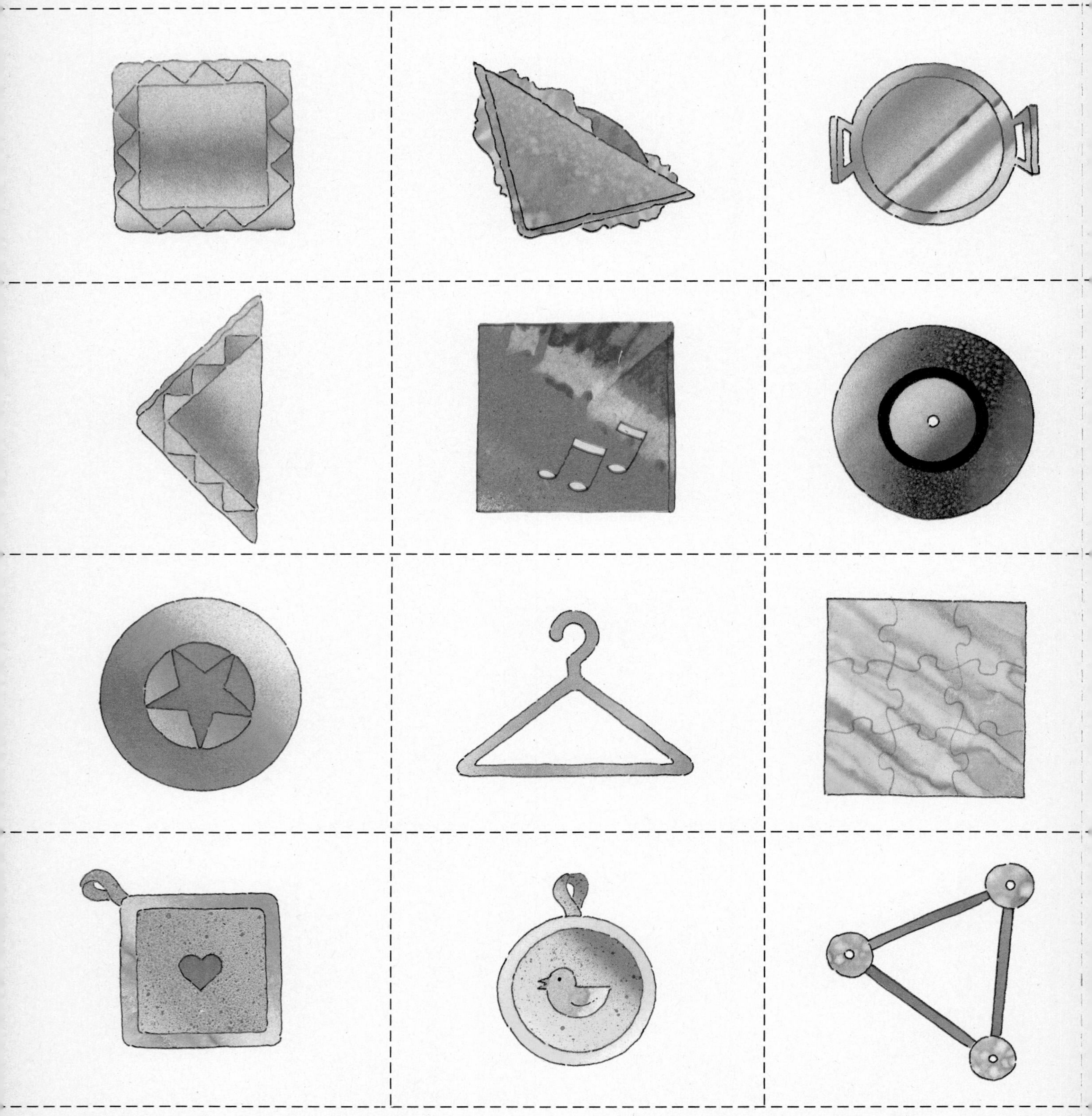

Name ______________________________

I can find ovals and rectangles.

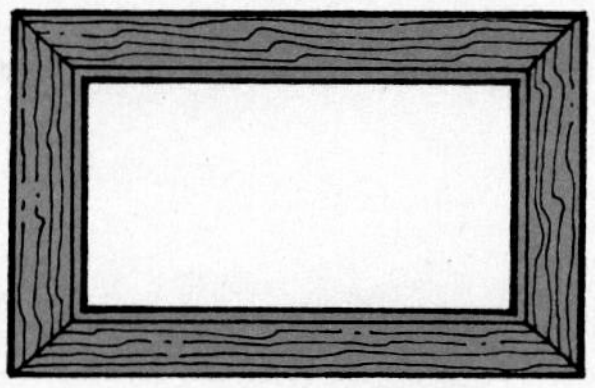

I can find matching shapes.

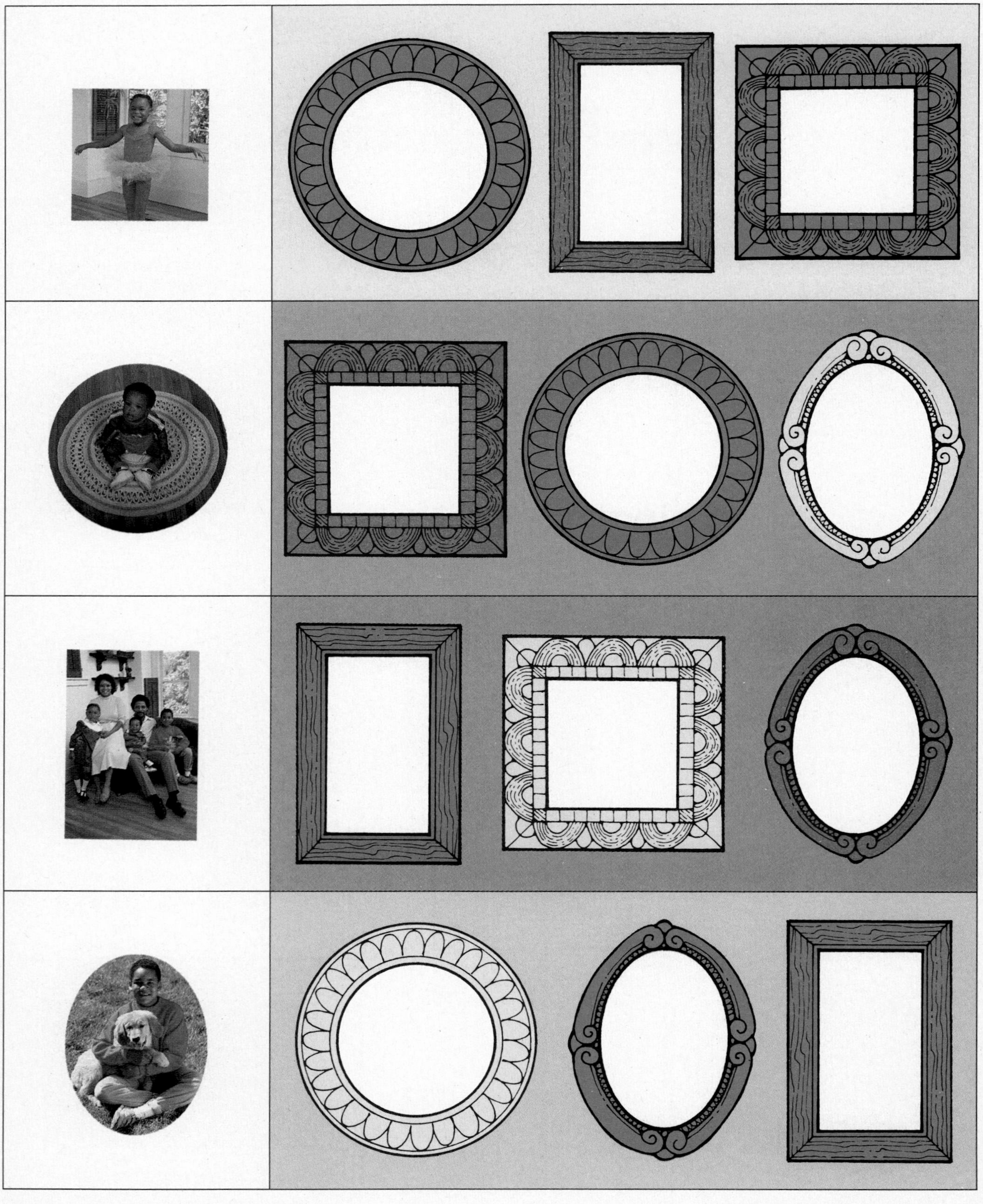

Name ______________________________

I can draw shapes.

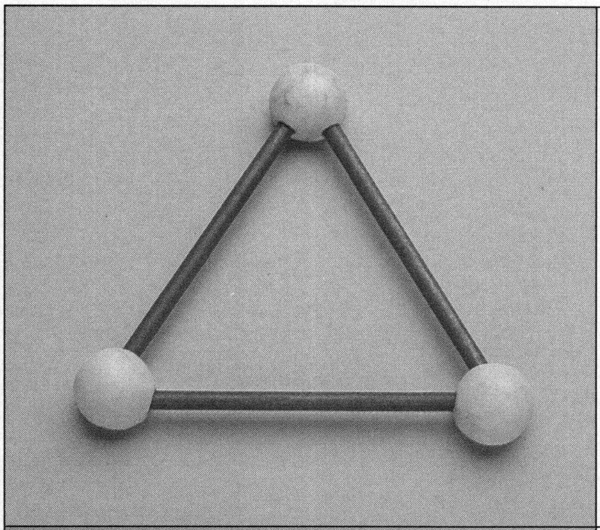

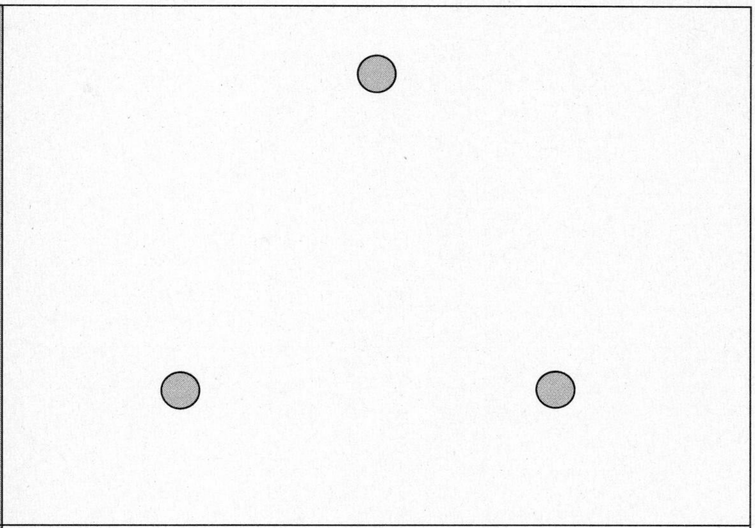

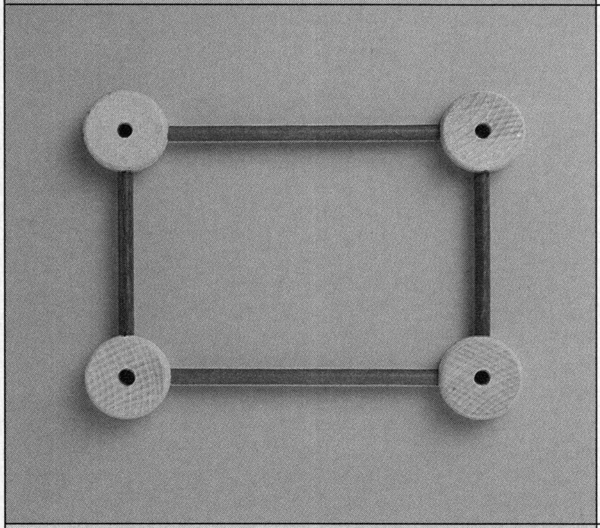

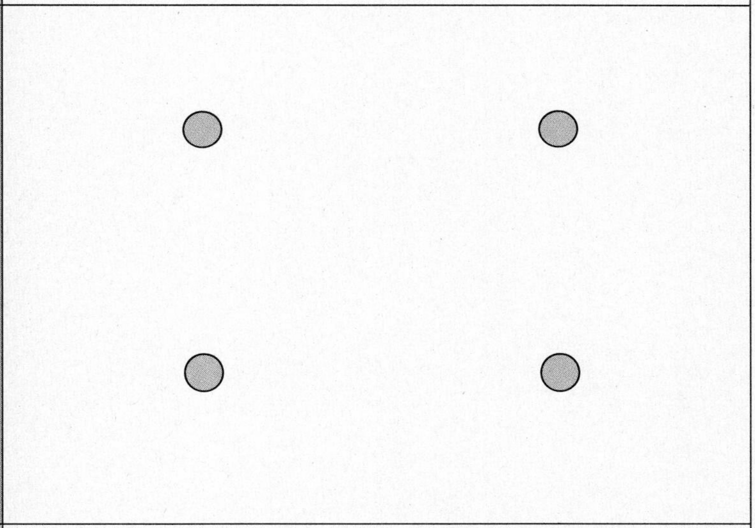

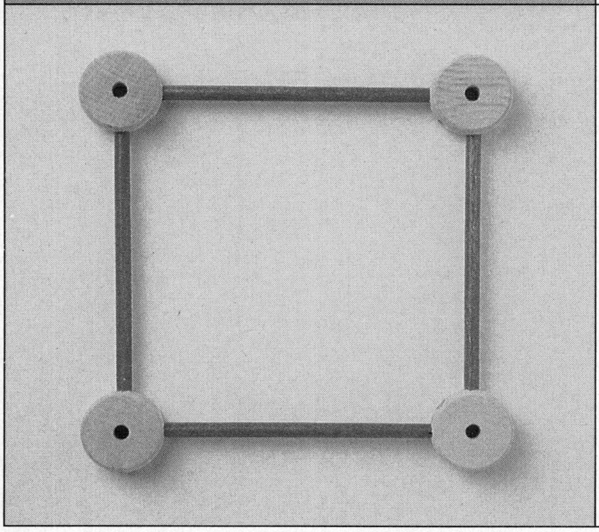

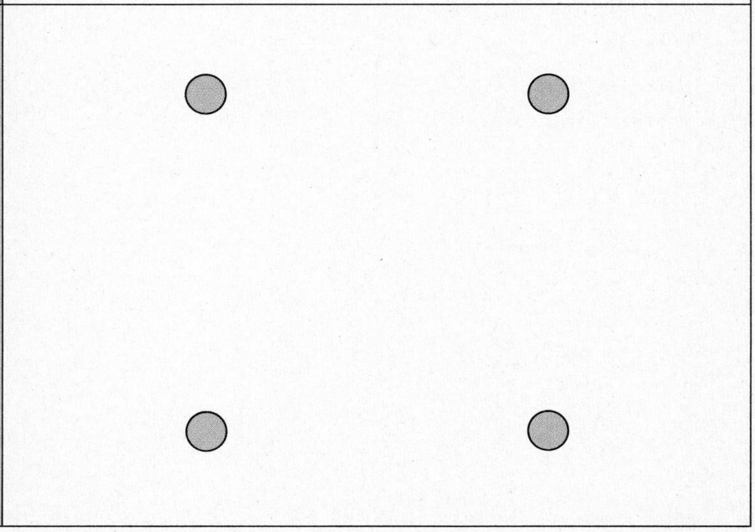

I can draw shapes.

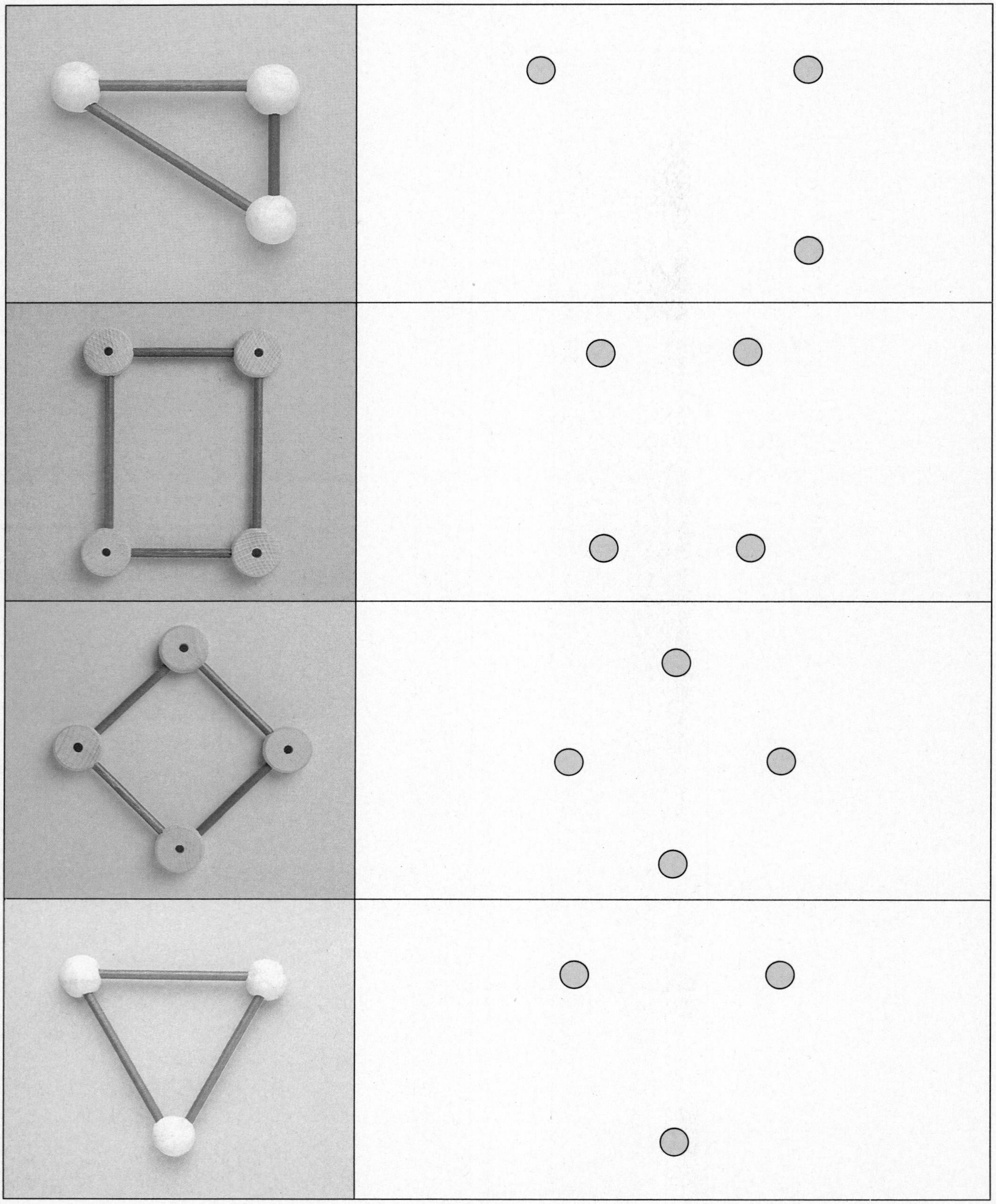

Name ____

I can make designs with shapes.

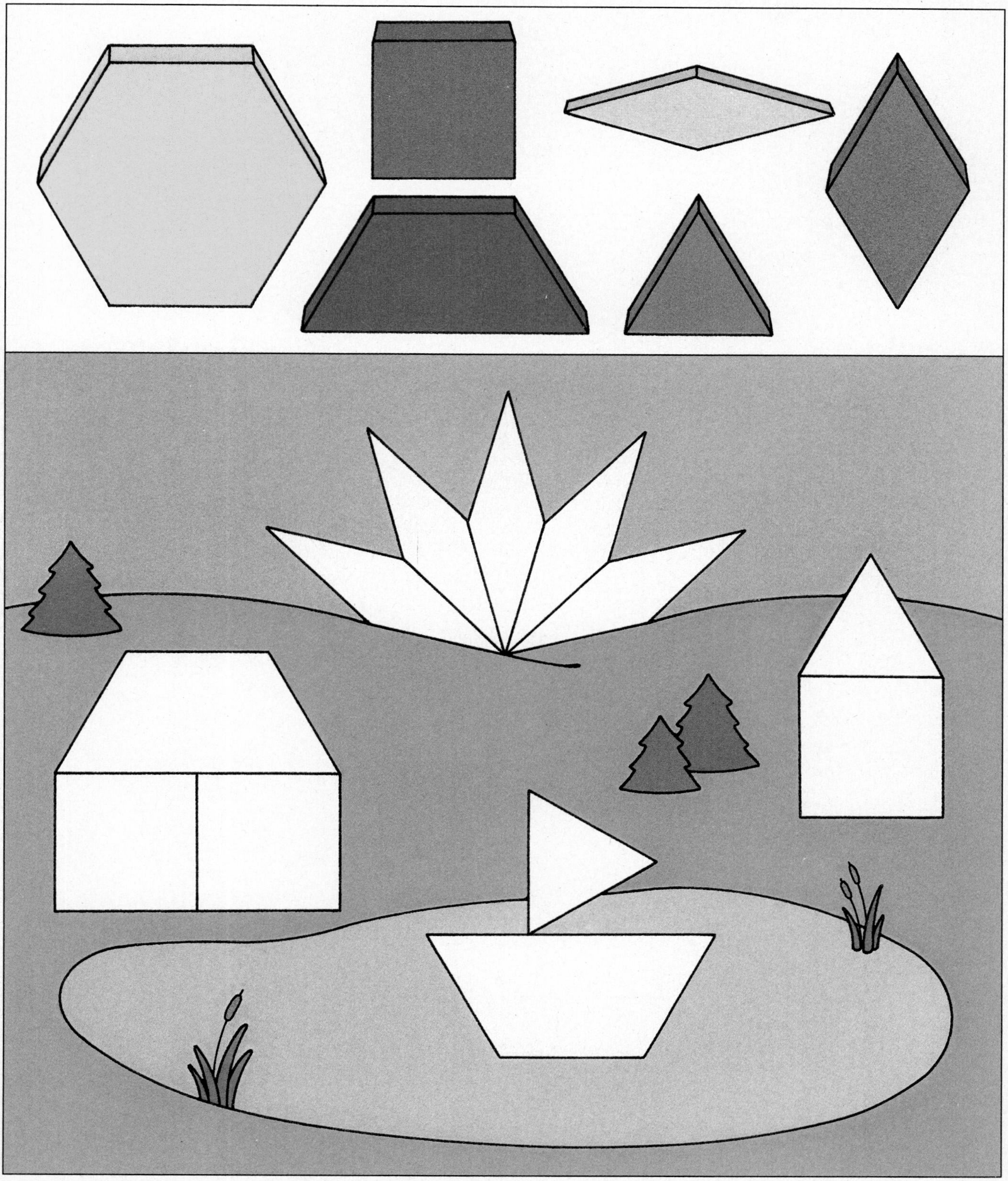

I can make designs with shapes.

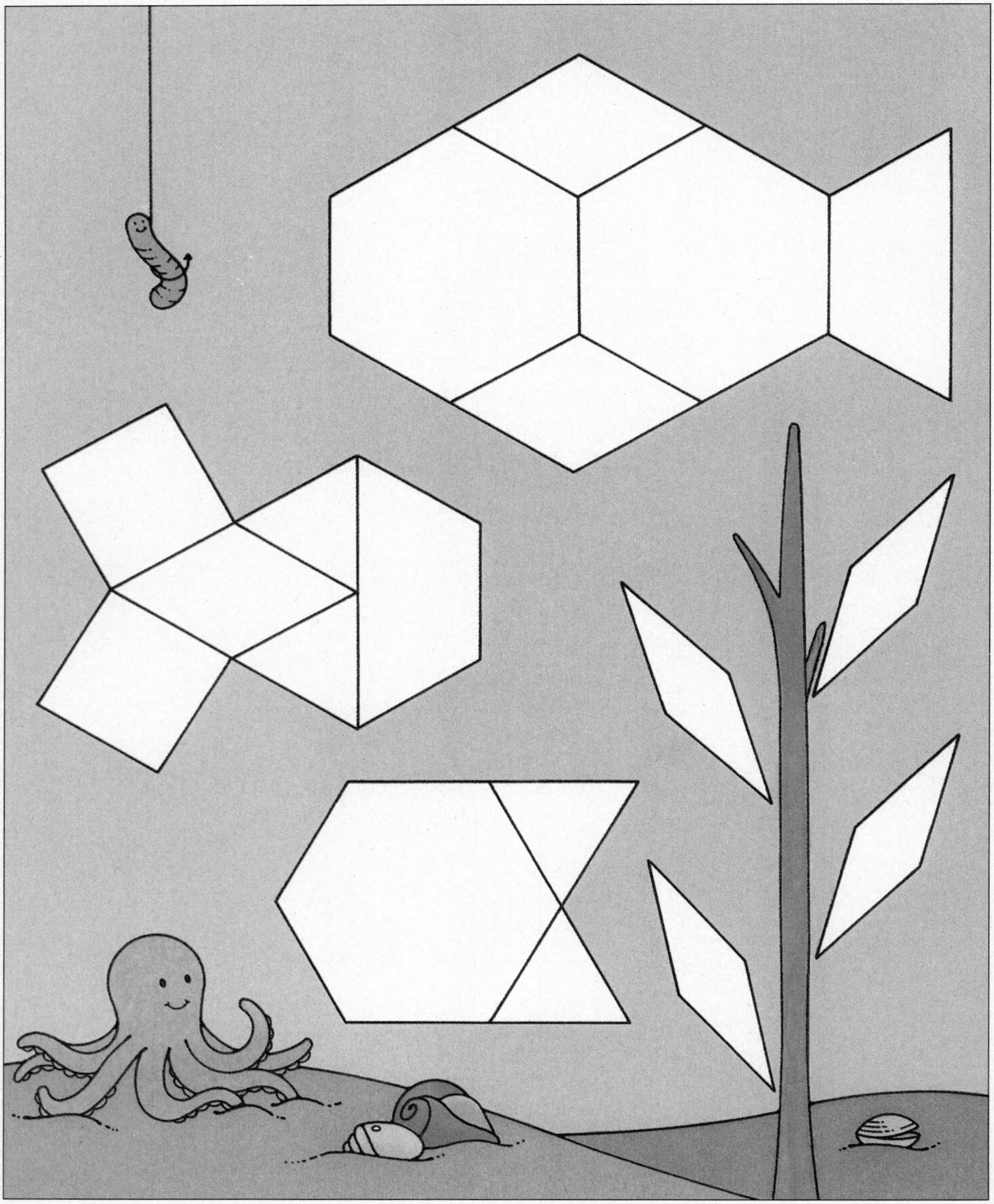

Name ______________________________

I can tell which blocks will cover the turtle's shell.

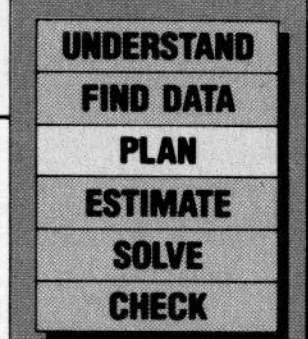

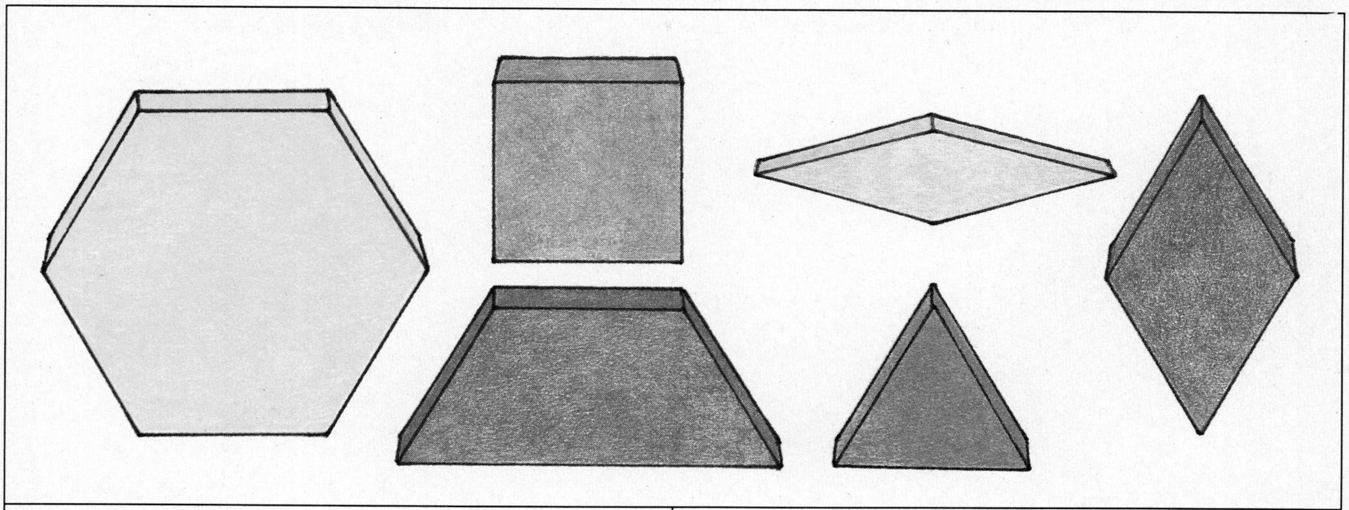

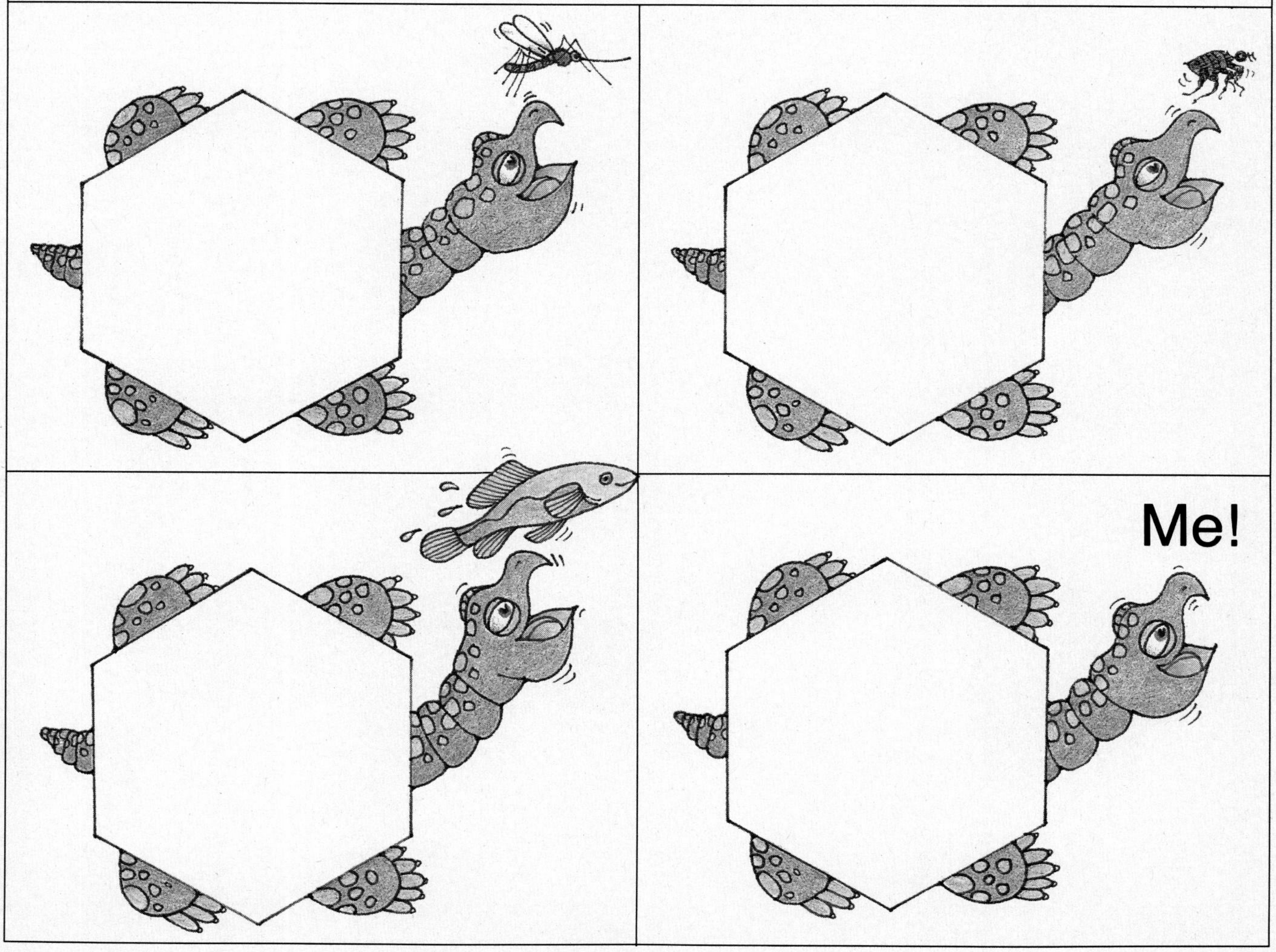

UNDERSTAND
FIND DATA
PLAN
ESTIMATE
SOLVE
CHECK

I can listen to a story.
I can show the path.

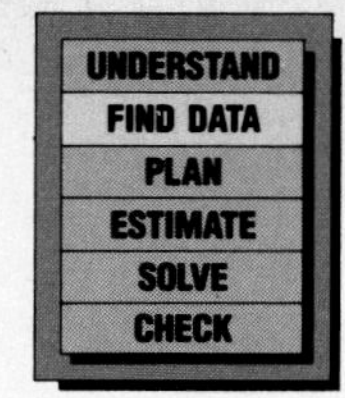

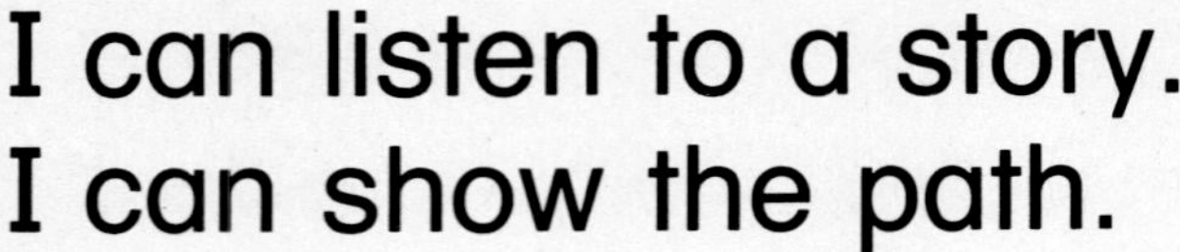

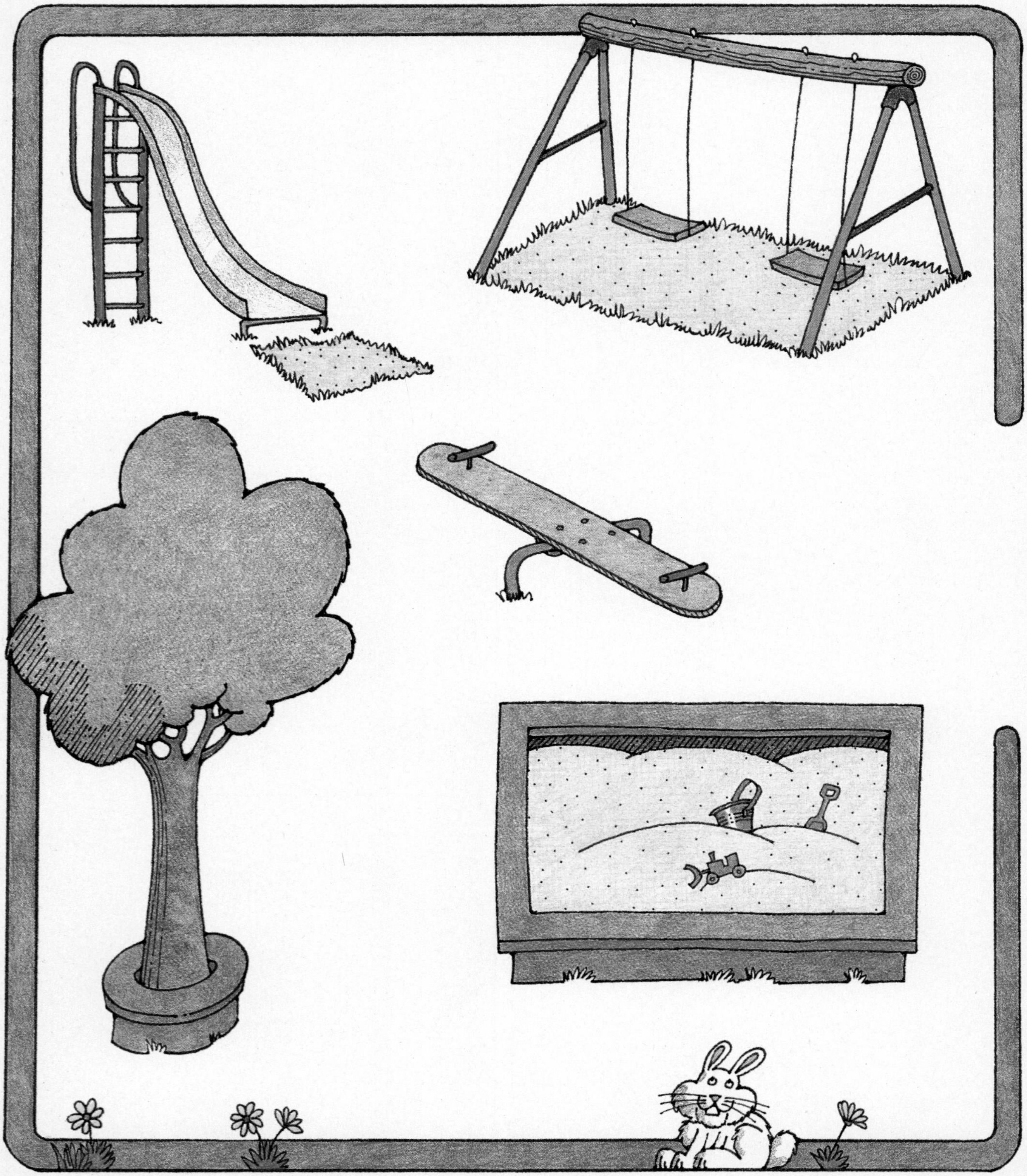

Name ______________________________

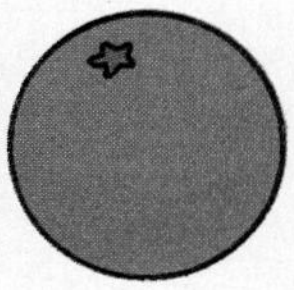

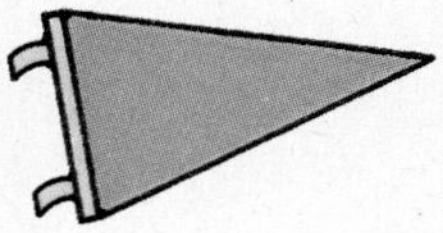

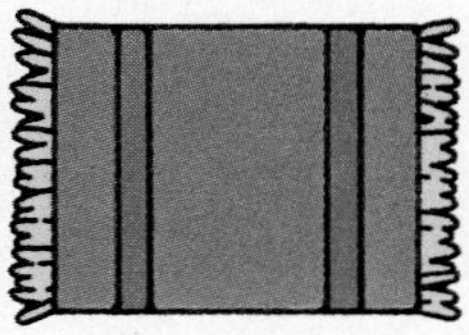

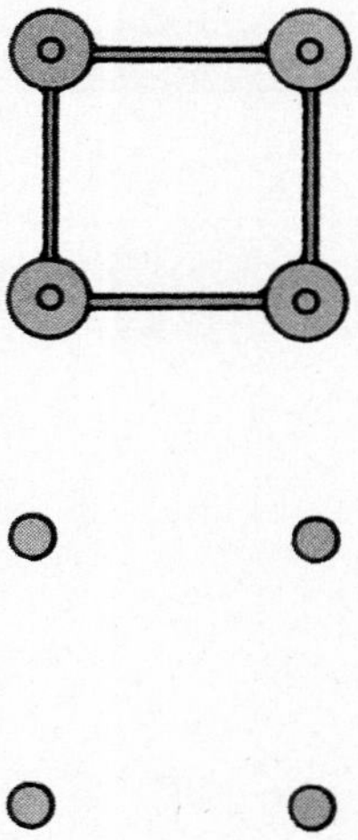
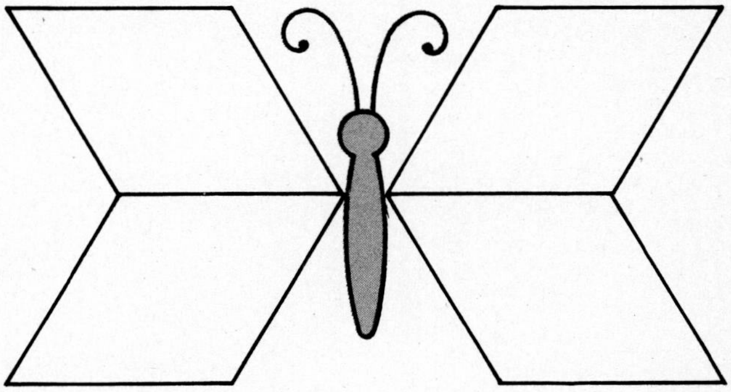

Name ______________________________

I can tell if I can build the shape.

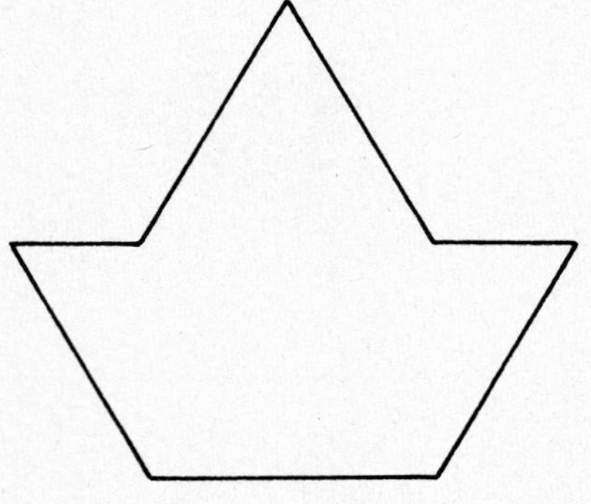

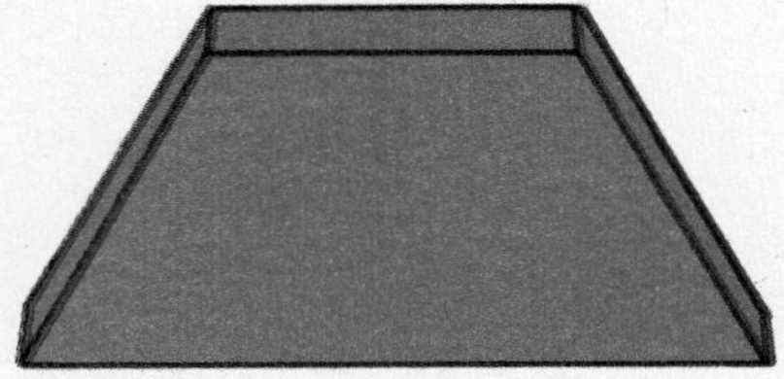

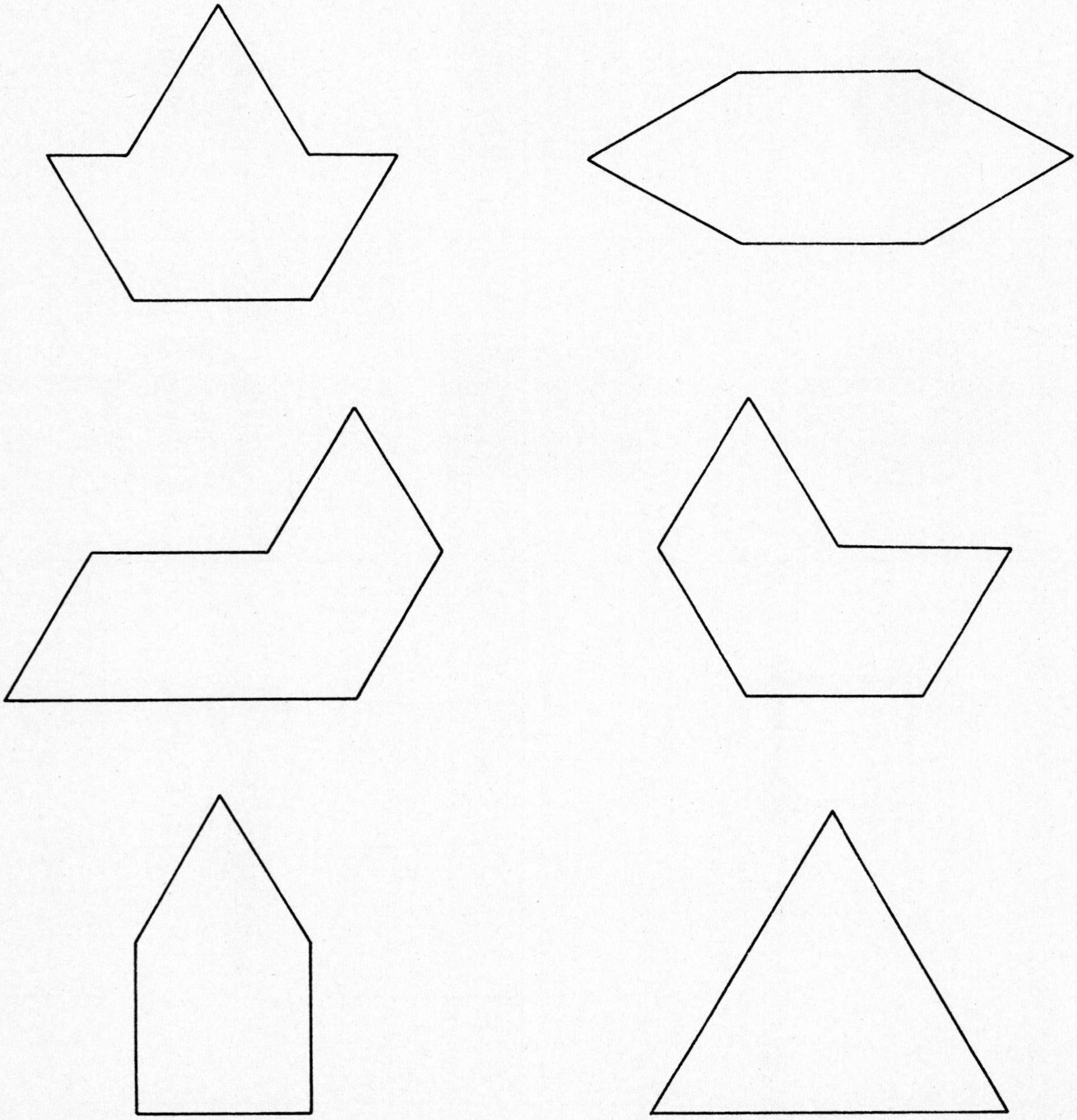

3
Patterns

Workmat

Theme: Music on Parade

Name ______________________________

I can follow patterns.
I can show what is missing.

Name ______________________________

I can follow color patterns.
I can show what comes next.

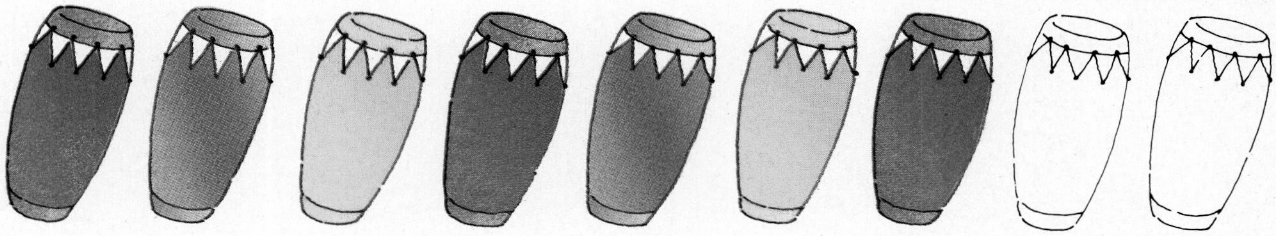

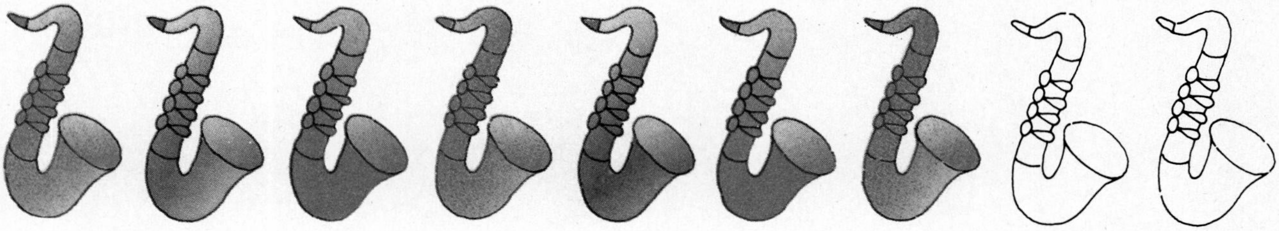

I can follow color patterns.
I can show what comes next.

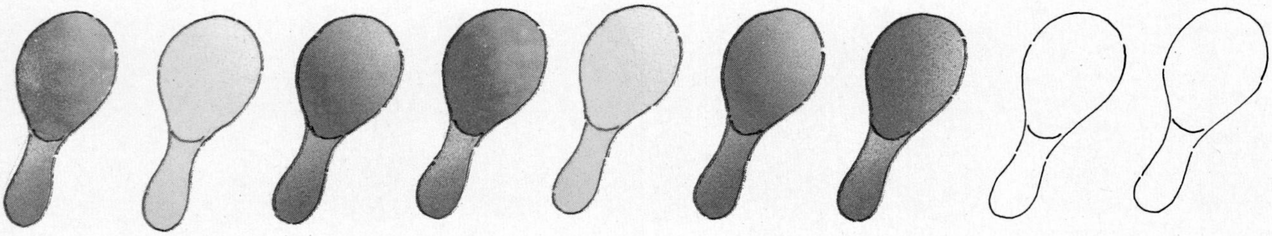

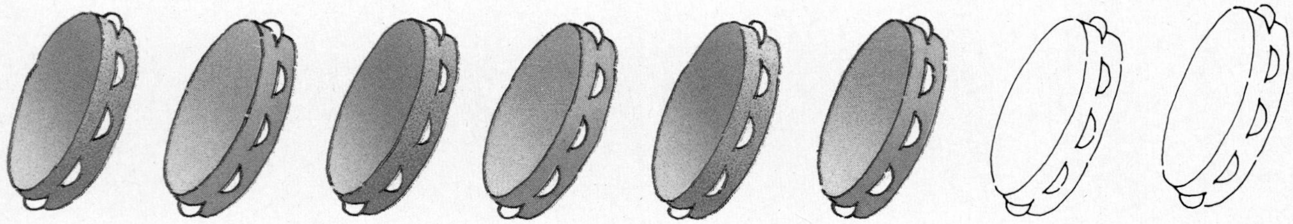

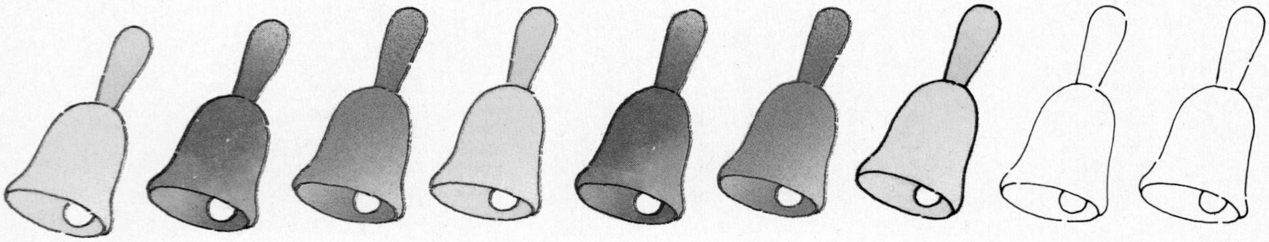

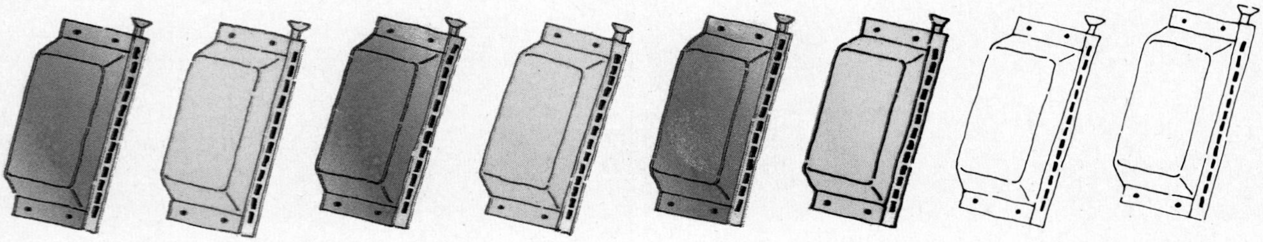

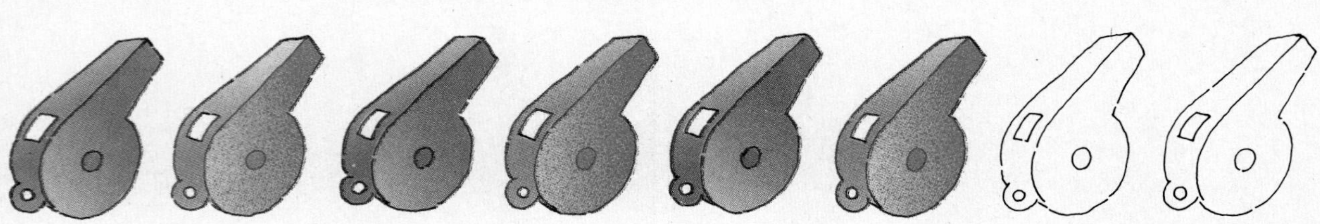

Name ________________________________

I can follow shape patterns.
I can show what comes next.

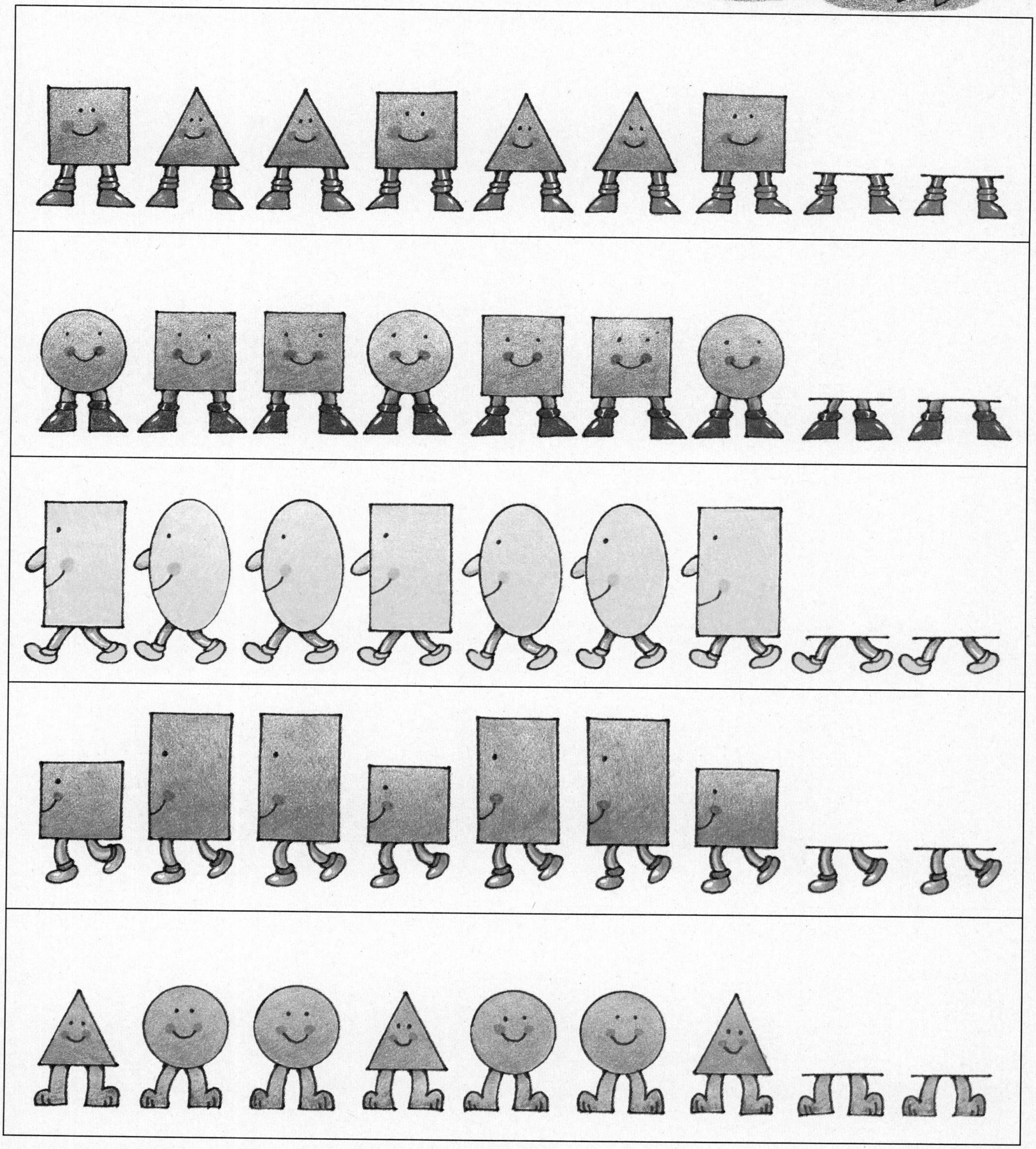

I can follow shape patterns.
I can show what comes next.

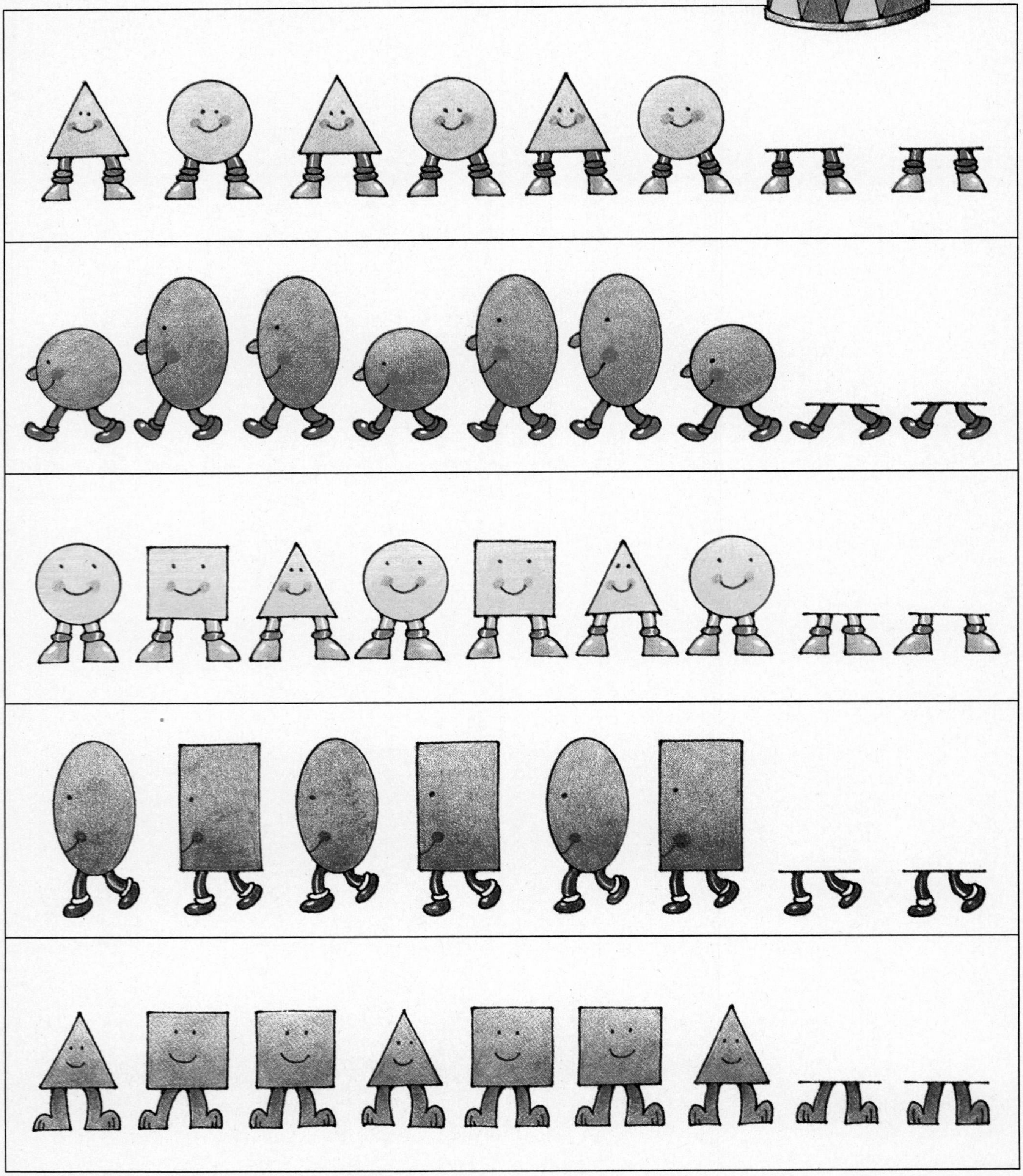

Name ______________________

I can follow patterns.
I can show what comes next.

I can follow patterns.
I can show what comes next.

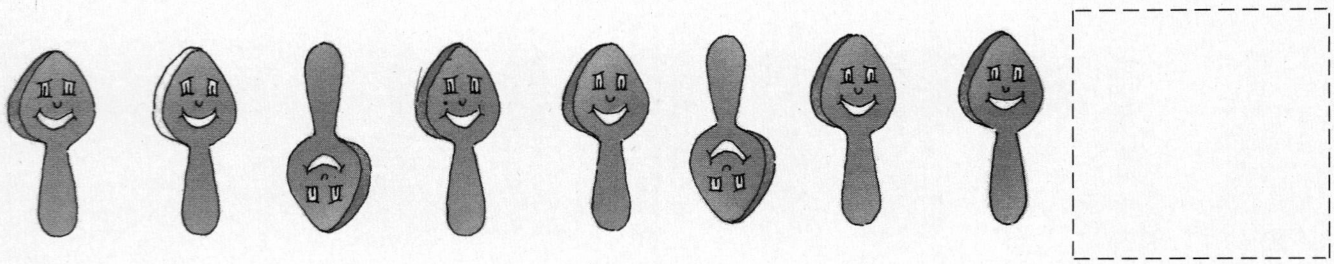

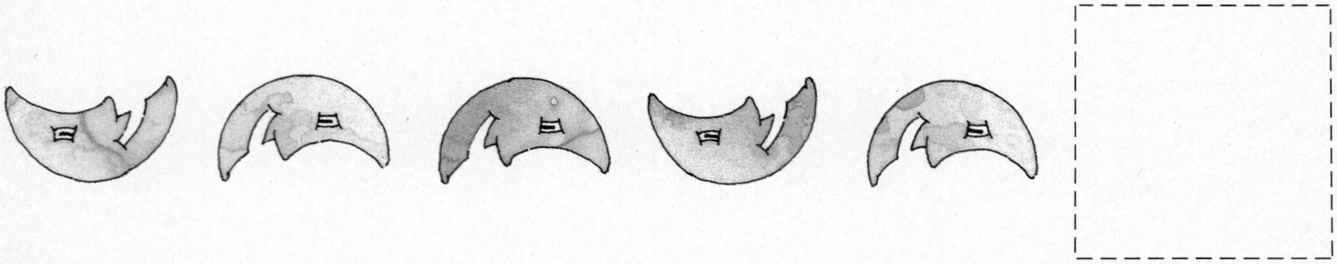

Name ______________________________

I can make a pattern.

I can make a pattern.

Name ____________________

I can listen to a story.
I can show the pattern.

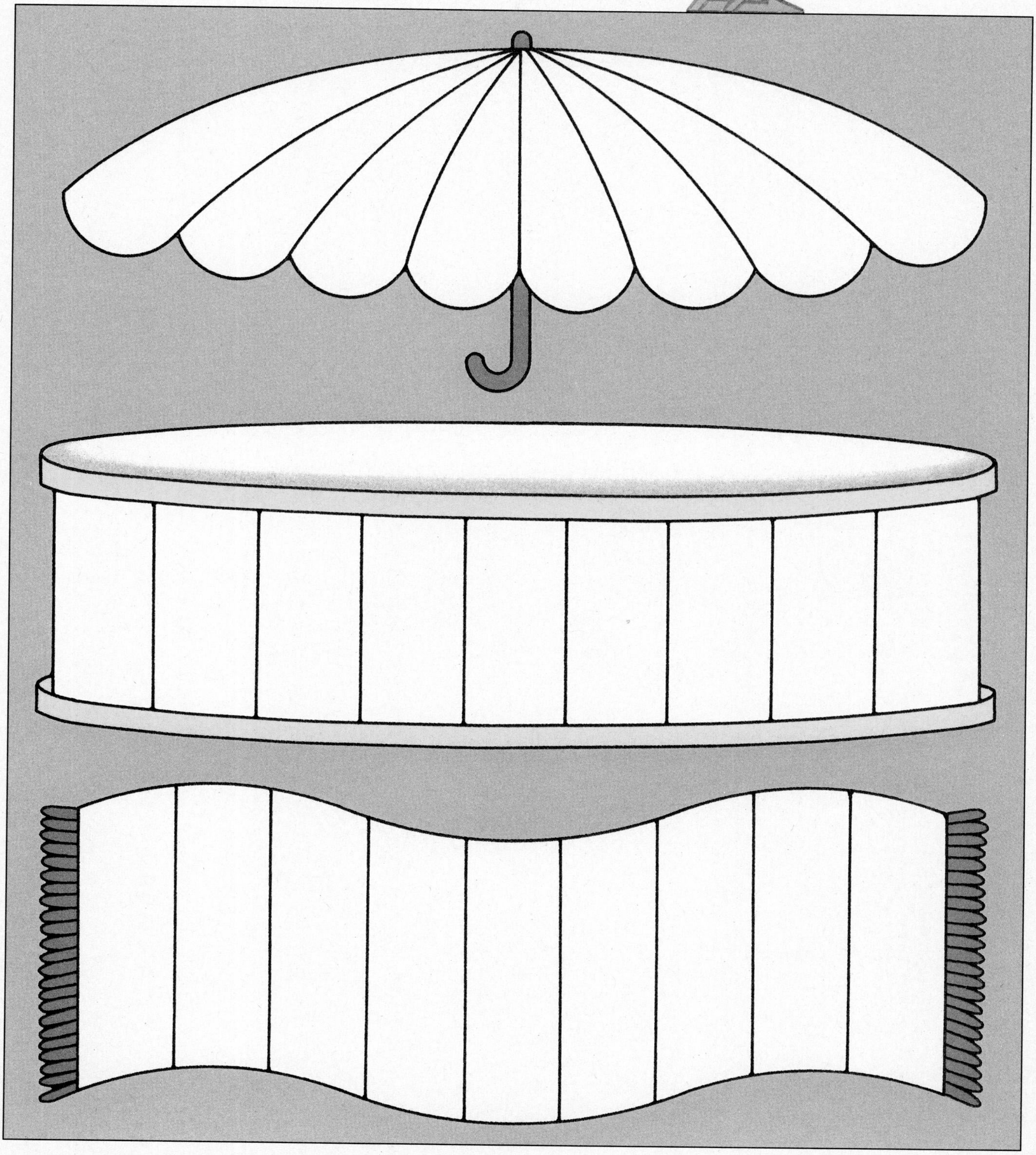

I can follow patterns.
I can show what comes next.

UNDERSTAND
FIND DATA
PLAN
ESTIMATE
SOLVE
CHECK

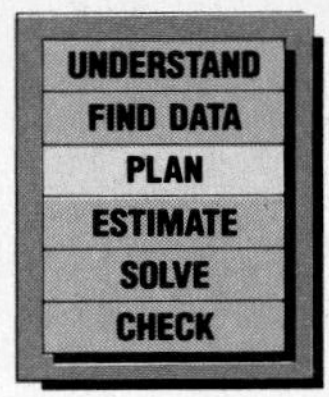

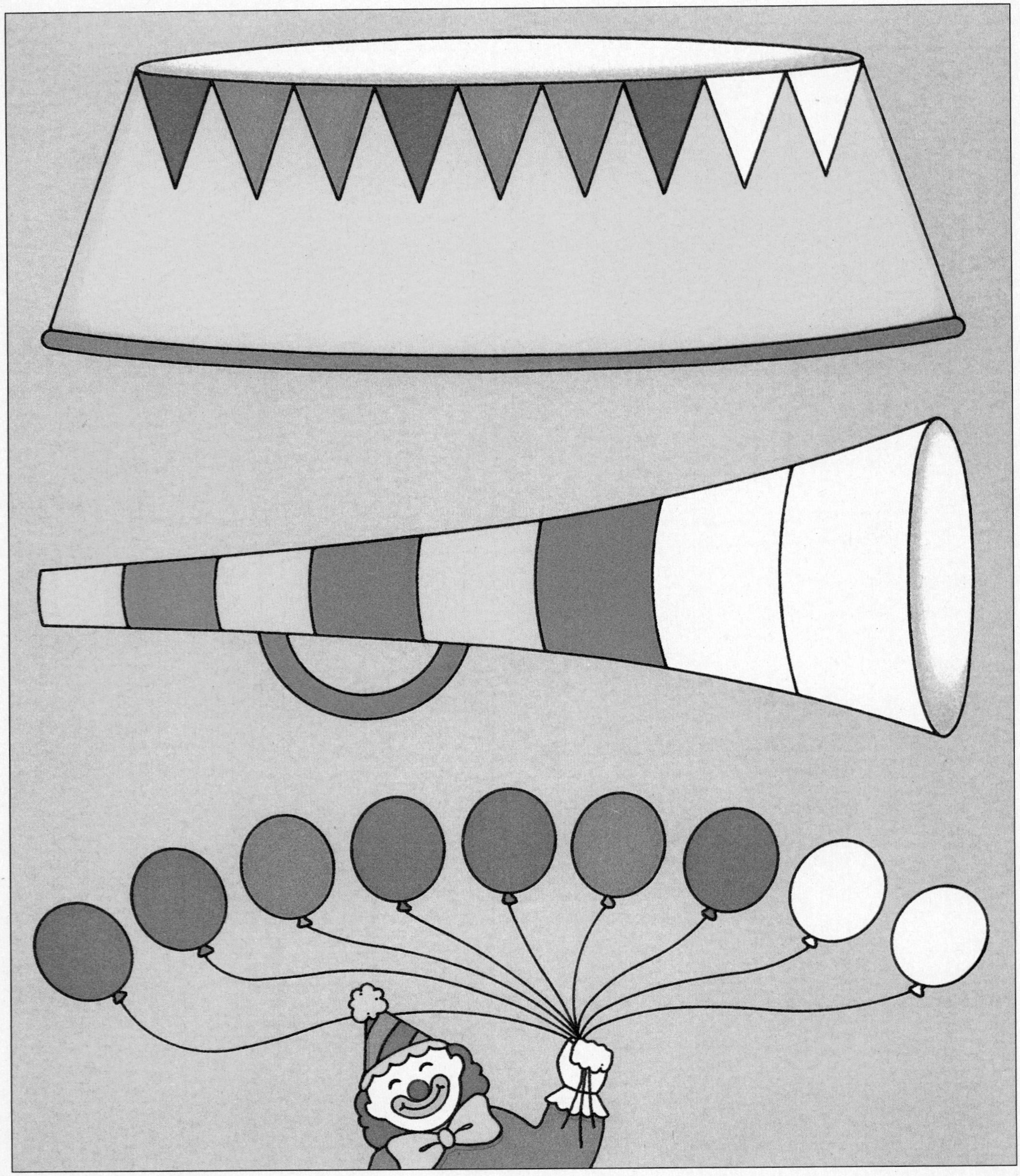

Name ______________________________

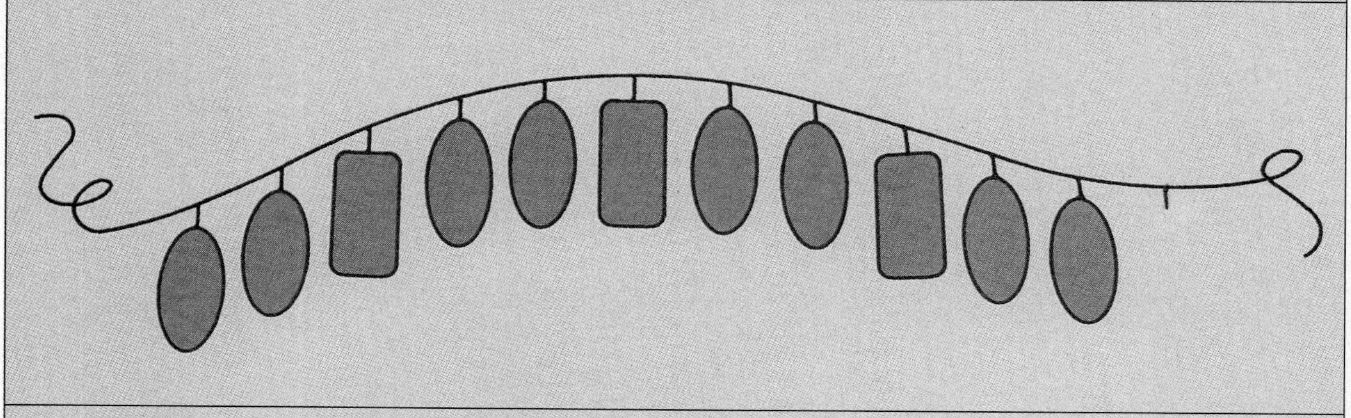

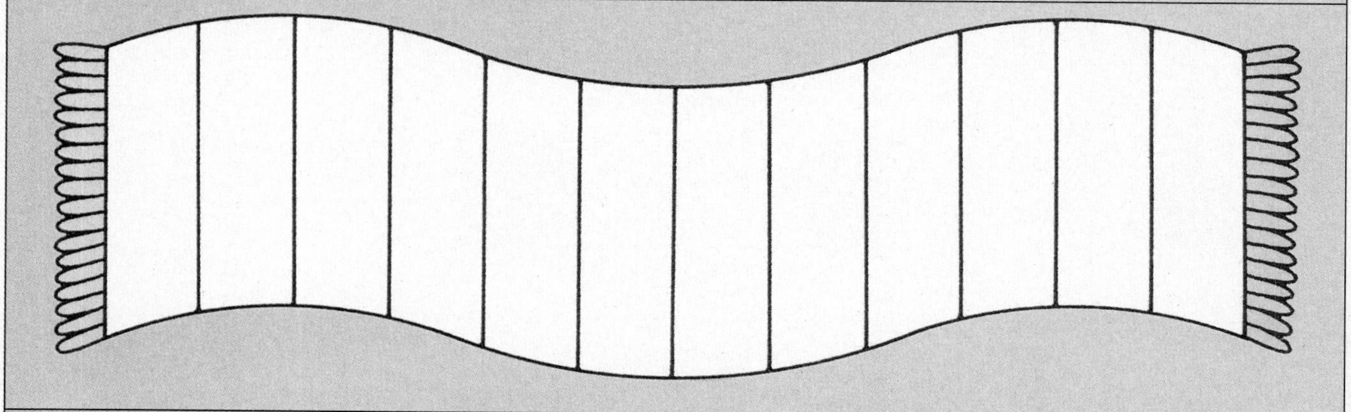

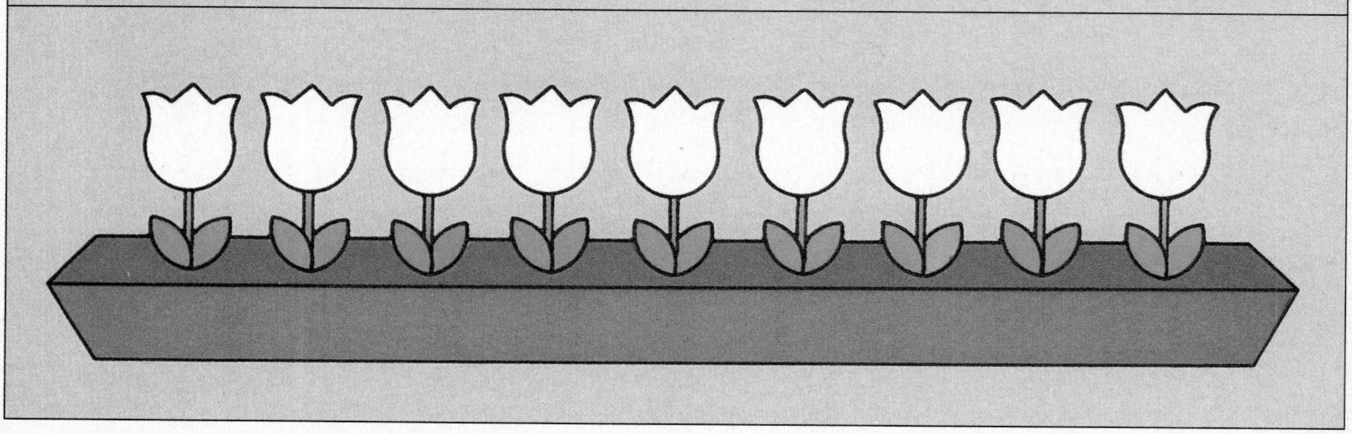

Name ______________________________

I can follow patterns.
I can show what is missing.

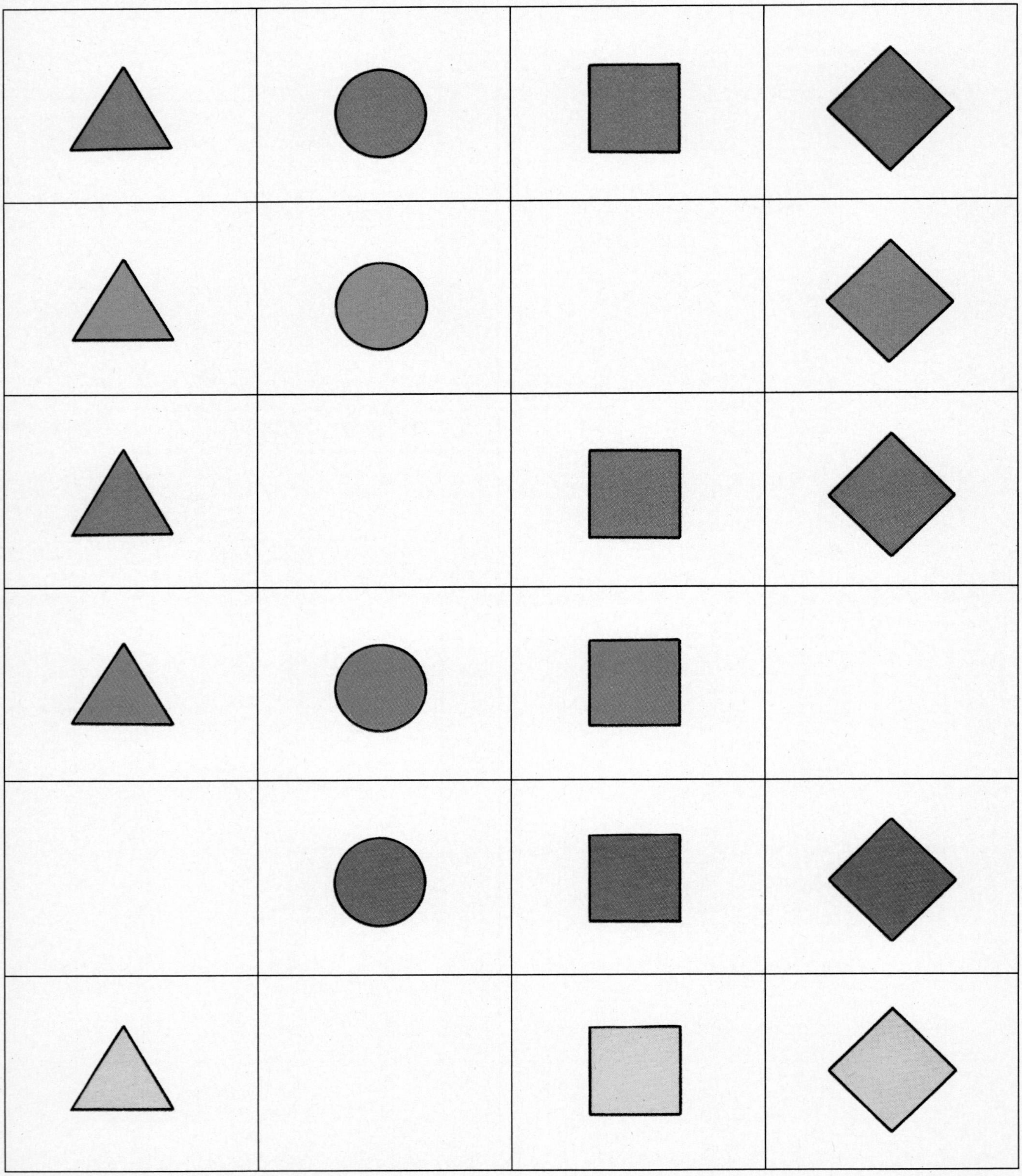

4

Comparing and Ordering

Workmat

Theme: Favorite Book Characters

Name ____________________

I can tell which is larger and which is smaller.

Name ________________________________

I can tell which hats are taller than the elf.

I can tell which hats are shorter than the elf.

Name ________________________________

I can tell which shoes are longer than the elf.

I can tell which shoes are shorter than the elf.

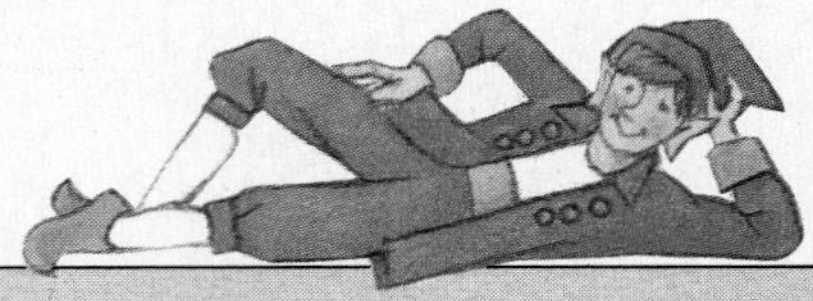

Name ______________________________

I can tell which things are taller than I am.

I can draw something taller than I am.

I can tell which things are shorter than my hand.

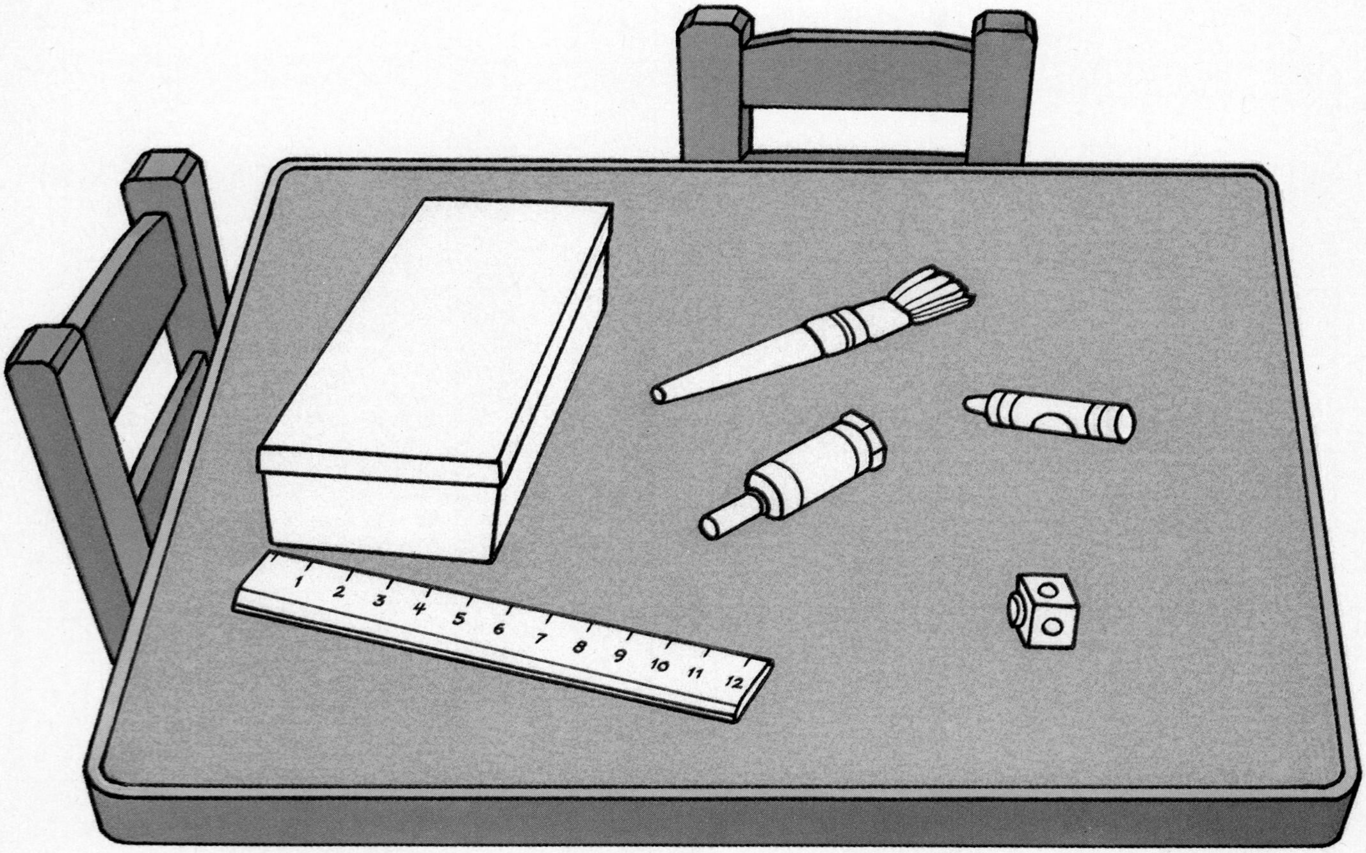

I can draw something shorter than my hand.

Name ____________________

I can put things in order from smallest to largest.

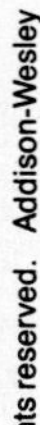

I can put things in order from largest to smallest.

Name ____

I can put things in order from shortest to tallest.

I can put things in order
from shortest to longest.

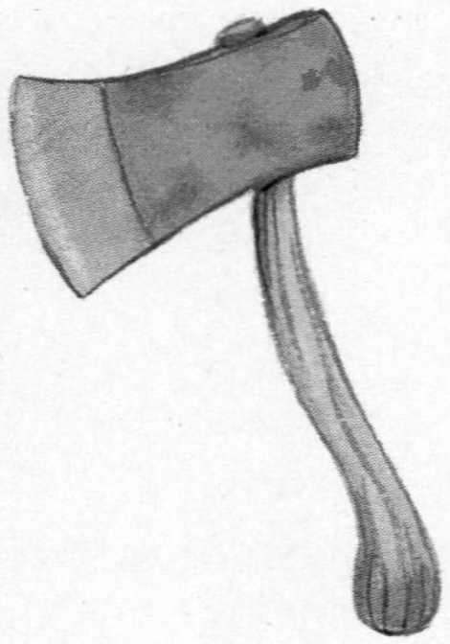

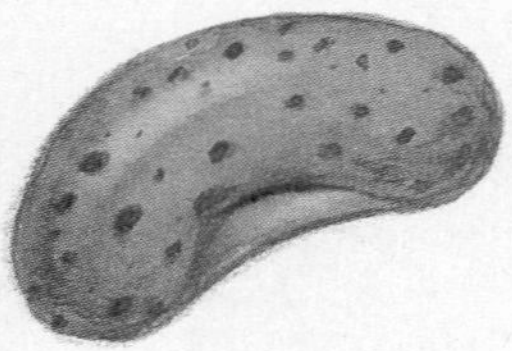

Name ____________________

UNDERSTAND
FIND DATA
PLAN
ESTIMATE
SOLVE
CHECK

I can listen to a story.
I can tell how the sizes compare.

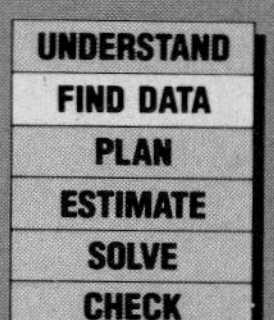

I can look for a pattern.
I can show what comes next.

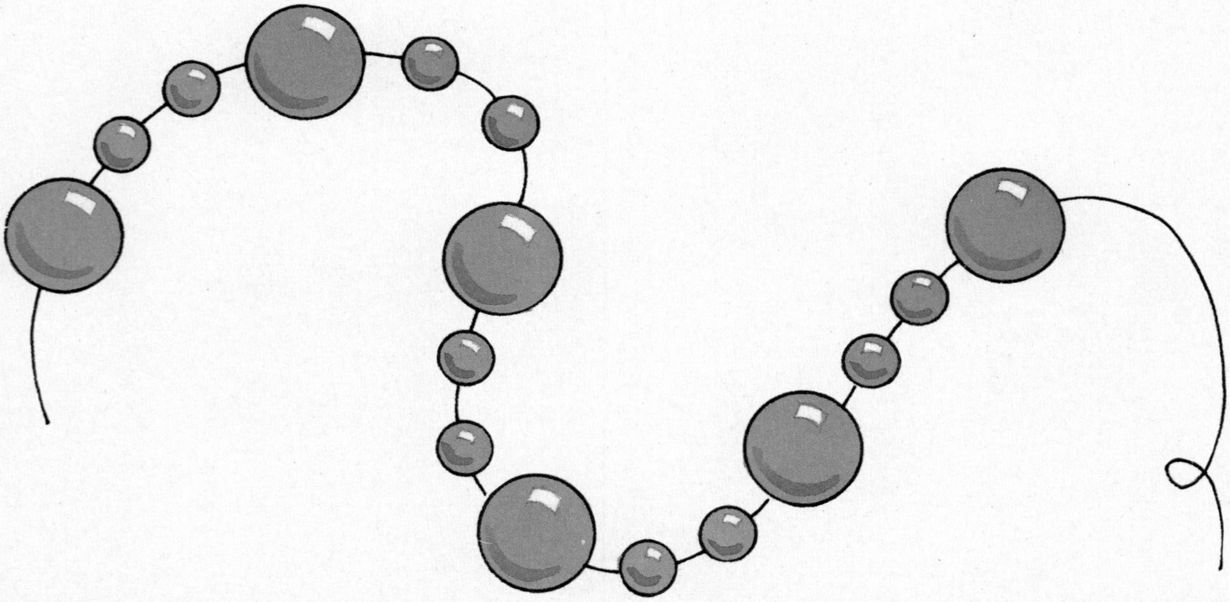

Name ______________________________

I can tell which ones are the same size and shape.

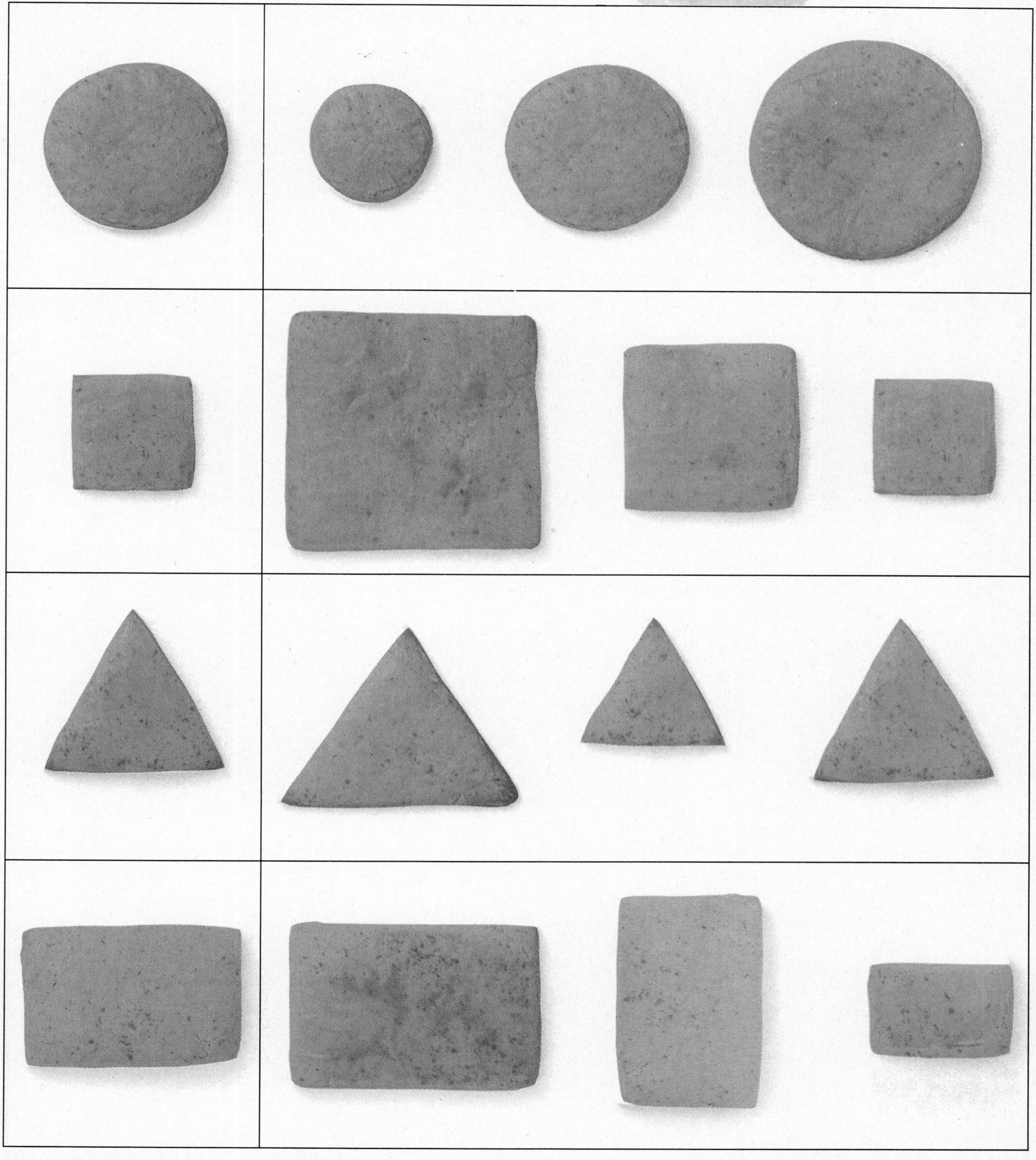

I can tell which ones are the same size and shape.

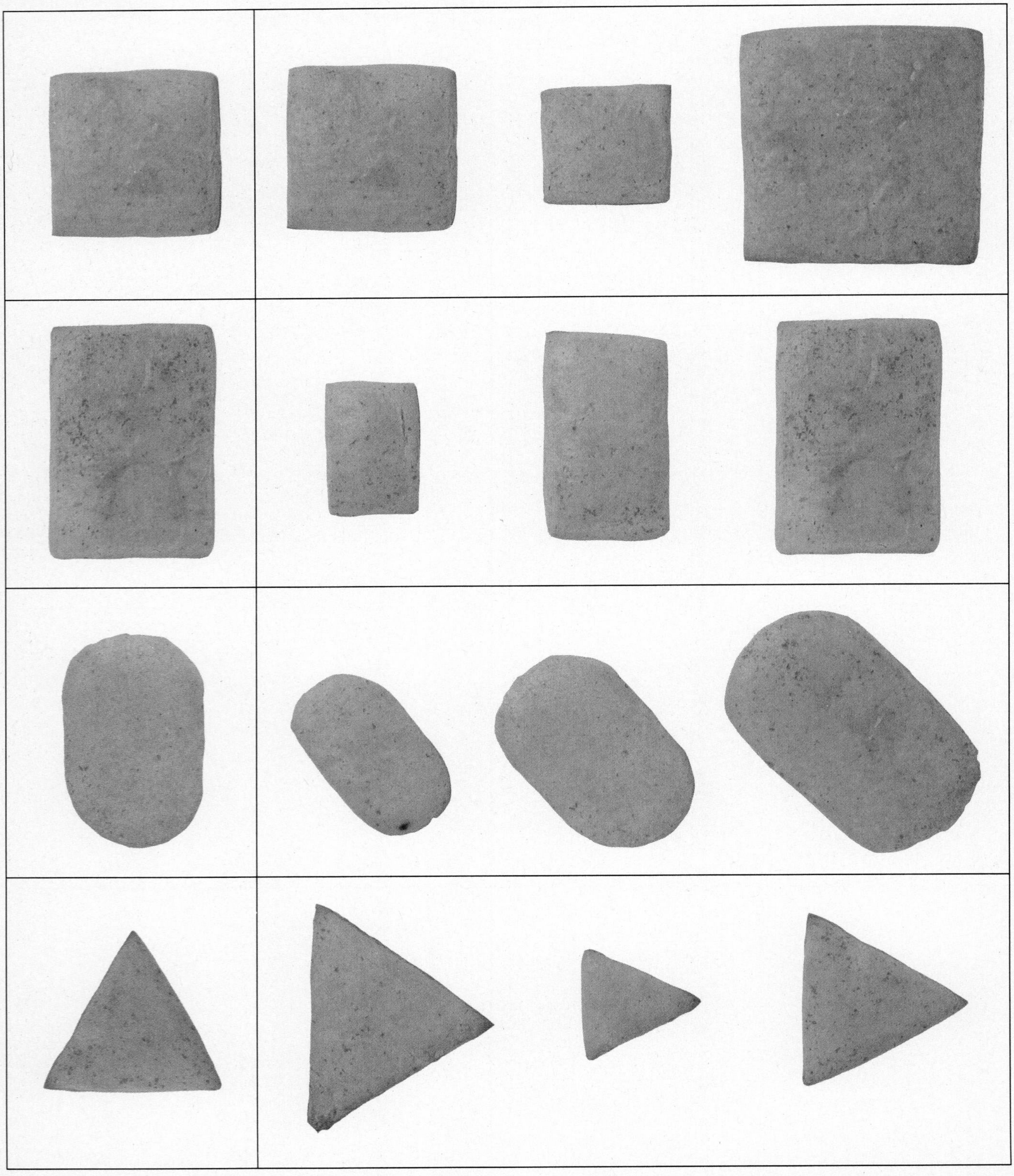

Name ______________________________

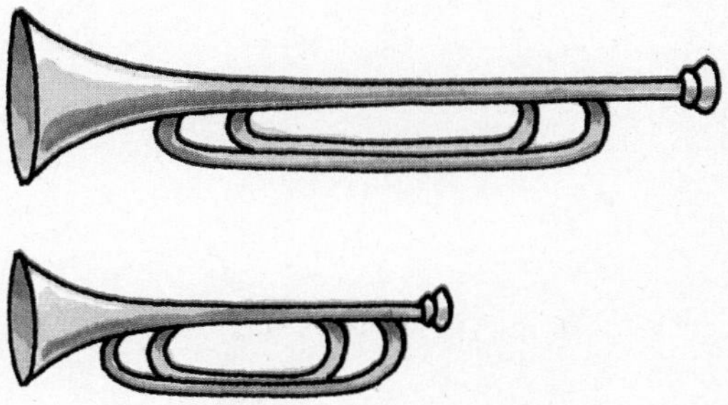

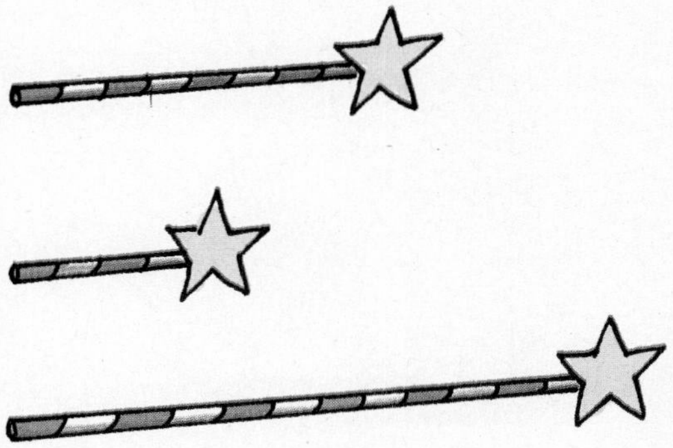

Name ________________________________

I can match kittens and mittens.

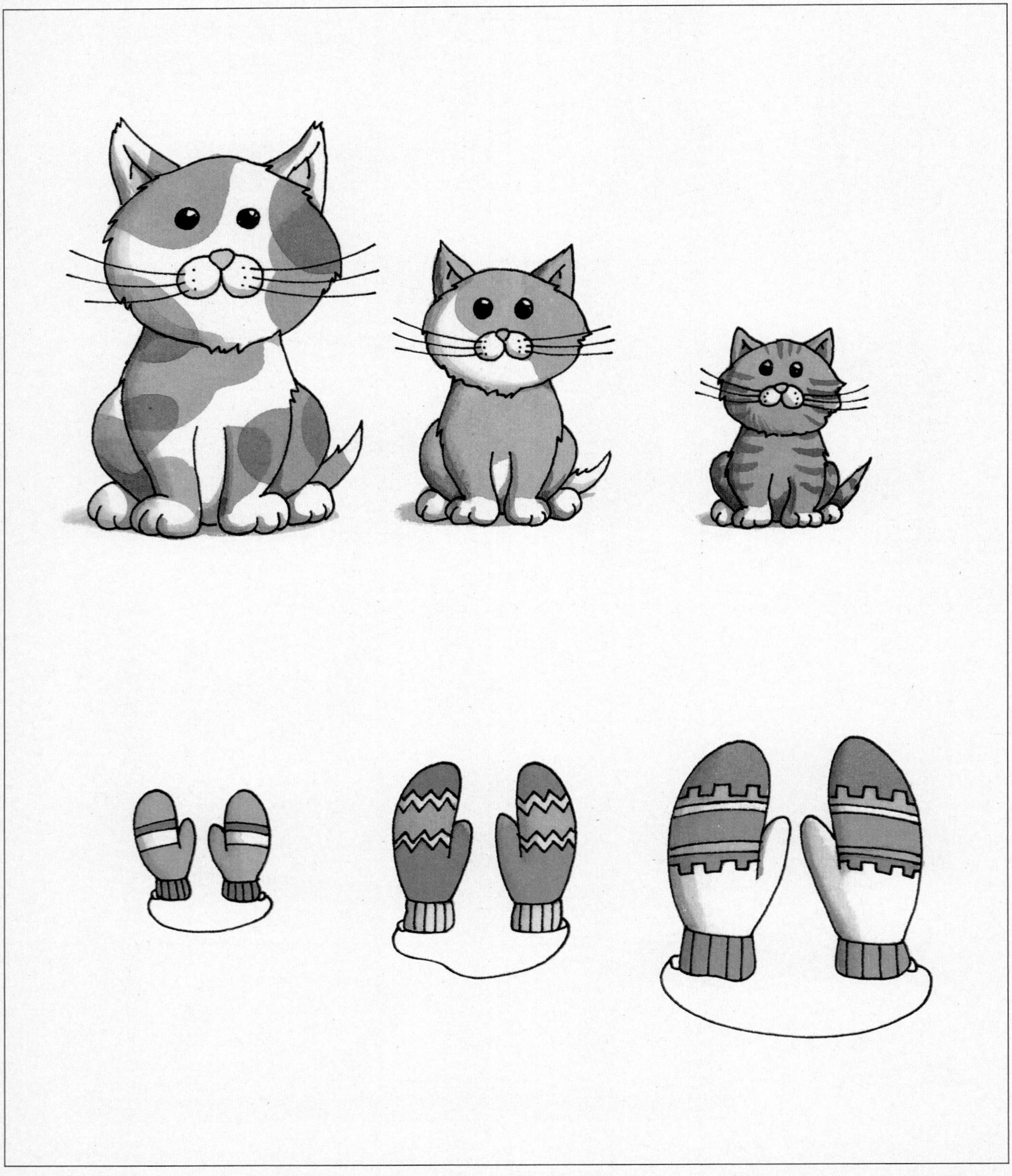

5

Comparing and Graphing

Workmat

Theme: At Play

Name ____________________

I can tell if the groups have the same number.

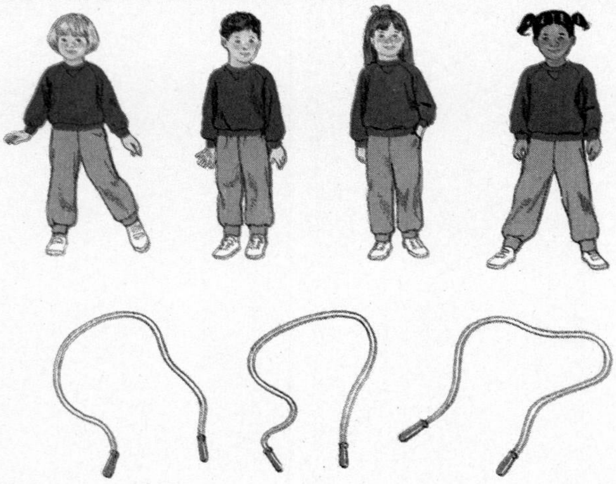

Name ______________________________

I can show the same number.

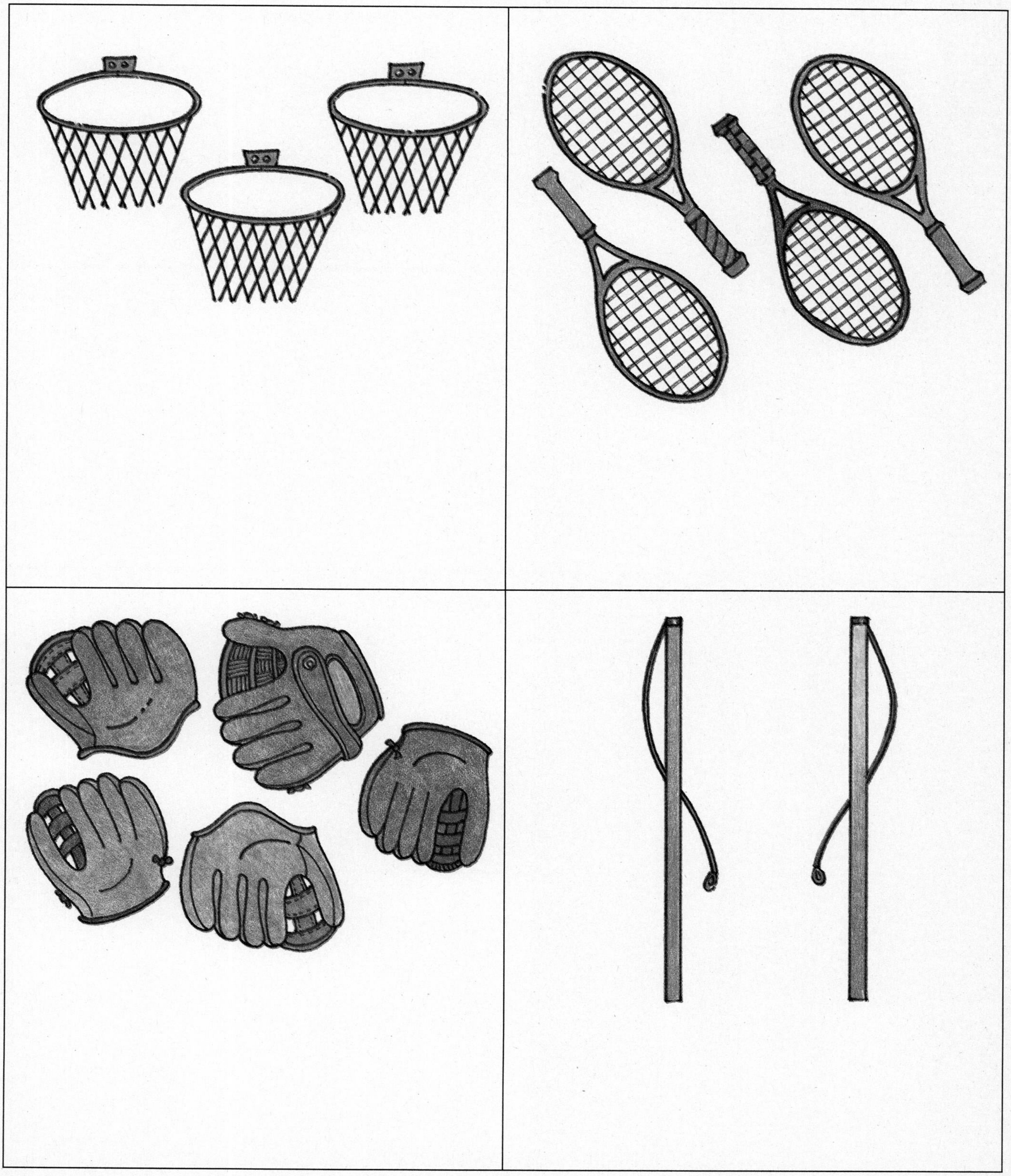

I can show the same number.

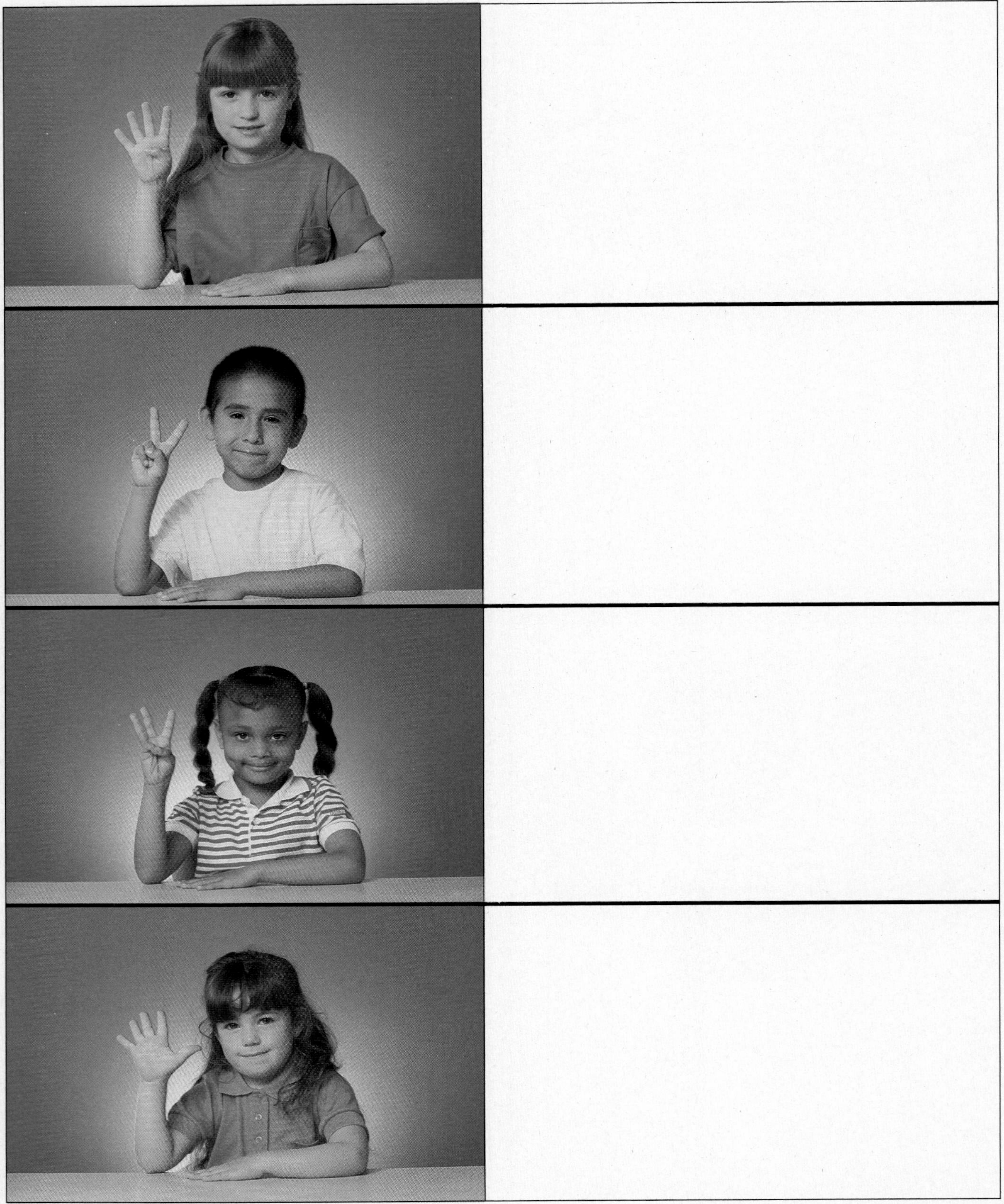

Name ______________________________

I can compare groups.
I can tell which box has more.

I can tell which box has less.

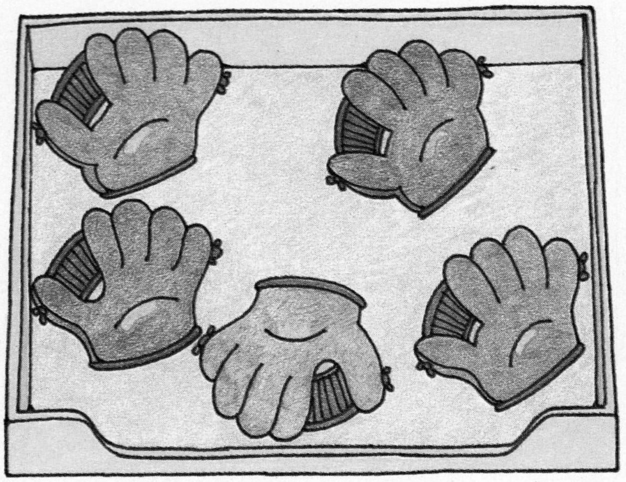
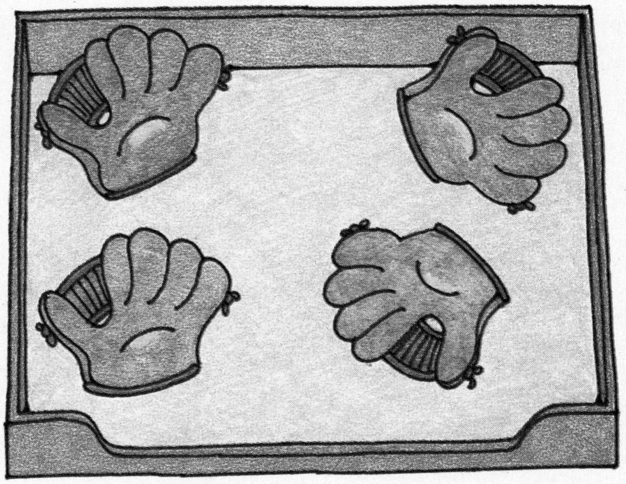

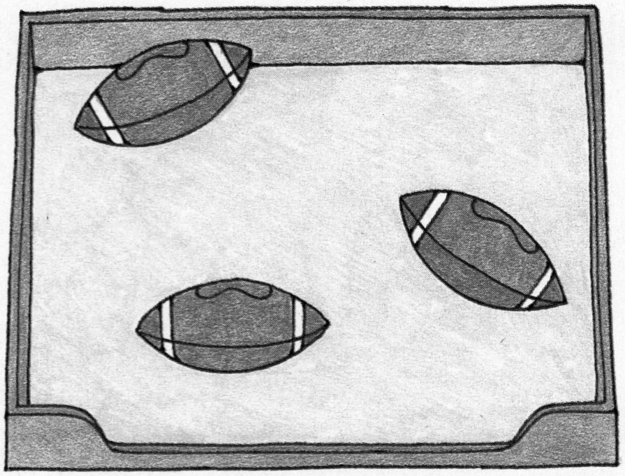
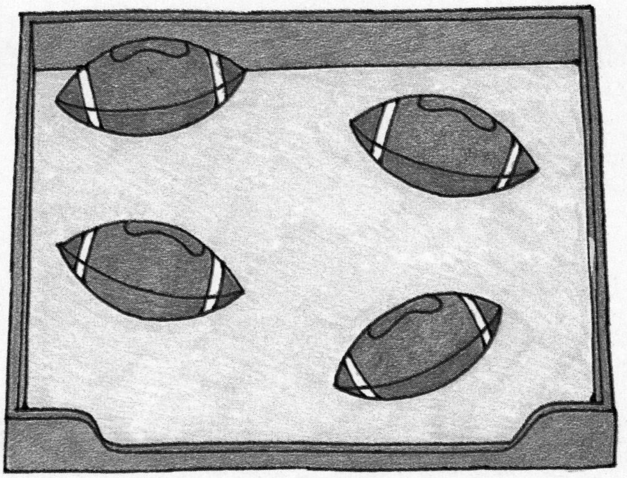

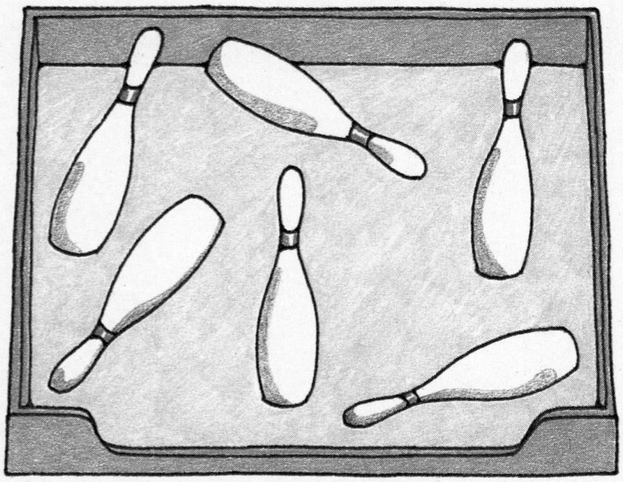
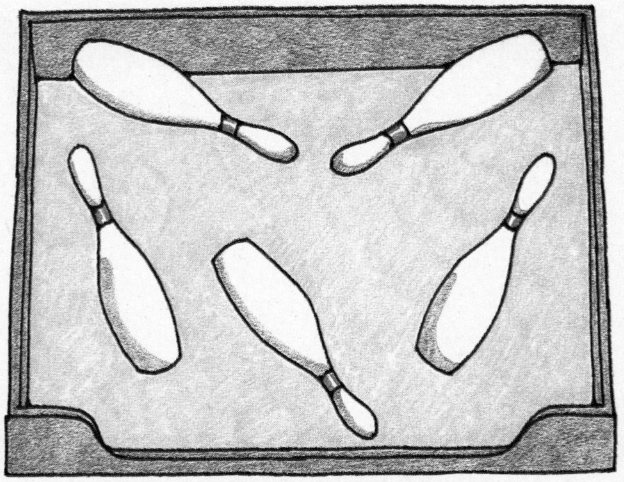

Name ______________________________

I can show more.

I can show less.

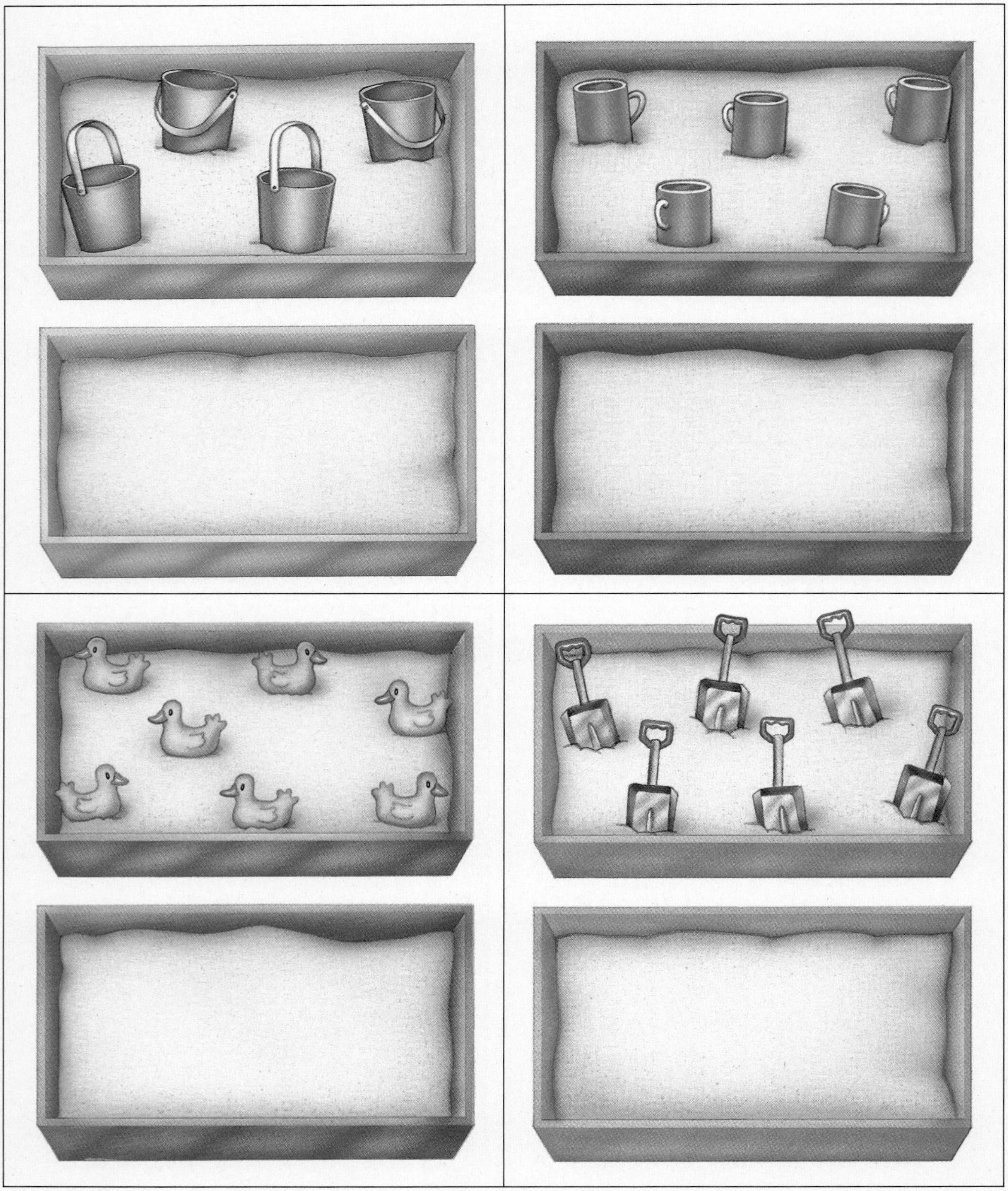

Name ____________________

I can make the groups equal.

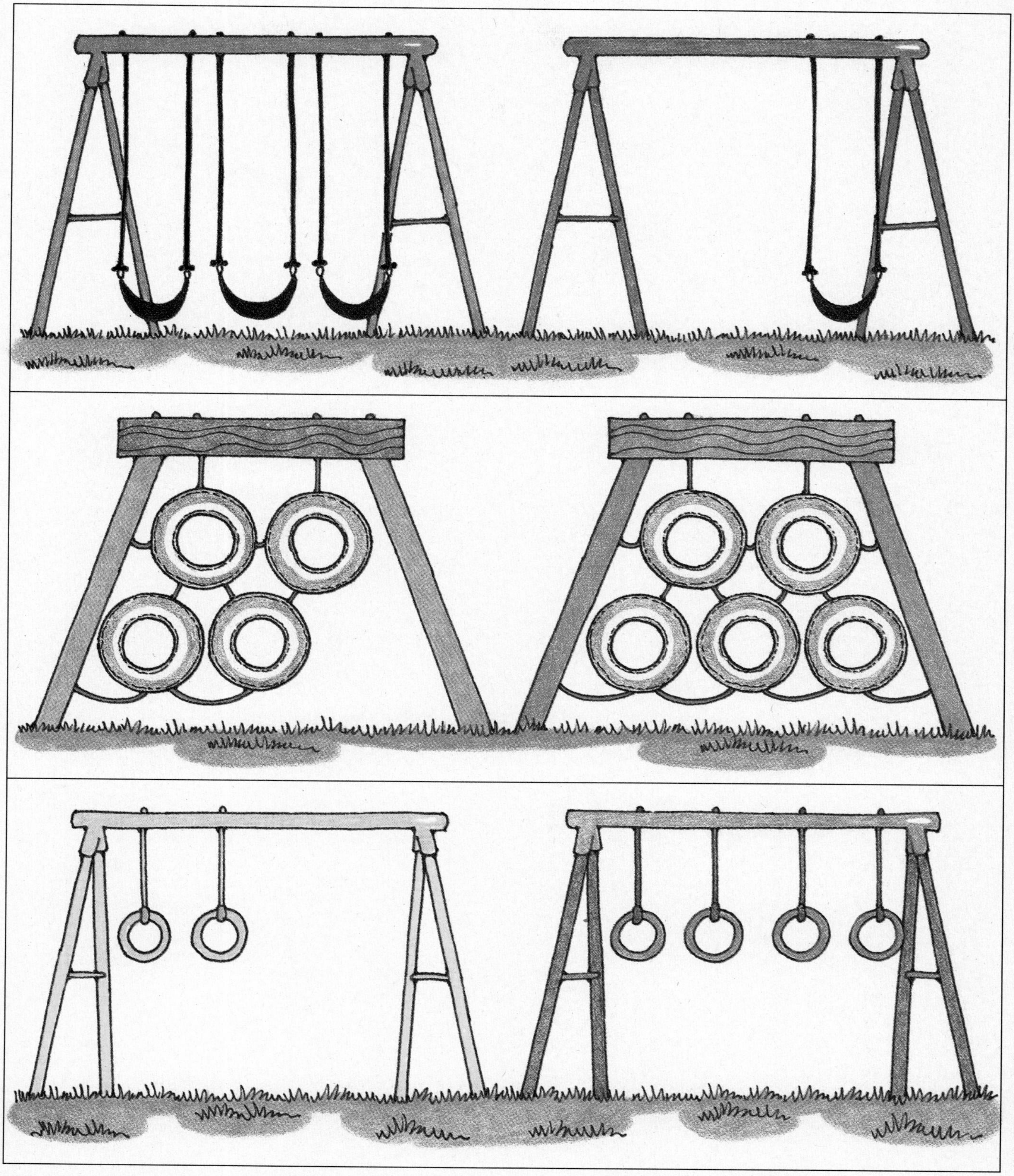

I can make the groups equal.

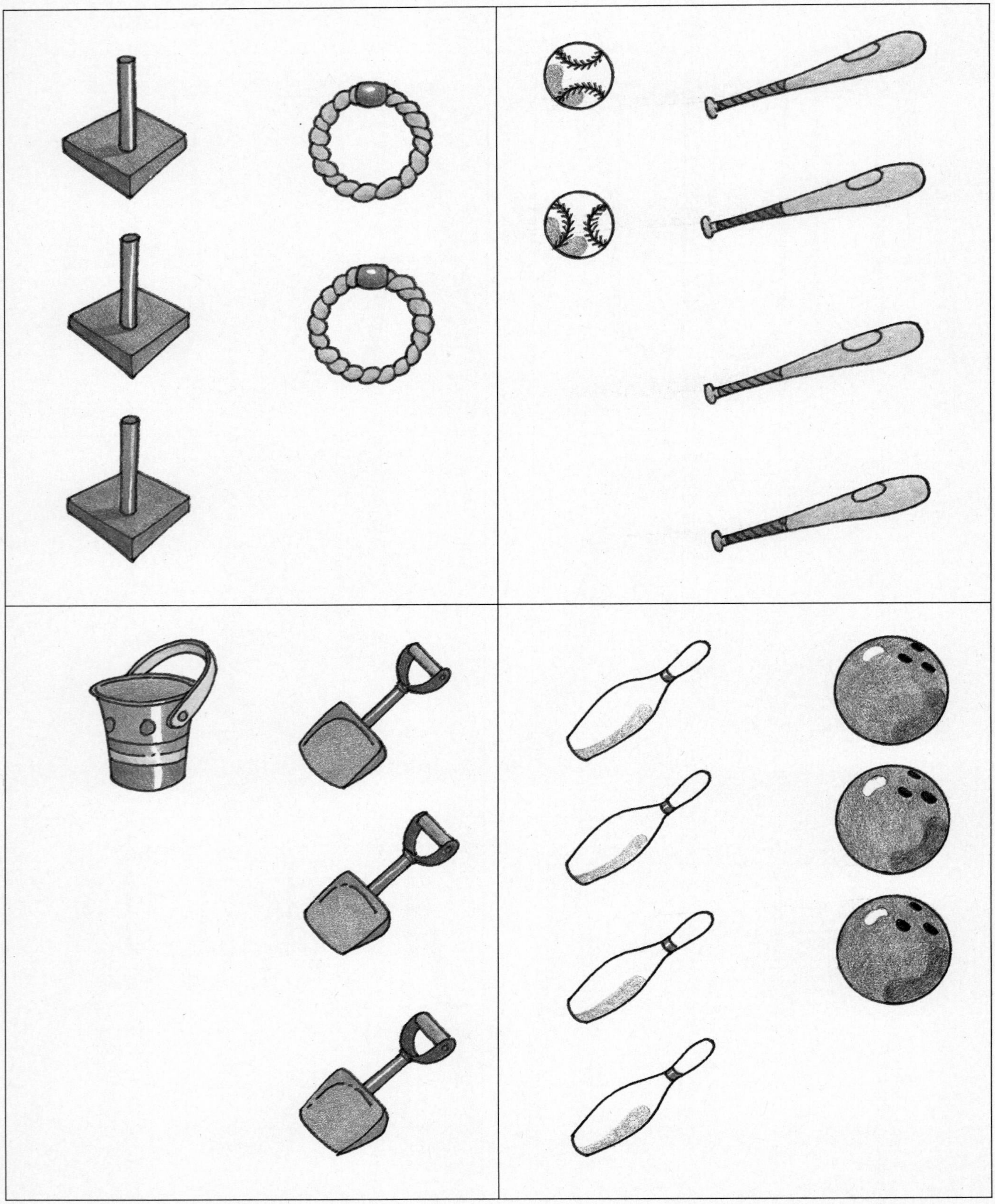

Name ____

I can make a graph.
I can tell what it shows.

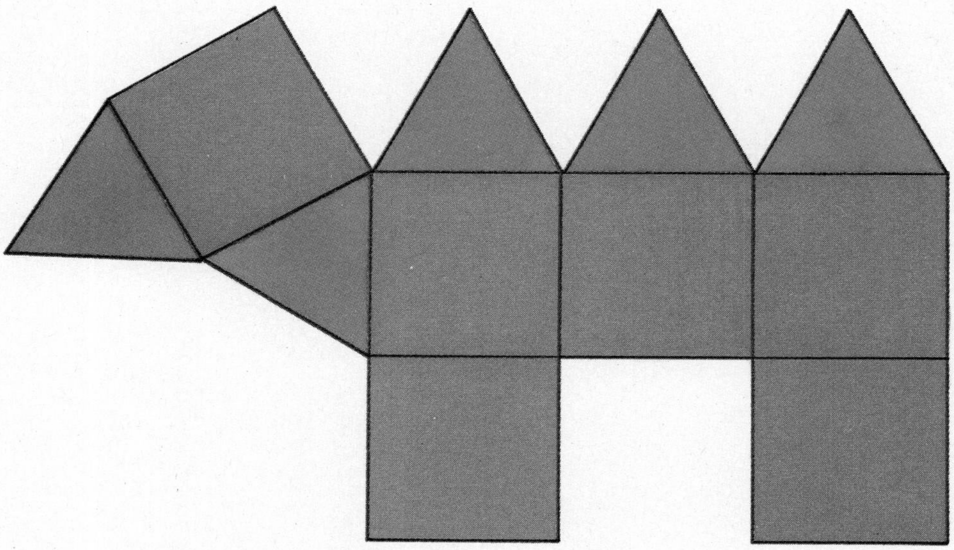

Pattern Block Graph

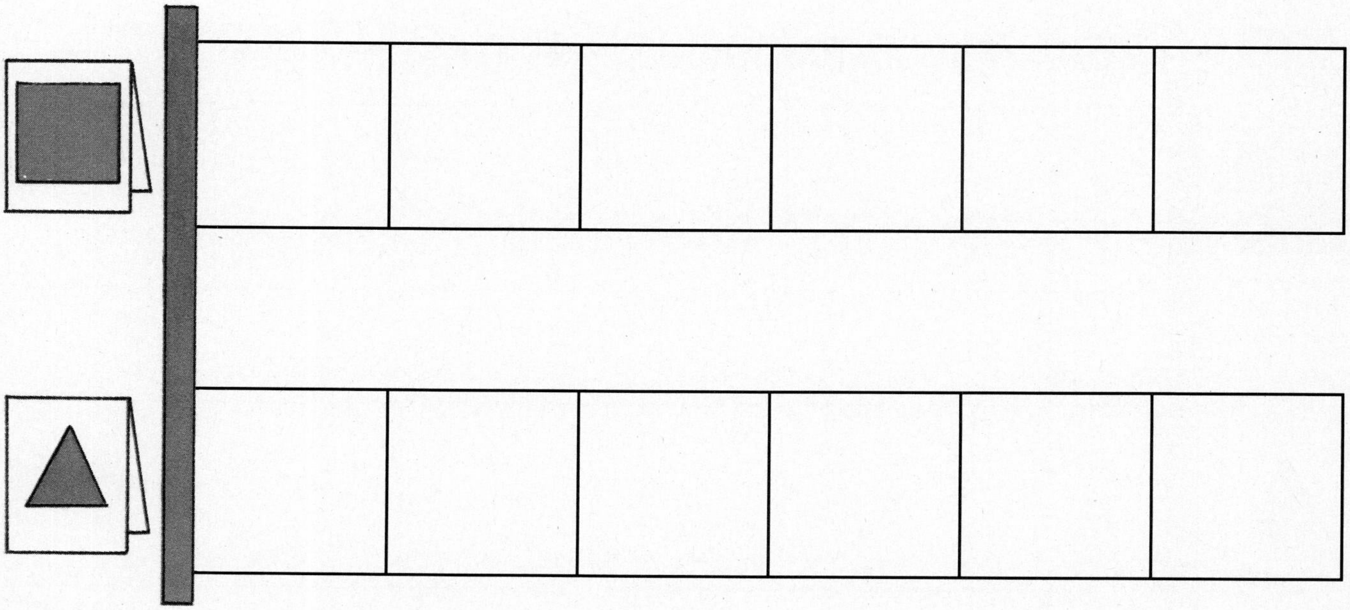

I can make a graph.
I can tell what it shows.

Pattern Block Graph

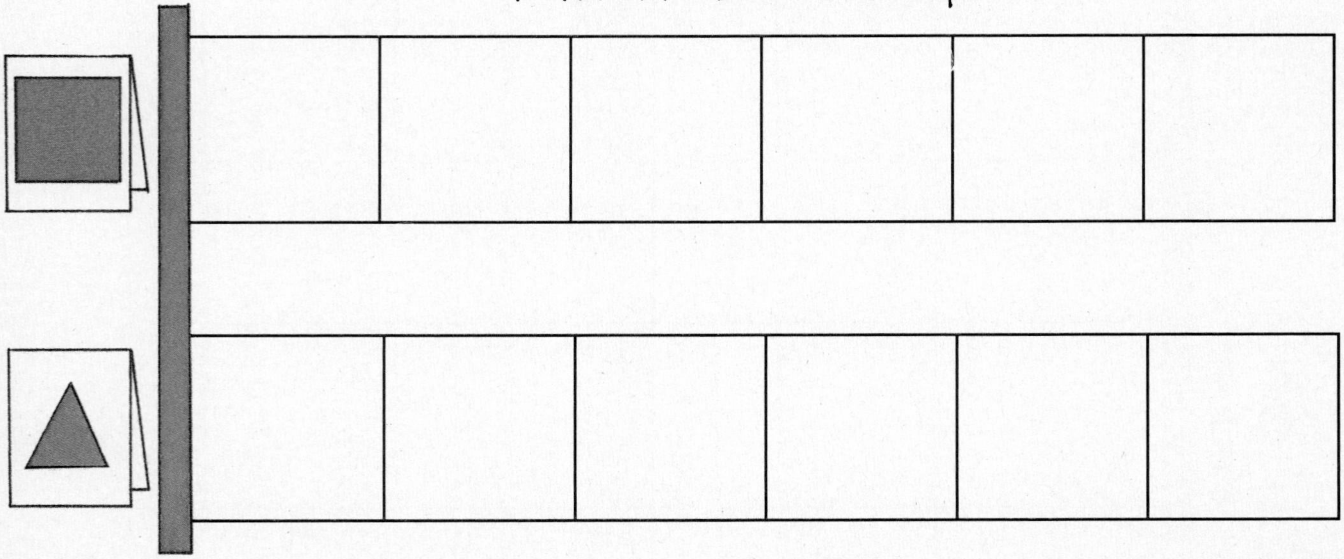

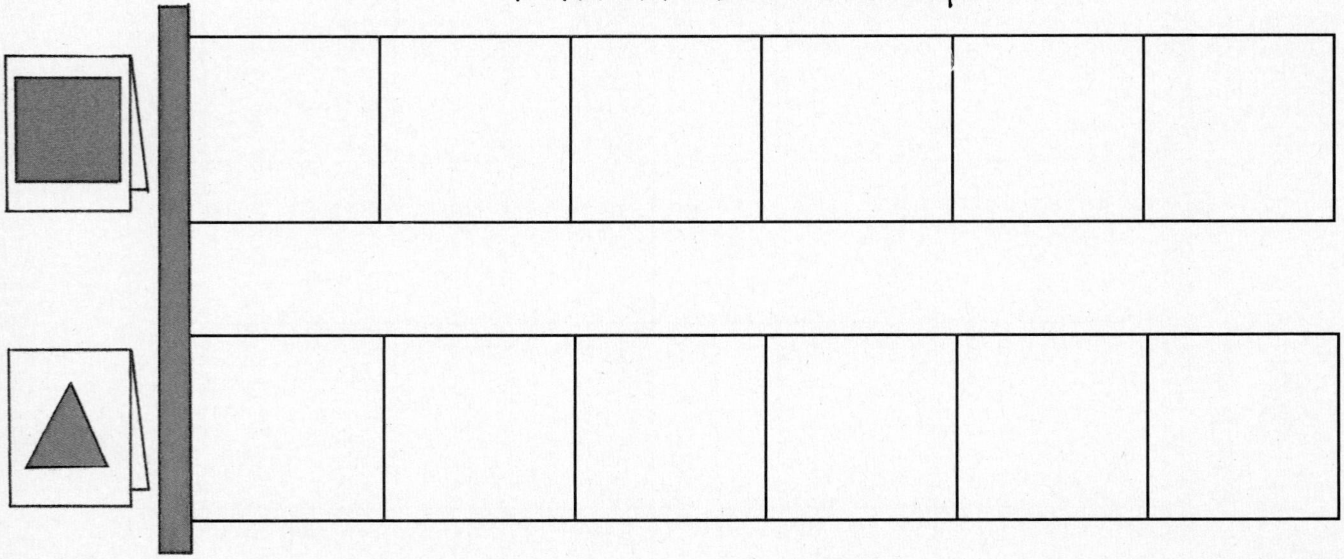

Name ______________________________

I can make a graph.
I can tell what it shows.

T-Shirt Graph

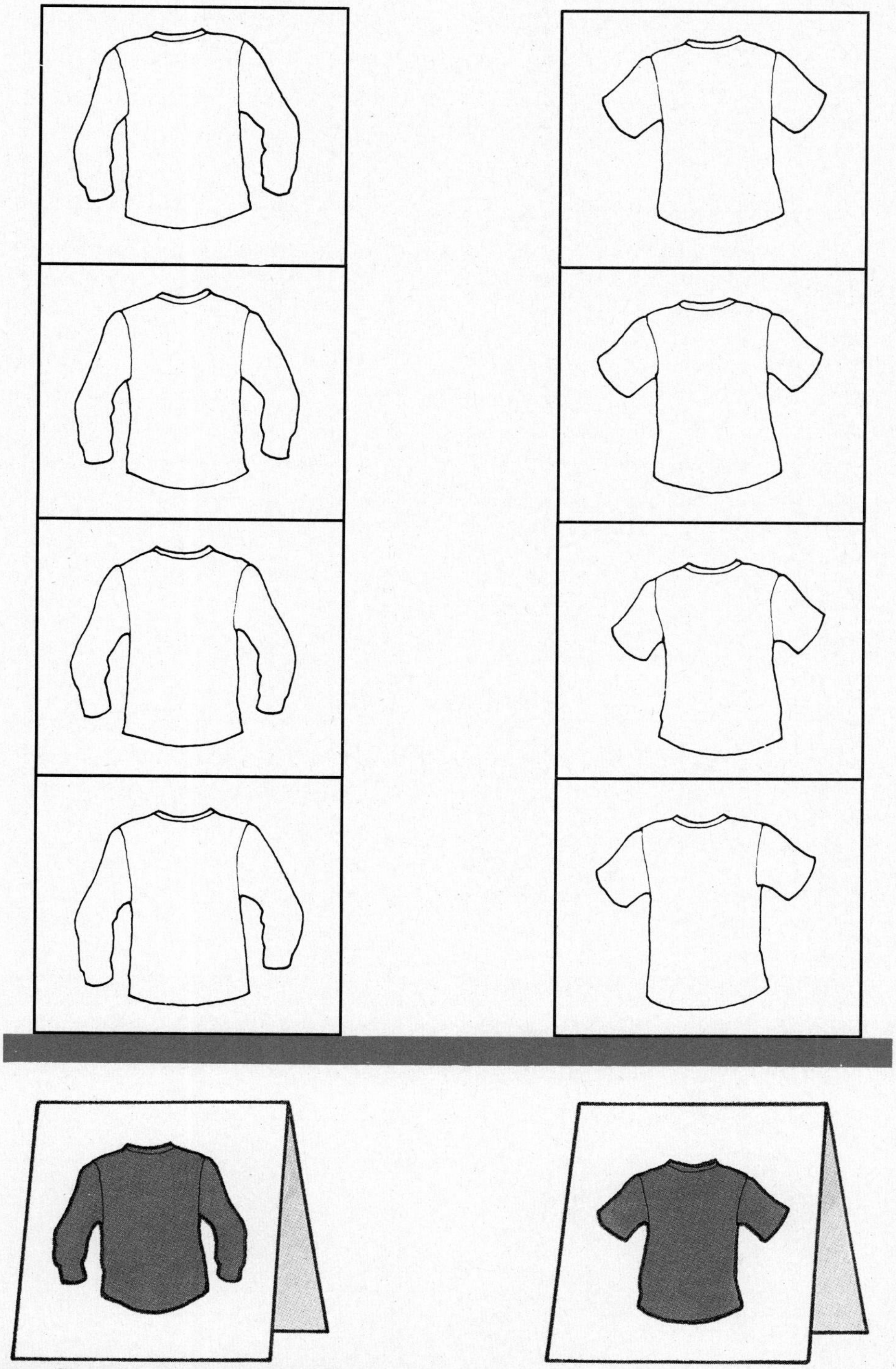

I can make a graph.
I can tell what it shows.

Jacket Graph

Name ______________________________

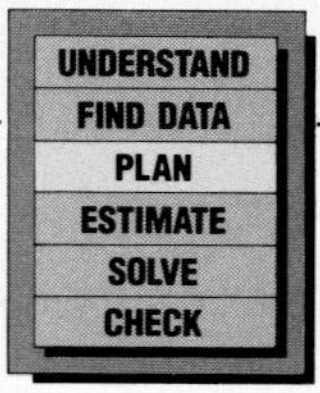

I can tell if there is a cap for each monkey.

I can make a graph.
I can tell what it shows.

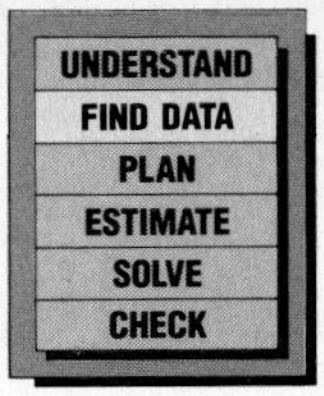

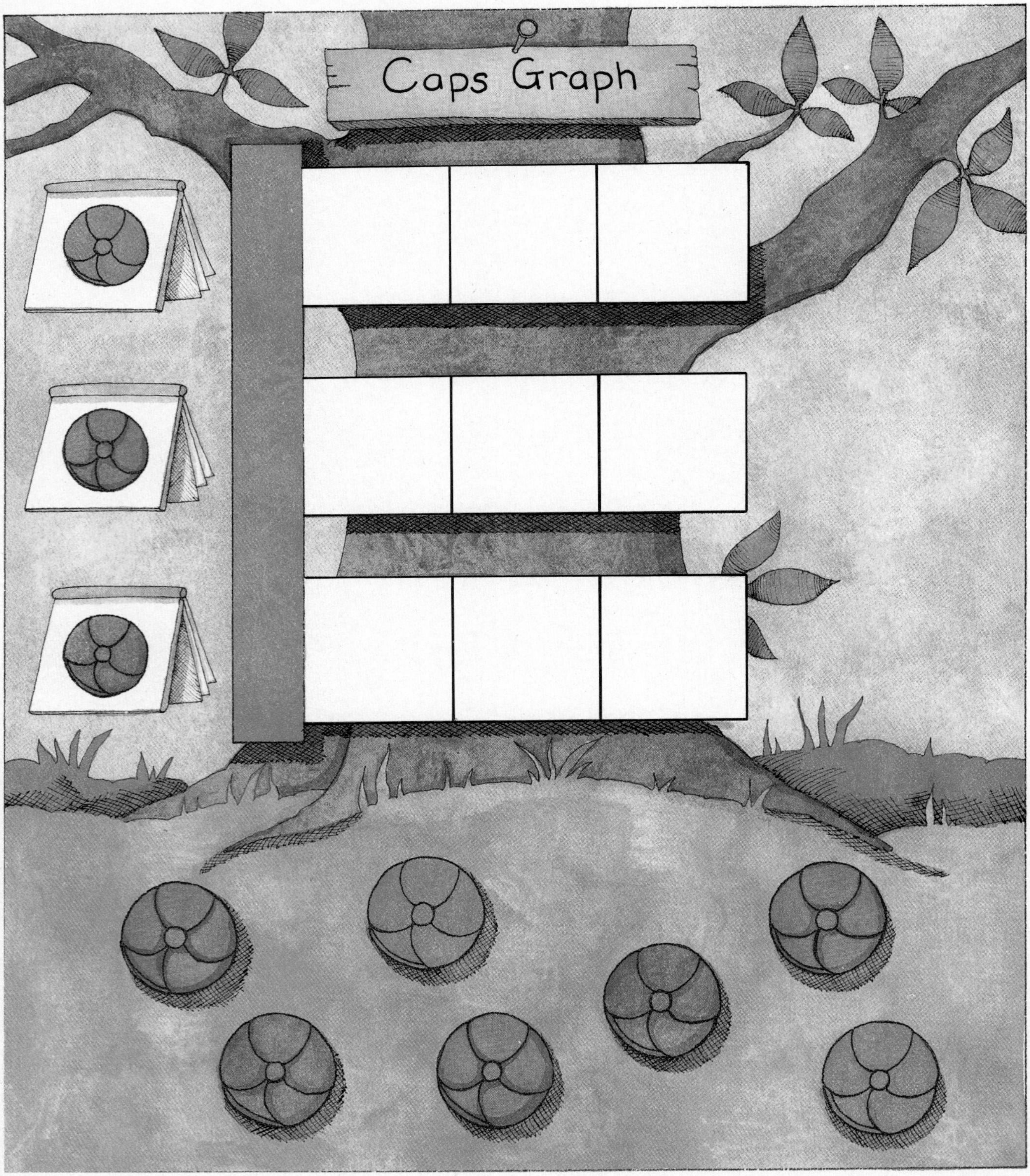

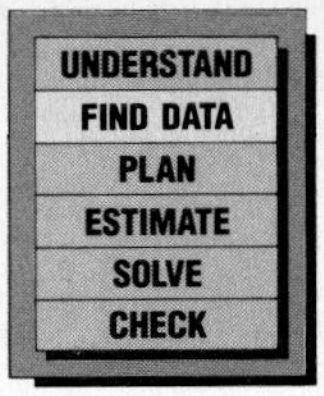

Name ______________________________

I can make a graph for an experiment.

Chipmunk Flips

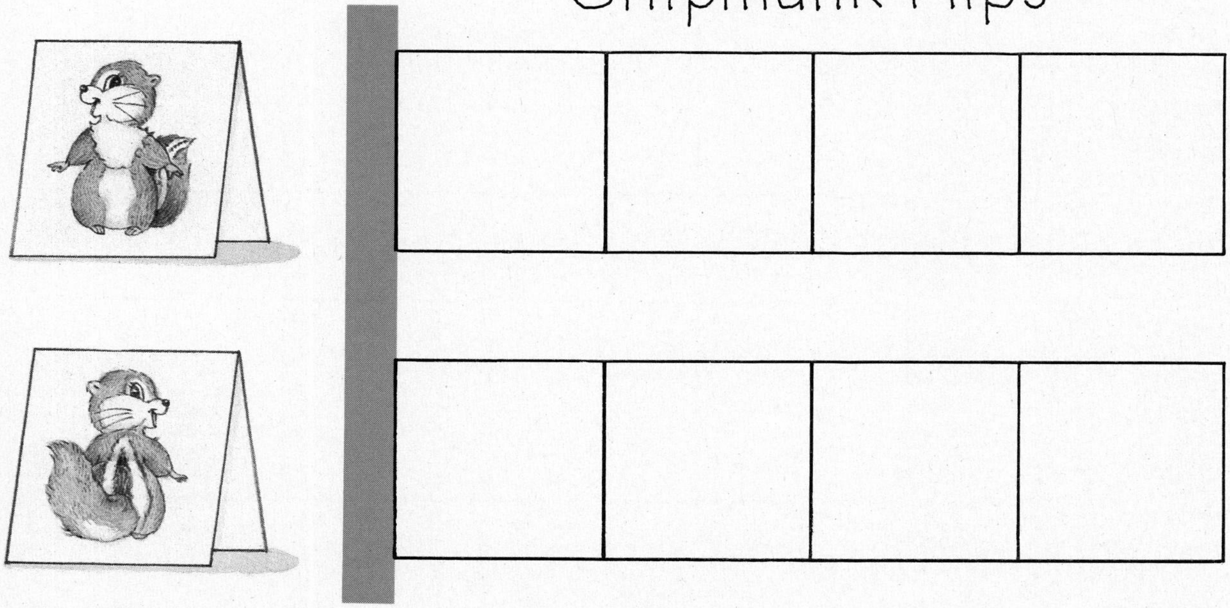

I can make a graph for an experiment.

Chipmunk Flips

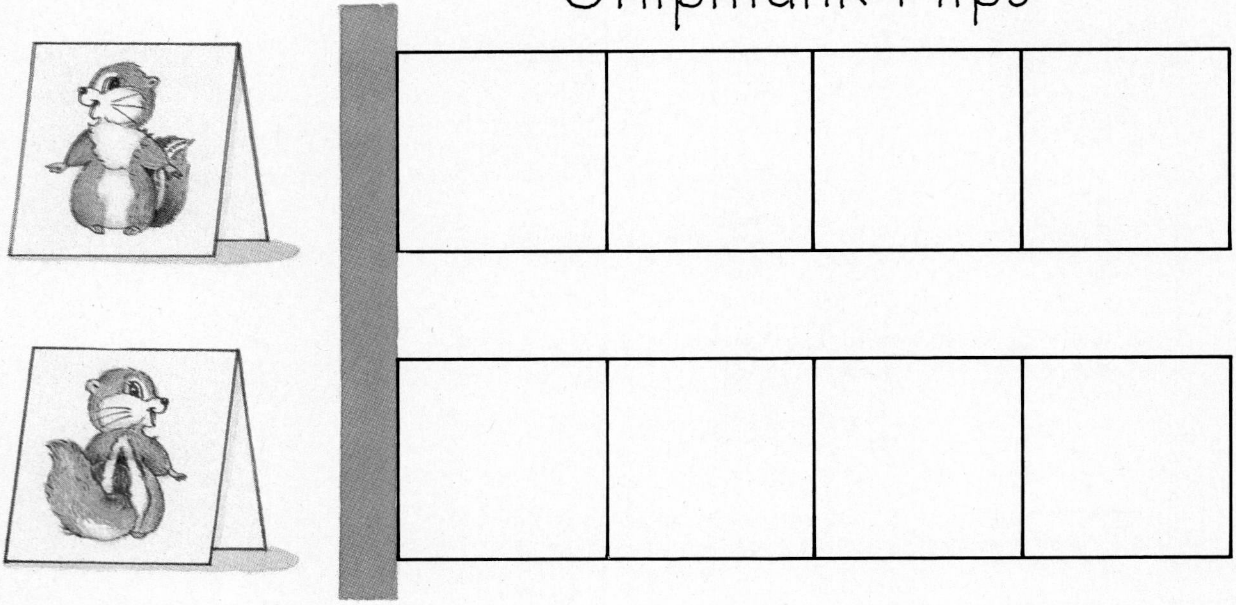

Chipmunk Flips

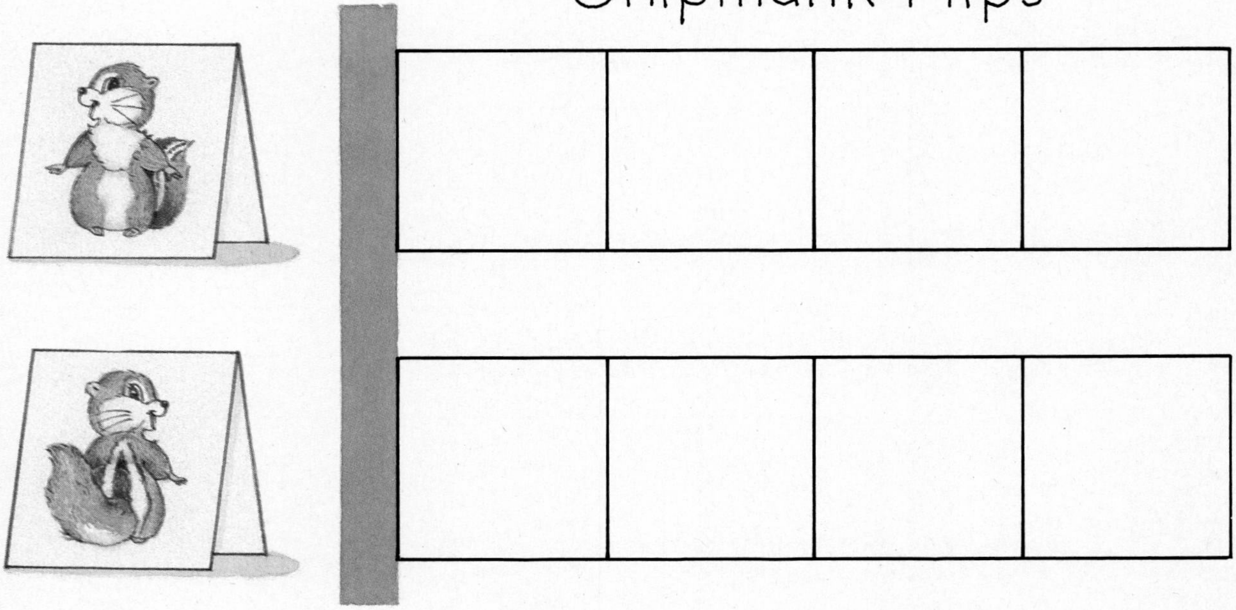

Name ________________________________

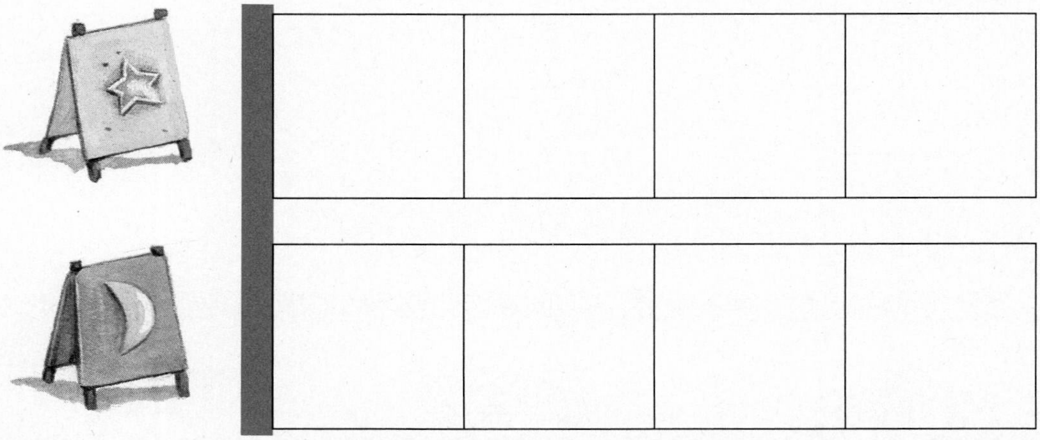

Name ____________________

I can make a graph.
I can tell what it shows.

What We Saw

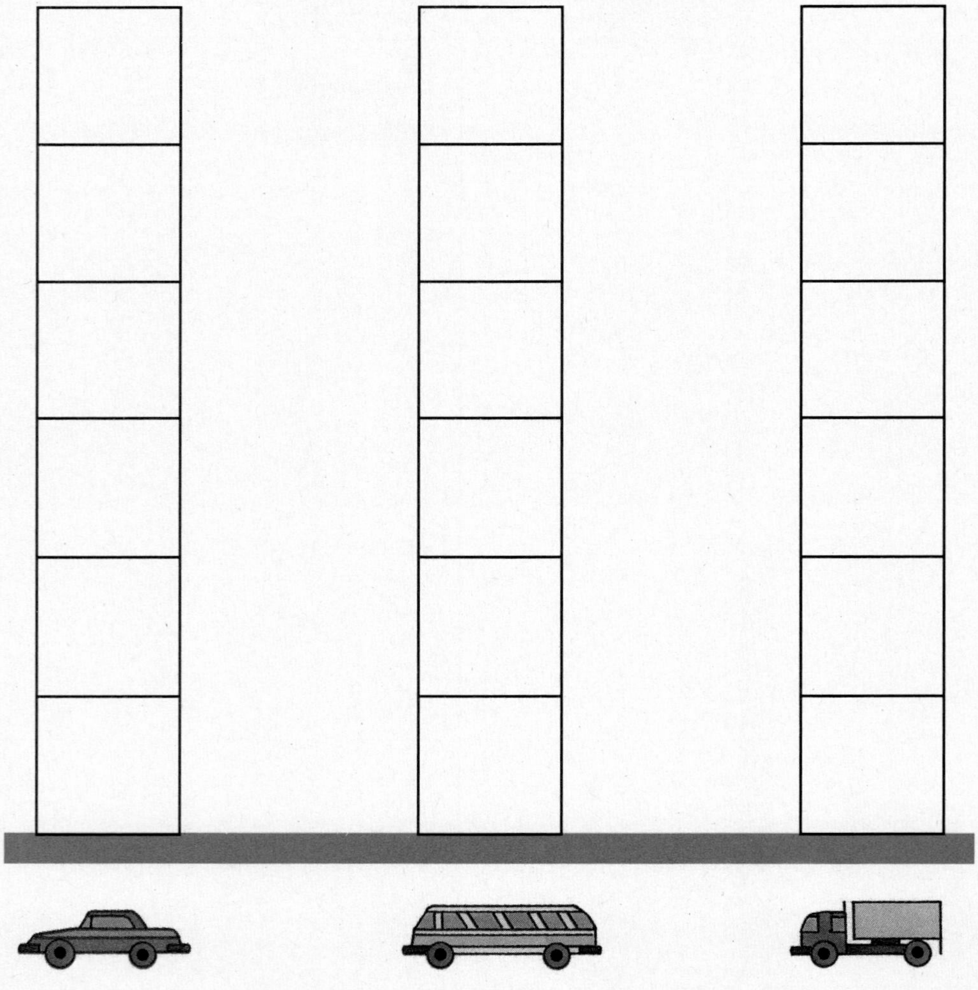

6
Numbers to 4

Workmat

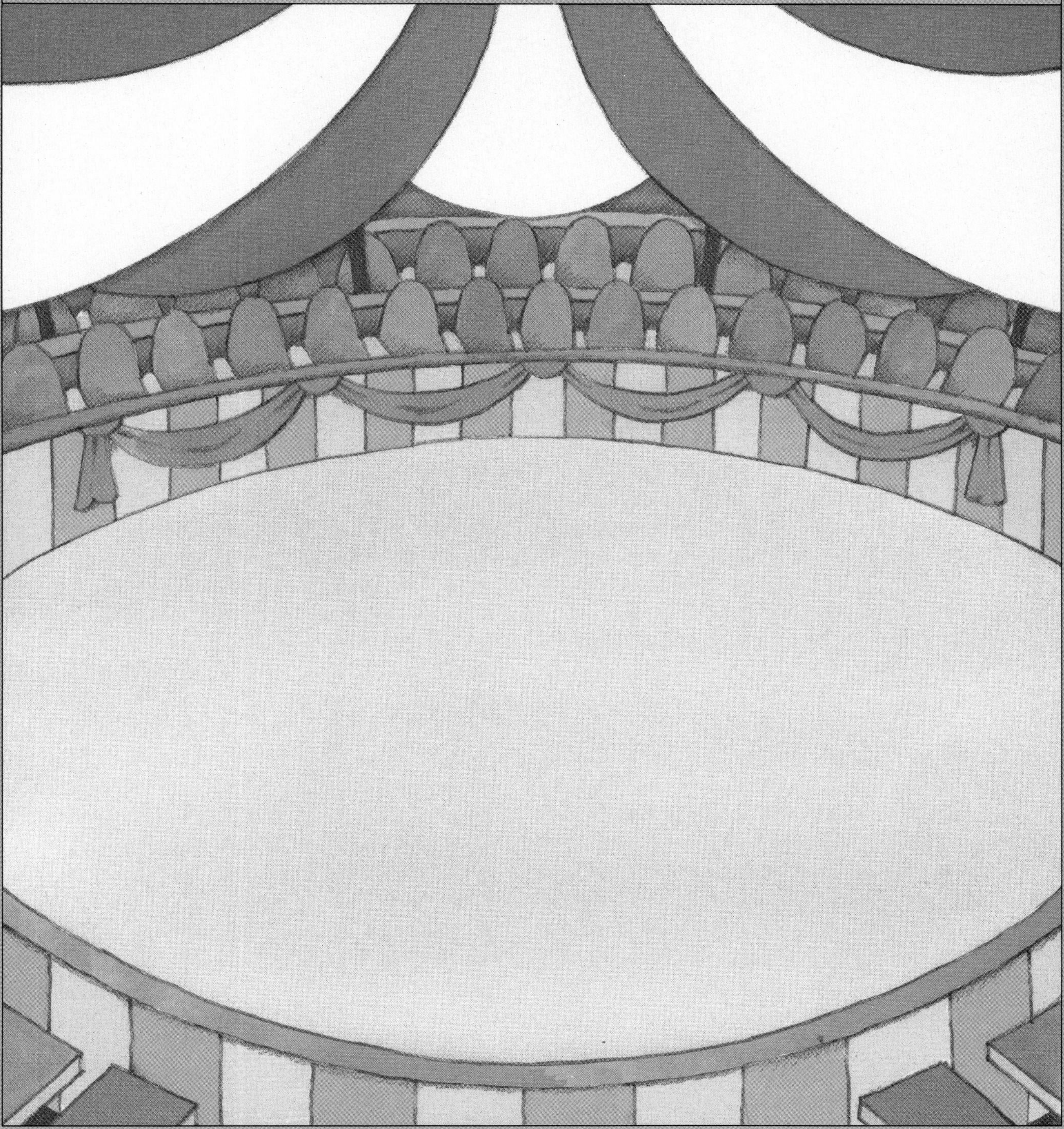

Theme: The Circus Comes to Town

Name ___________________________

I can explore numbers to 4.
I can show groups with one more.

Name ____________________

I can show groups of 1.

I can show groups of 2.

Name ______________________________

I can write numbers to show how many.

1 1 1
1 1 1

2 2 2
2 2 2

1

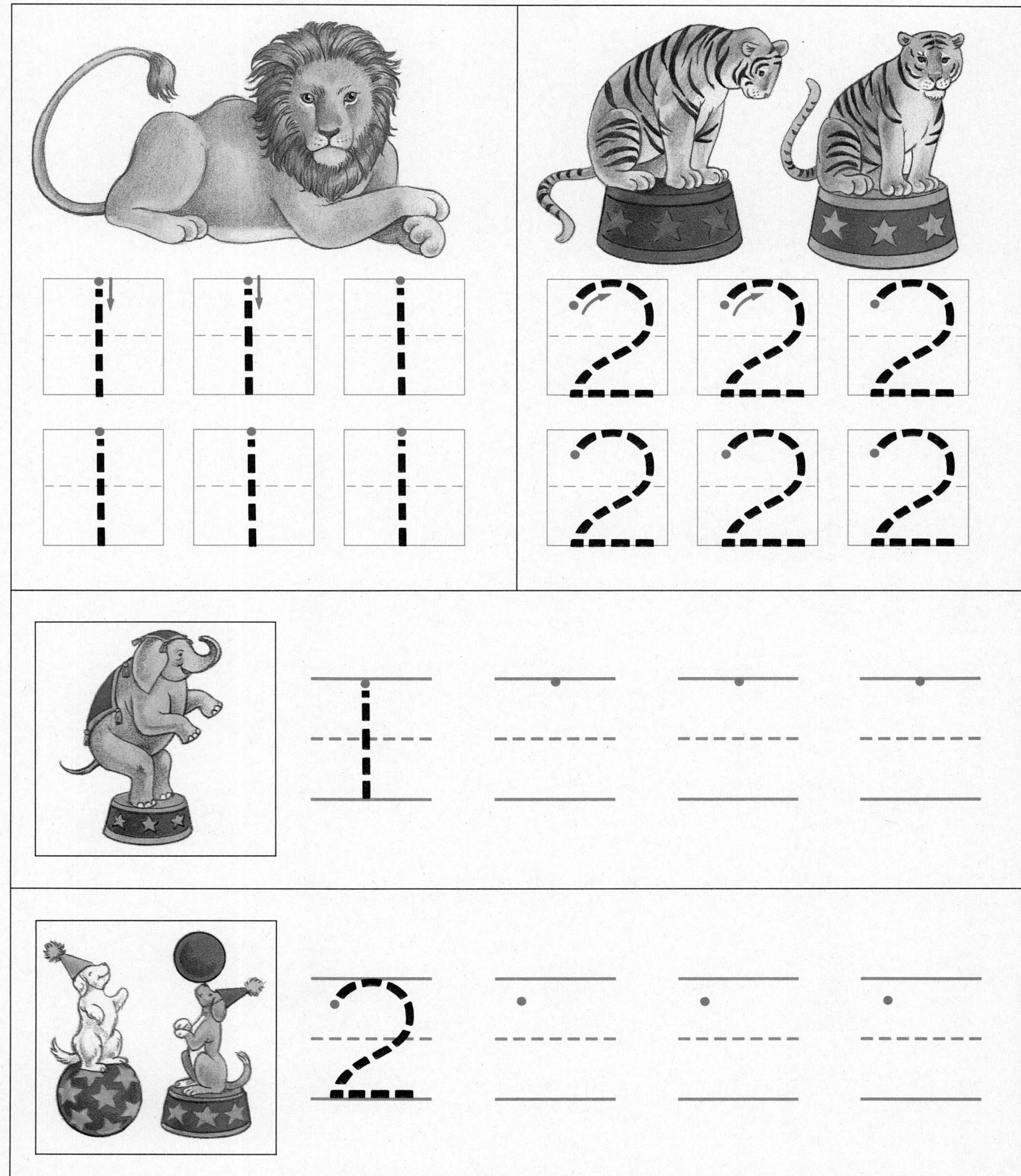

2

I can read and write number patterns.

1 2 1 2

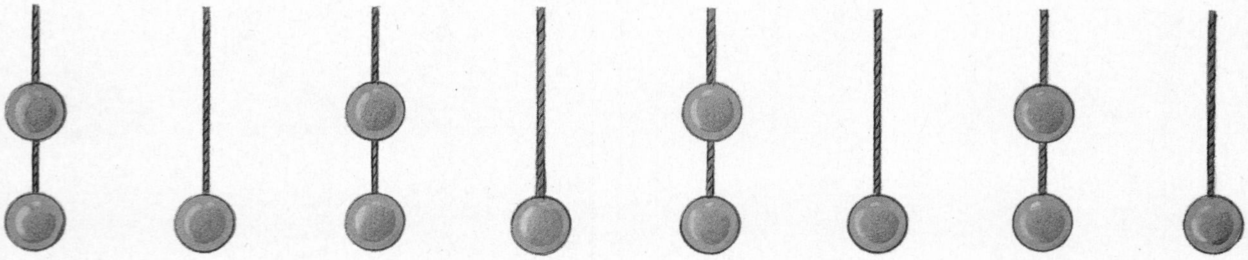

2 1 2 1

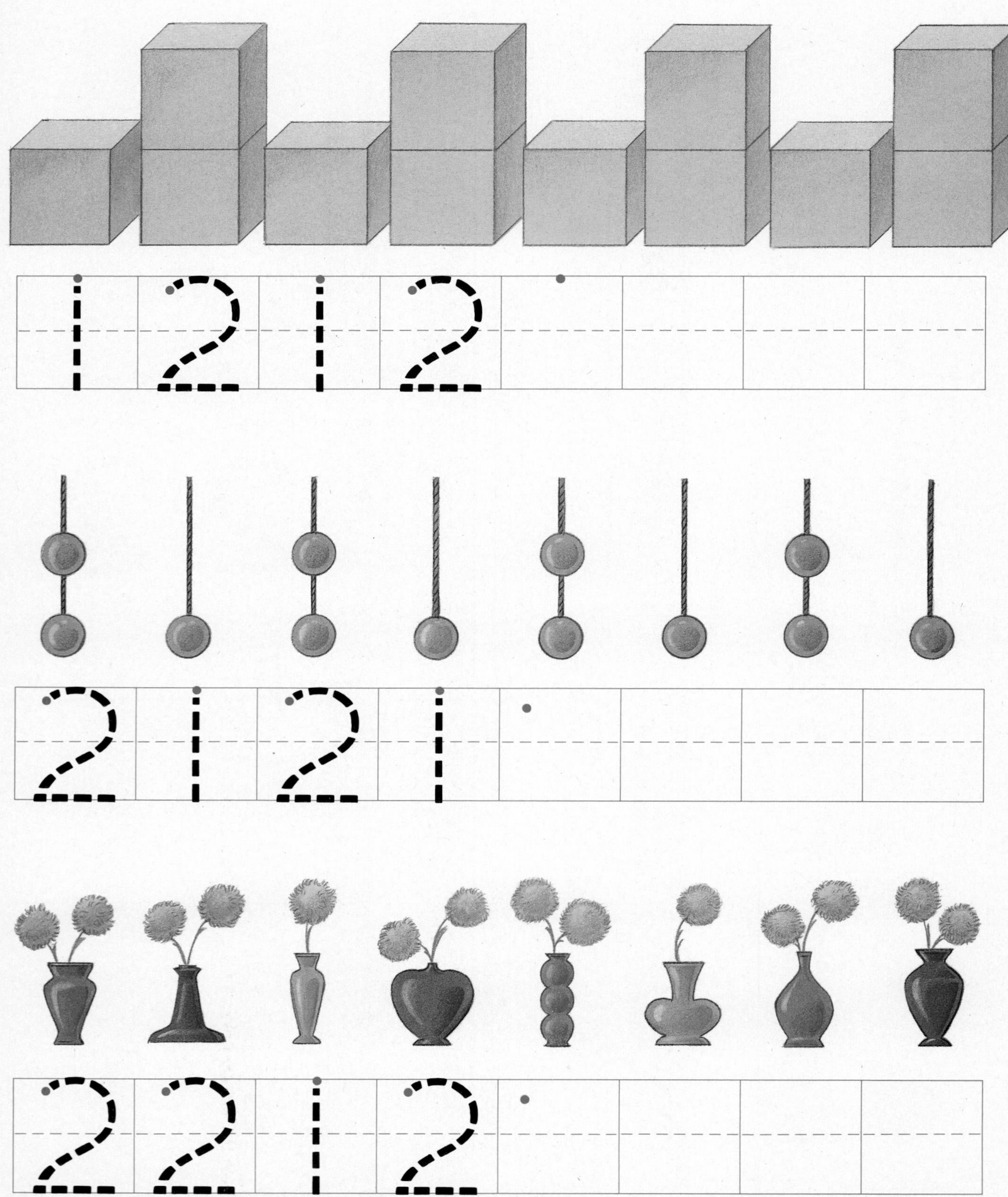

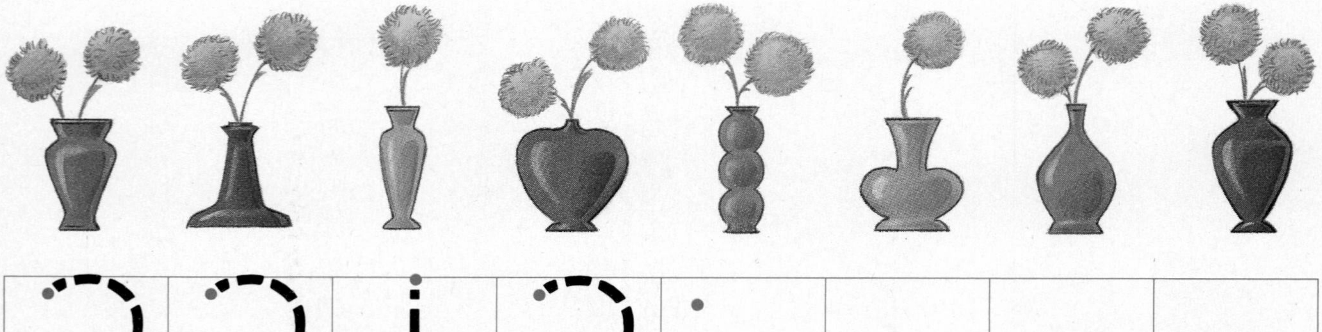

2 2 1 2

Name ________________________________

I can show groups of 3.

I can show groups of 4.

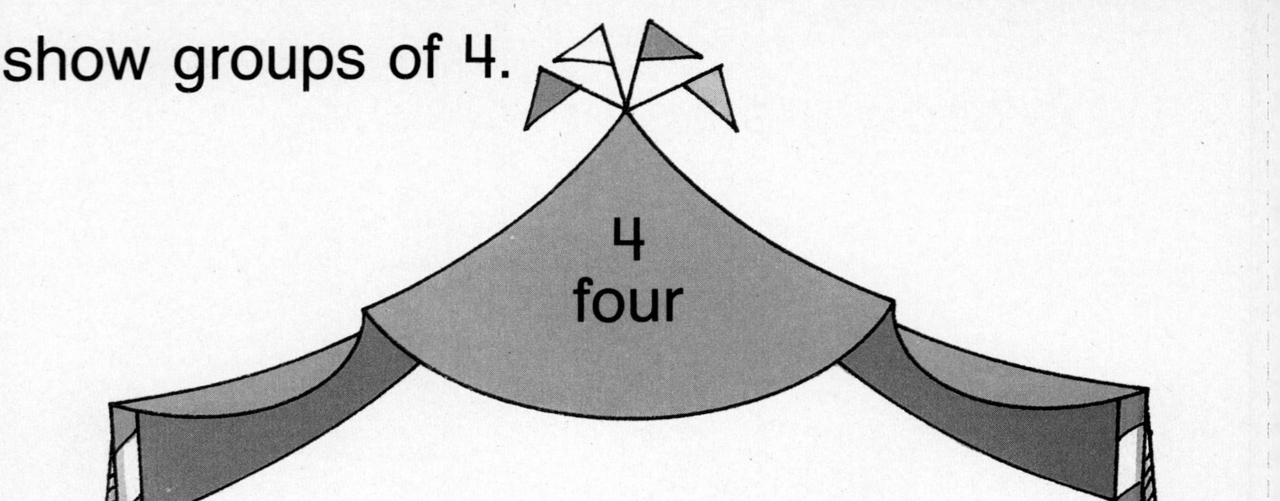

Name ____________________

I can write numbers to show how many.

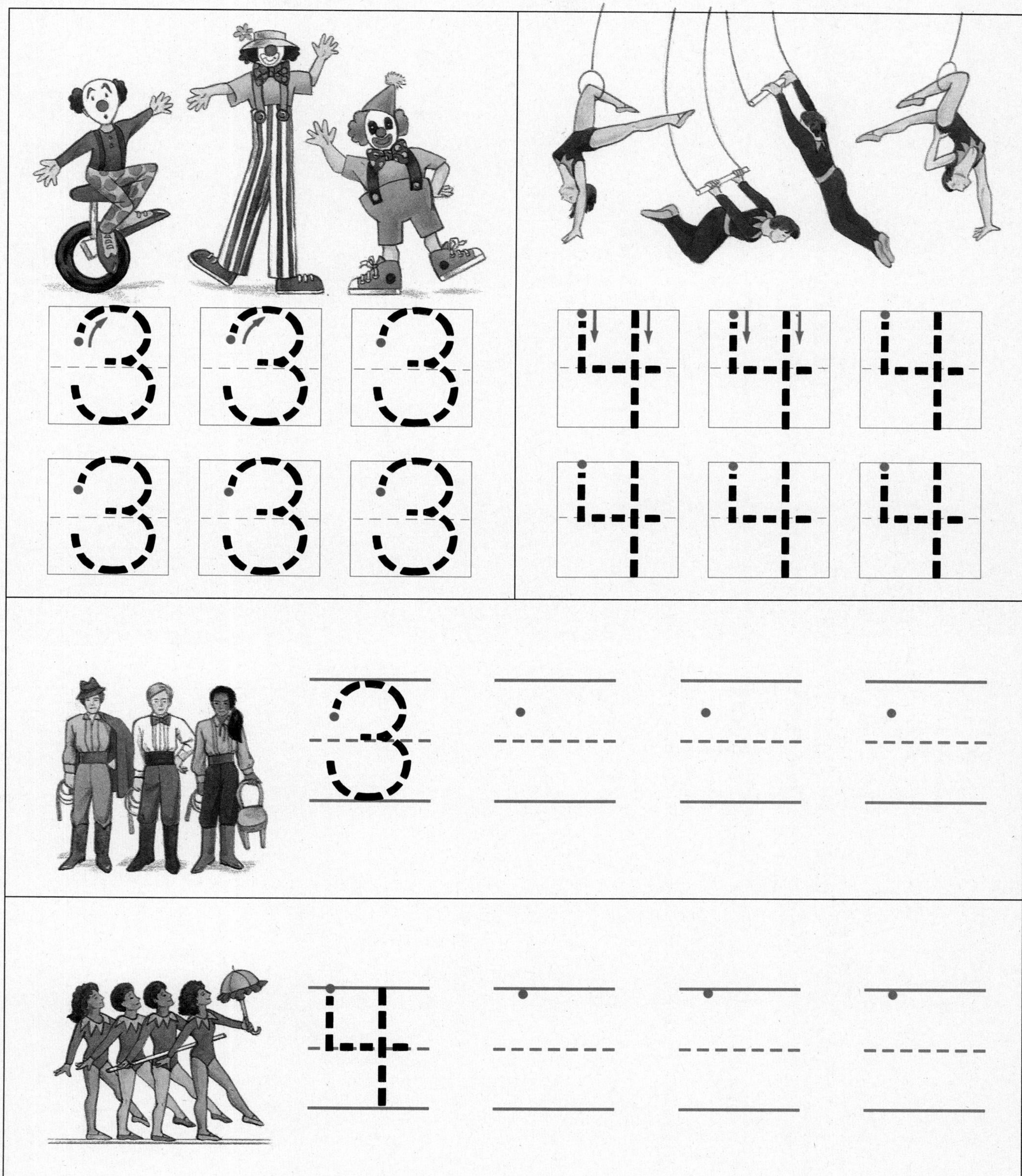

I can read and write number patterns.

3	4	3	4				

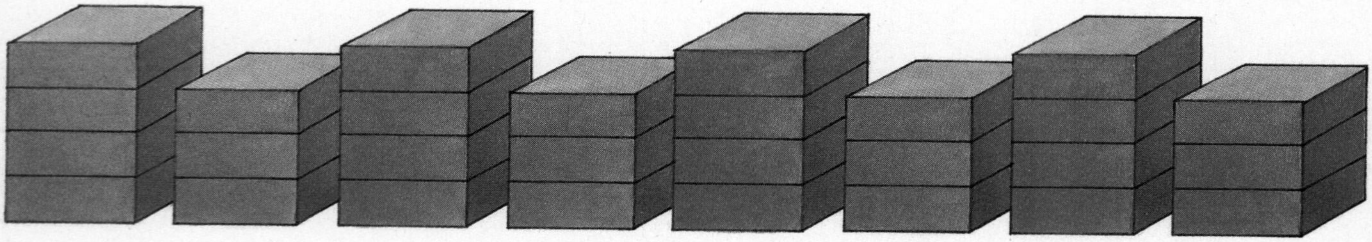

4	3	4	3				

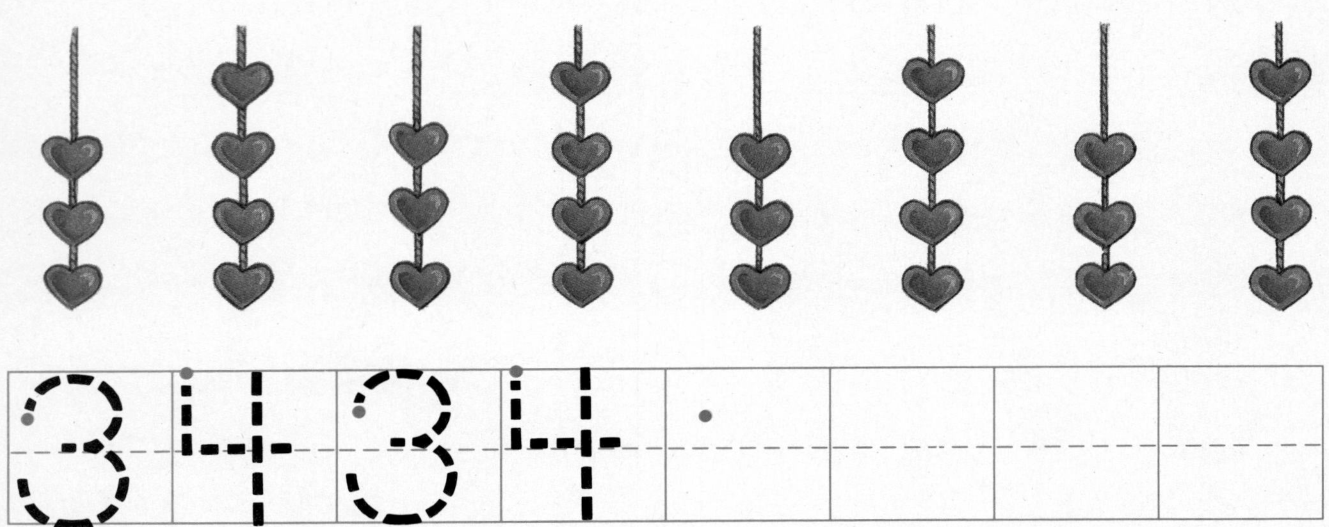

4	4	3	4				

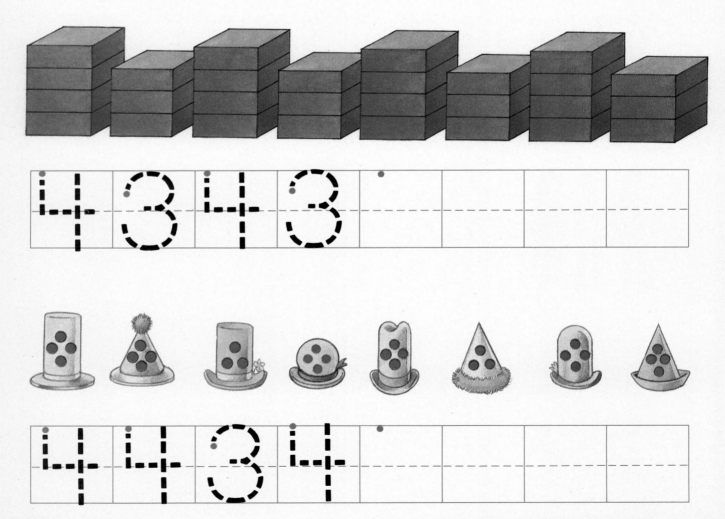

Name ______________________________

I can sort groups of 1, 2, 3, and 4.

______________'s
Tiny Book
of
1

______________'s
Tiny Book
of
2

______________'s
Tiny Book
of
3

______________'s
Tiny Book
of
4

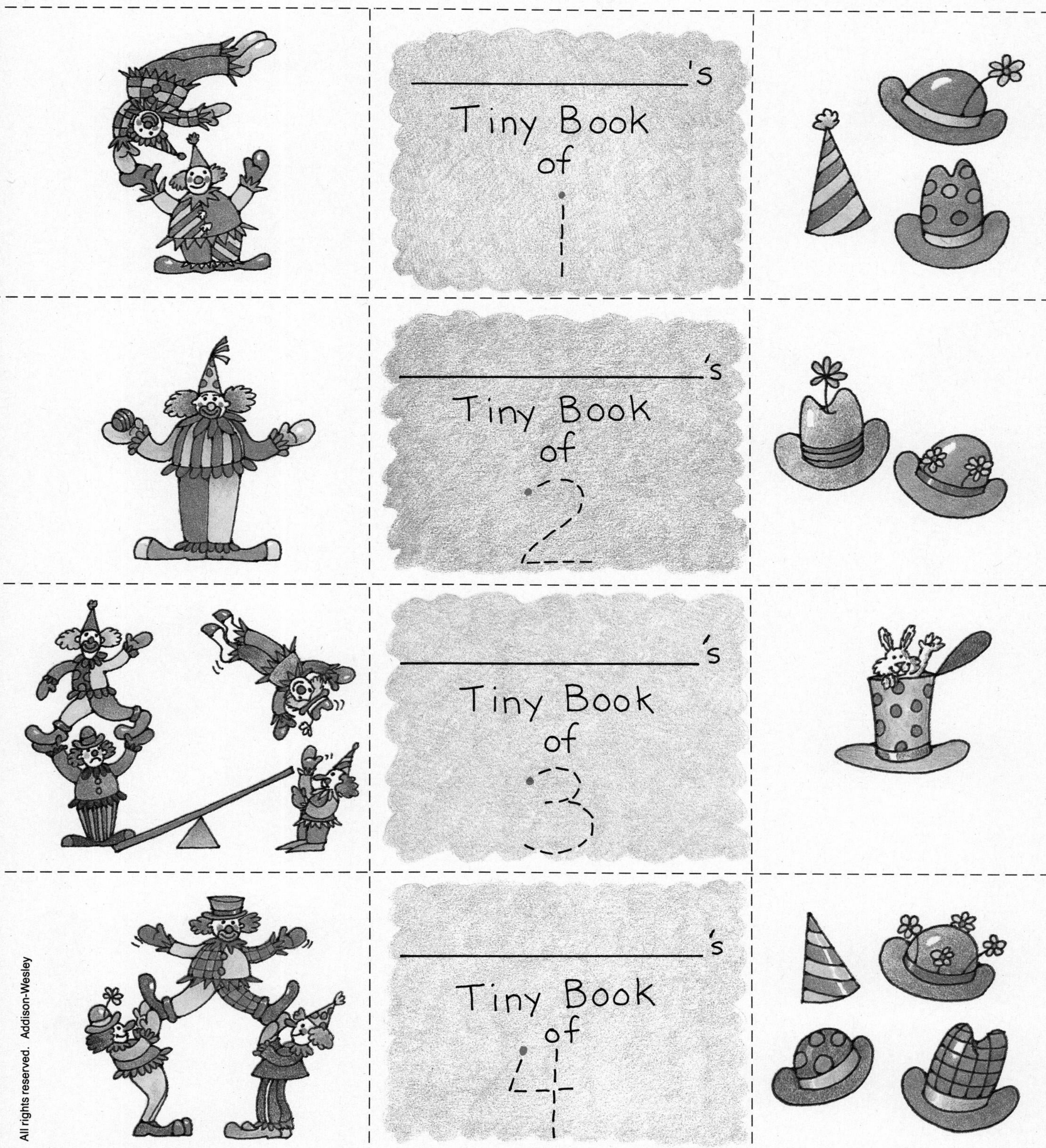

I can sort groups of 1, 2, 3, and 4.

Name ____________________

UNDERSTAND
FIND DATA
PLAN
ESTIMATE
SOLVE
CHECK

I can draw a picture for a story.
I can tell what it shows.

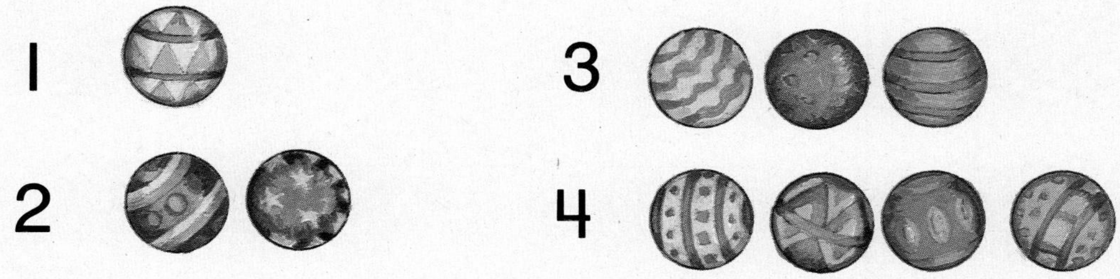

______

______ balls

______

______ flowers

______

______ ball

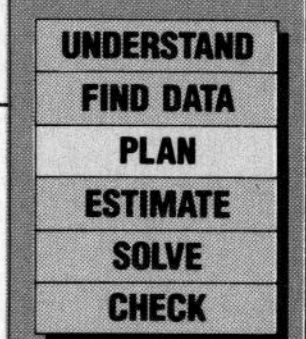

______

______ hoops

UNDERSTAND
FIND DATA
PLAN
ESTIMATE
SOLVE
CHECK

I can color to show how many.

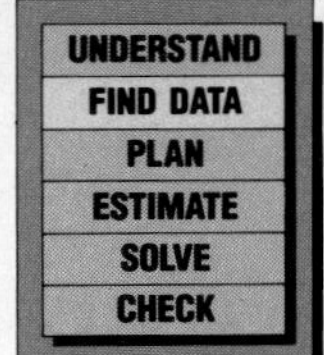

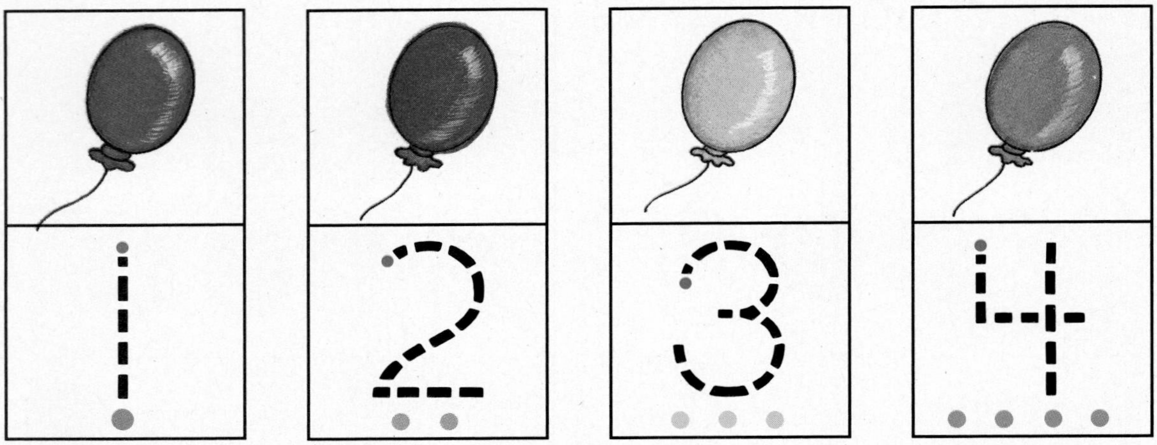

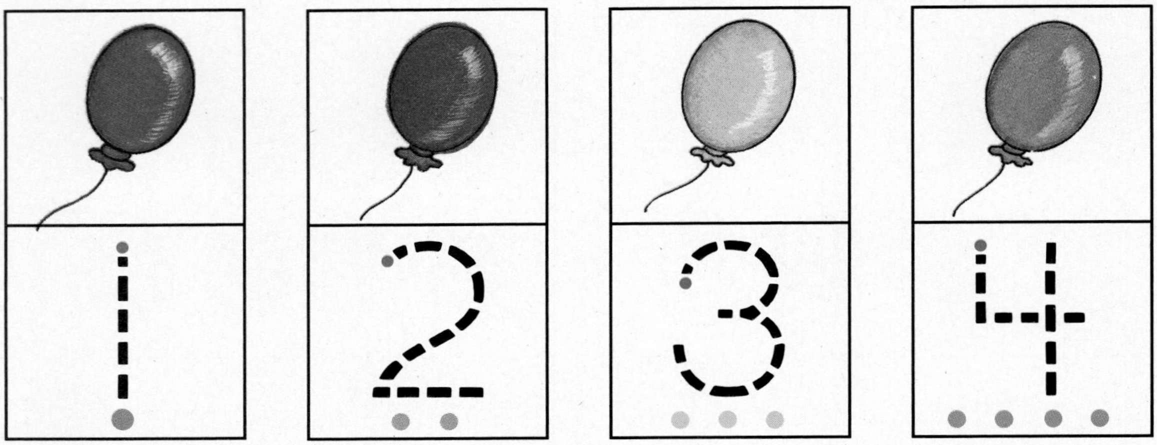

Name ______________________

I can make groups of 1, 2, 3, and 4.

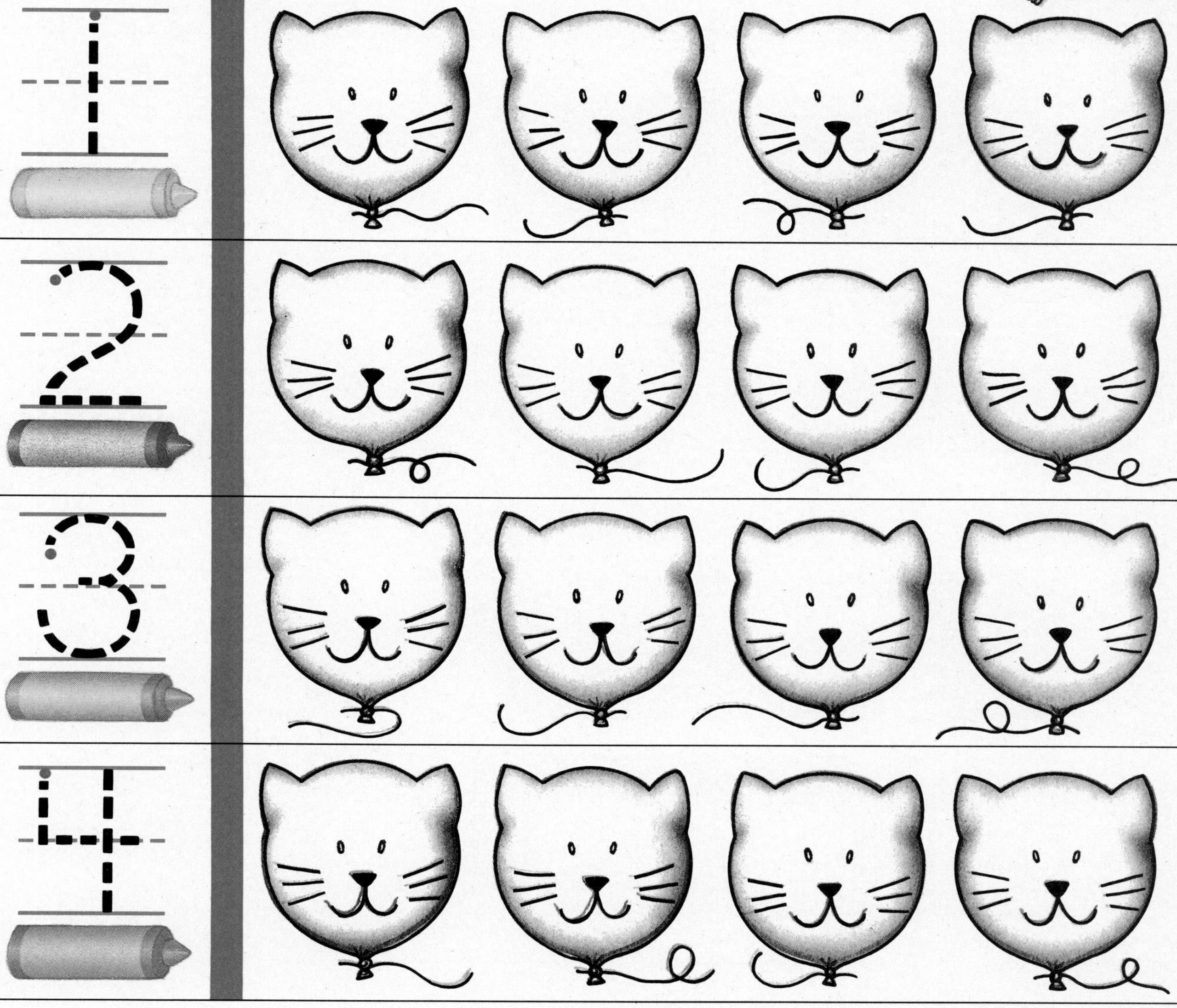

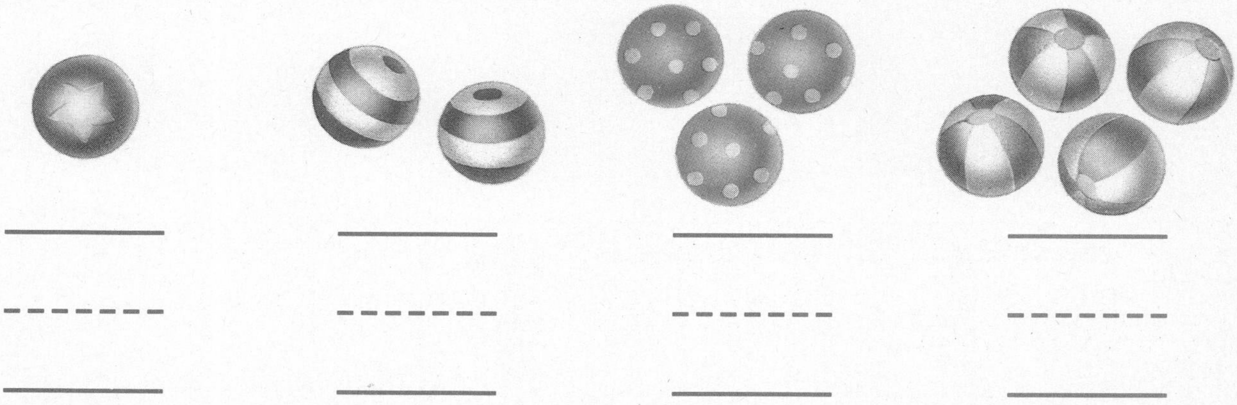

I can make groups of one more.

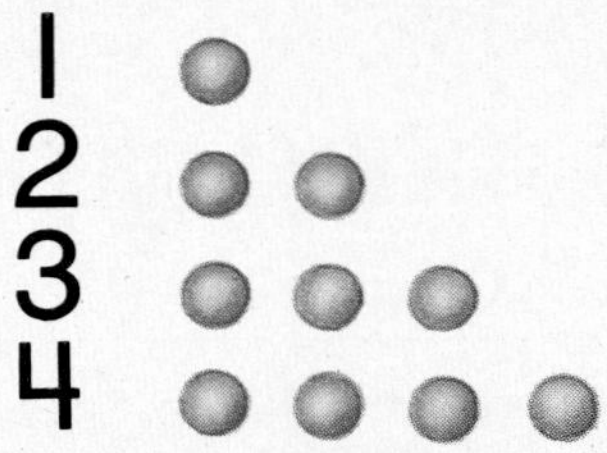

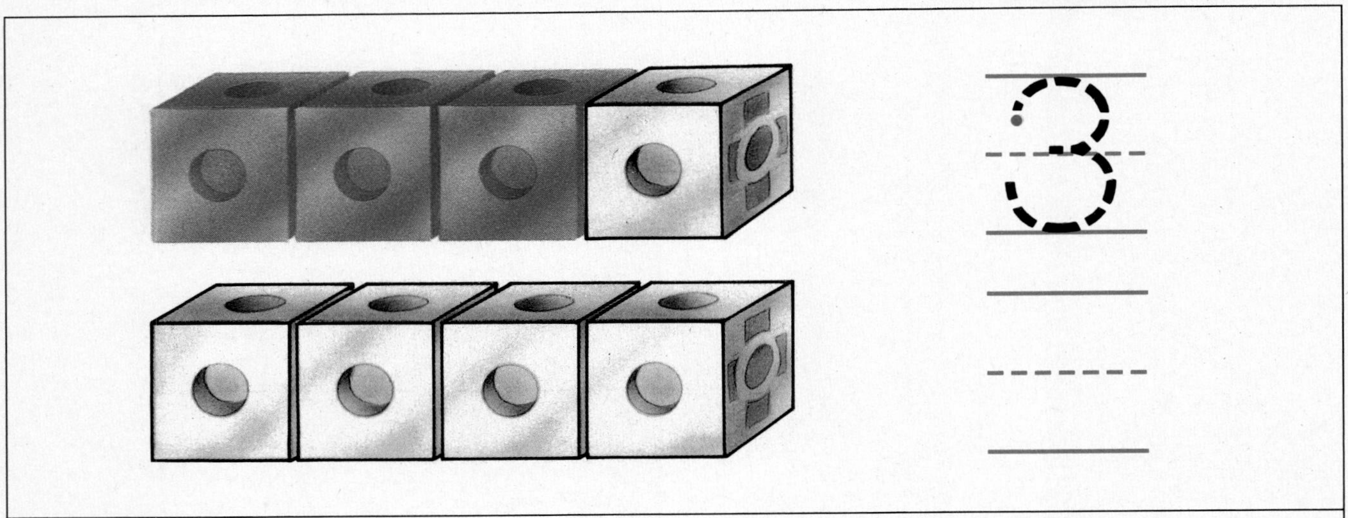

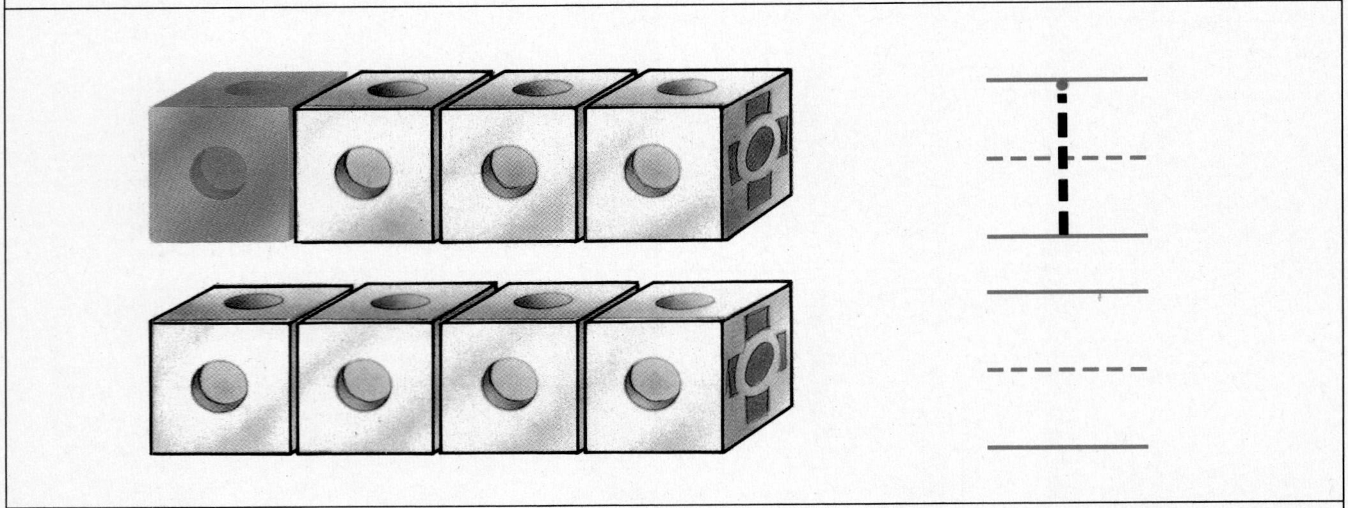

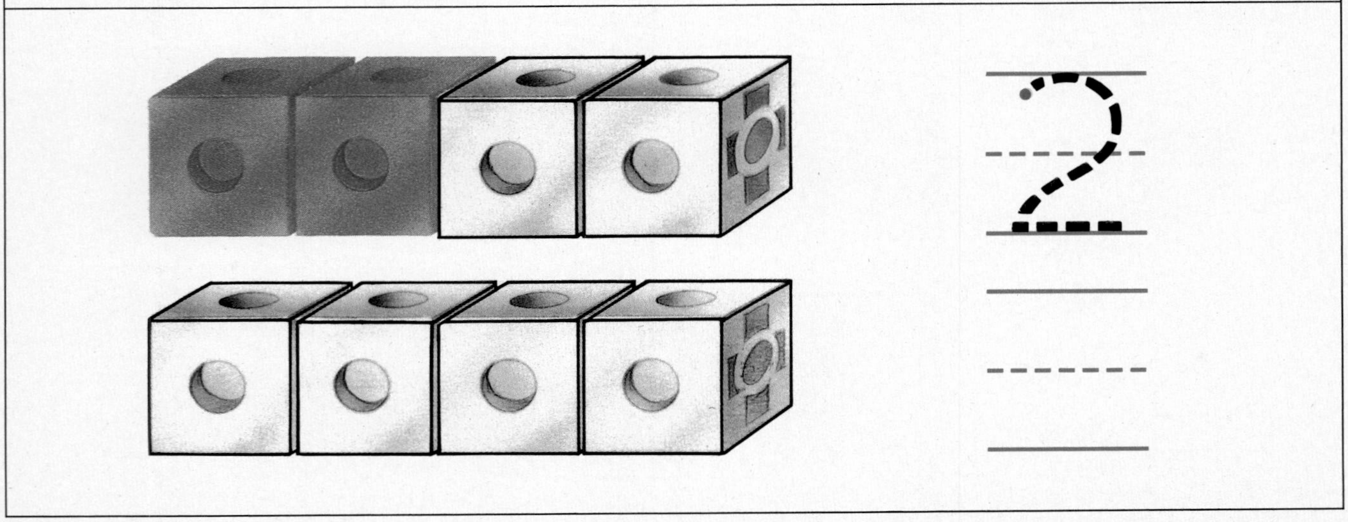

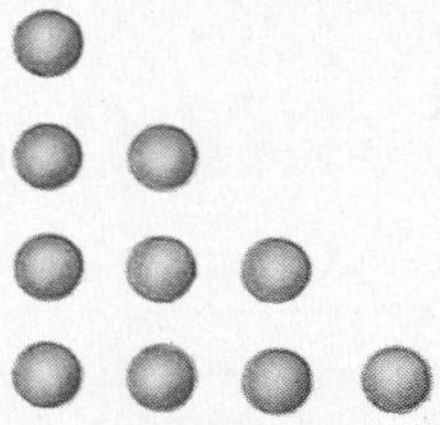

Name ______________________________

I can make groups of 4, 3, 2, 1, and 0.

0 0 0

2

1

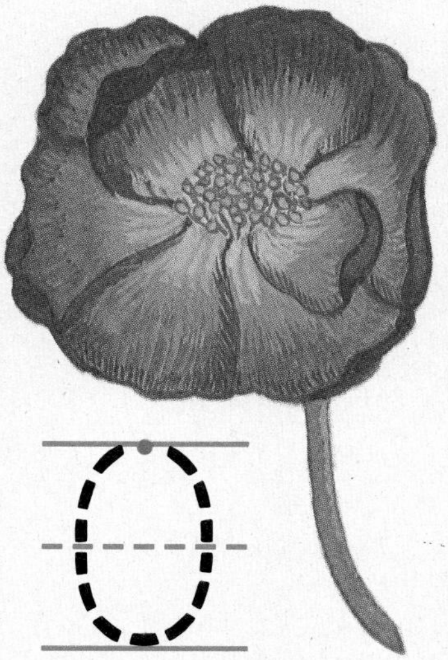

0

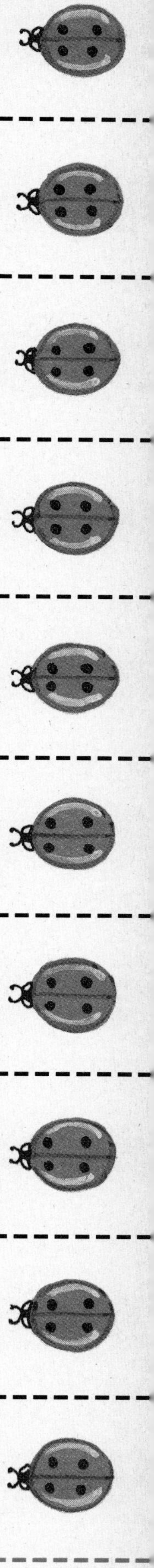

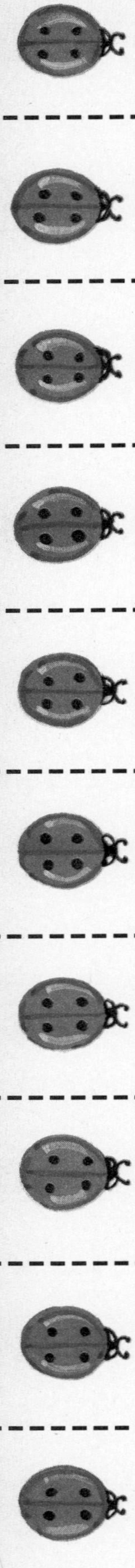

I can make groups of 4, 3, 2, 1, and 0.

0

3

4

0

Name ______________________________

I can tell how many blocks I need.

0	1	2	3	4

I can tell how many blocks I need.

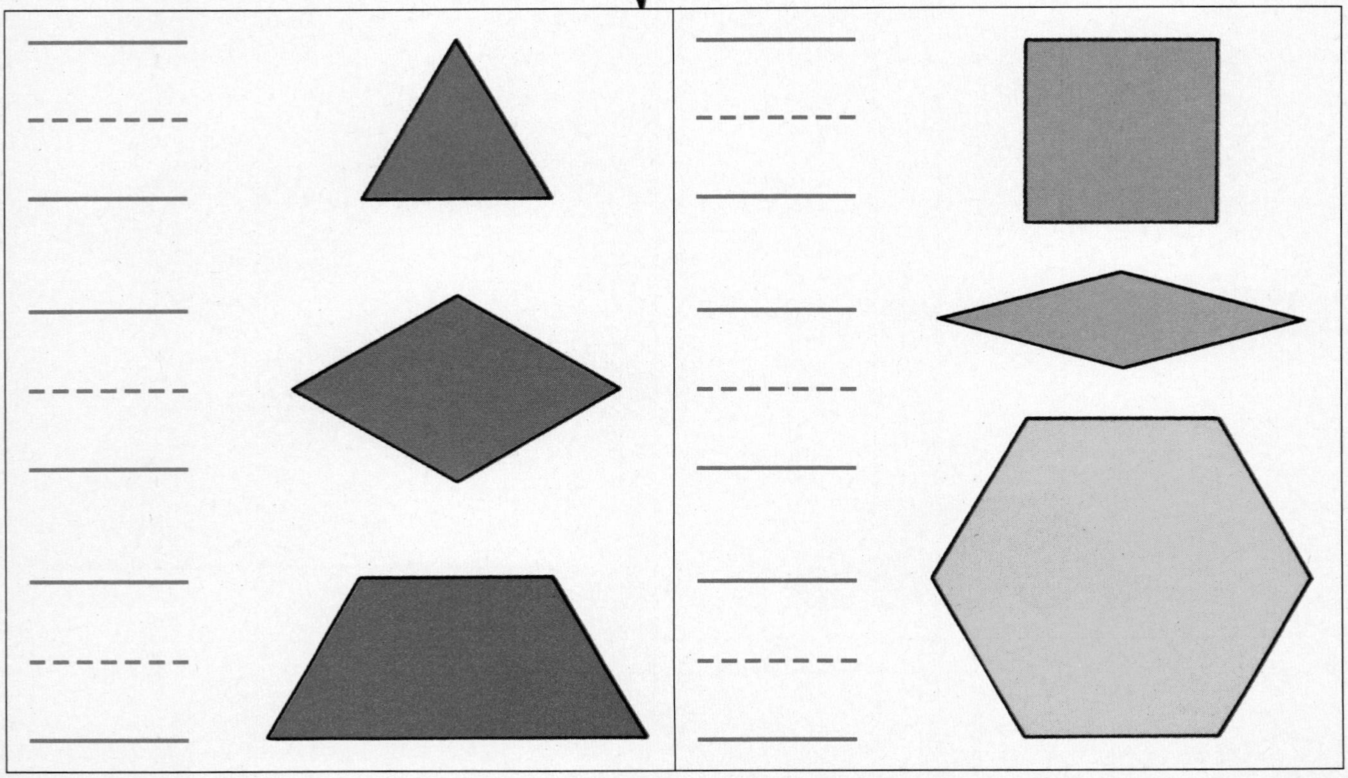

Name ______________________________

I can make a graph.
I can tell what it shows.

Things in Our Room

______ 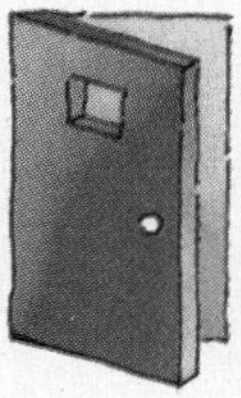	______ 
______ 	______ 

0 1 2 3 4

I can compare numbers.
I can tell which one is less.

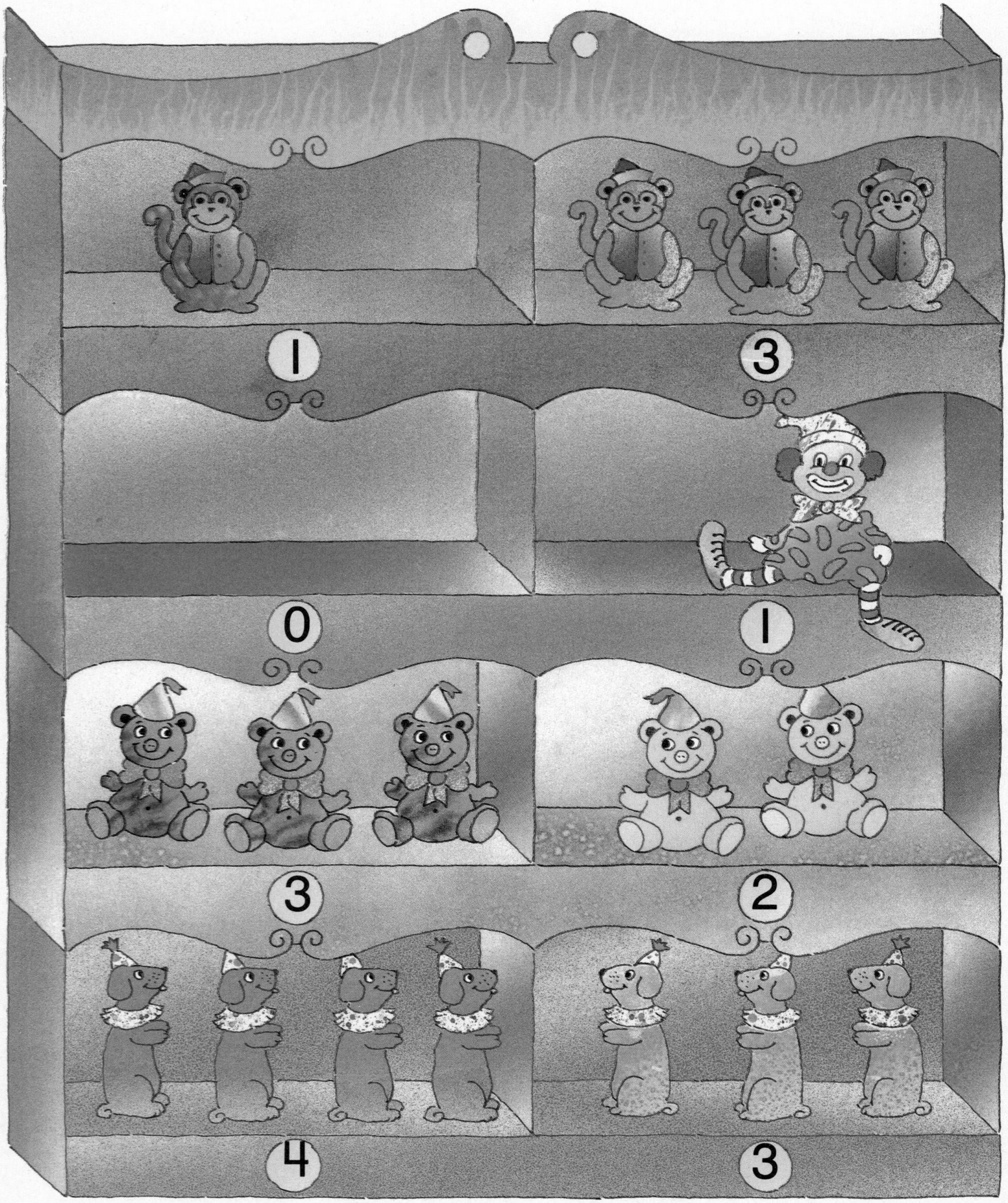

Name ______________________________

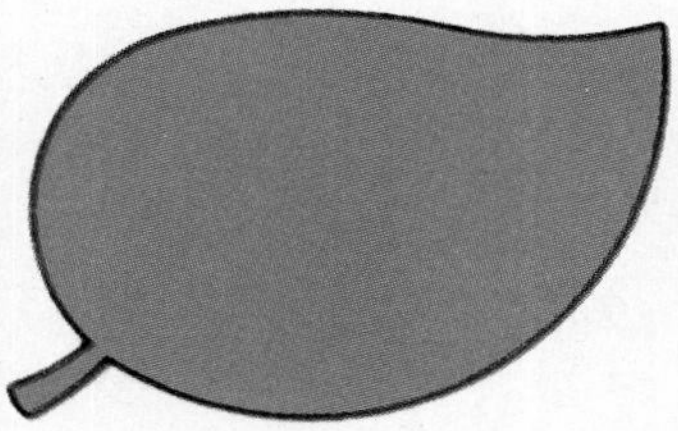

1	2

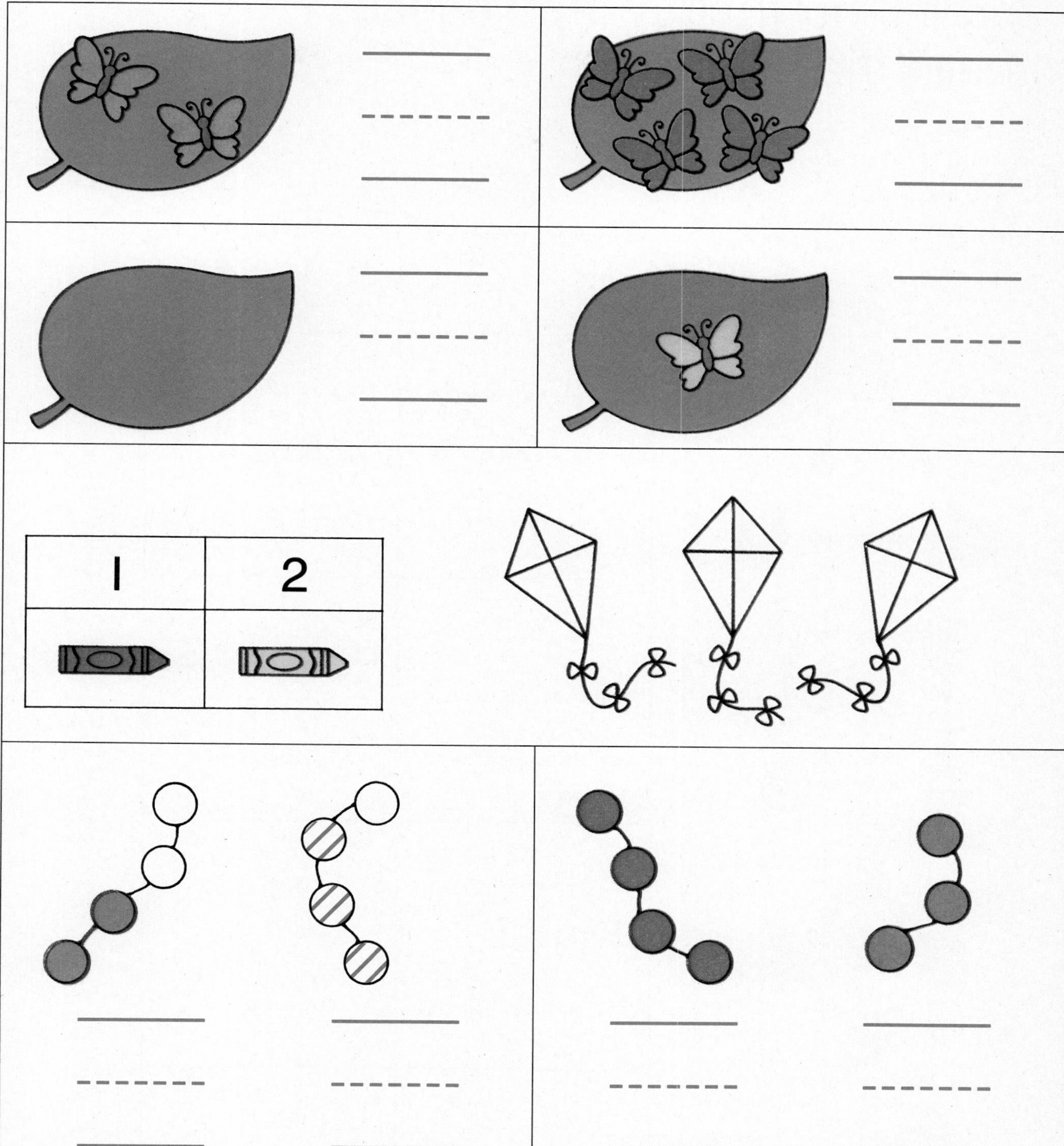

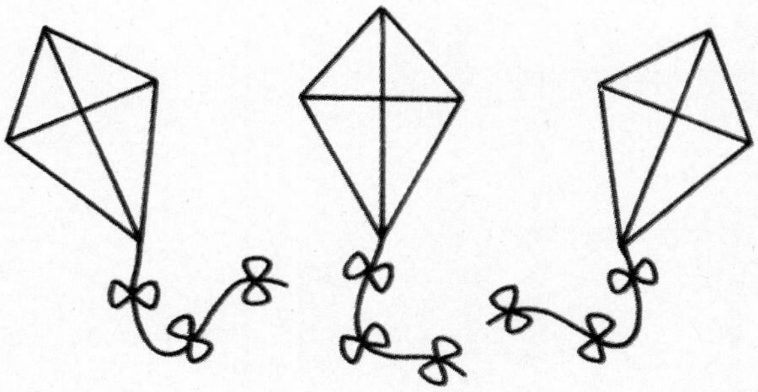

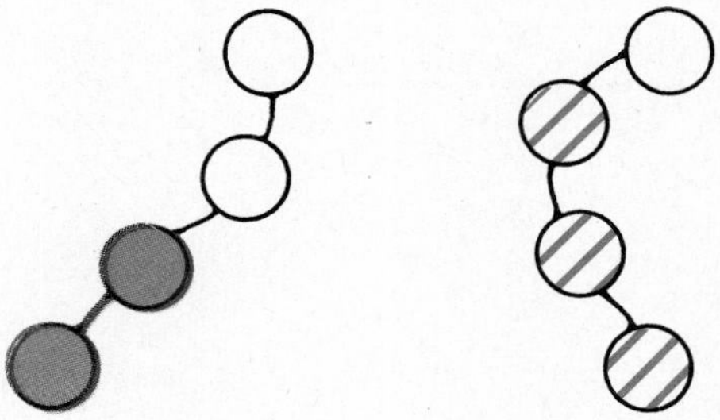

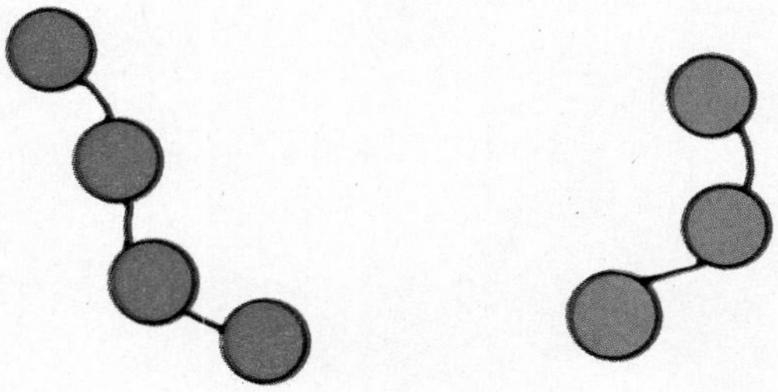

0 1 2 3 4

Name ______________________________

I can tell how many are needed to build the shape.

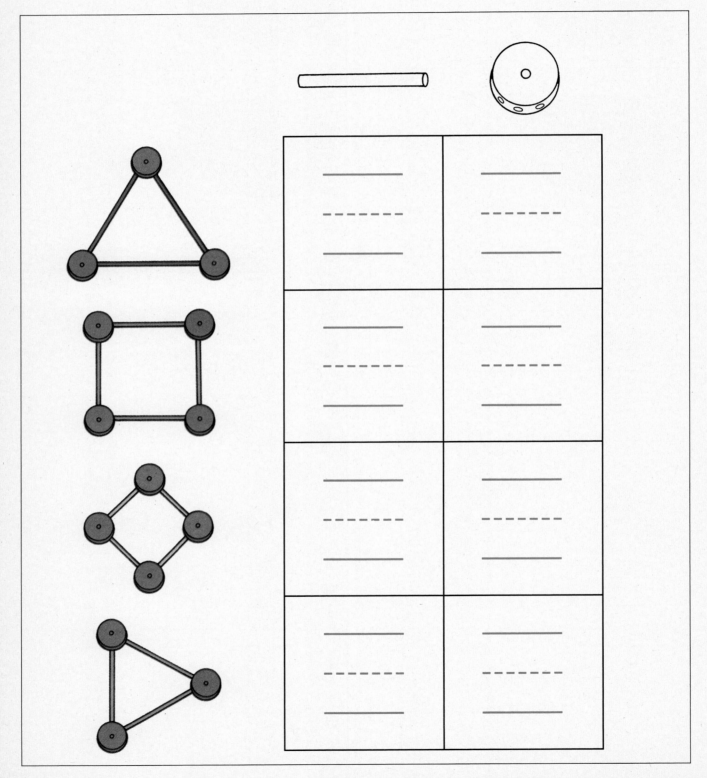

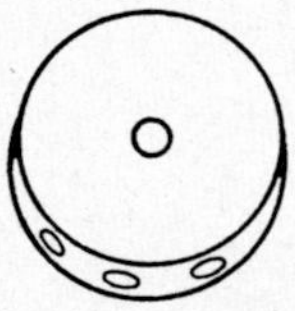

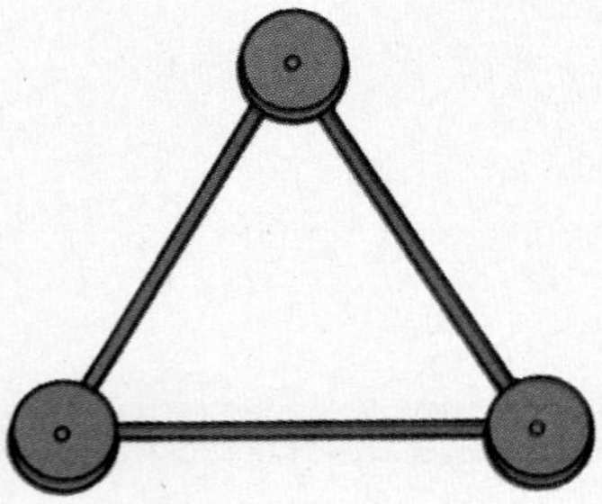

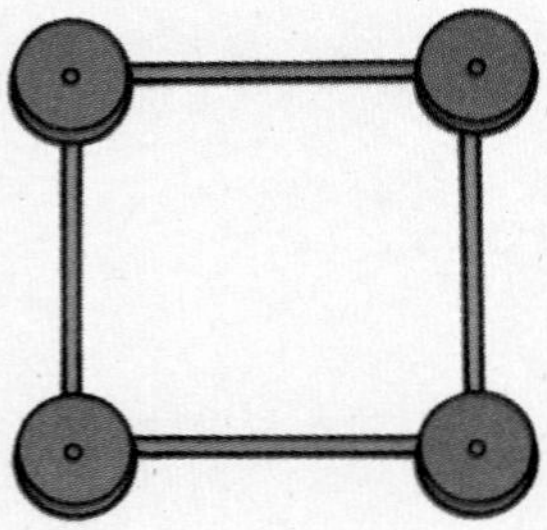

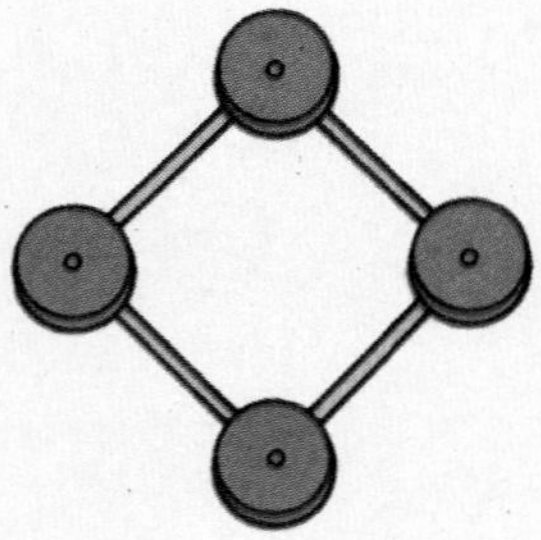

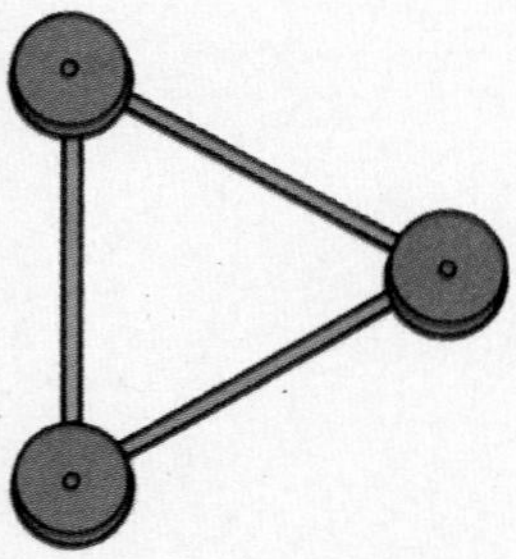

7
Numbers to 8

Workmat

Theme: Home and Neighborhood

Name ______________________________

I can explore numbers to 8.
I can show groups with one more.

Name ____________________

I can show groups of 5.

I can find groups of 5.

Name ______________________________

I can show groups of 6.

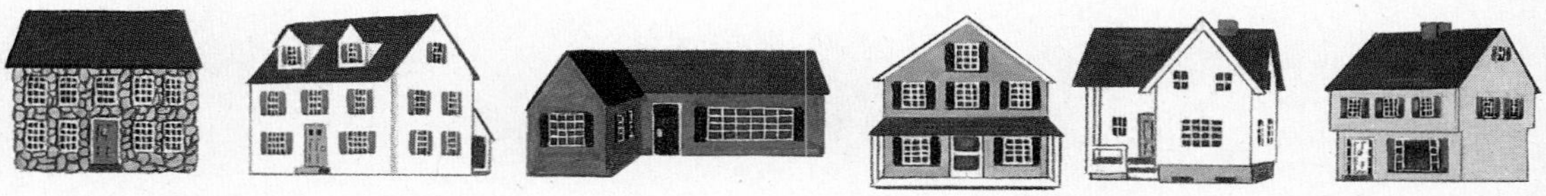

I can find groups of 6.

Name ______________________________

I can write numbers to show how many.

5 5 5

5 5 5

6 6 6

6 6 6

5 ___ ___ ___

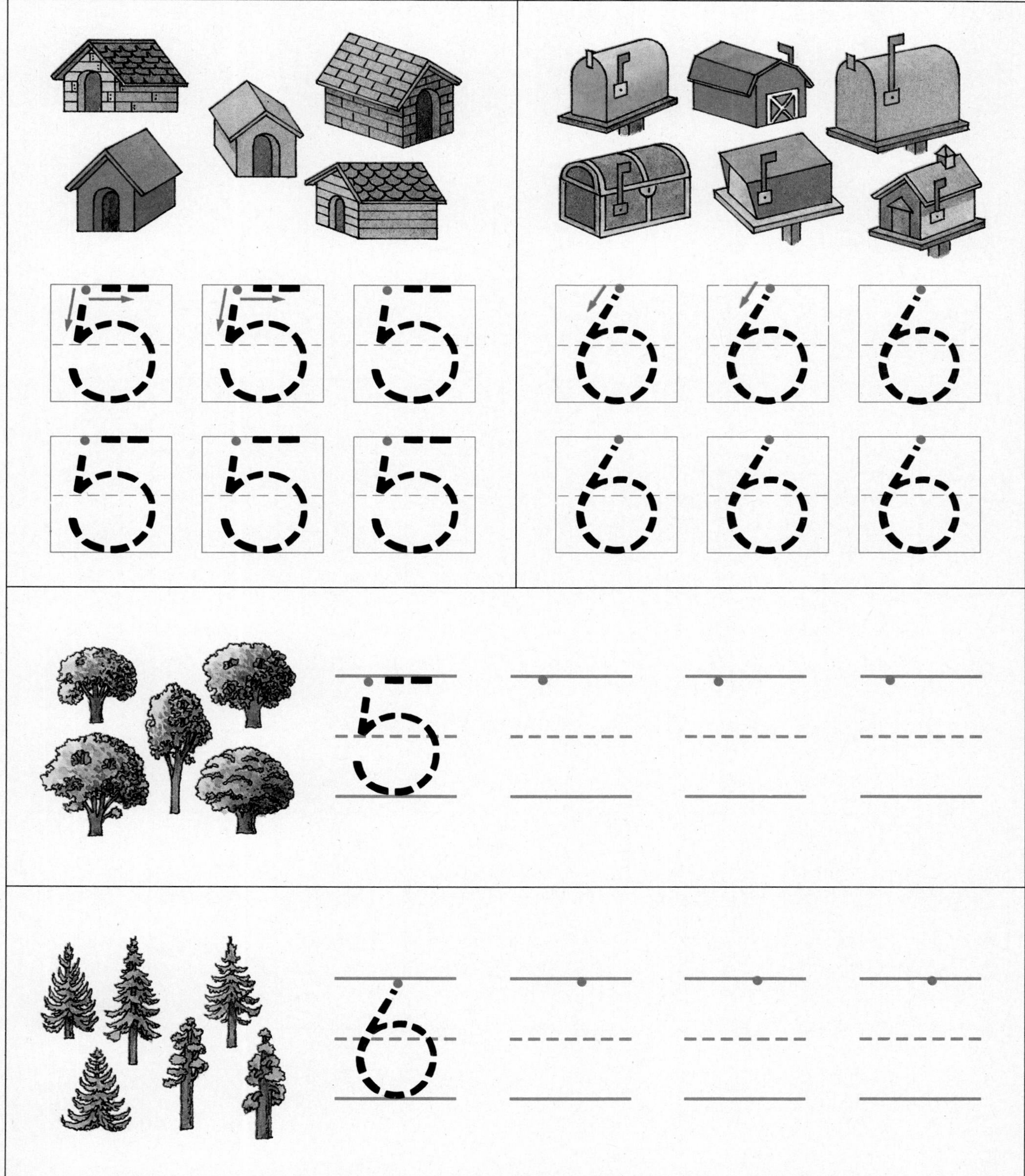

6 ___ ___ ___

I can read and write number patterns.

5	6	5	6				

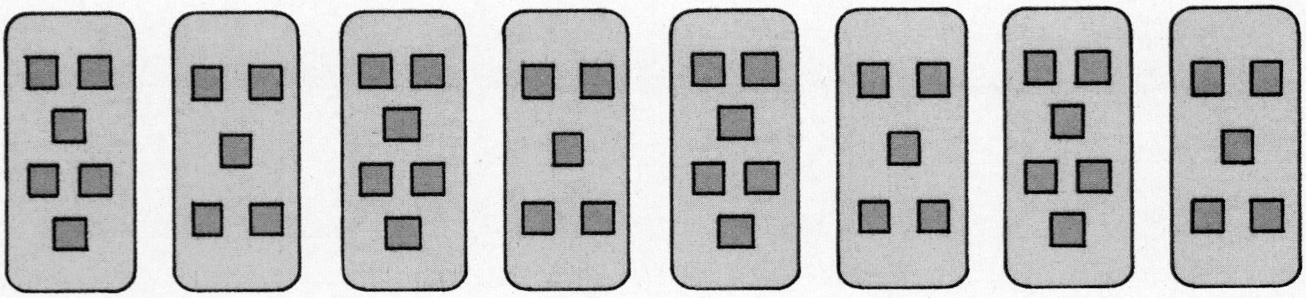

6	5	6	5				

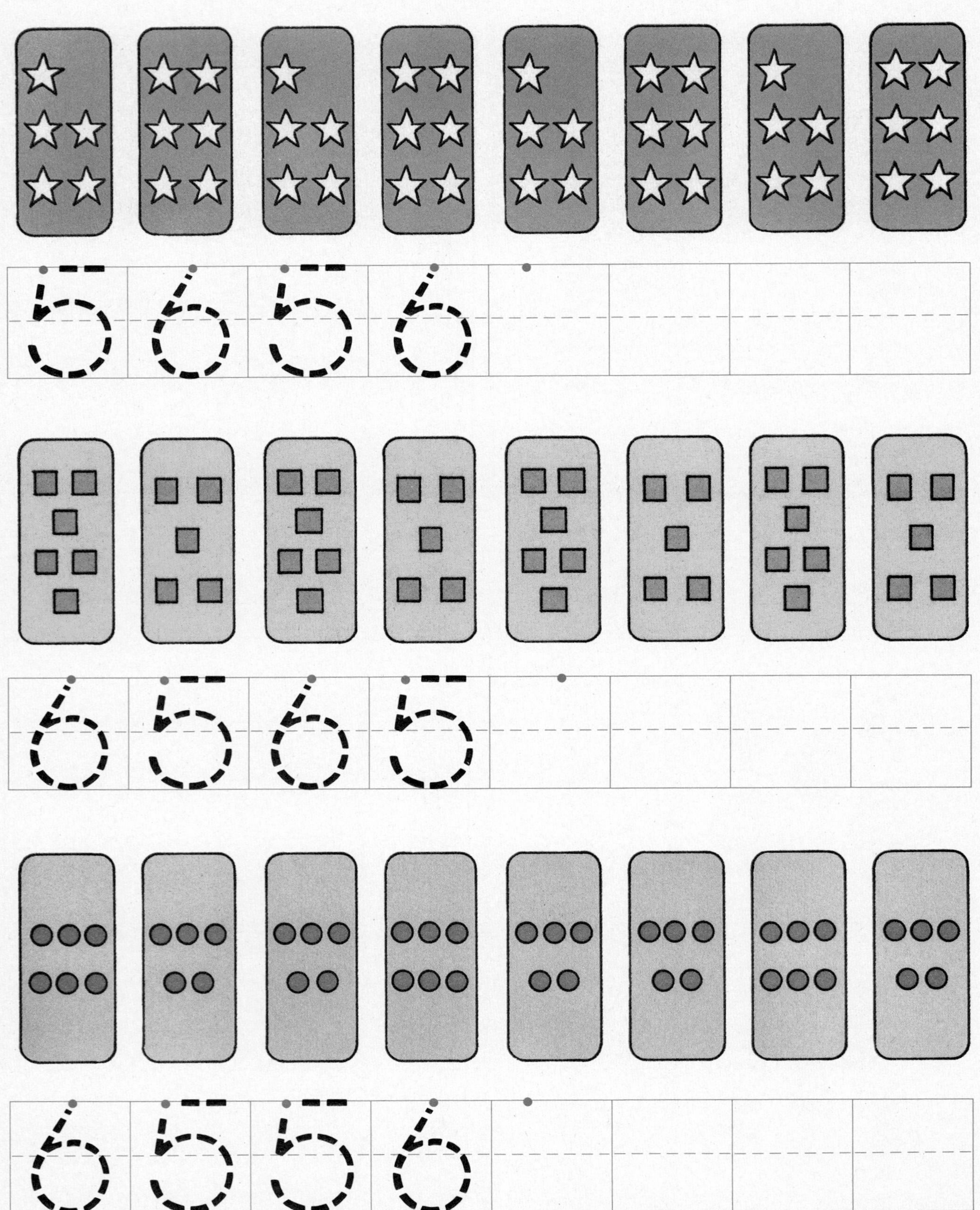

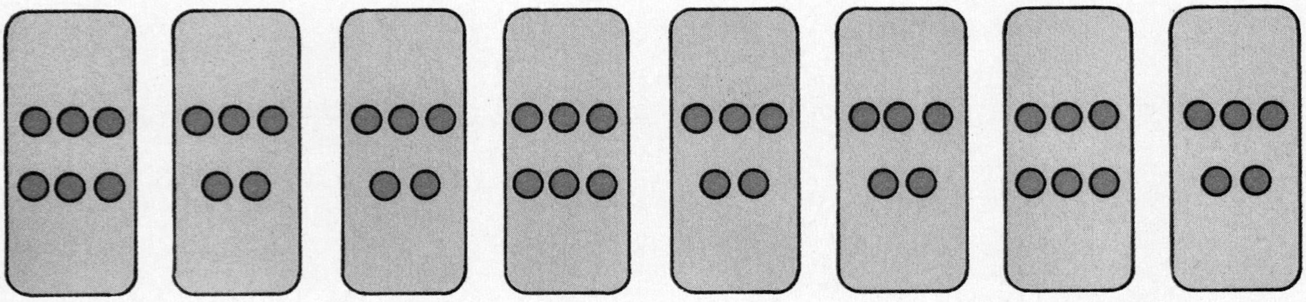

6	5	5	6				

Name ____________________

I can make groups of 5 in many ways.

0 1 2 3 4 5

I can make groups of 6 in many ways.

0	1	2	3	4	5	6

Name ______________________________

I can show groups of 7.

7
seven

I can find groups of 7.

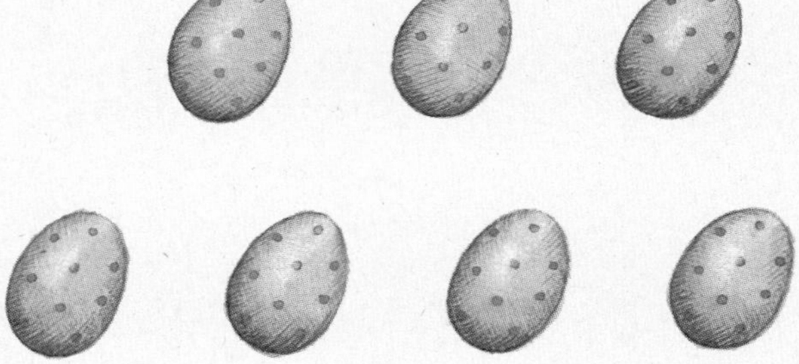

Name ______________________________

I can show groups of 8.

I can find groups of 8.

Name ______________________________

I can write numbers to show how many.

7 7 7

7 7 7

8 8 8

8 8 8

7

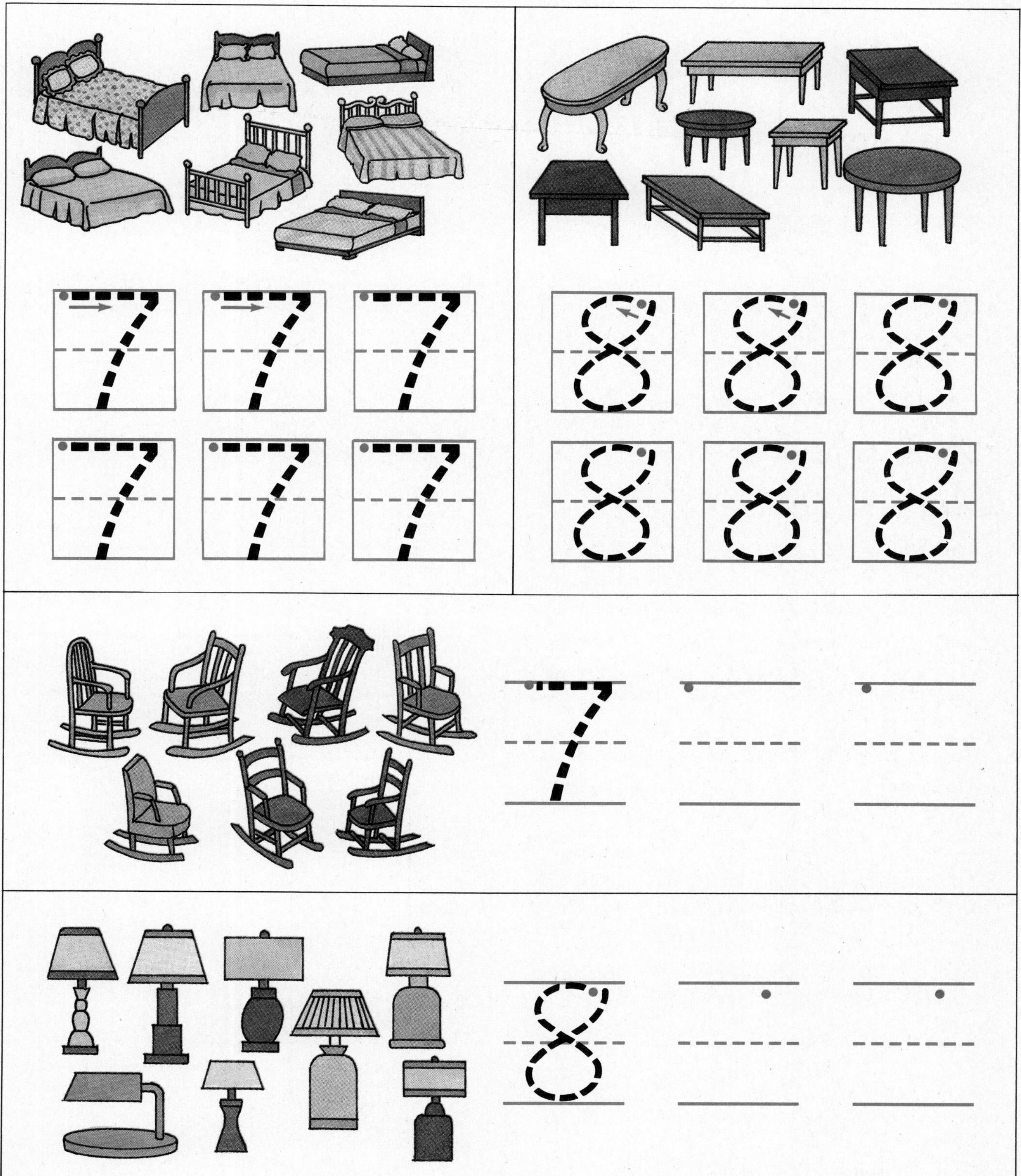

8

I can read and write number patterns.

7 8 7 8

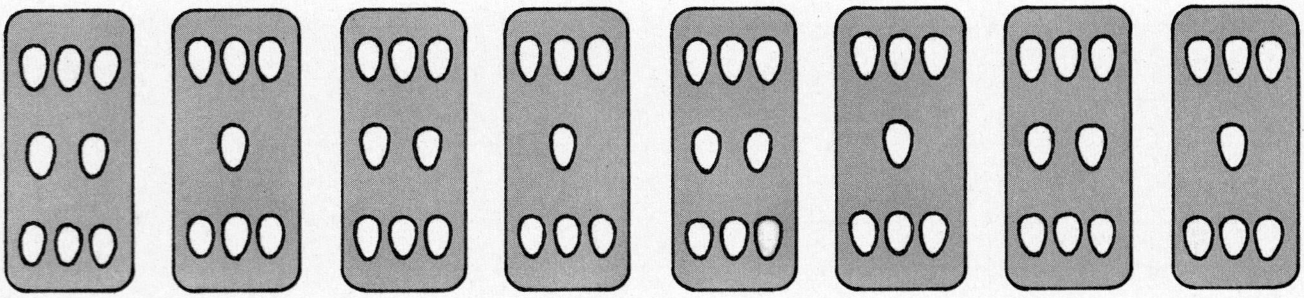

8 7 8 7

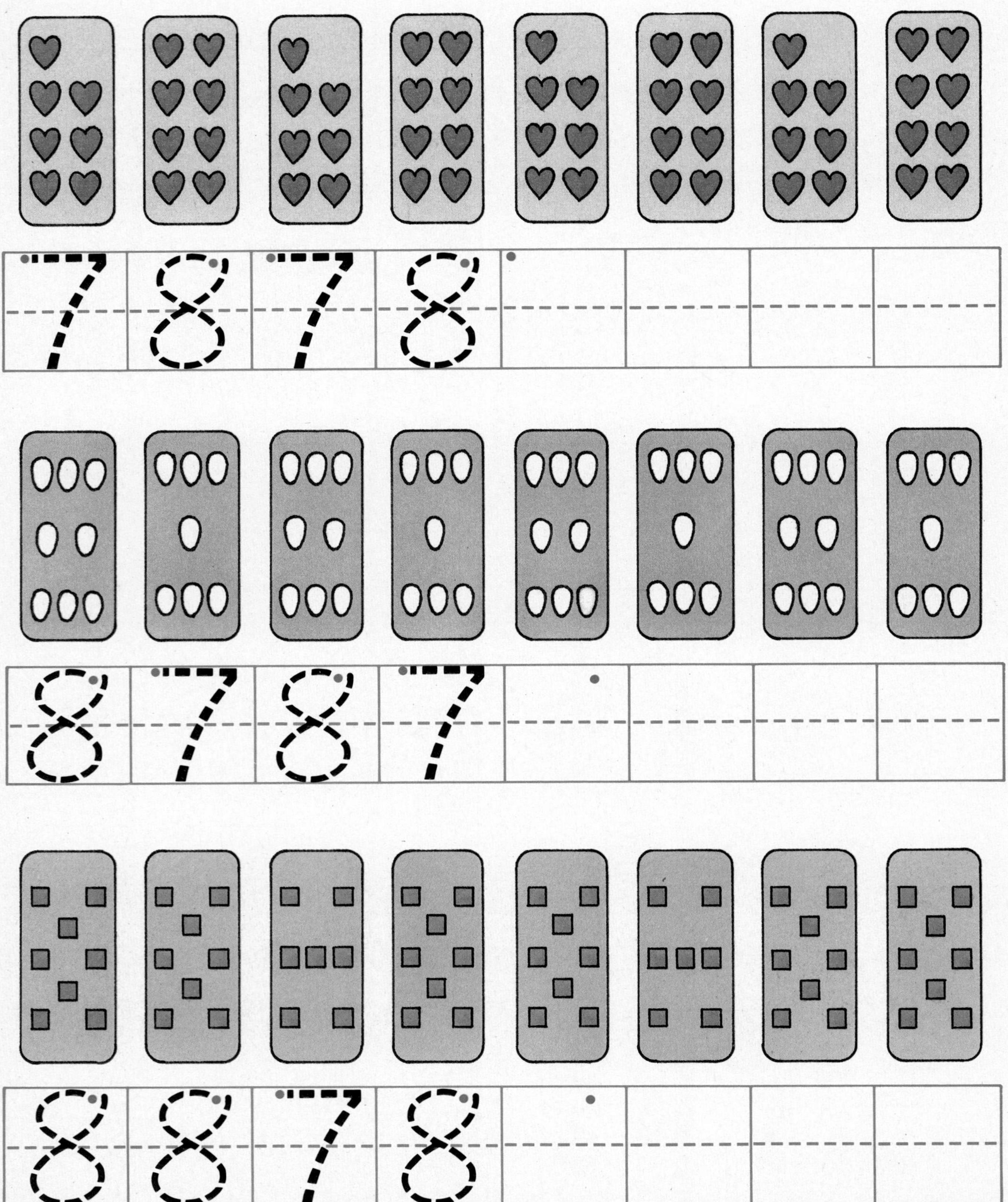

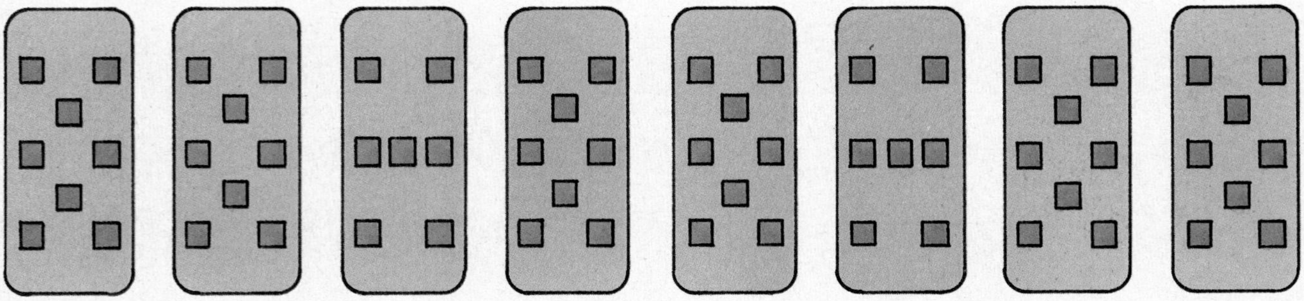

8 8 7 8

Name ____

UNDERSTAND
FIND DATA
PLAN
ESTIMATE
SOLVE
CHECK

I can tell who is first, second, third, fourth, and fifth in a story.

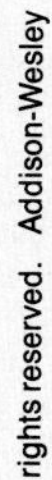

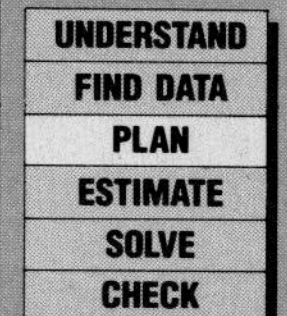

UNDERSTAND
FIND DATA
PLAN
ESTIMATE
SOLVE
CHECK

I can tell how many are in the picture.

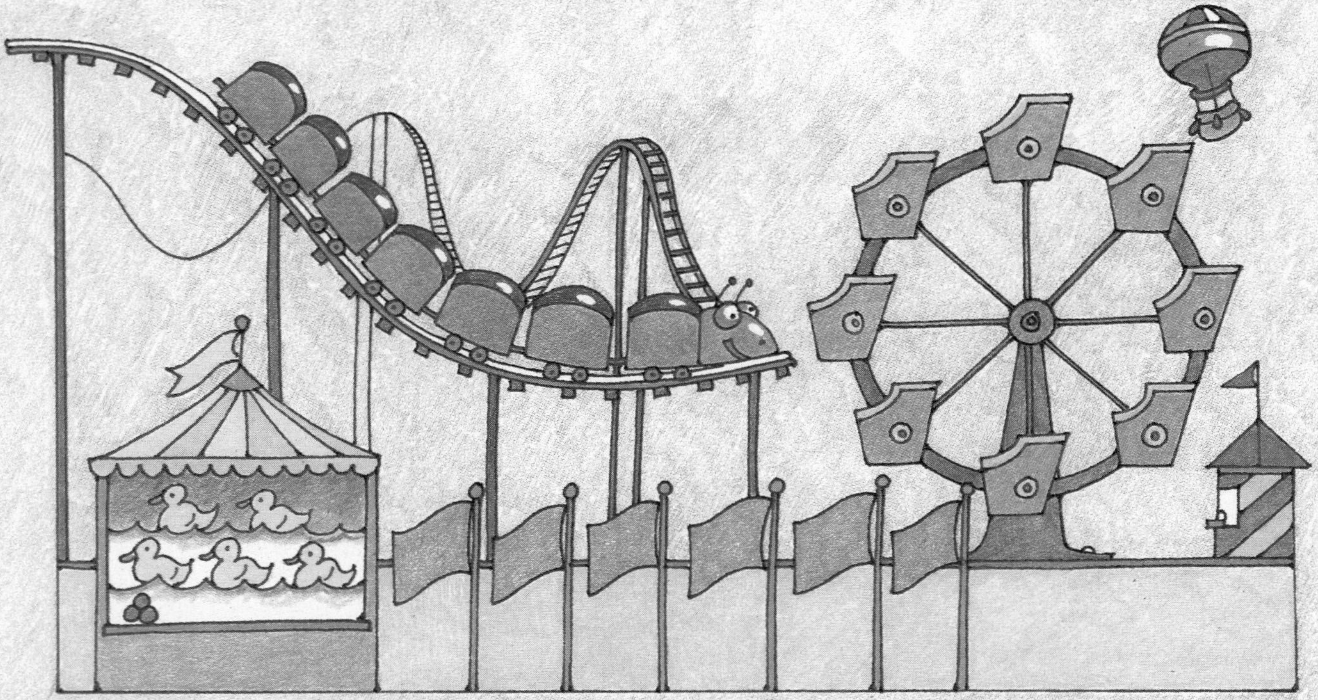

	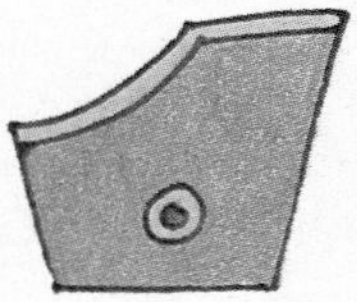

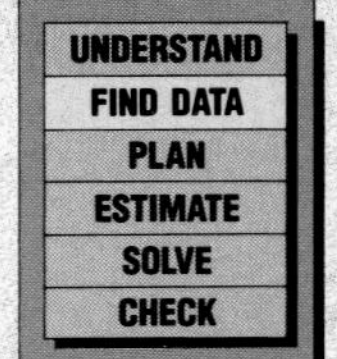

1 2 3 4 5 6 7 8

Name ______________________

I can tell how many there are.

1	2	3	4	5	6	7	8

I can tell how many there are.

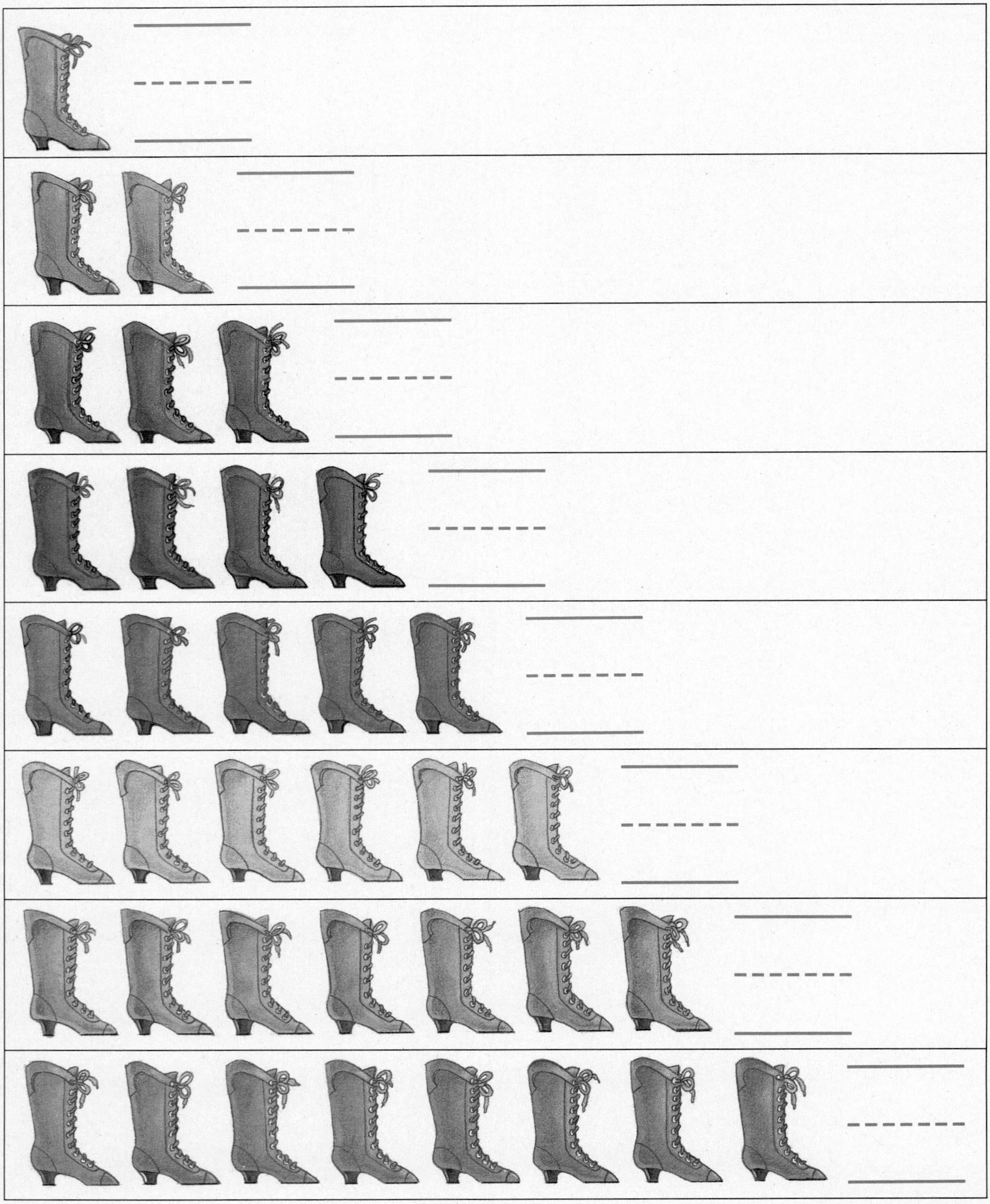

Name ______________________________

I can tell how many there are.

1	2	3	4	5	6	7	8

I can tell how many there are.

Name ____________________

I can make tallies.
I can tell which number is more.

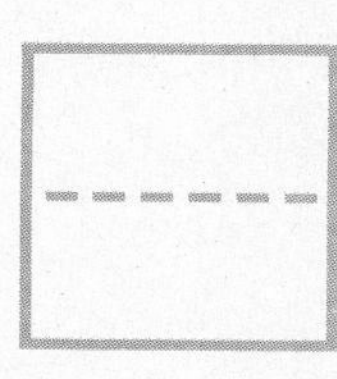

1 2 3 4 5 6 7 8

I can compare numbers.
I can tell which one is less.

7 

5 

8 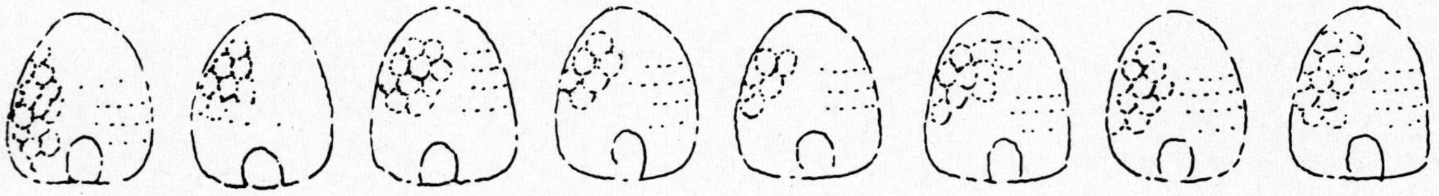

6 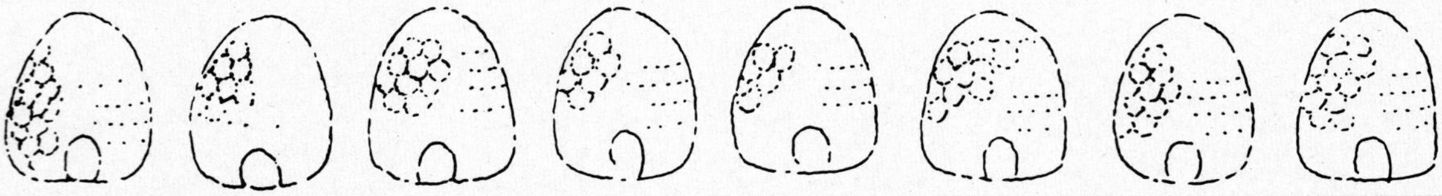

5 

6 

8 

7 

Name ______________________________

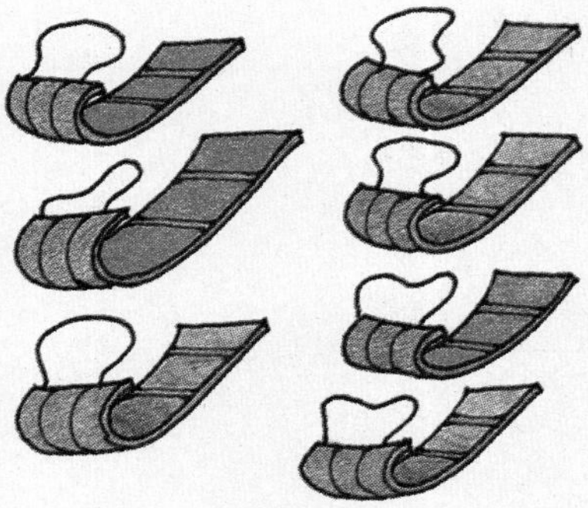

6

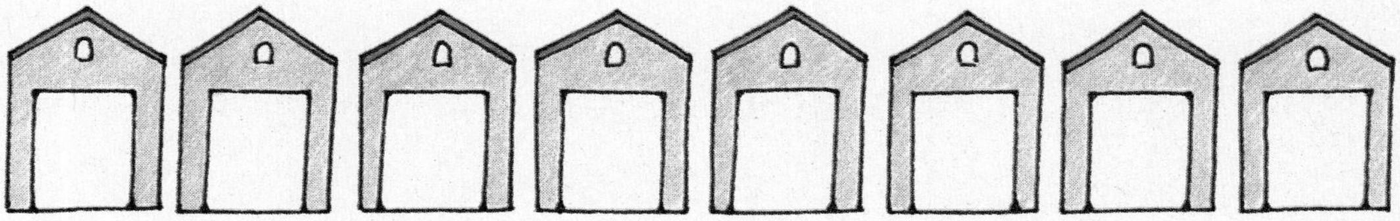

8

1	2	3	4	5	6	7	8

Name ______________________________

I can tell which is closer.

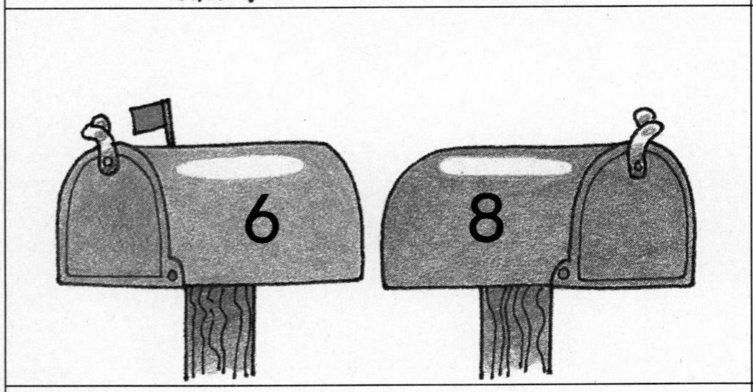

8

Numbers to 12

Workmat

Theme: Picnic in the Park

Name ____________________

I can explore numbers to 12.
I can show groups with one more.

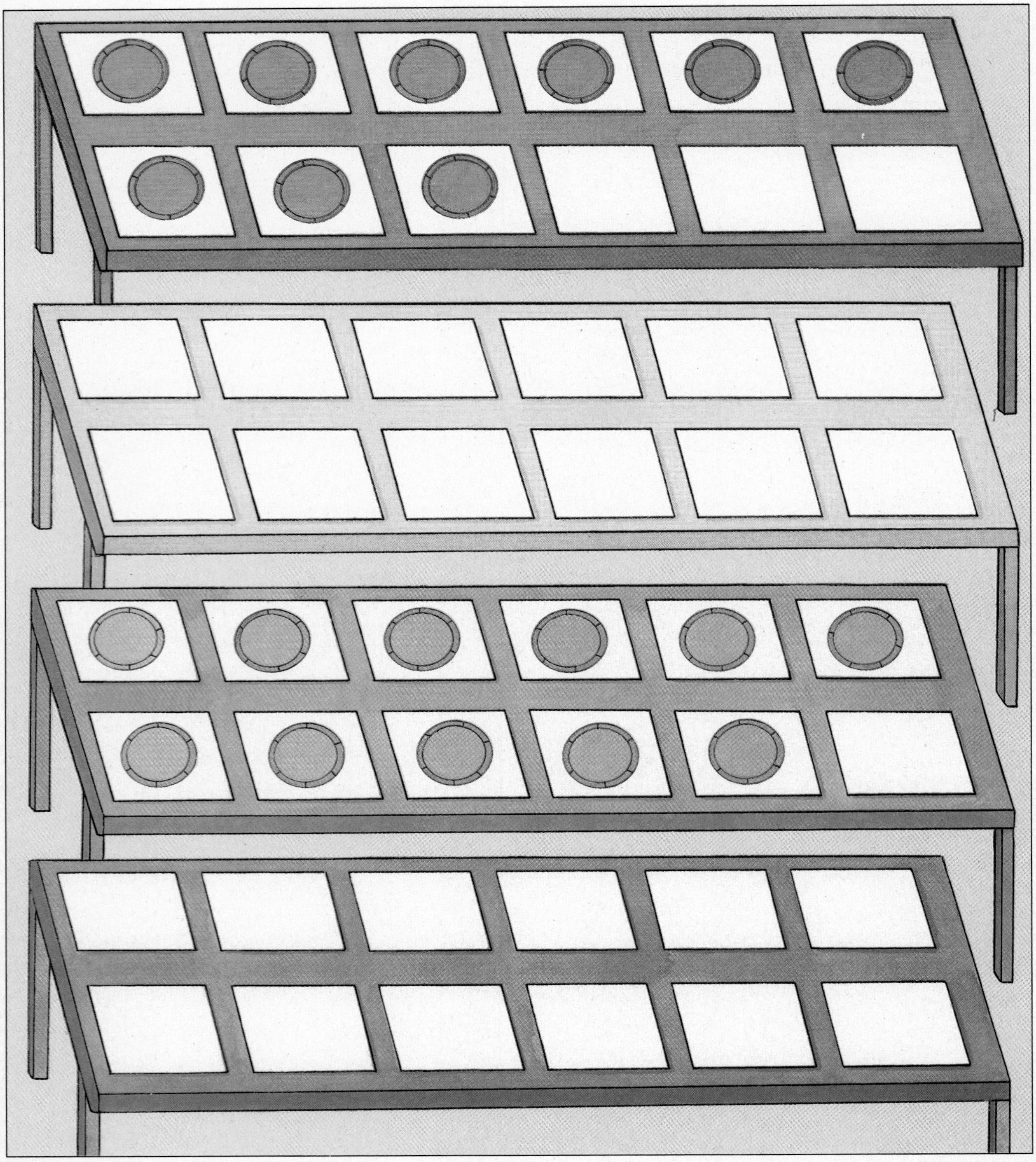

Name ________________________________

I can show groups of 9.

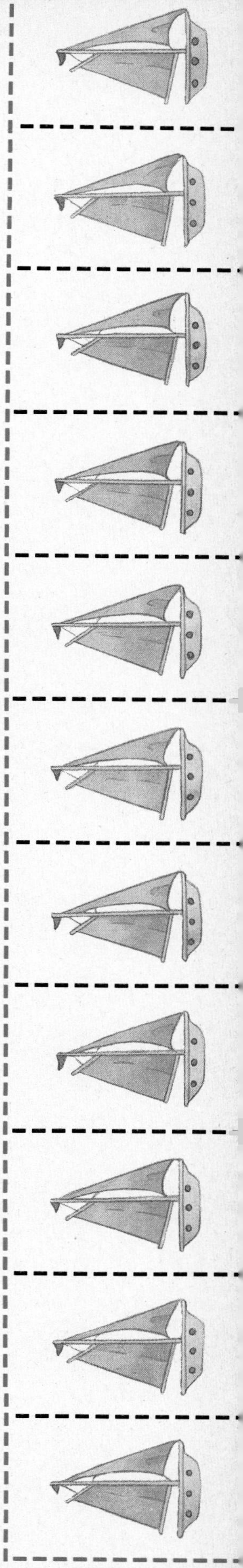

I can find groups of 9.

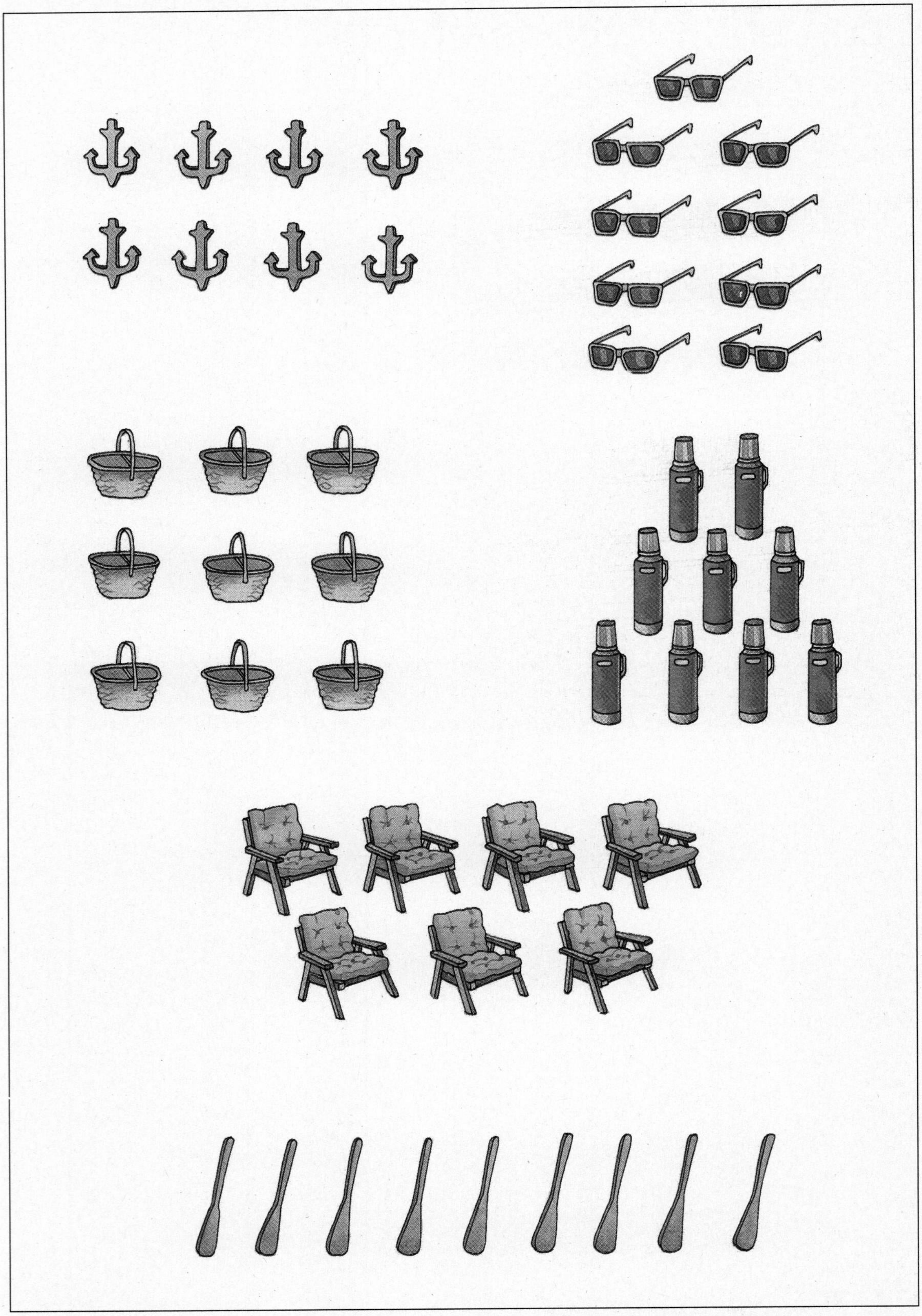

Name ______________________________

I can write numbers and number patterns.

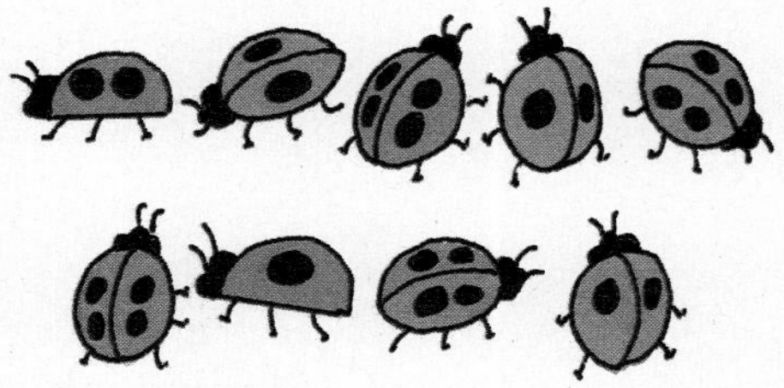

9 9 9 9

9 9

8 9 8 9

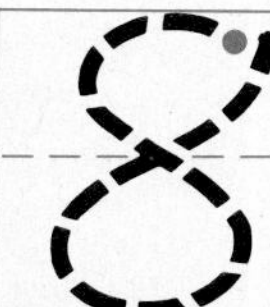

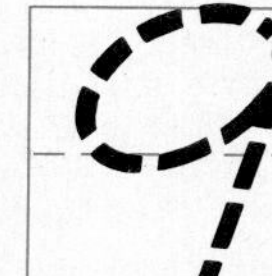

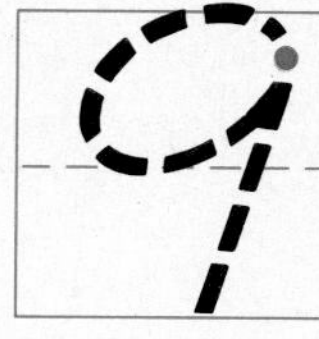

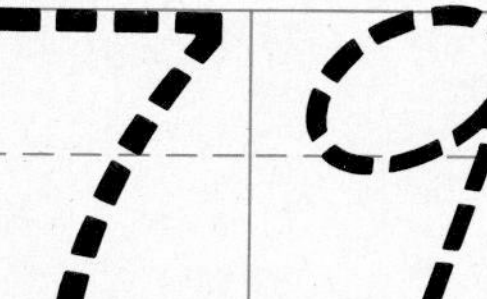

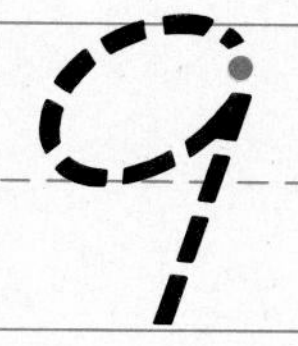

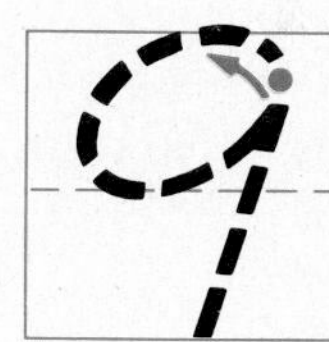

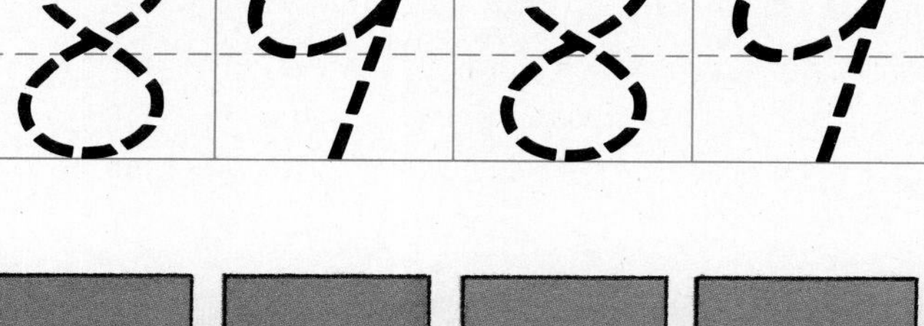

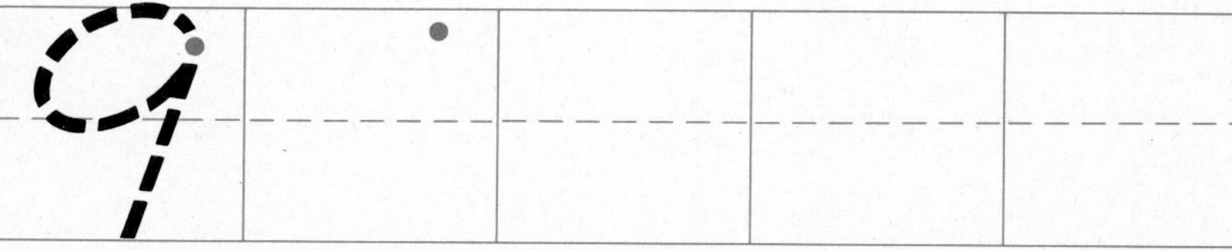

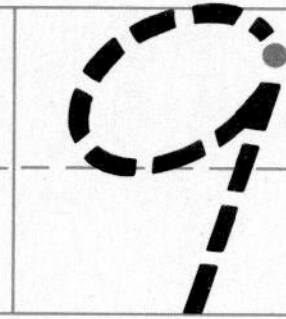

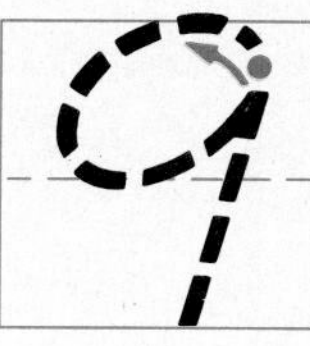

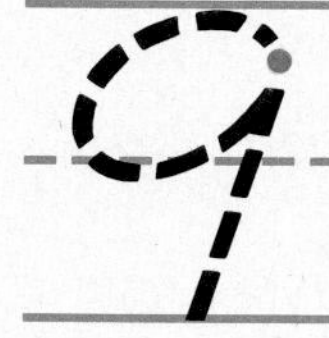

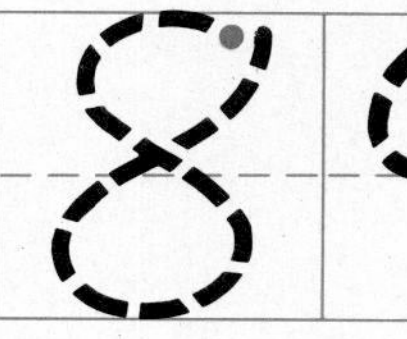

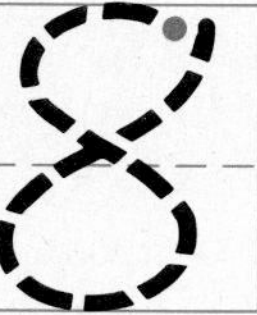

9 8 7 9

I can read and write number patterns.

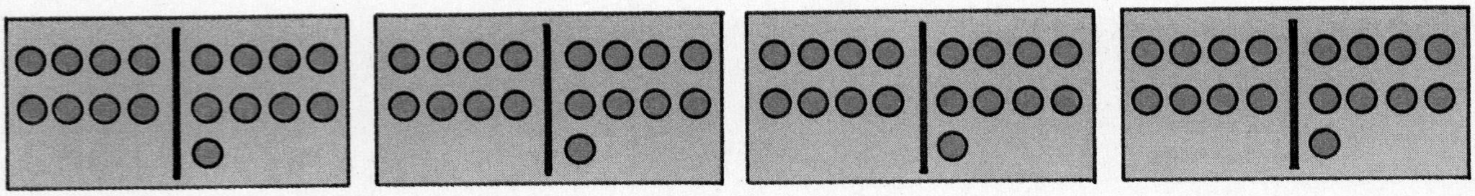

8	9	8	9				

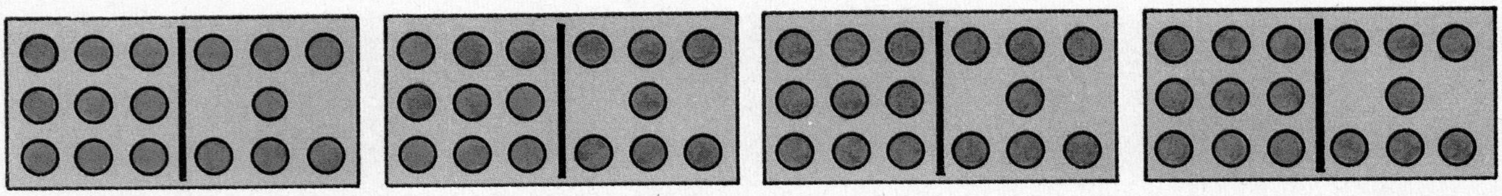

9	7	9	7				

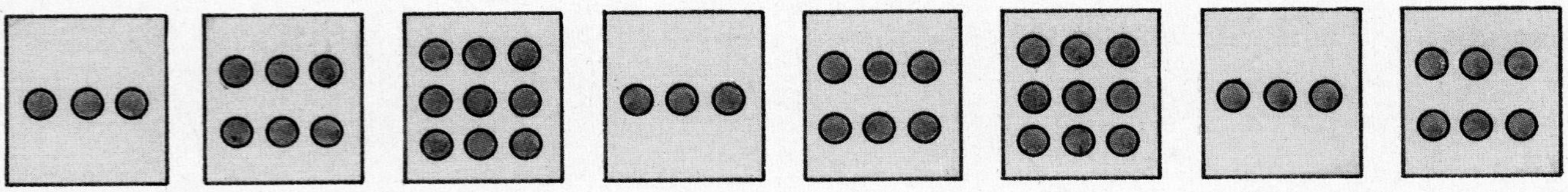

3	6	9	3				

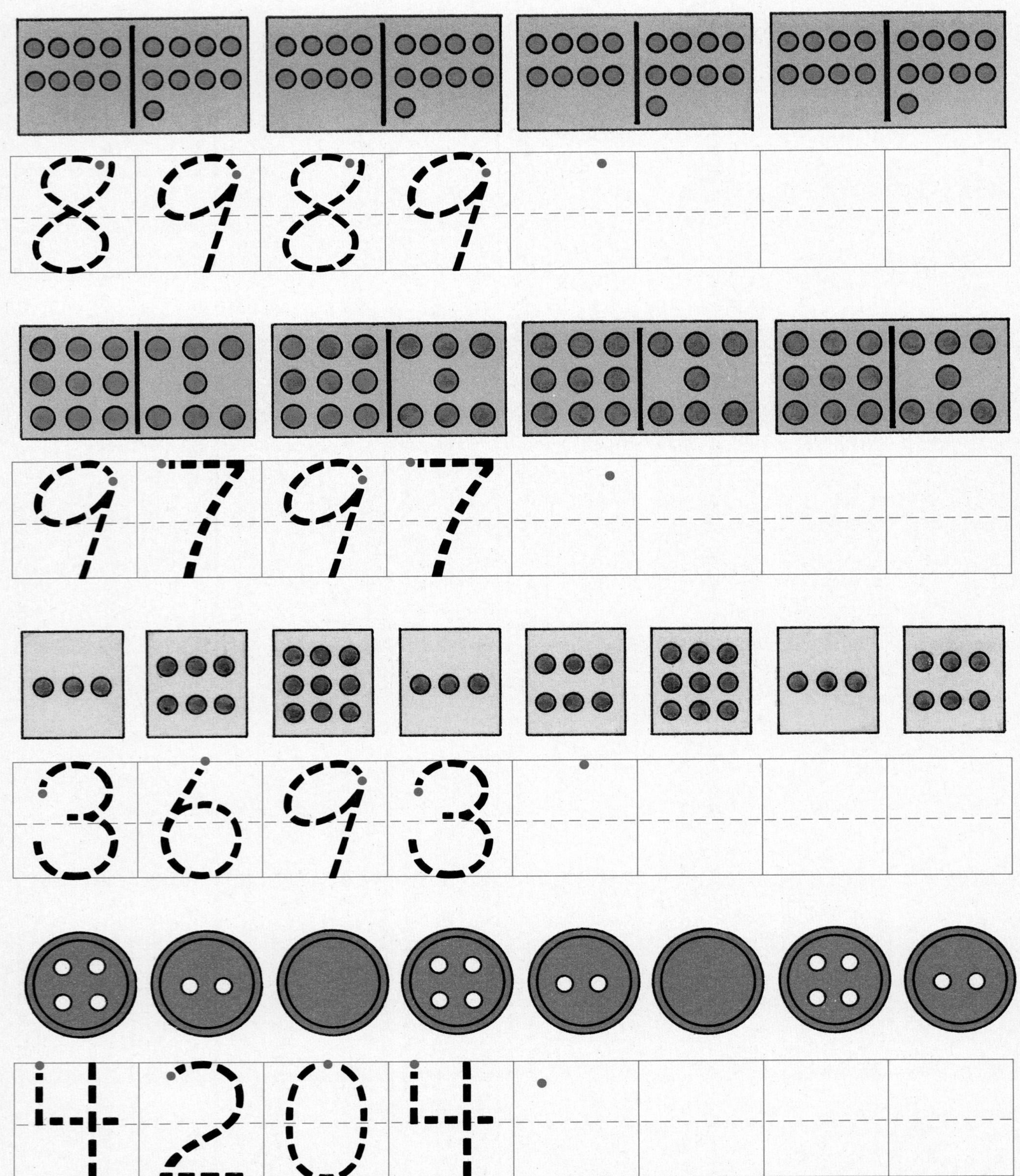

4	2	0	4				

Name

I can show groups of 10.

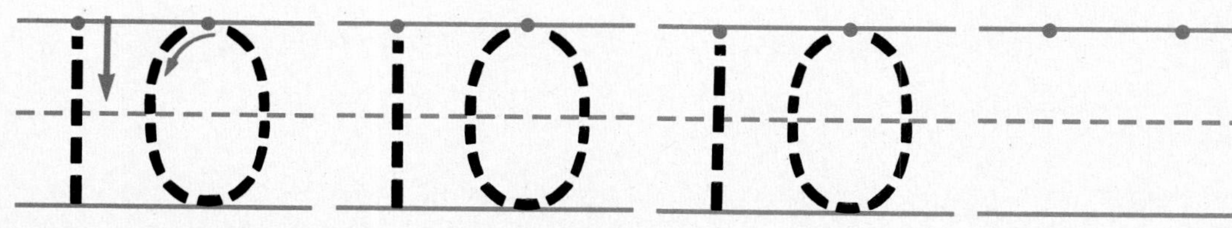

10 10 10

I can find groups of 10.

Name

I can show groups of 11.

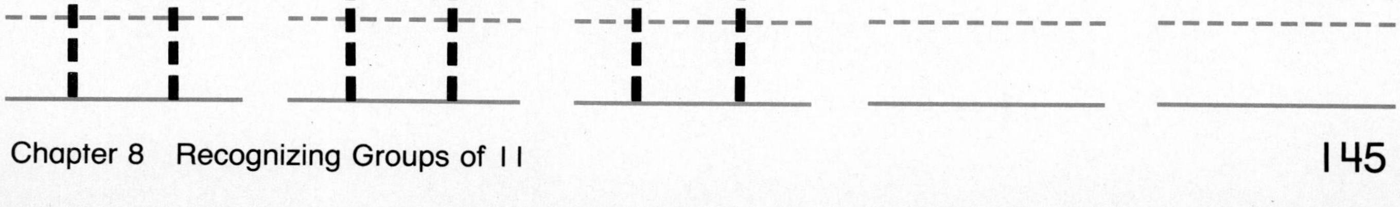

I can find groups of 11.

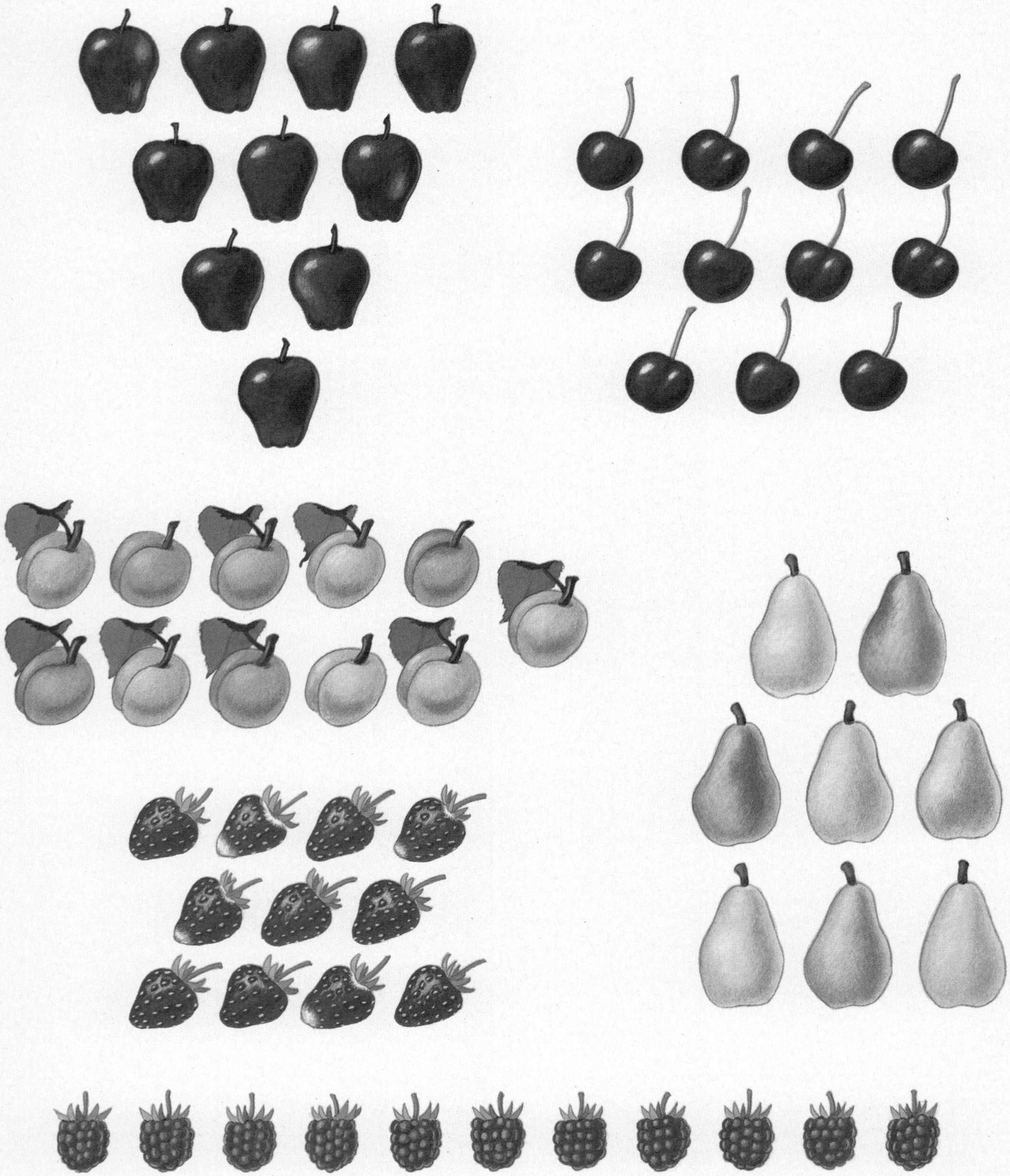

Name ____________________

I can show groups of 12.

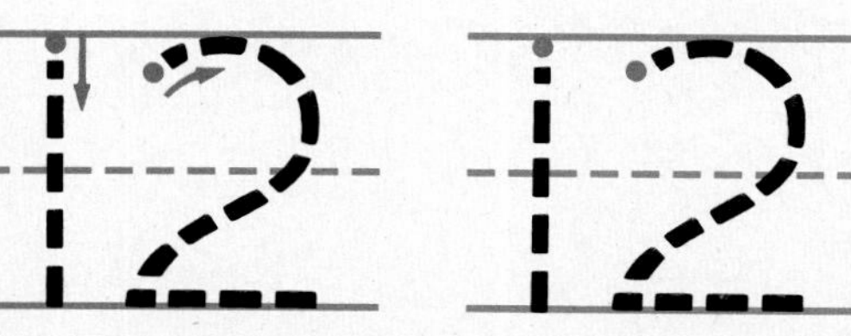

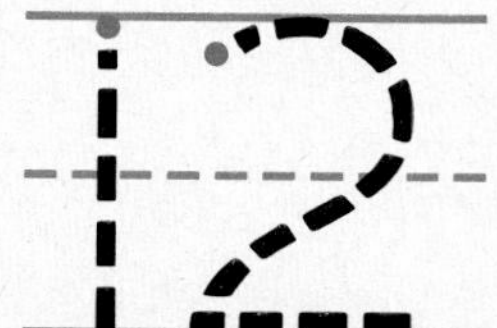

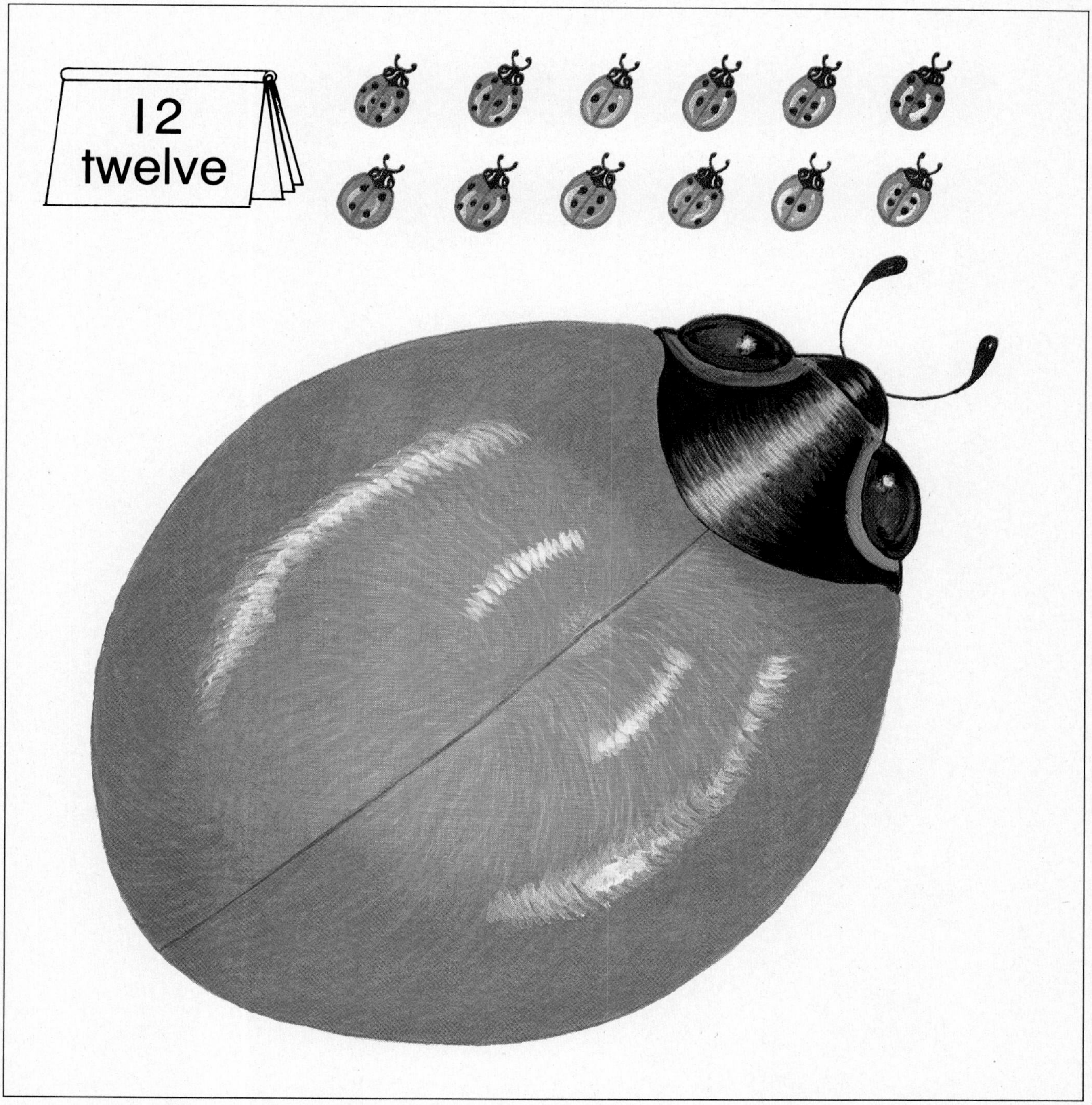

12 12 12

I can find groups of 12.

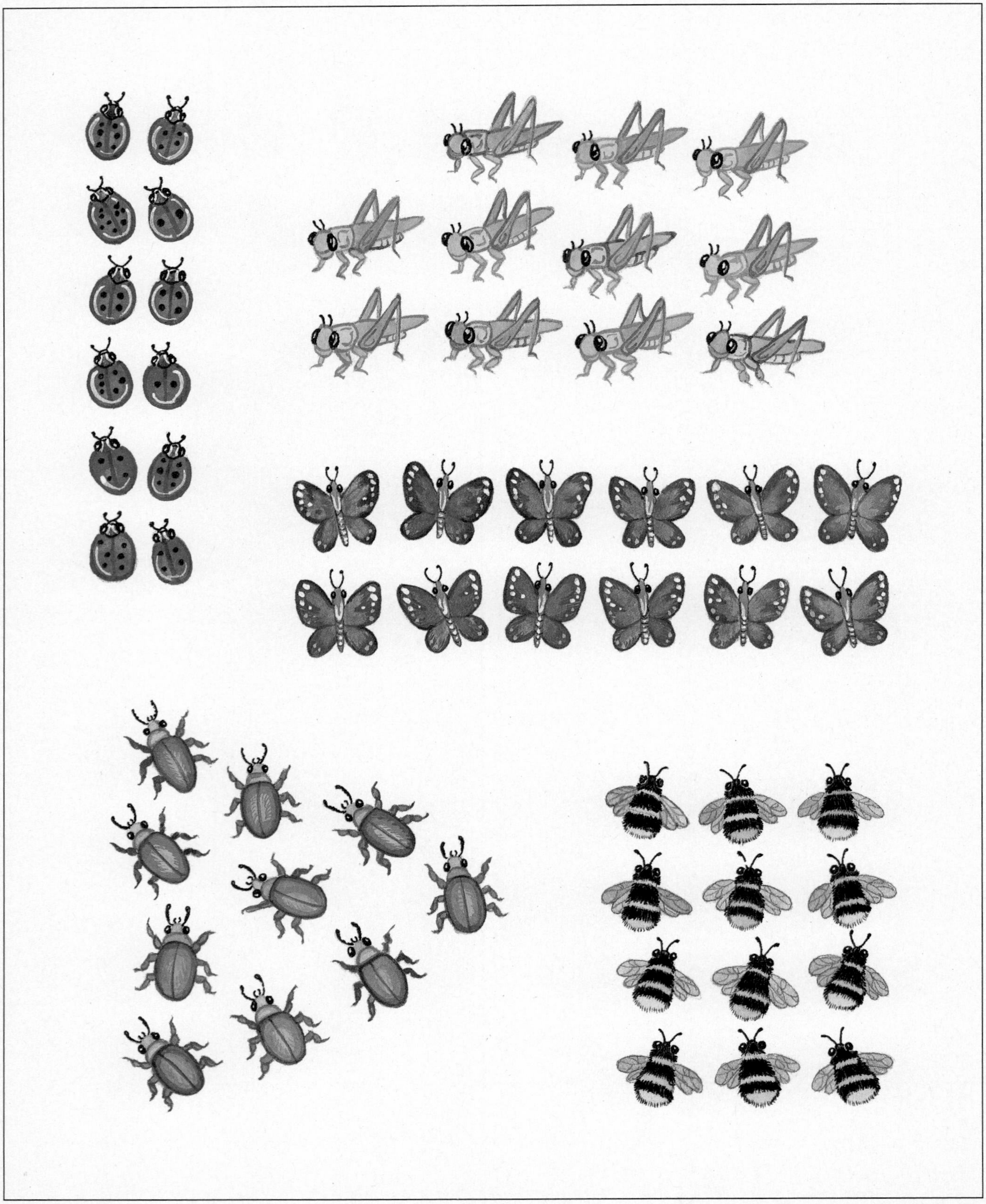

Name ______________________________

I can show a number.

10

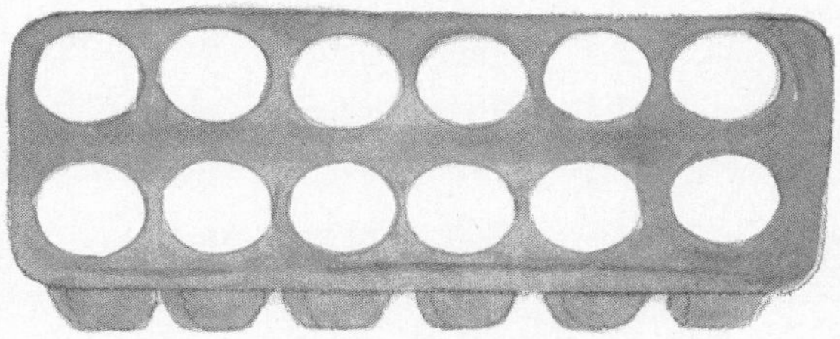

12

11

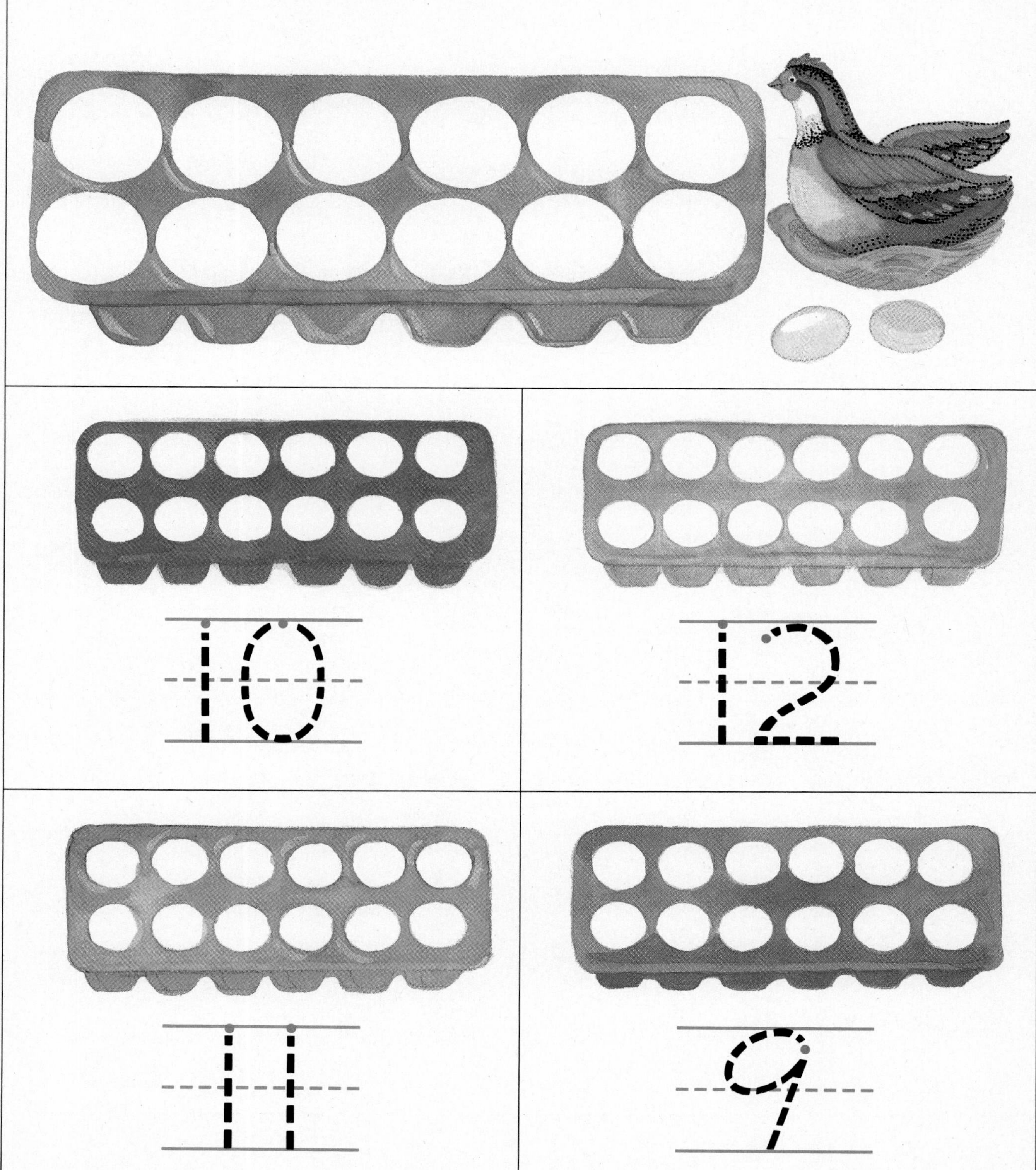

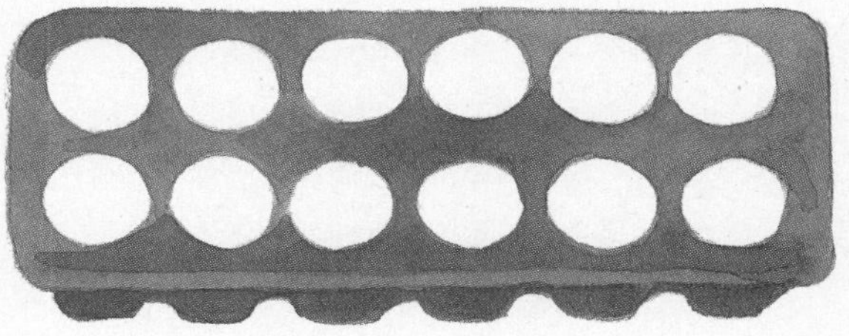

9

I can tell how many there are.

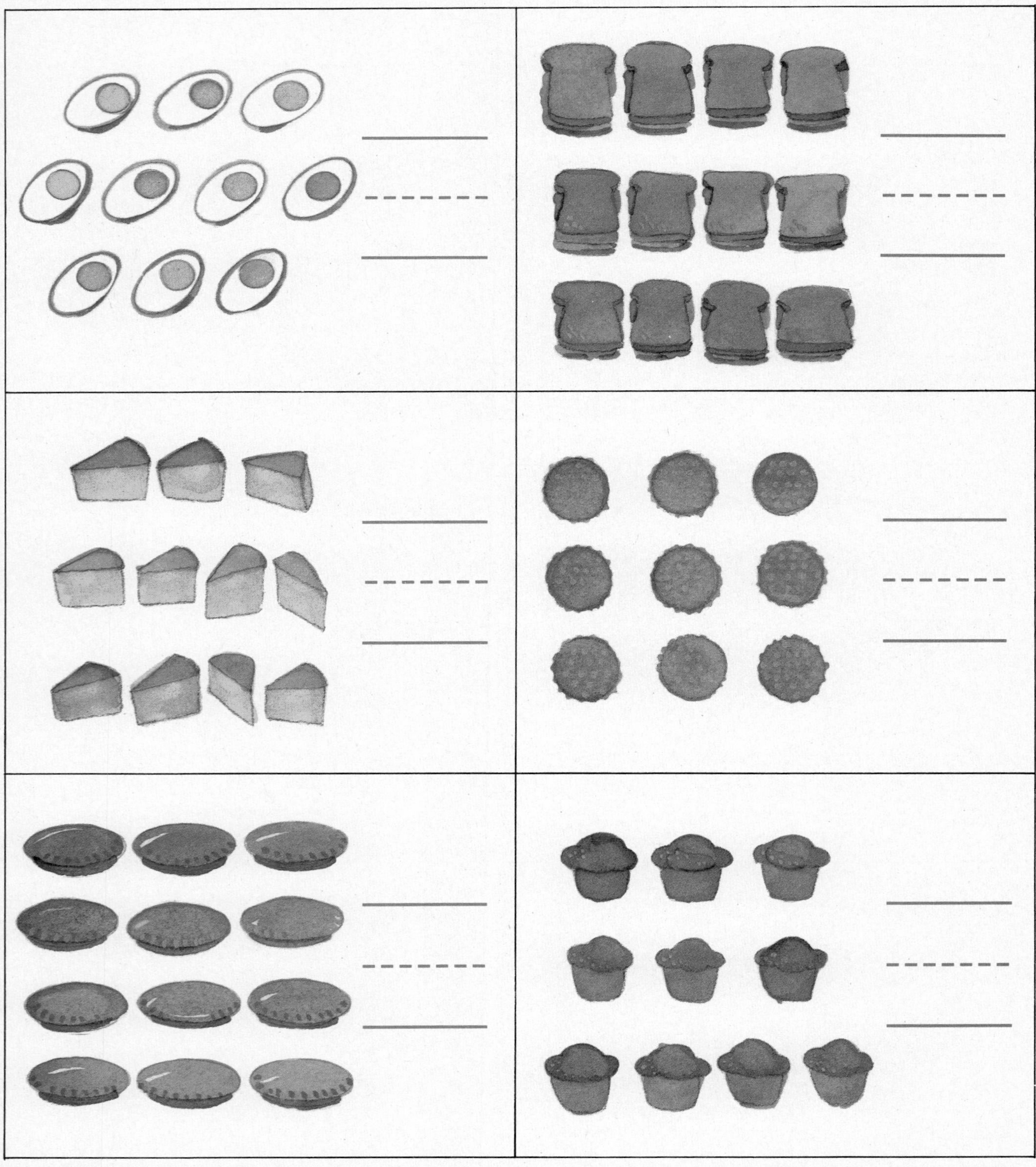

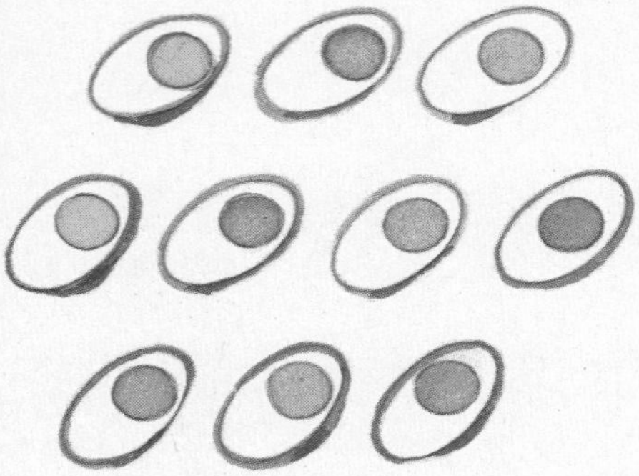

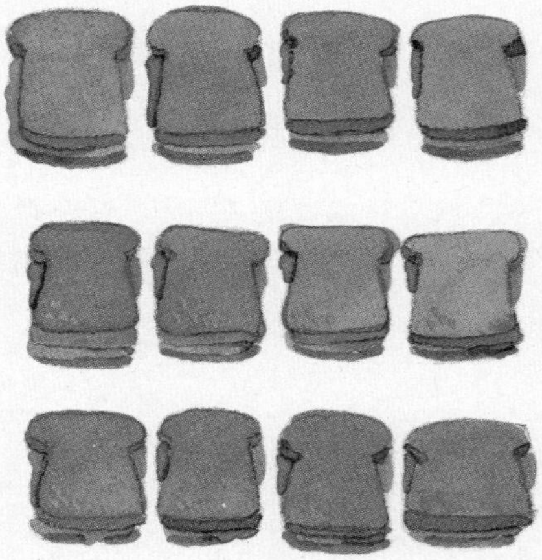

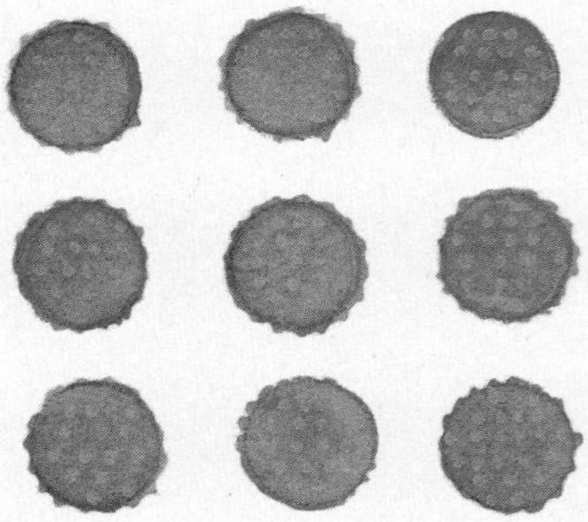

1	2	3	4	5	6	7	8	9	10	11	12

Name ______________________

I can listen to a story.
I can show how many there are.

______ animals

______ badgers

______ bugs

1 2 3 4 5 6 7 8 9 10 11 12

UNDERSTAND
FIND DATA
PLAN
ESTIMATE
SOLVE
CHECK

I can count how many.
I can count again to check.

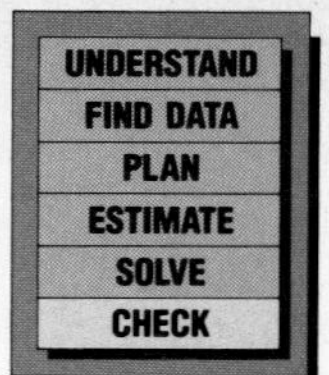

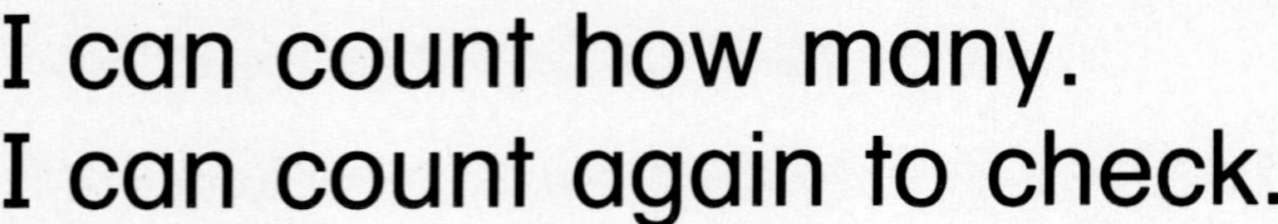

1 2 3 4 5 6 7 8 9 10 11 12

Name ______________________

I can count how many.
I can tell if there are enough.

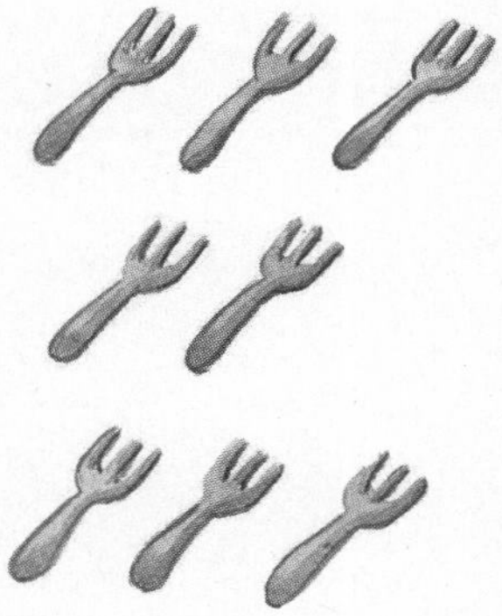 ______	 ______
 ______	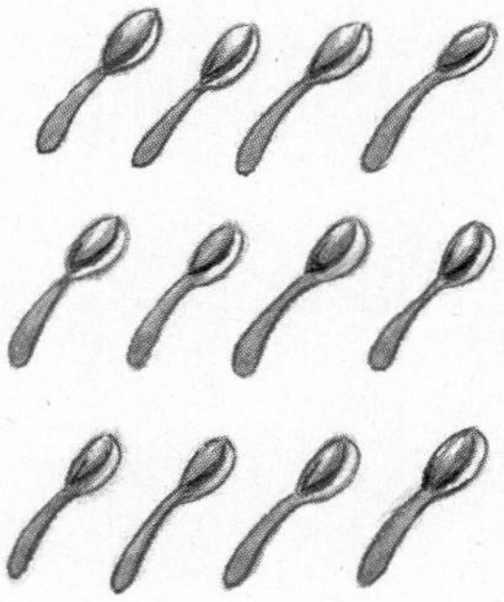 ______

1 2 3 4 5 6 7 8 9 10 11 12

I can count how many.
I can tell if there are enough.

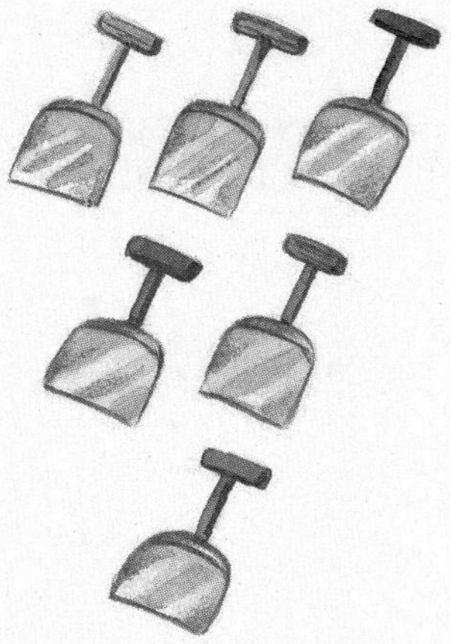

1	2	3	4	5	6	7	8	9	10	11	12

Name ______________________________

I can show the numbers 1 to 12 in order.

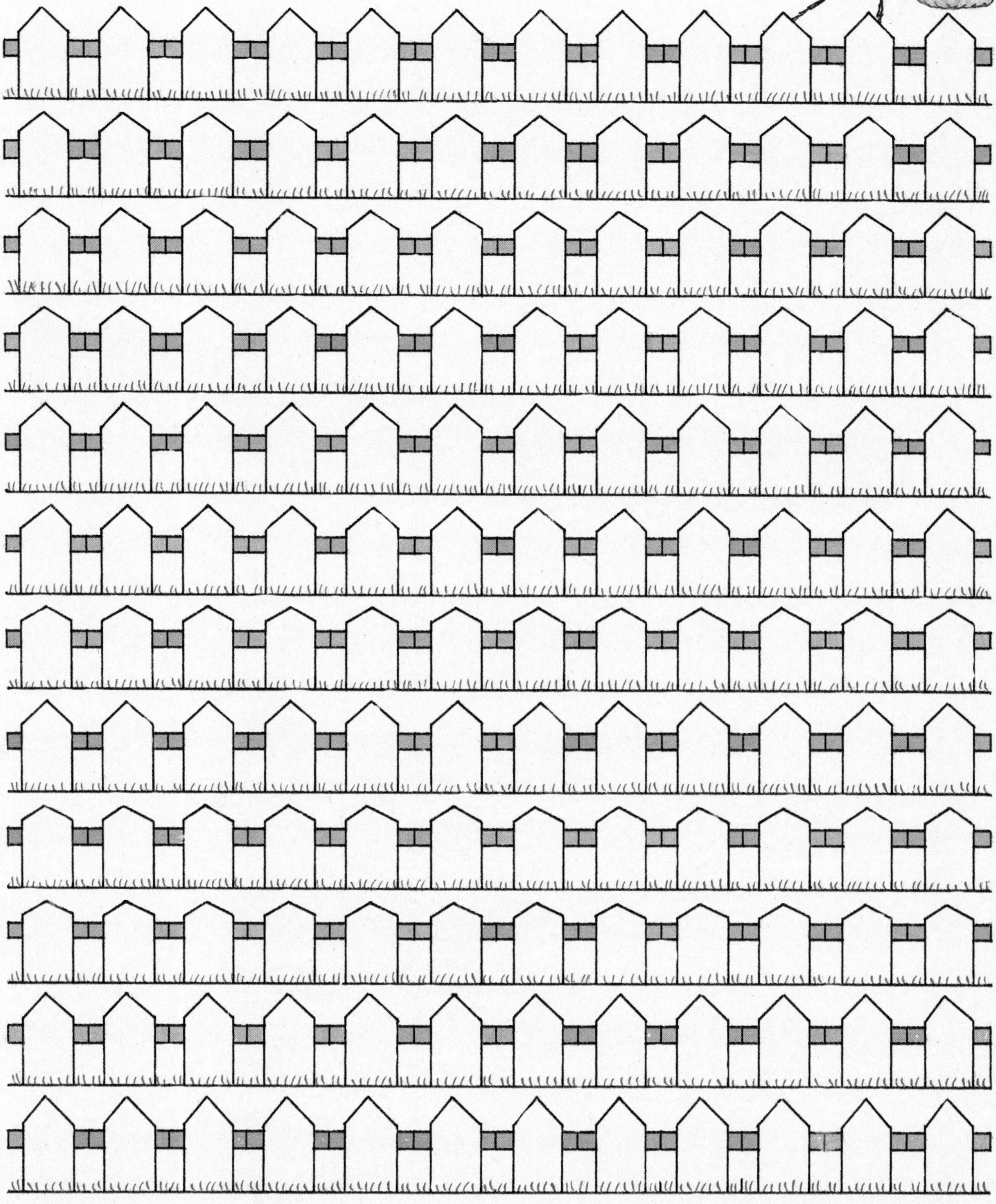

1
2
3
4
5
6
7
8
9
10
11
12

I can connect numbers in order.

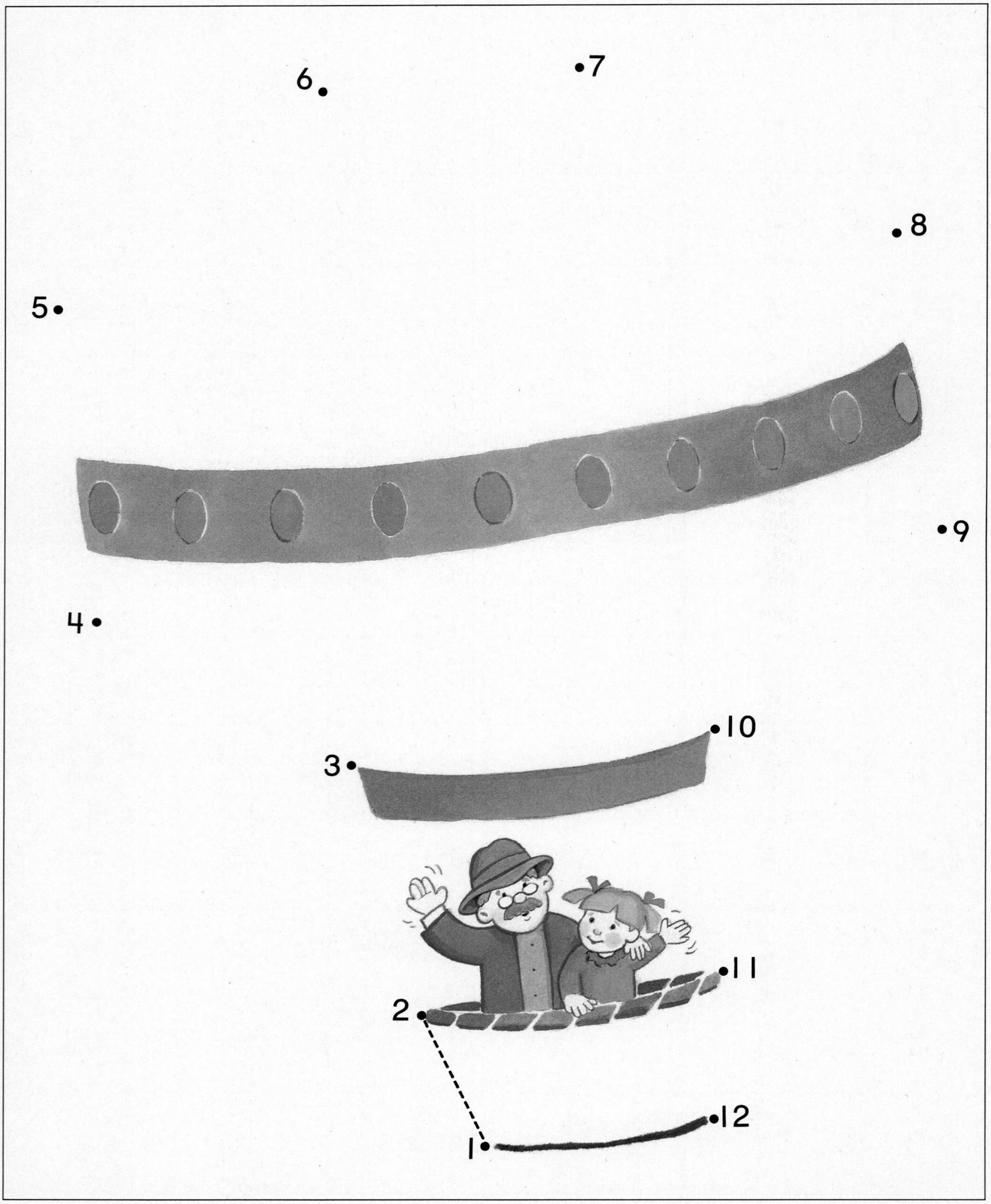

Name ______________________________

I can write my numbers.

I can write my numbers.

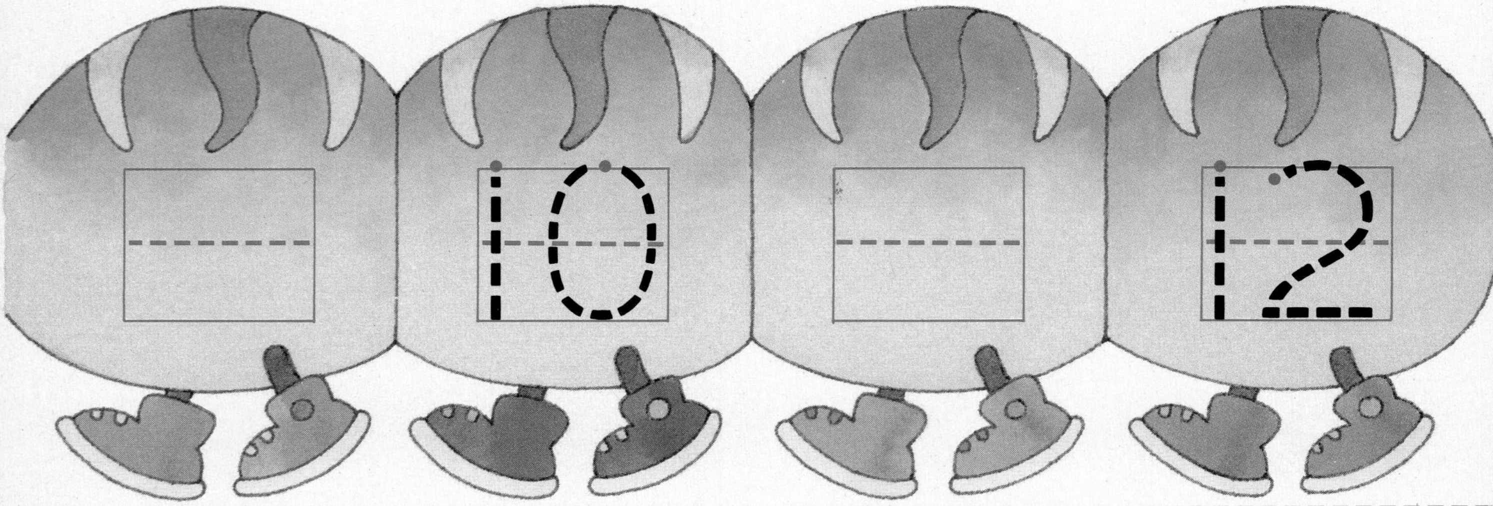

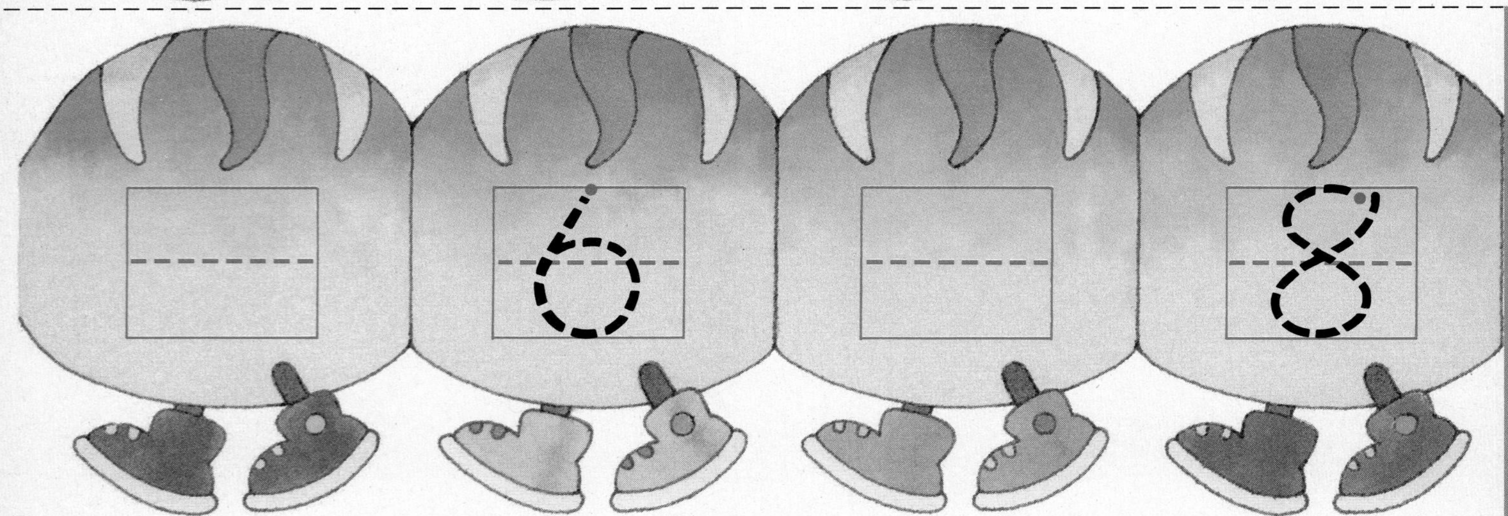

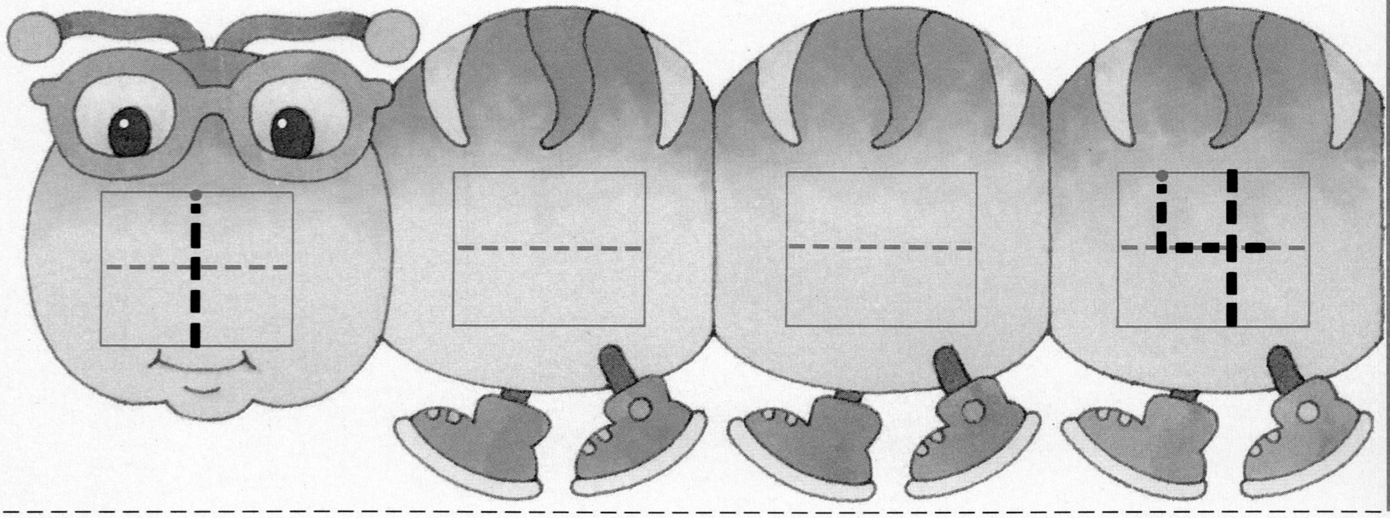

Name ____________________

I can compare numbers.
I can tell which one is more.

11 	9 
7 	10 
10 	12 
8 	9 
11 	8 

I can compare numbers.
I can tell which one is less.

12 	9 
7 	9 
11 	10 
6 	9 
8 	10 

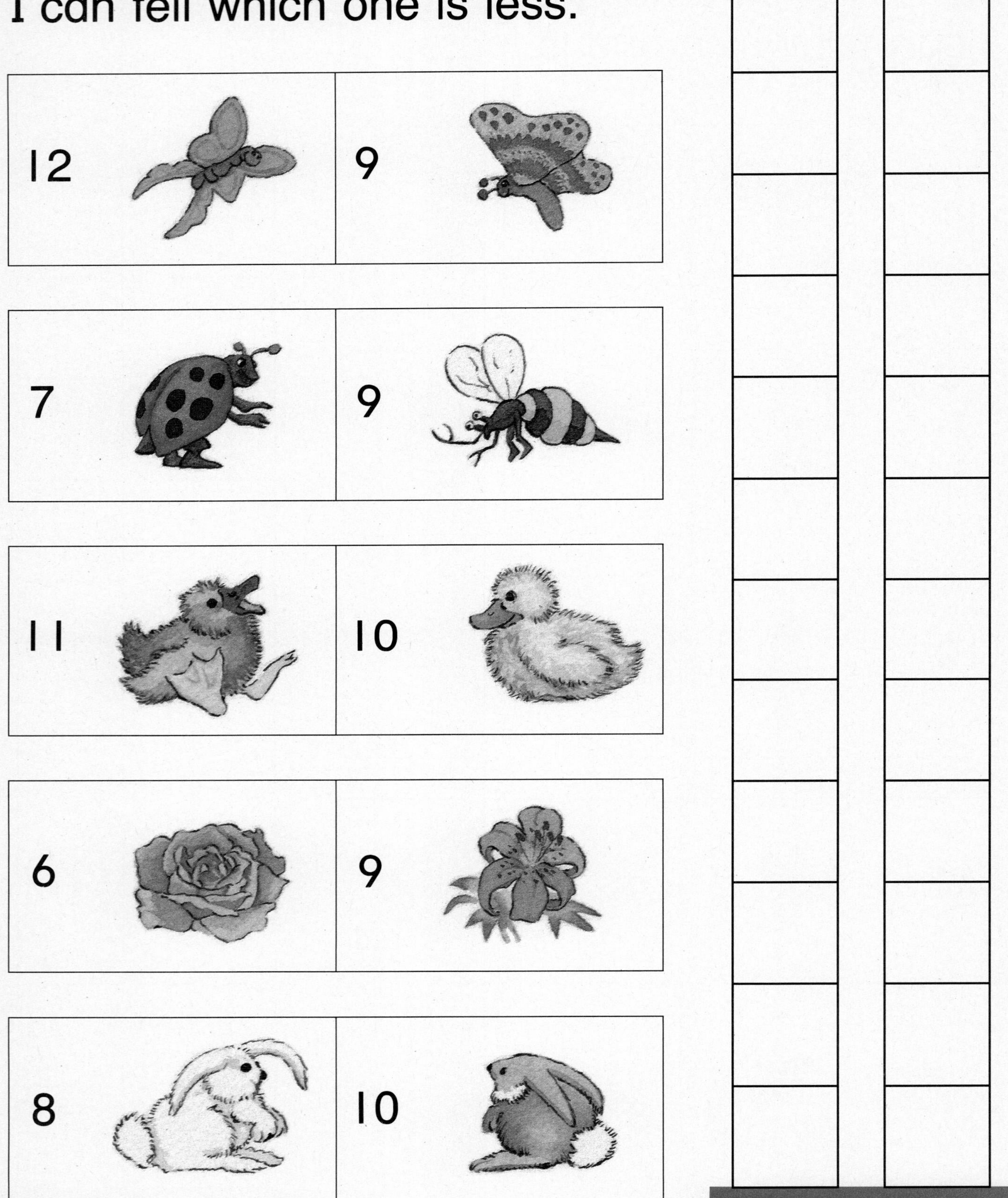

Name ______________________________

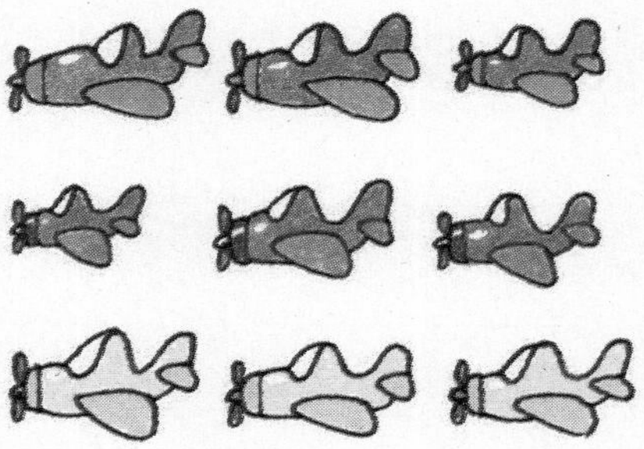

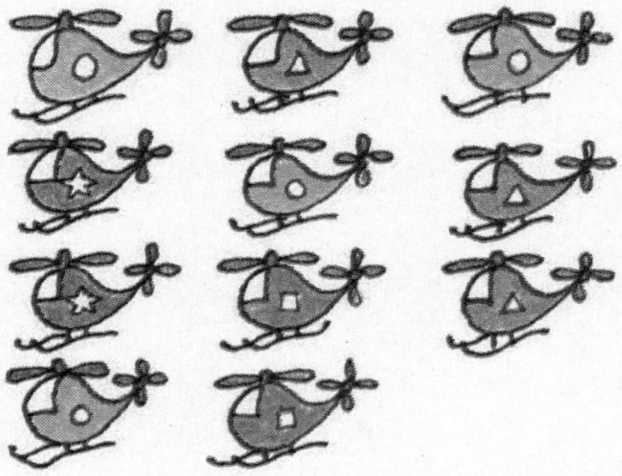

1 2 3 4 5 6 7 8 9 10 11 12

Name ______________________________

I can guess about how many fill the container.

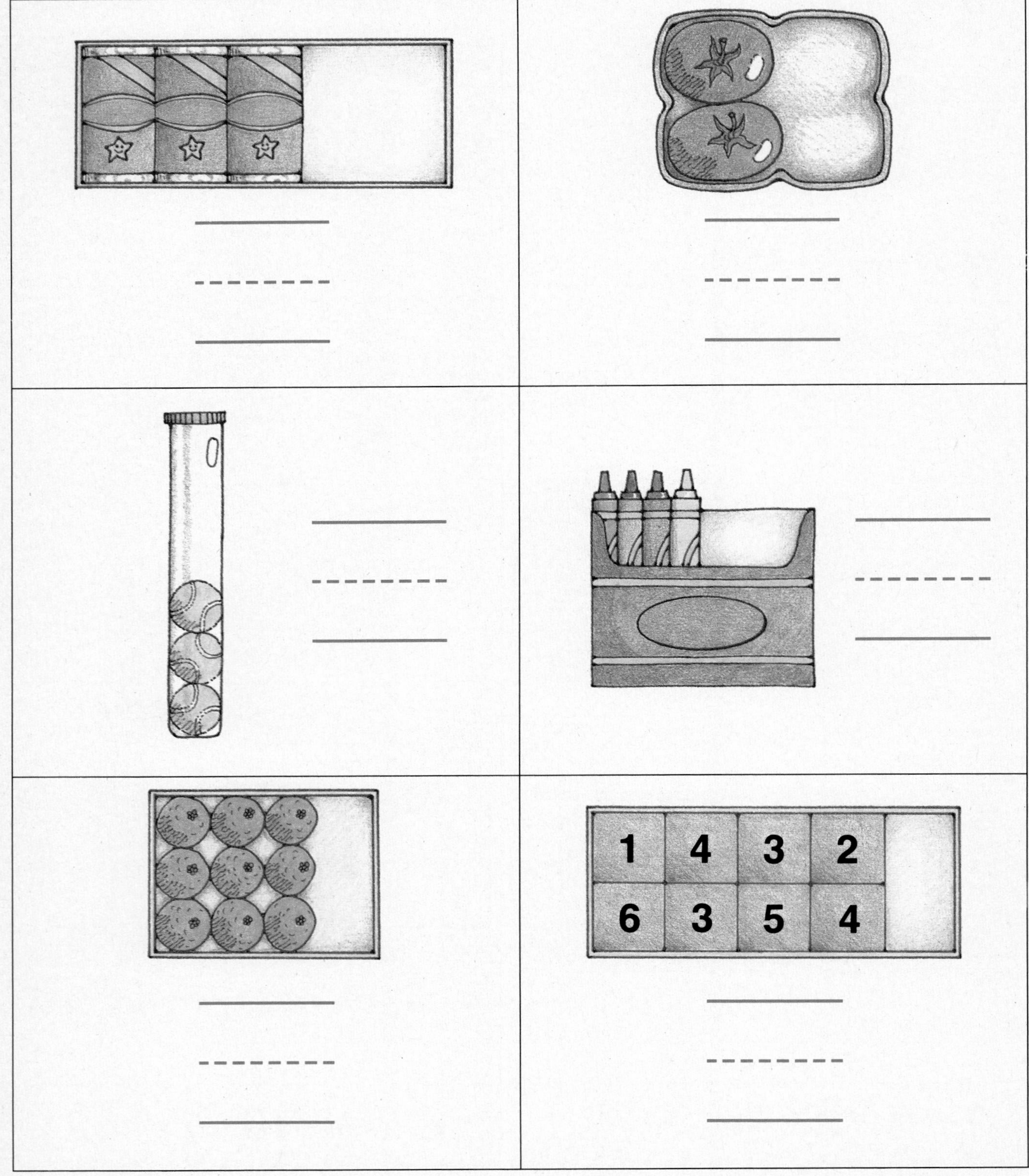

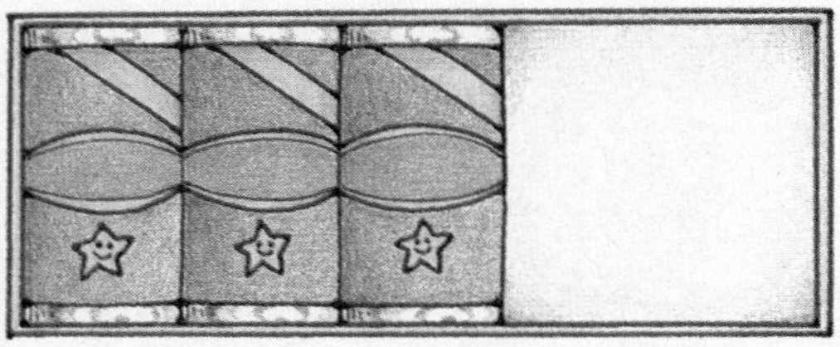

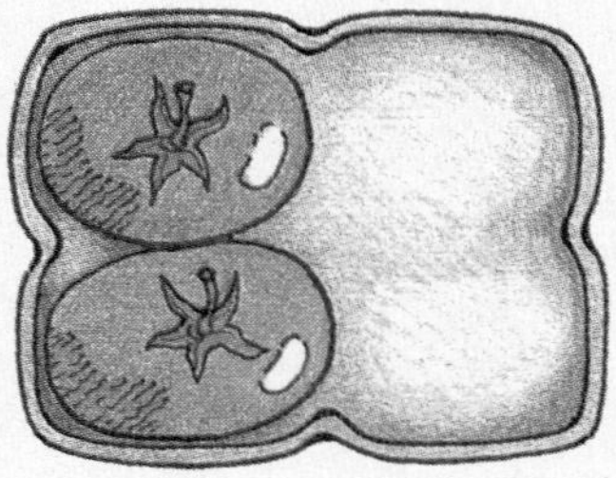

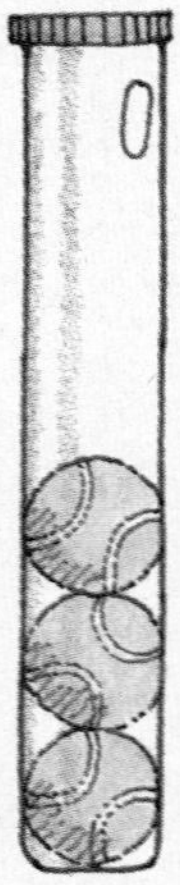

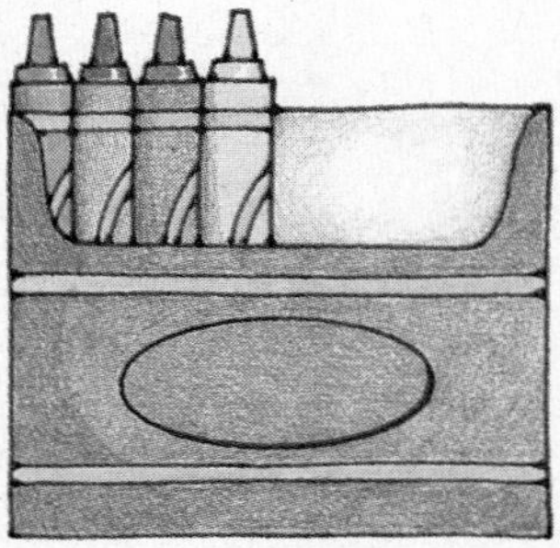

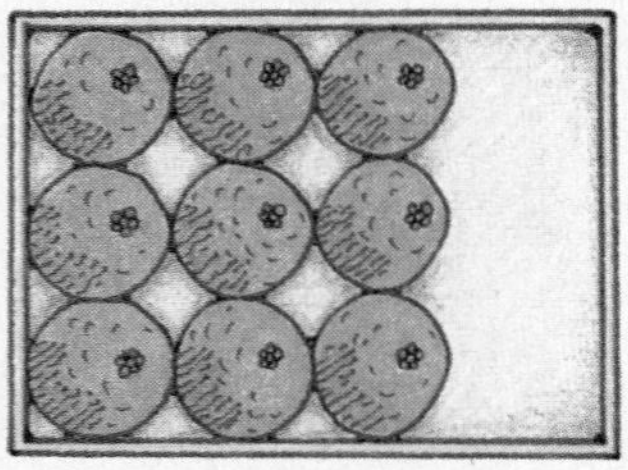

9 Measuring

Workmat

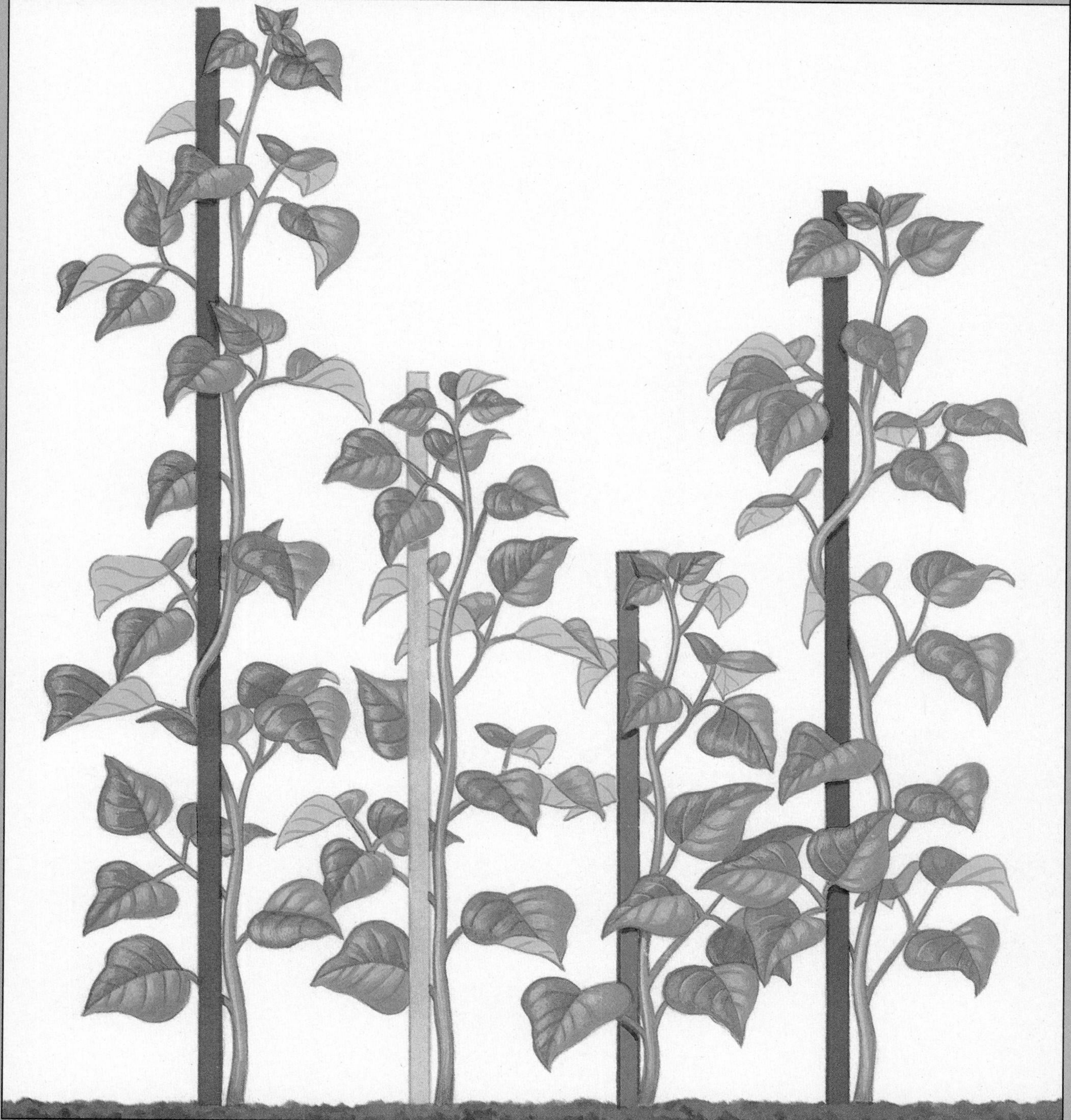

Theme: How Does Your Garden Grow?

Name ______________________________

I can tell how tall it is.

Guess

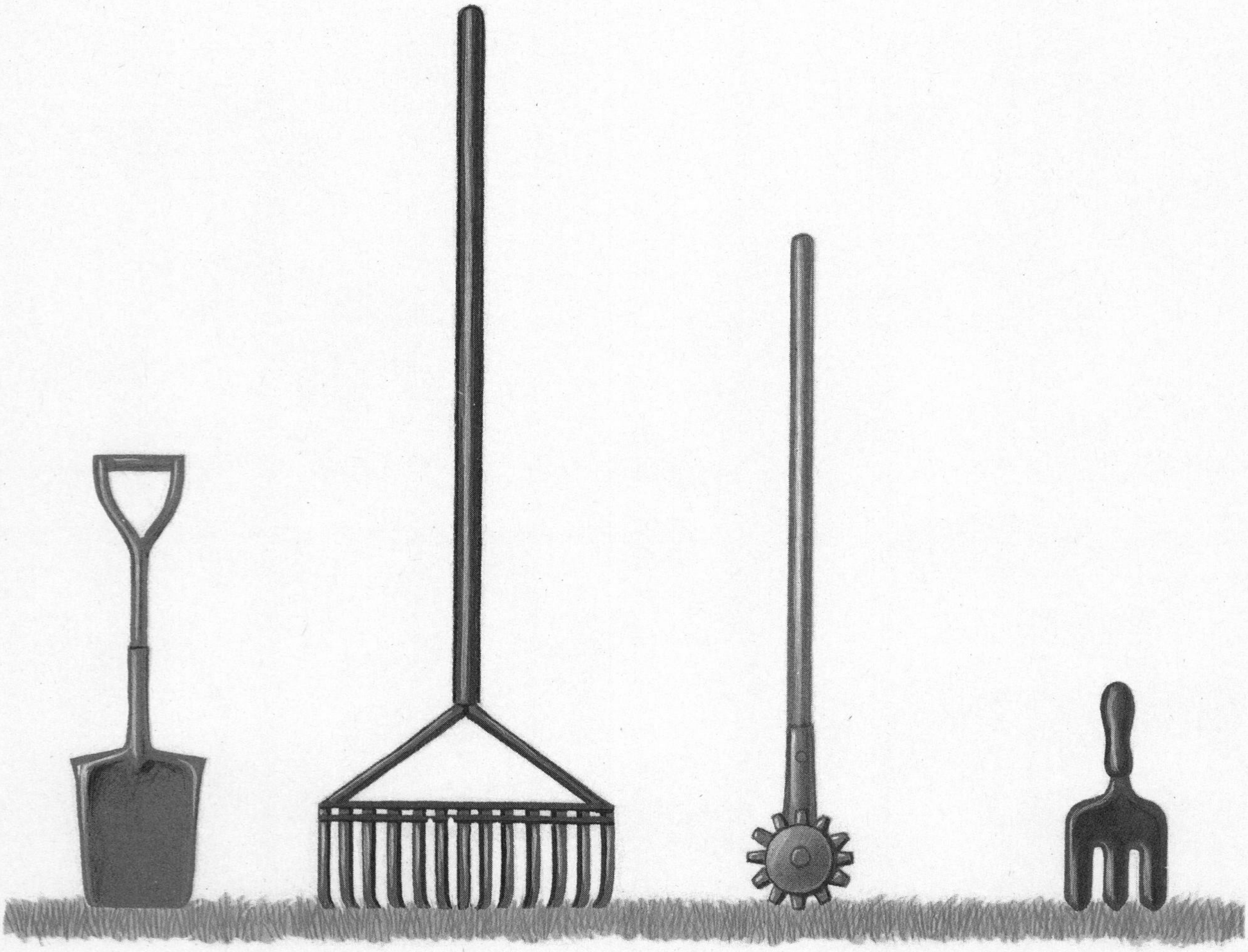

Measure

Name ______________________

I can tell how long it is.

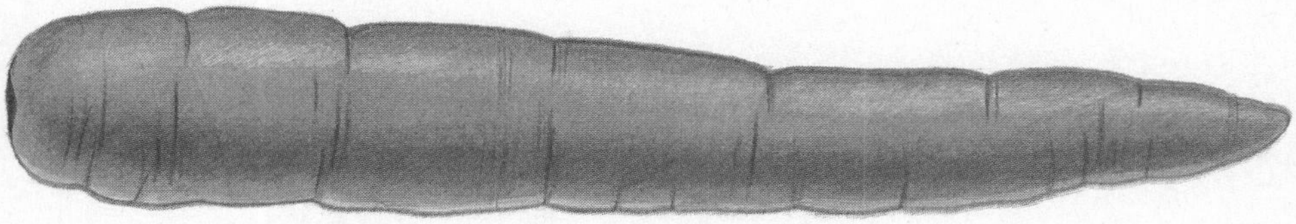

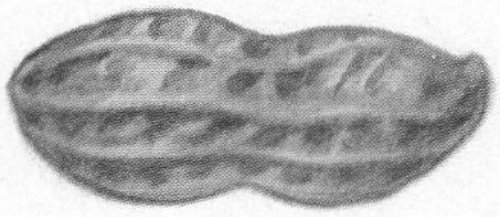

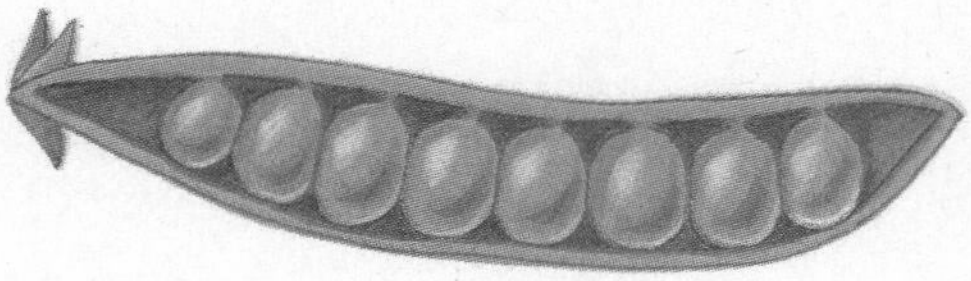

I can tell how long it is.

Guess | Measure

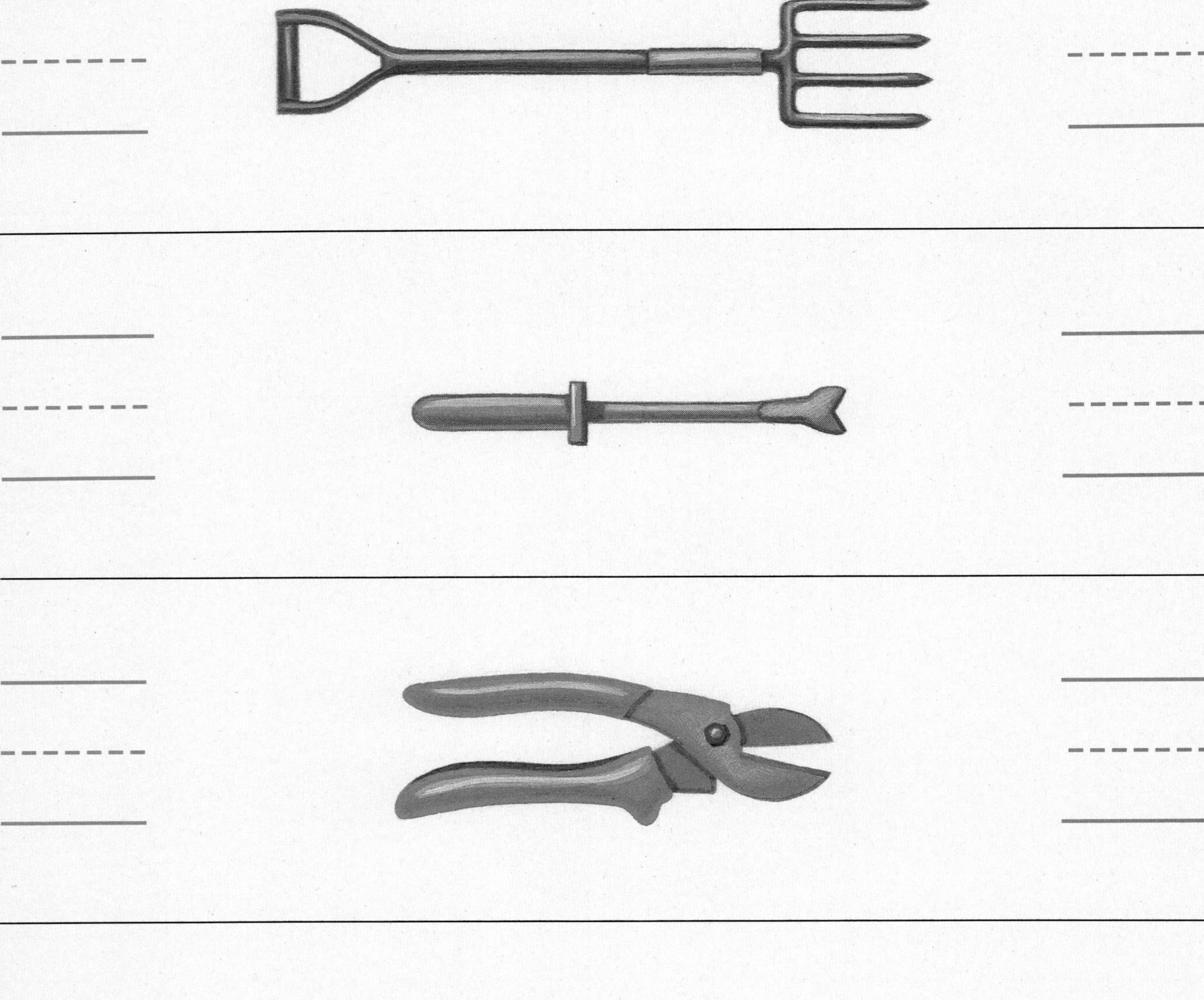

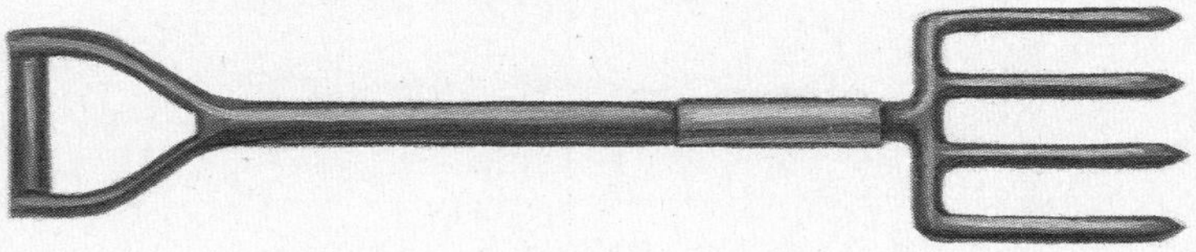

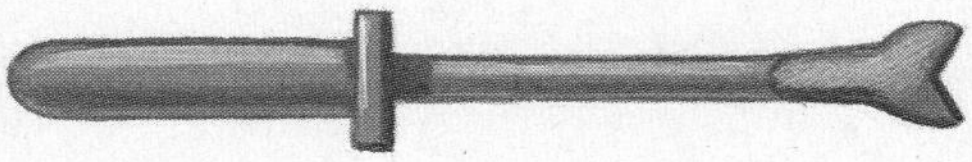

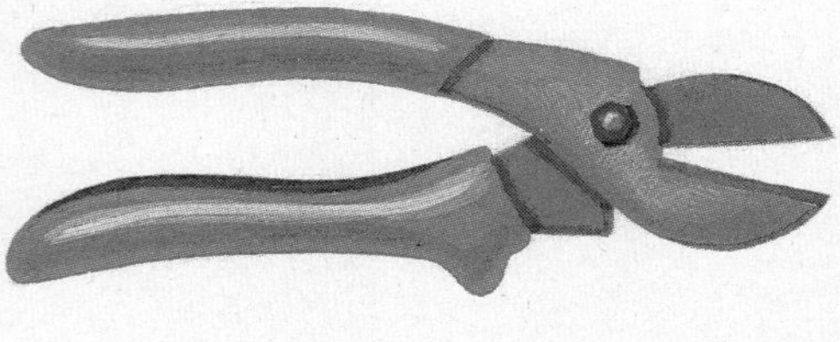

Name ____________________

I can measure my own things.
I can tell about how long they are.

Guess

Measure

my crayon

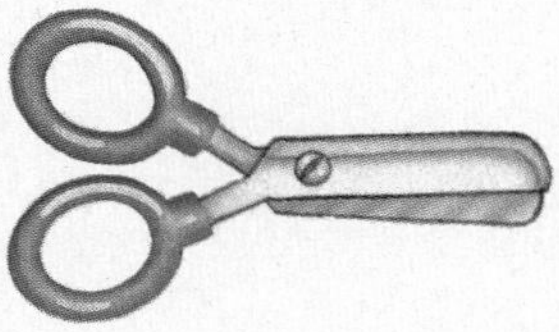

my scissors

my shoe

my choice

1	2	3	4	5	6	7	8	9	10	11	12

I can find something shorter and longer.

Name ______________________________

I can tell about how far it is.

1	2	3	4	5	6	7	8	9	10	11	12

I can tell about how far it is.

Name ______________________________

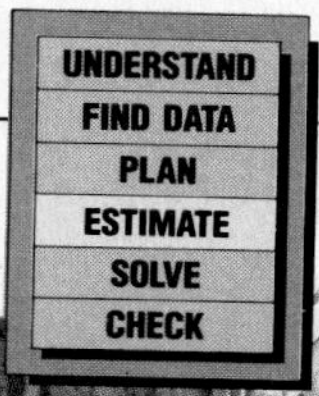

I can tell which path is the shortest one.

I can show the rabbit the way out of the garden.

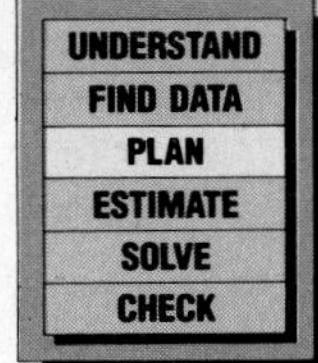

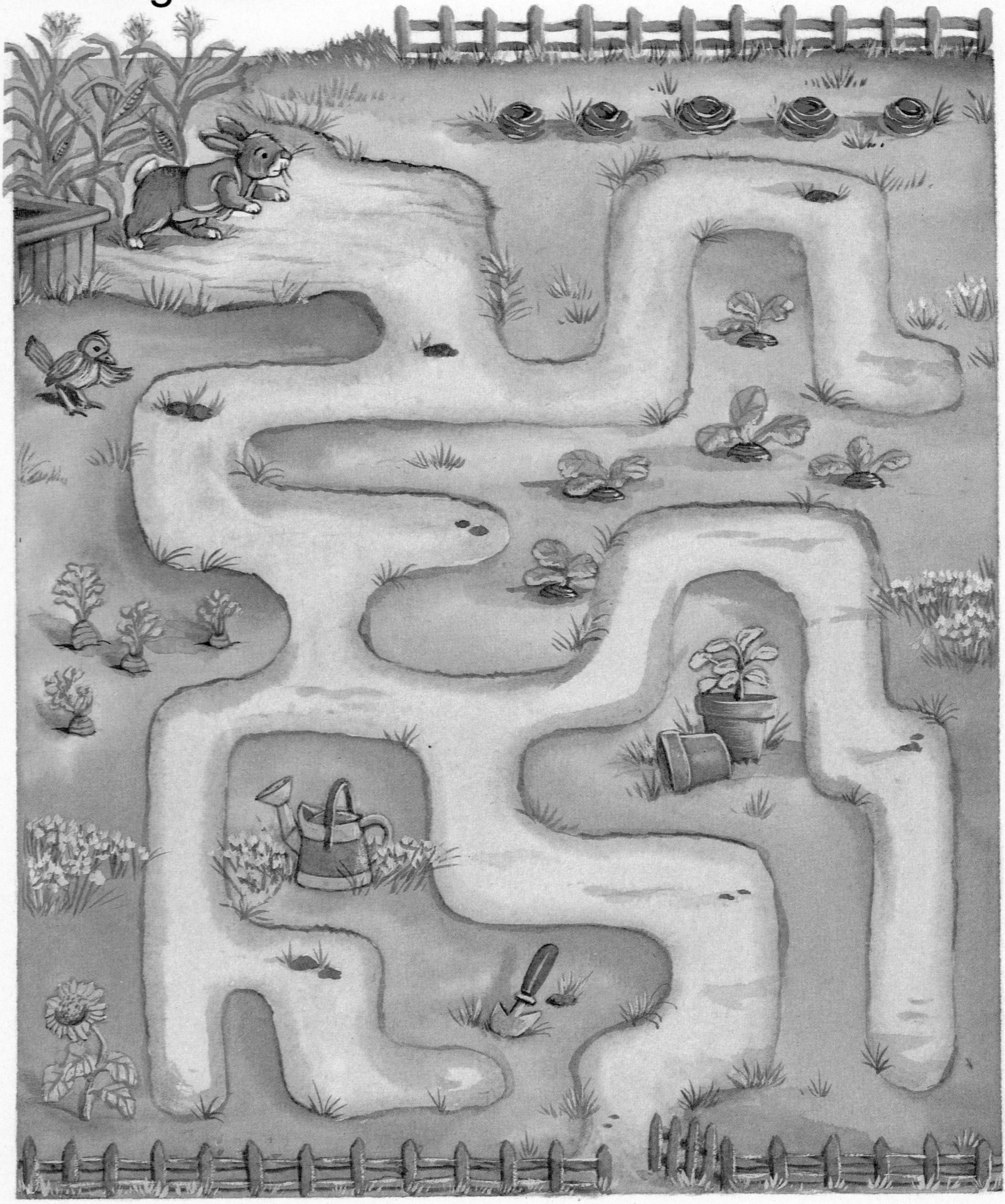

Name ______________________________

I can tell how many tiles cover the garden.

Guess — Measure

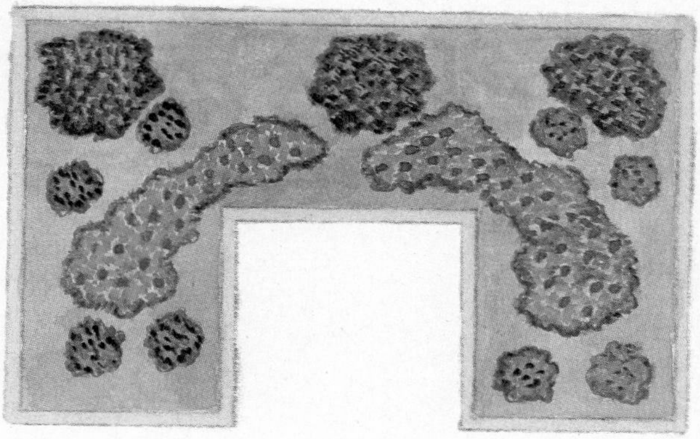

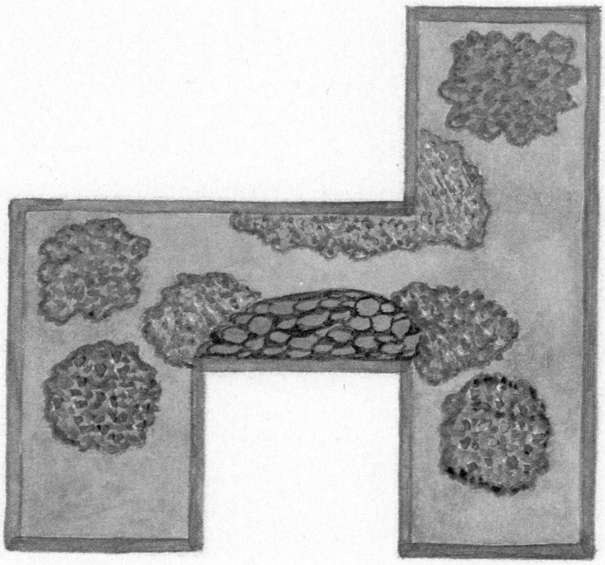

1	2	3	4	5	6	7	8	9	10	11	12

I can tell which garden is larger.

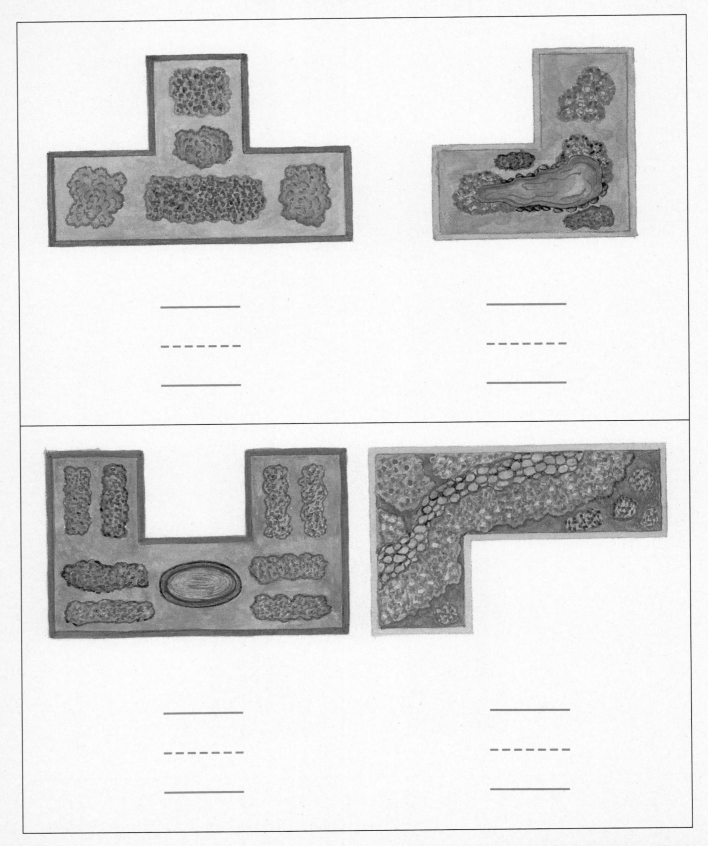

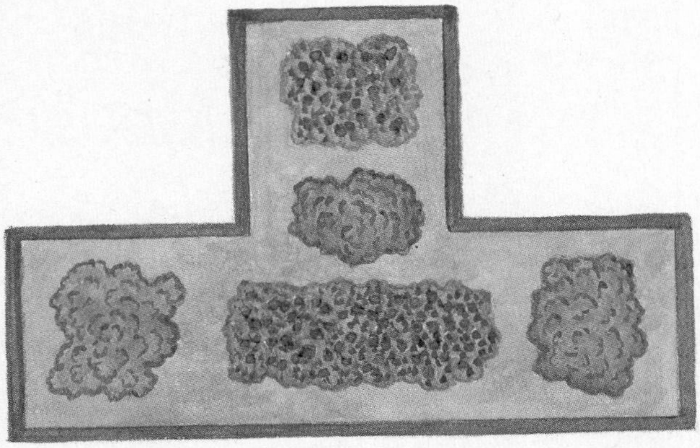

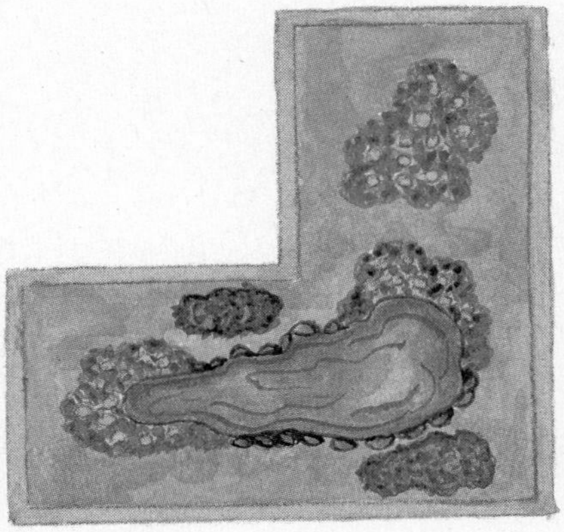

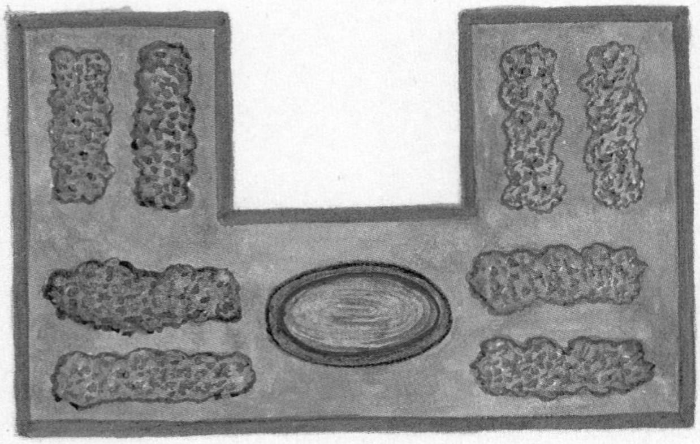

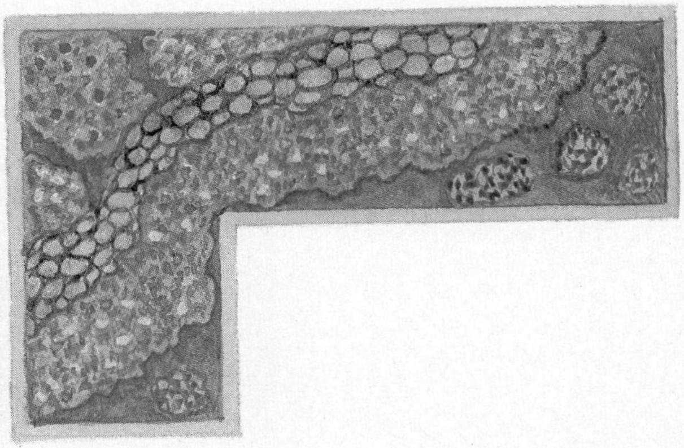

Name ______________________________

I can tell which one holds more.

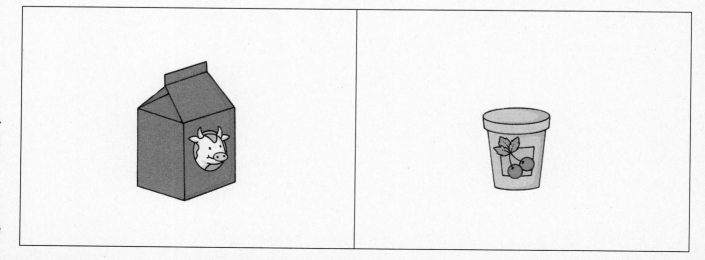

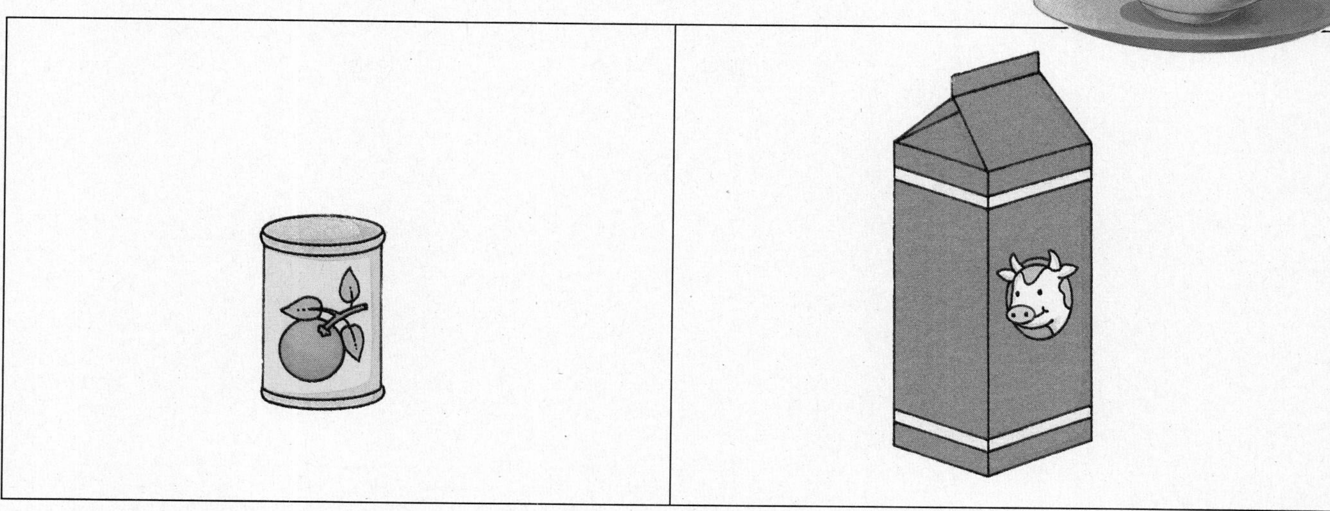

I can tell which one holds less.

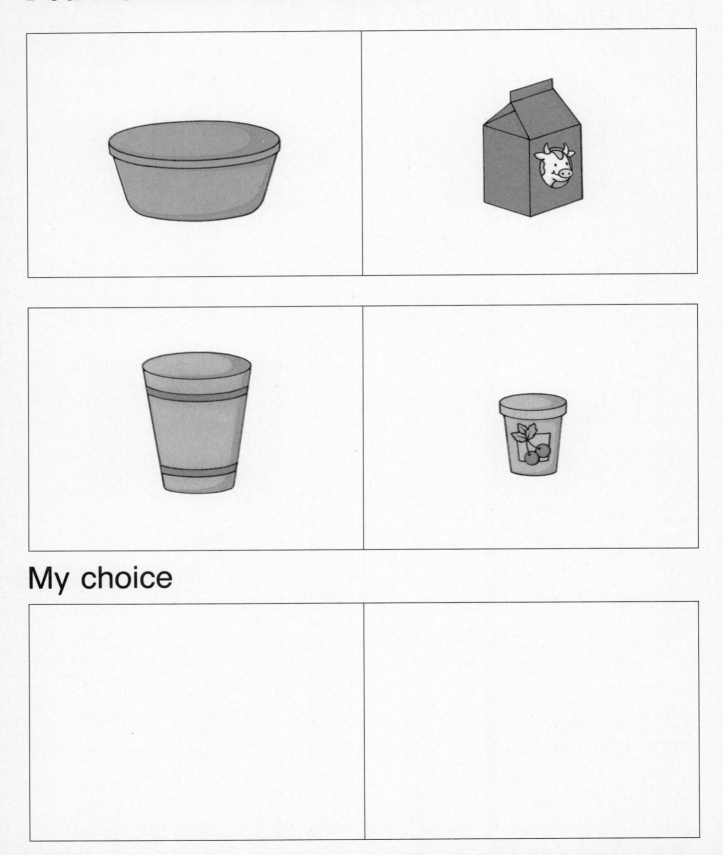

My choice

Name ______________________________

I can tell which objects are heavier or lighter.

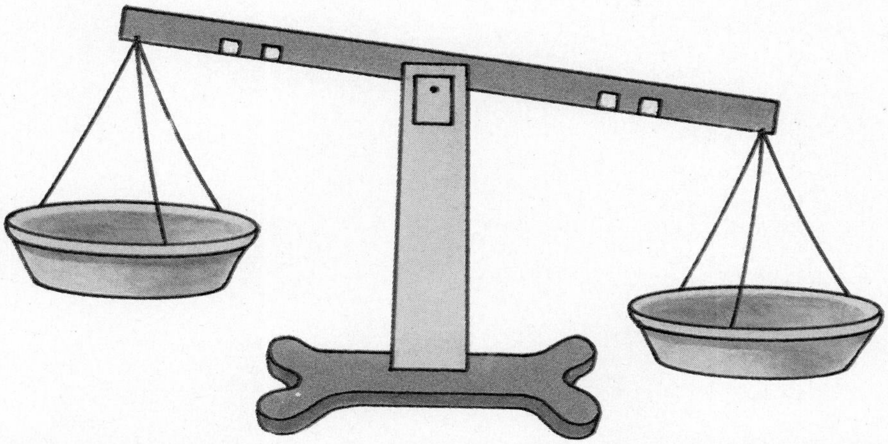

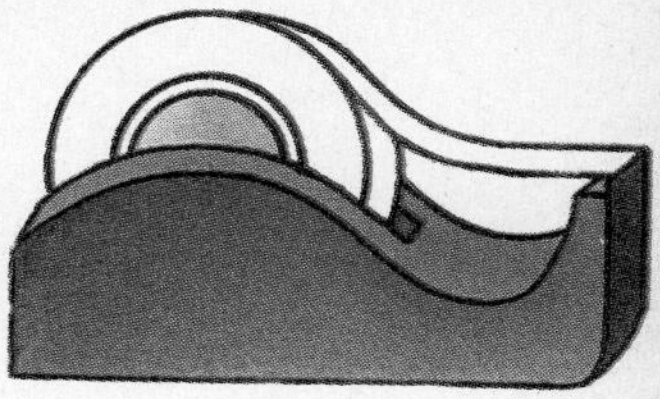

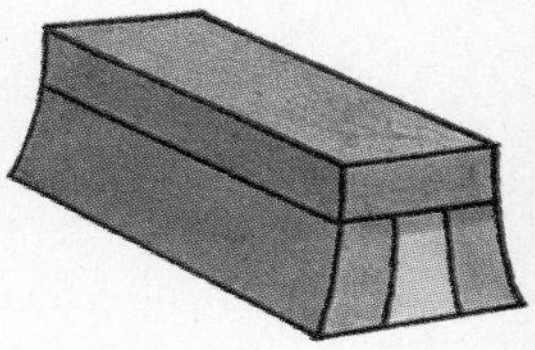

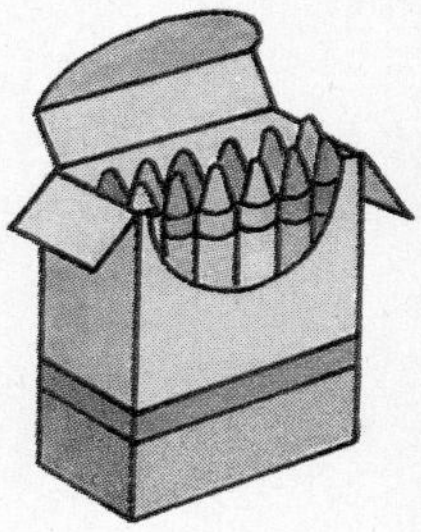

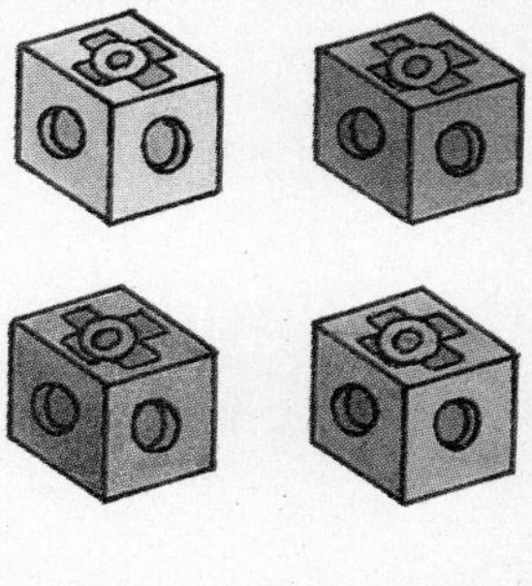

I can find something heavier or lighter.

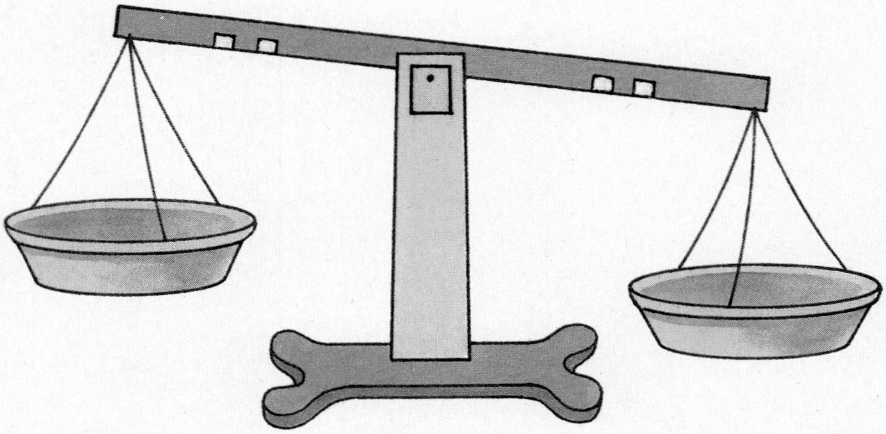

Name ________________________________

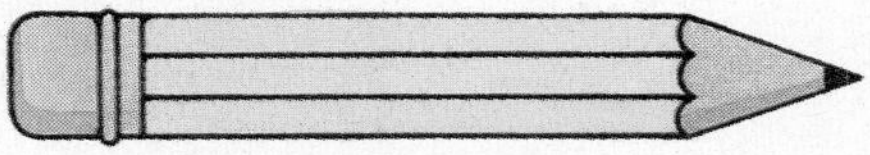

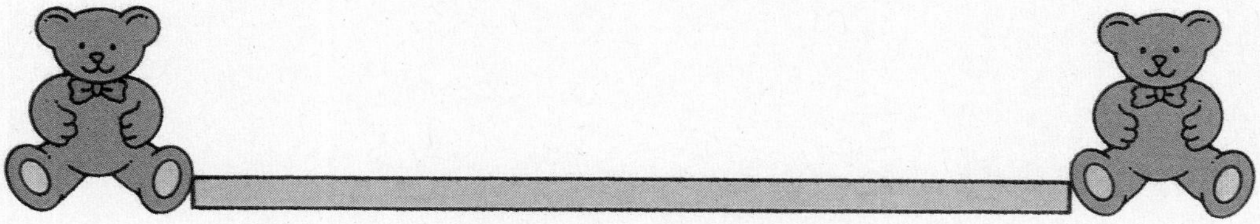

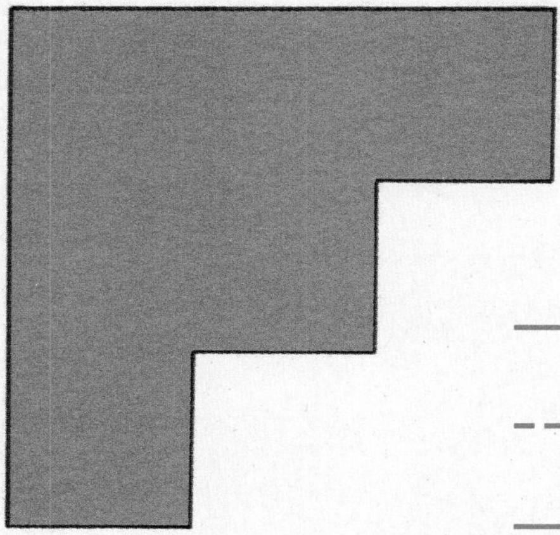

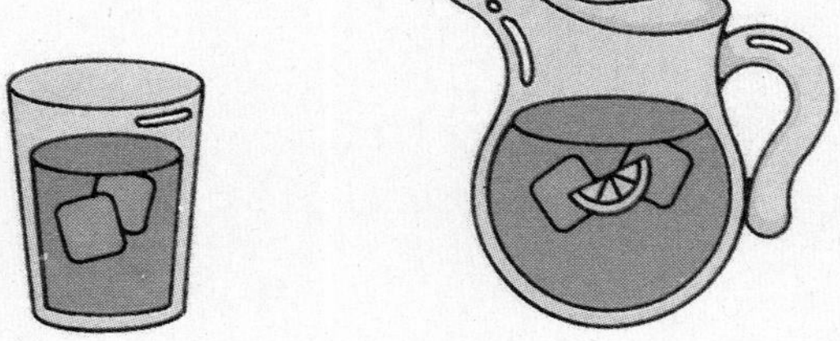

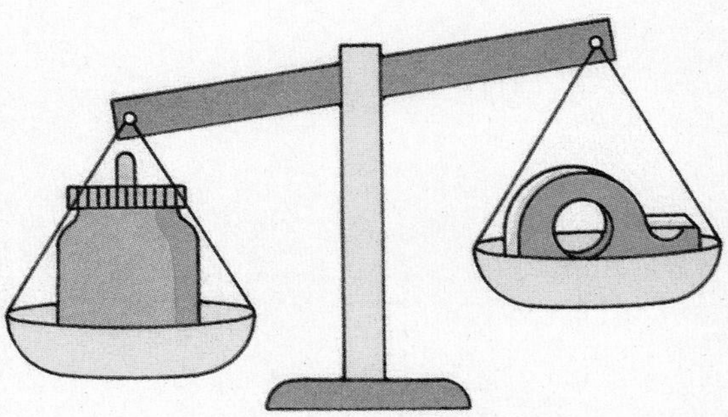

1	2	3	4	5	6	7	8	9	10	11	12

Name ____

I can tell how long the fence is.

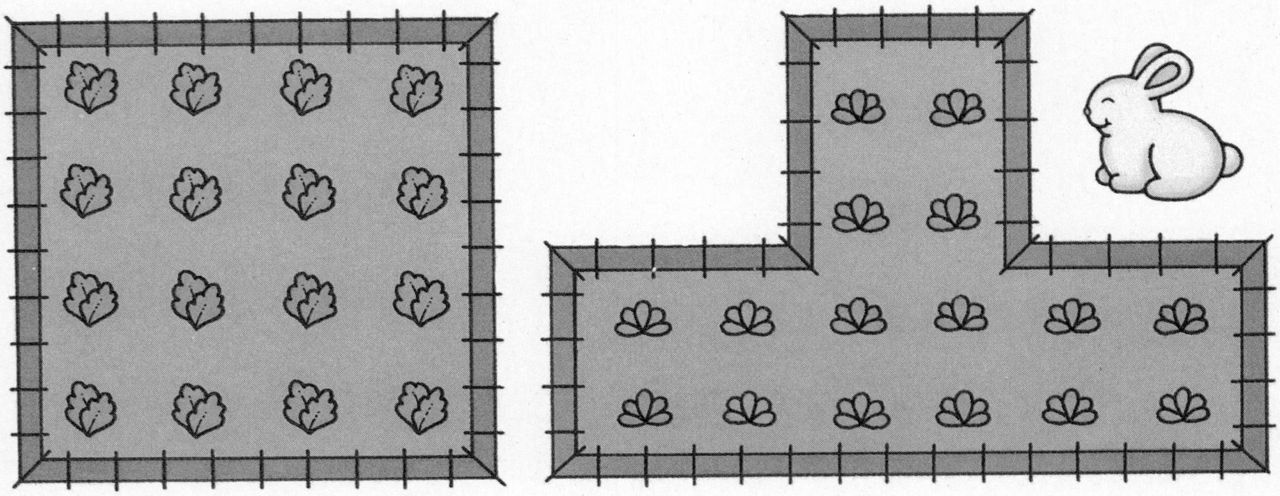

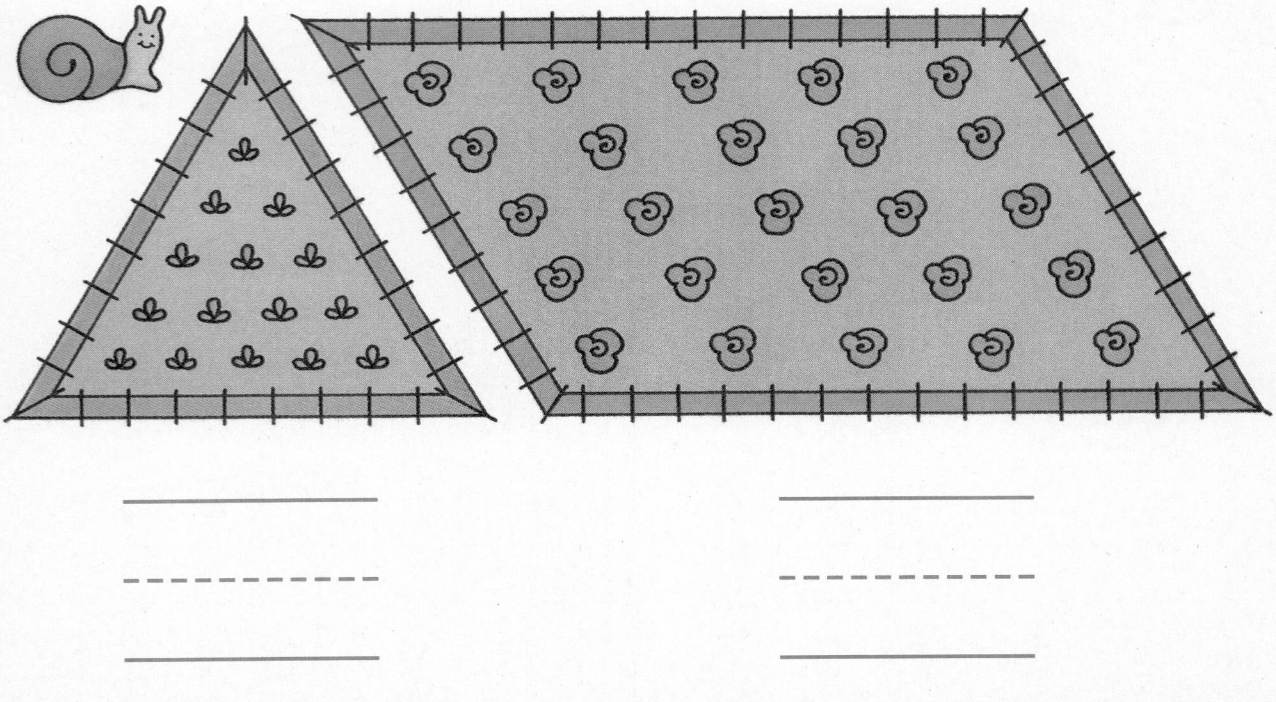

10
Time and Money

Workmat

Theme: Day at the Shops

Name ______________________________

I can tell what happened before and after.

Name ______________________________

I can tell what happened first, next, and last.

I can tell what happened first, next, and last.

Name ______________________________

I can guess which takes more time.

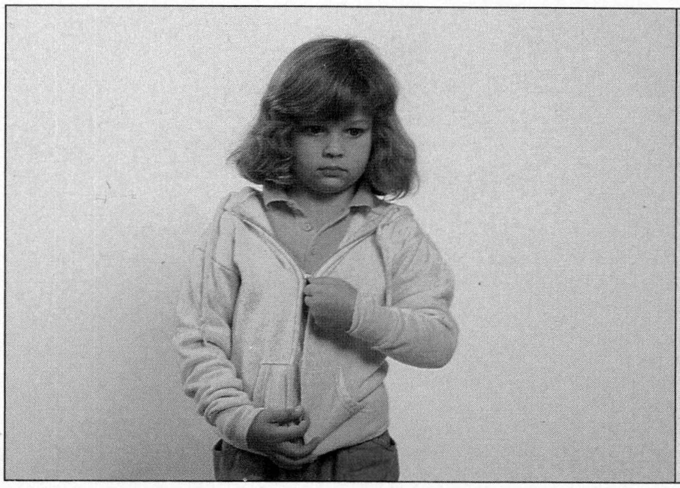

I can guess which takes less time.

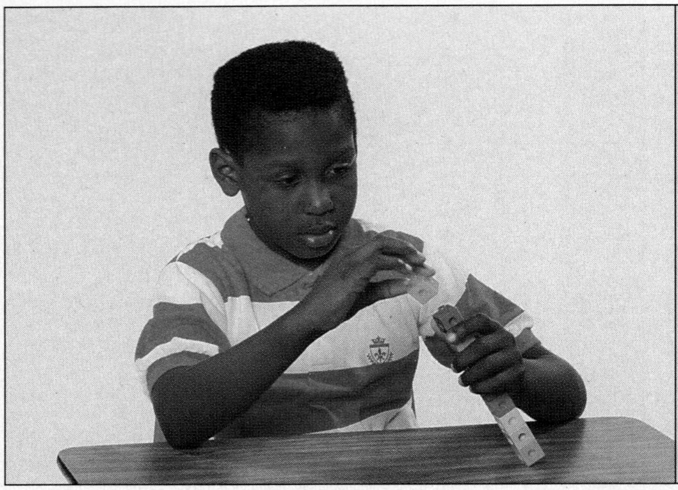

My choice

Name ________________________________

I can tell time on the hour.

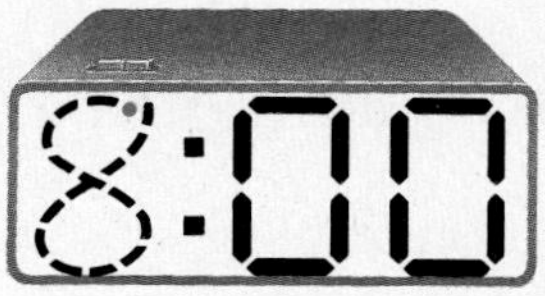

8 o'clock

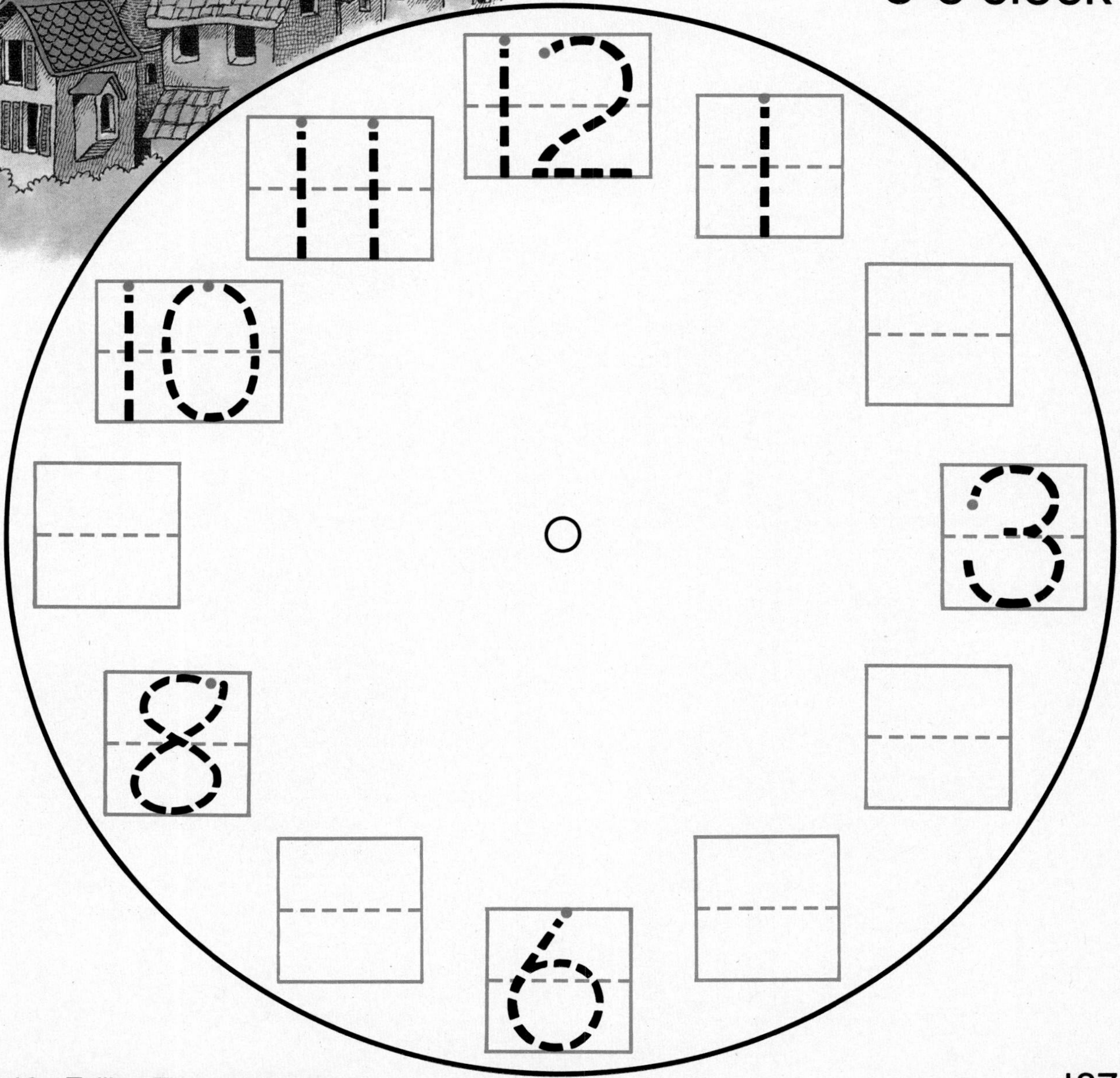

I can tell time on the hour.

Name ______________________________

I can count pennies.

penny

1¢

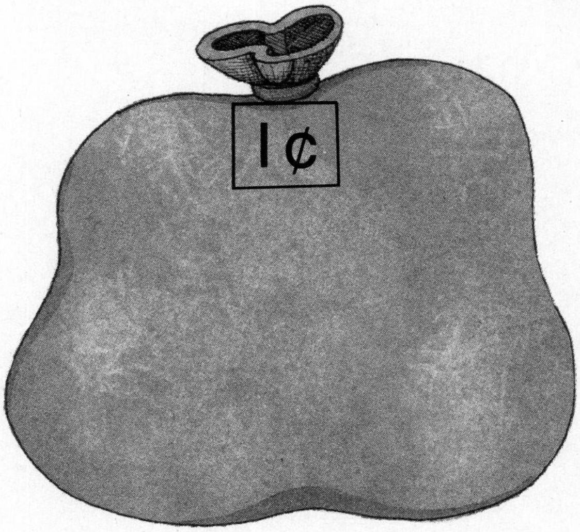

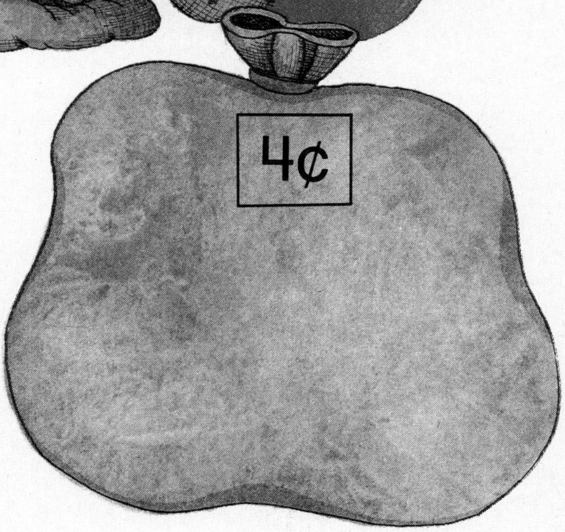

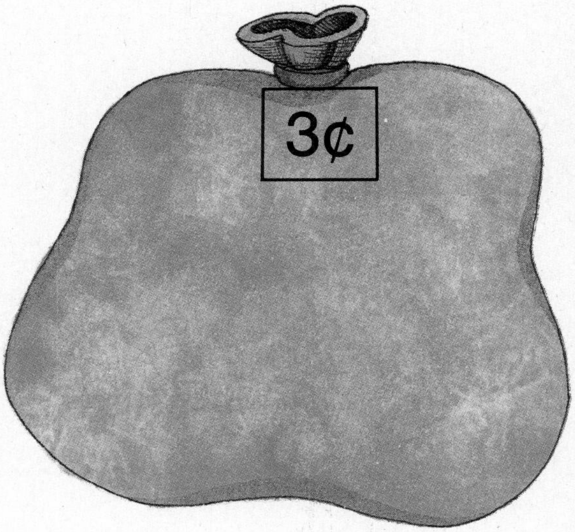

I can tell how much money there is.

_____ ¢

_____ ¢

_____ ¢

_____ ¢

1	2	3	4	5	6	7	8	9	10	11	12

Name ______________________________

UNDERSTAND
FIND DATA
PLAN
ESTIMATE
SOLVE
CHECK

I can read a graph.
I can tell who has more.

______ ¢

______ ¢

______ ¢

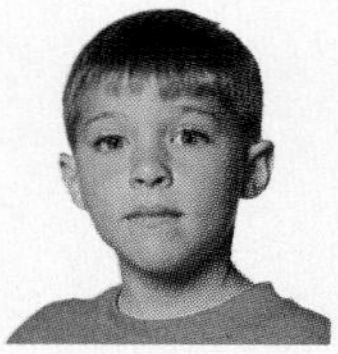
______ ¢

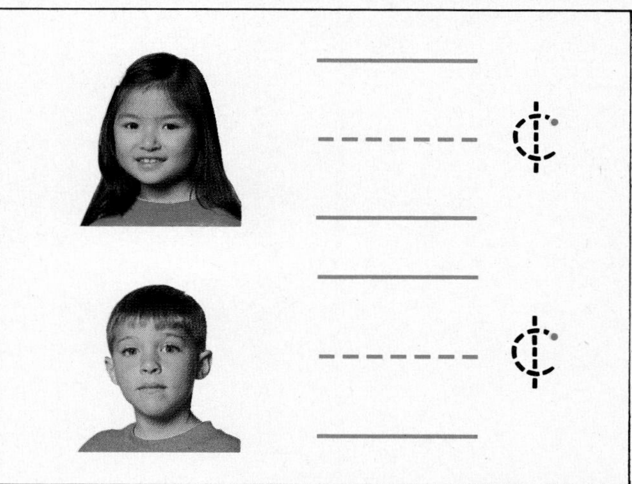

1 2 3 4 5 6 7 8 9 10 11 12

UNDERSTAND
FIND DATA
PLAN
ESTIMATE
SOLVE
CHECK

I can tell which costs less.

Name ______________________________

I can show what I can buy for 8¢.

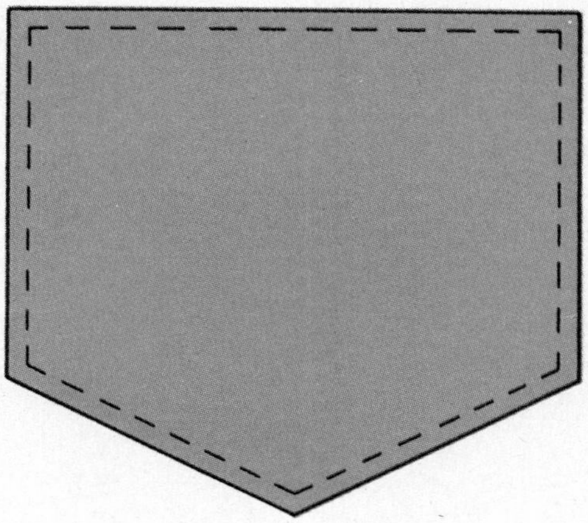	
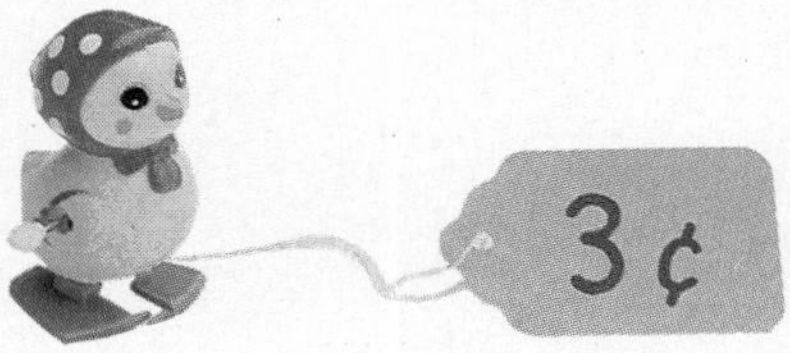	
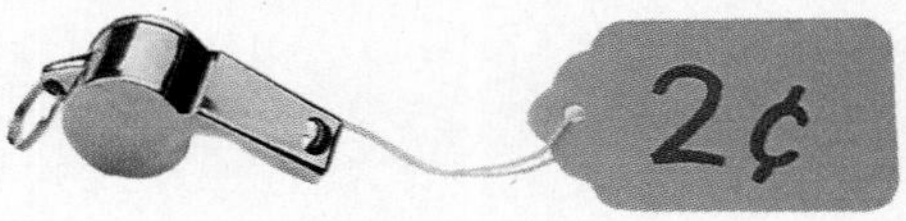	

I can tell if there is enough money in the pocket.

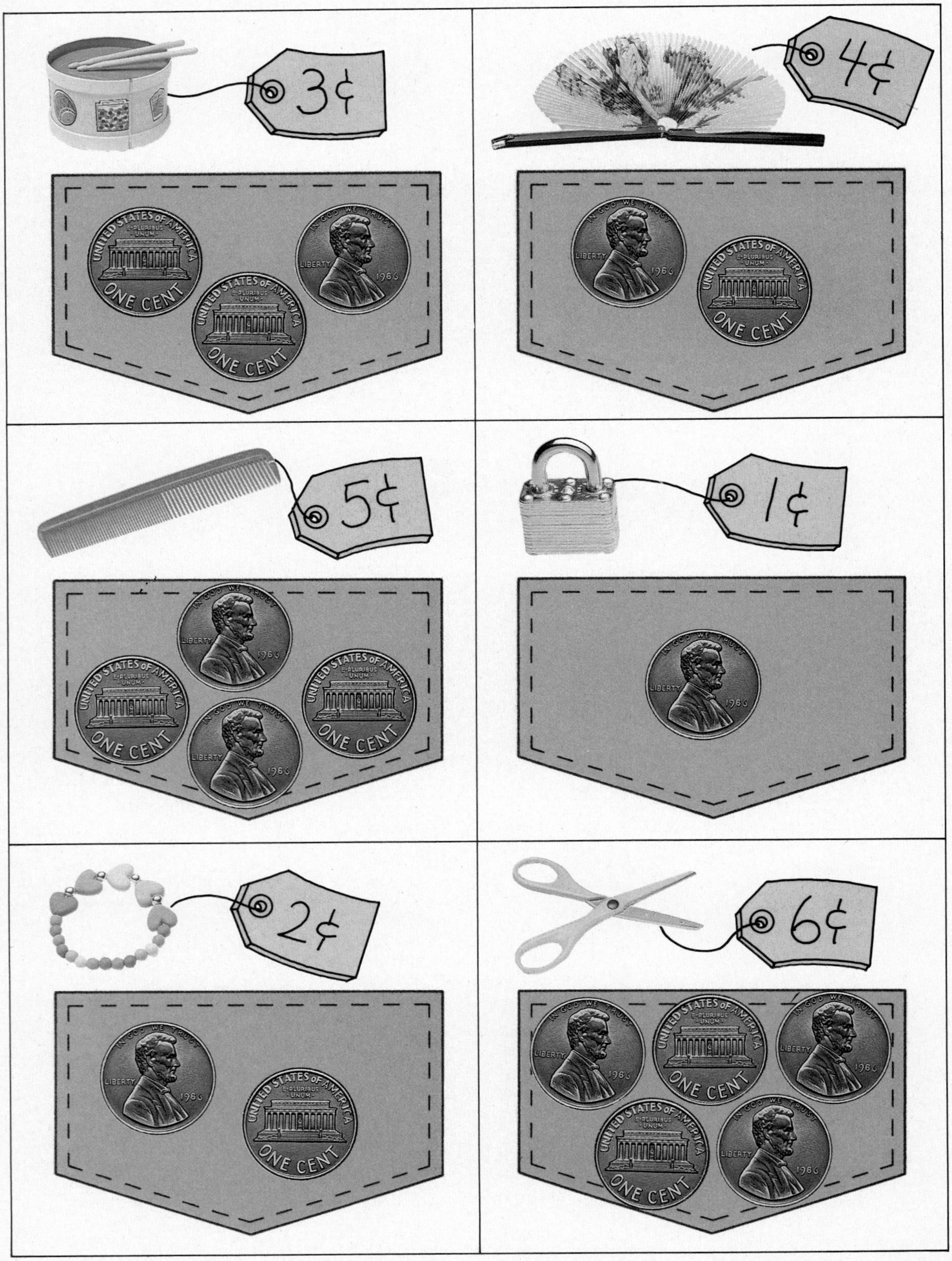

Name ____________________

I can play a game.
I can trade 5 pennies for 1 nickel.

nickel

5¢

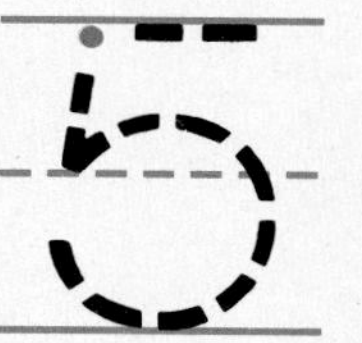

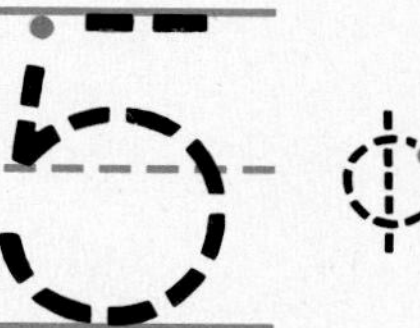

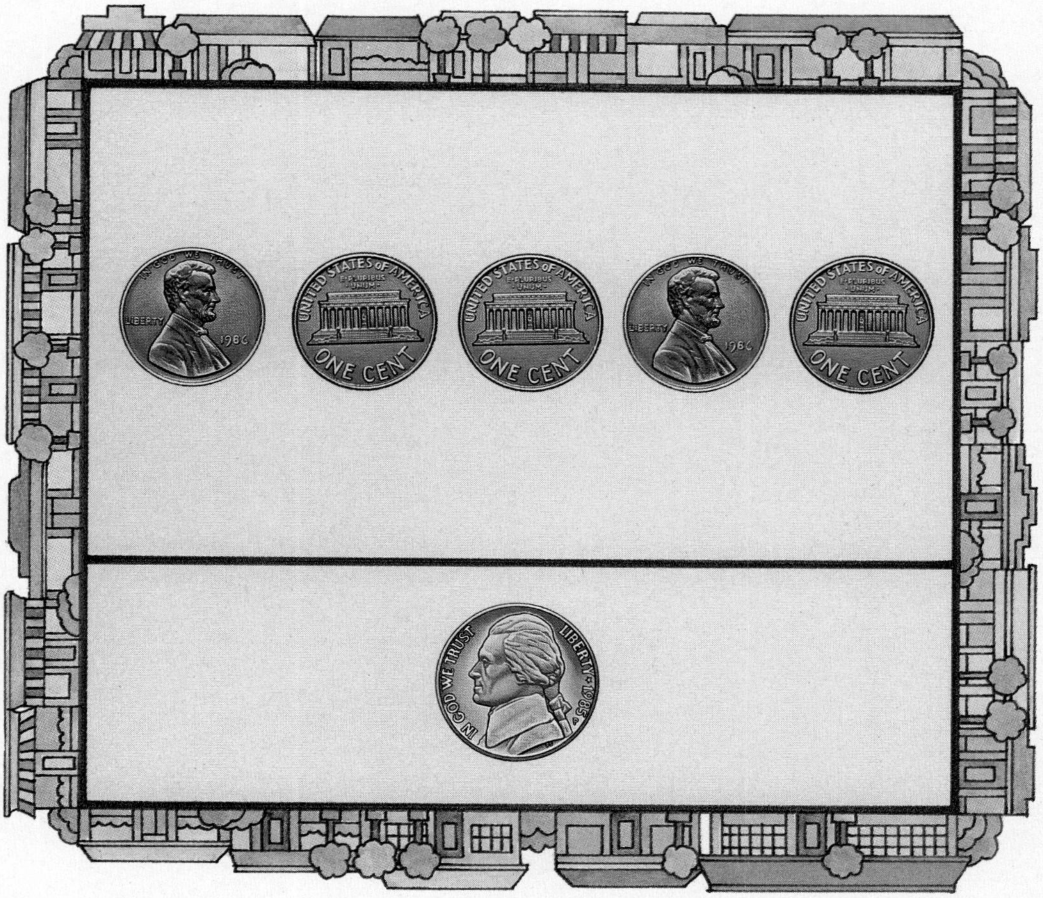

5¢

5¢

How Many Trades?

I can show 5¢.

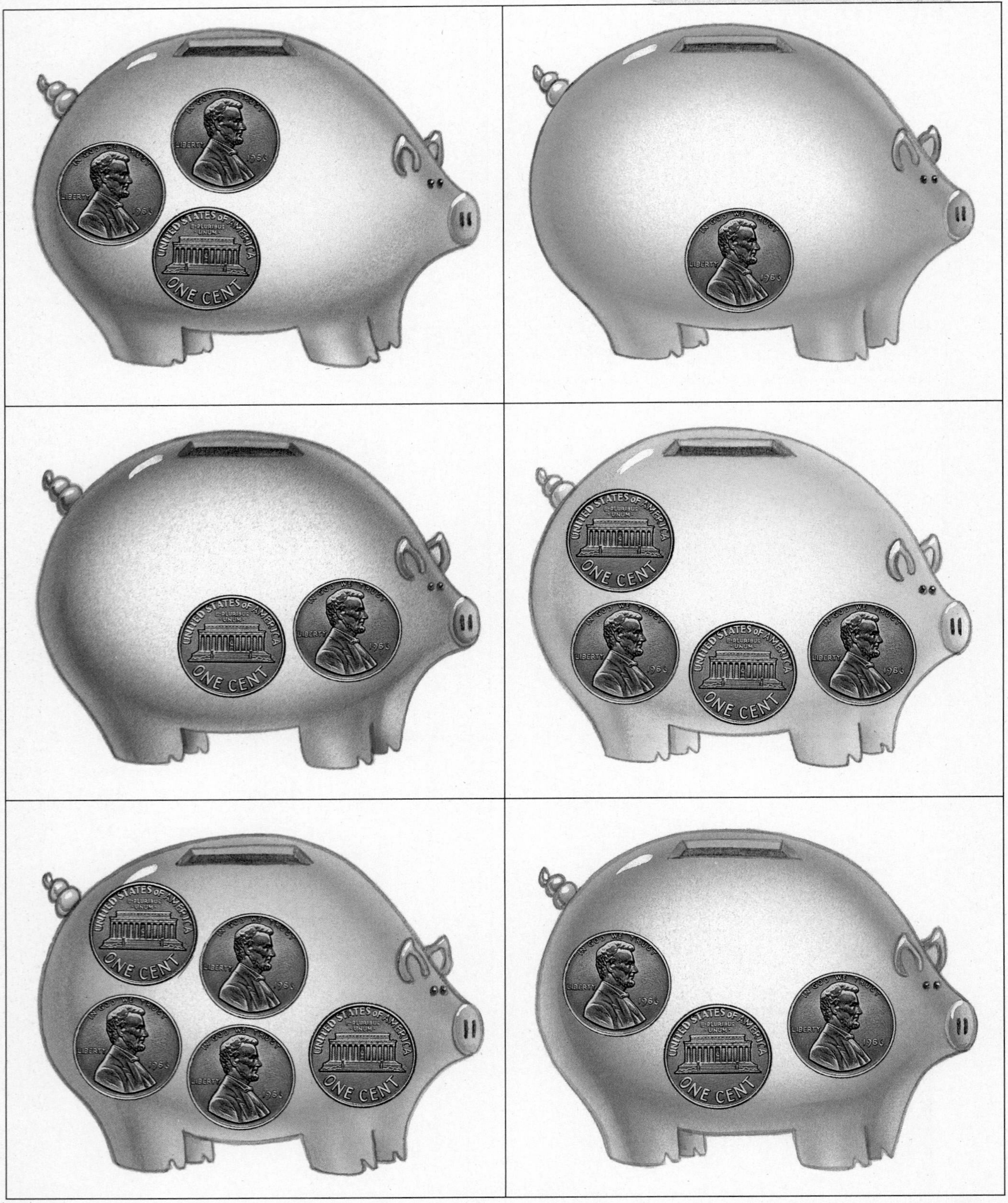

IN GOD WE TRUST
LIBERTY
UNITED STATES OF AMERICA
E PLURIBUS UNUM
ONE CENT

Name ____________________

I can play a game.
I can trade 10 pennies for 1 dime.

dime

10¢

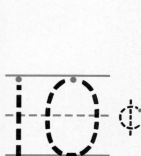

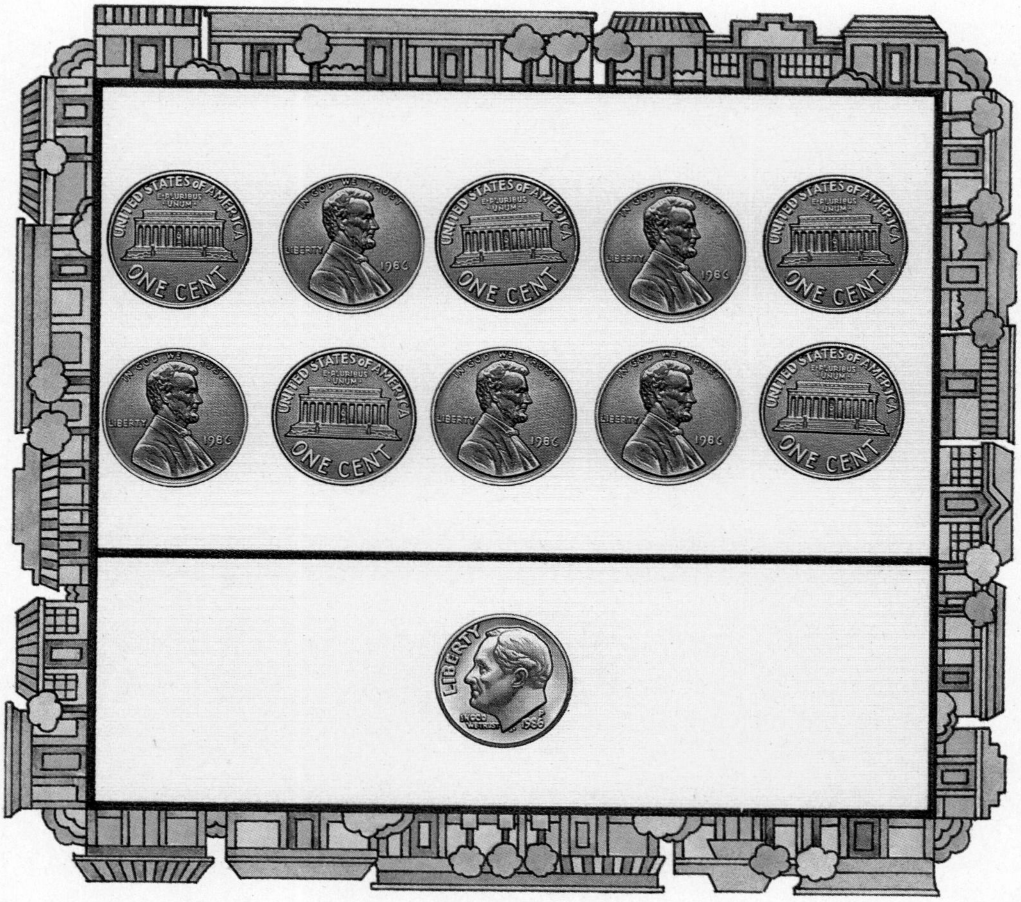

10¢

10¢

How Many Trades?

I can tell how much money it costs.

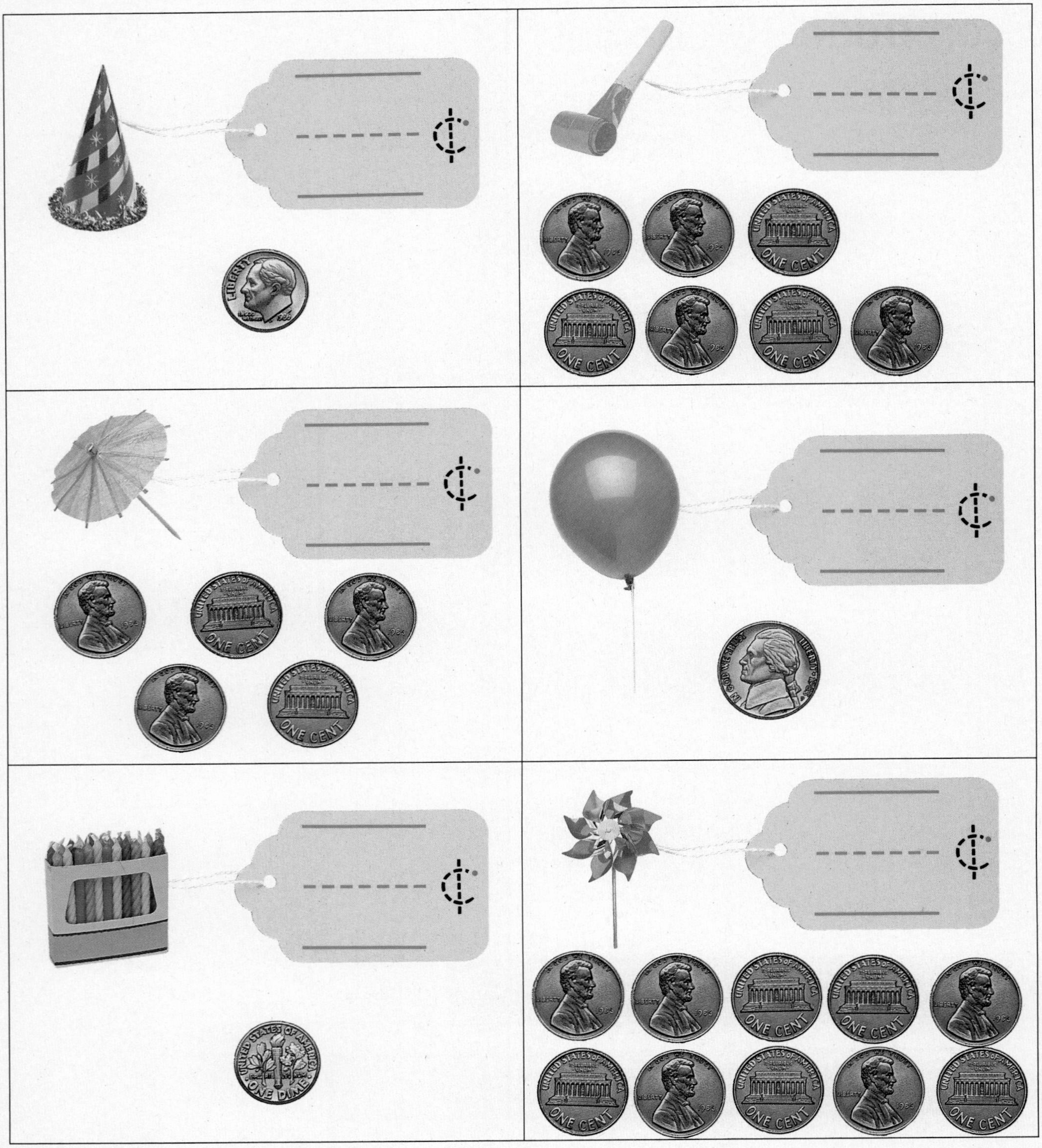

1 2 3 4 5 6 7 8 9 10 11 12

Name ______________________________

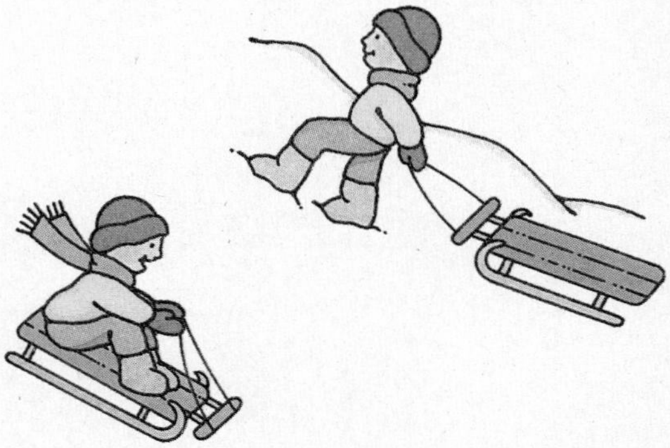

10:00

7:00

4:00

1¢

6¢

4¢

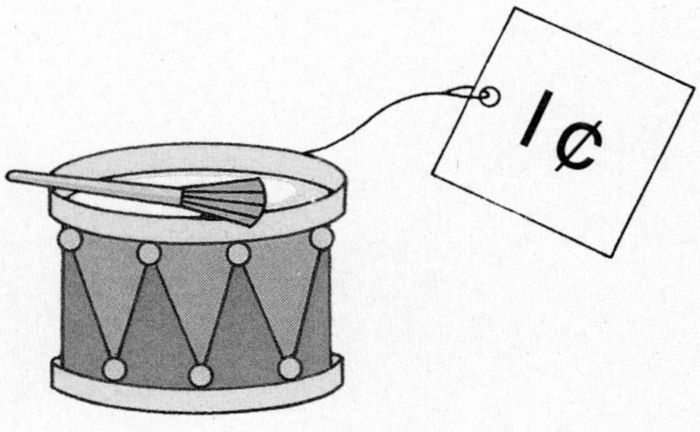

1¢

5¢

10¢

1¢

5¢

10¢

Name ______________________________

I can take a survey.

Seasons We Like Best

Spring

Summer

Fall

Winter

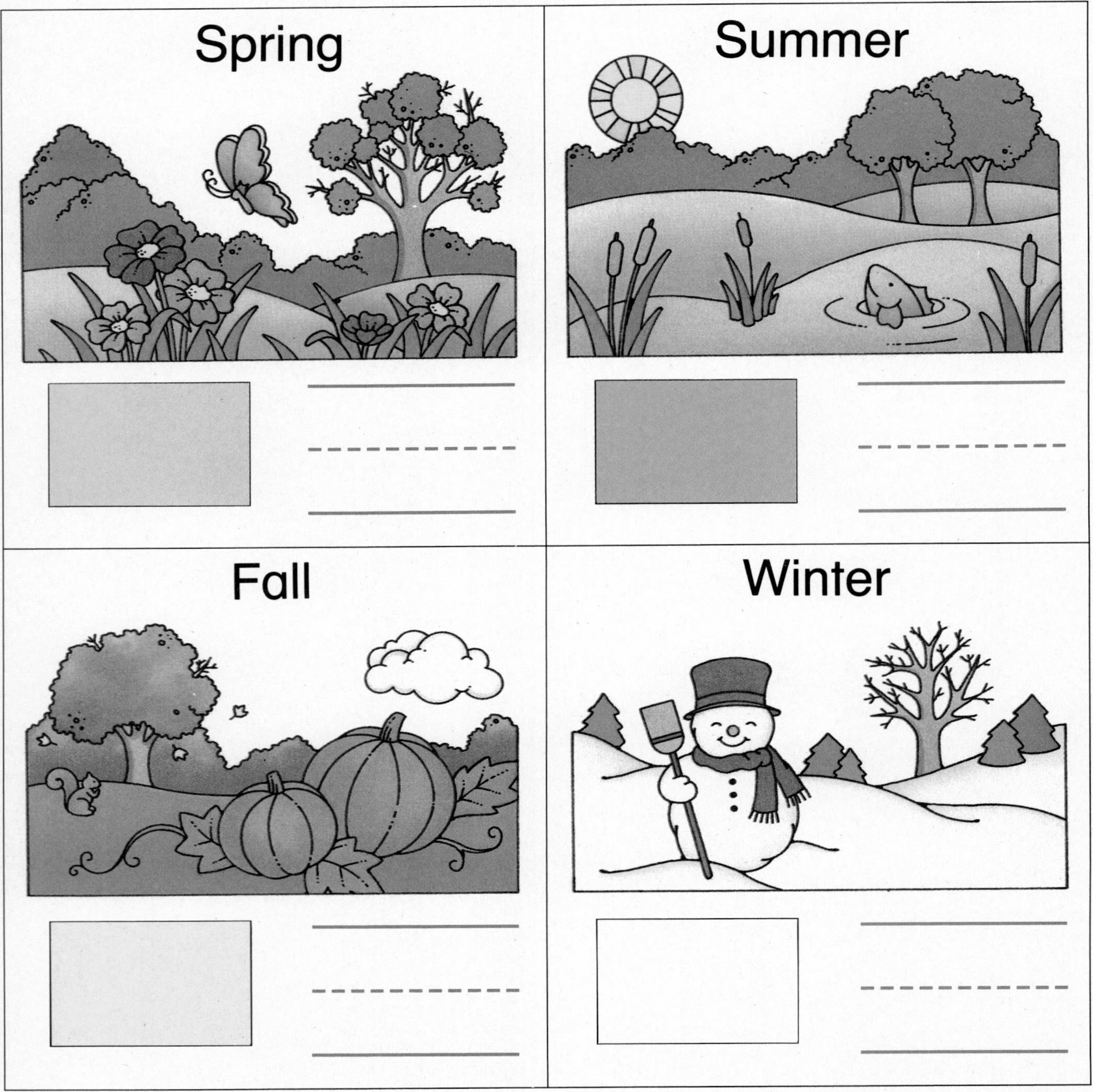

1	2	3	4	5	6	7	8	9	10	11	12

11
Putting Together

Workmat

Theme: Pets

Name ______________________________

I can put in some more.
I can tell how many in all.

Name ____________________

UNDERSTAND
FIND DATA
PLAN
ESTIMATE
SOLVE
CHECK

I can listen to a story.
I can tell how many in all.

the  story

treats

the  story

bones

the  story

hamsters

the  story

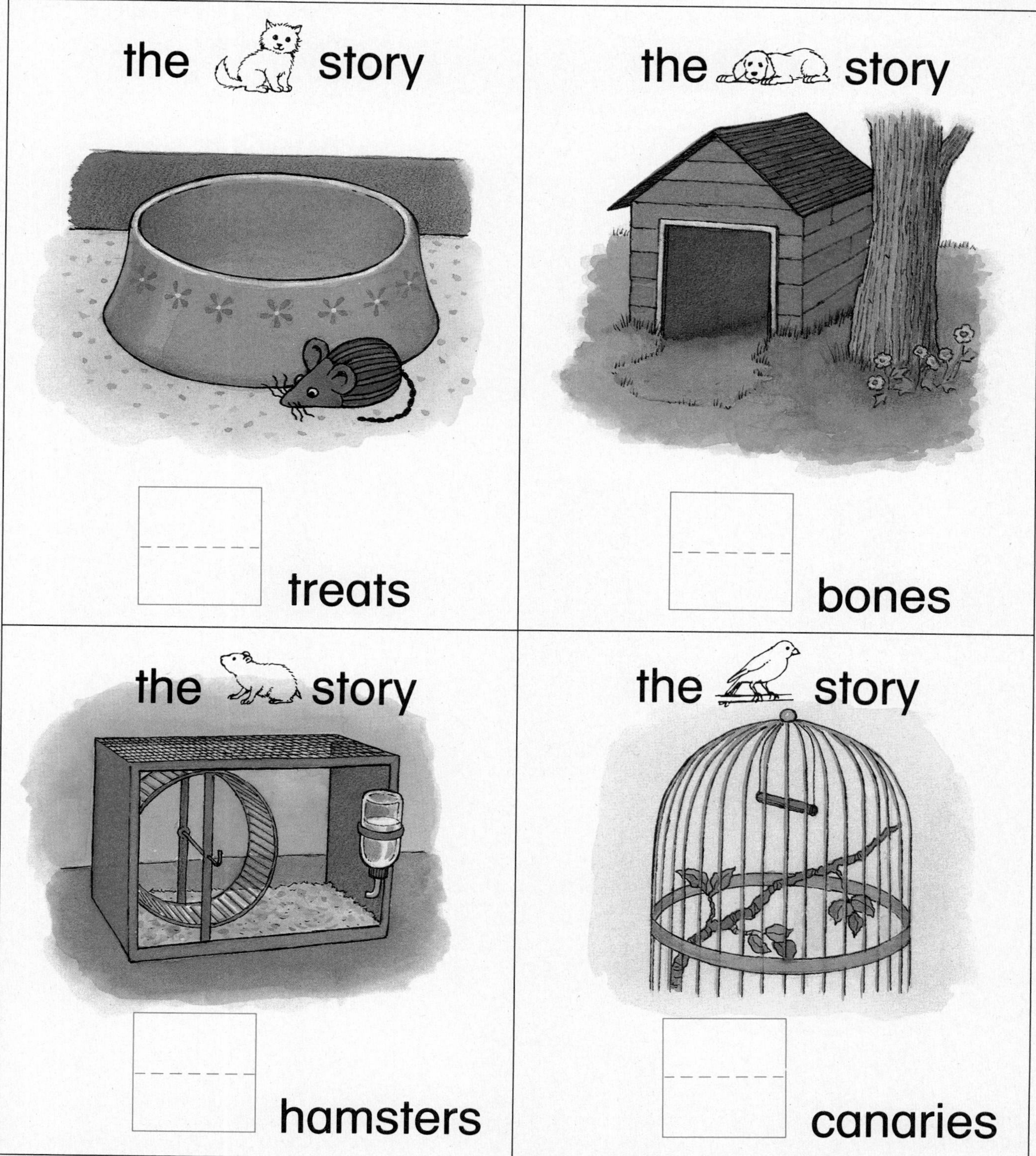

canaries

I can make a table.
I can tell how many in all.

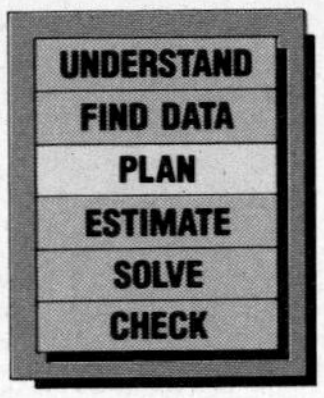

Pets	In All

Name ______________________________

I can show how many are added.

3 + 1

2 + 2

1 + 3

3 + 2

I can tell how many there are of each kind.

+

+

+

+

Name ______________________________

I can show ways to make 5.

5 in all

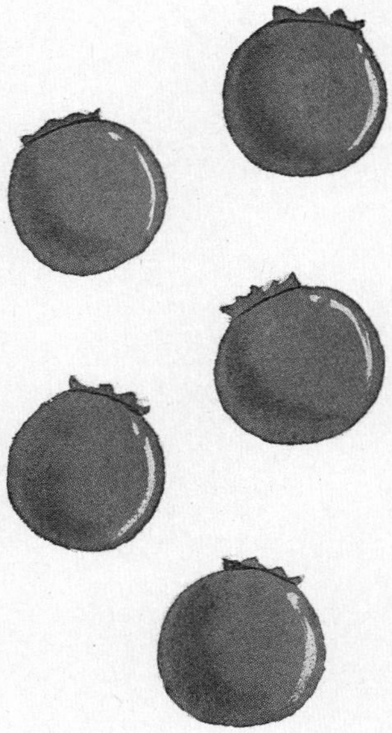

☐ + ☐

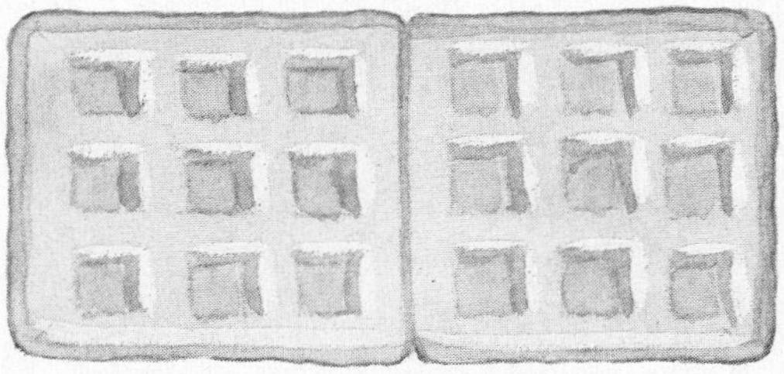

☐ + ☐

☐ + ☐

☐ + ☐

I can show ways to make 6.

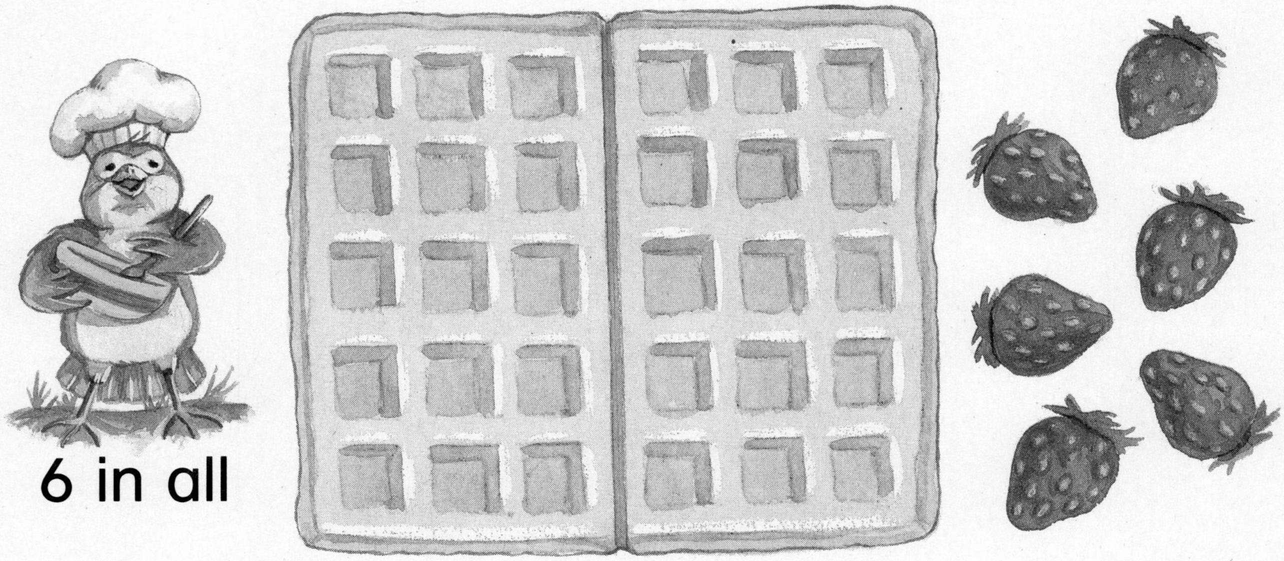

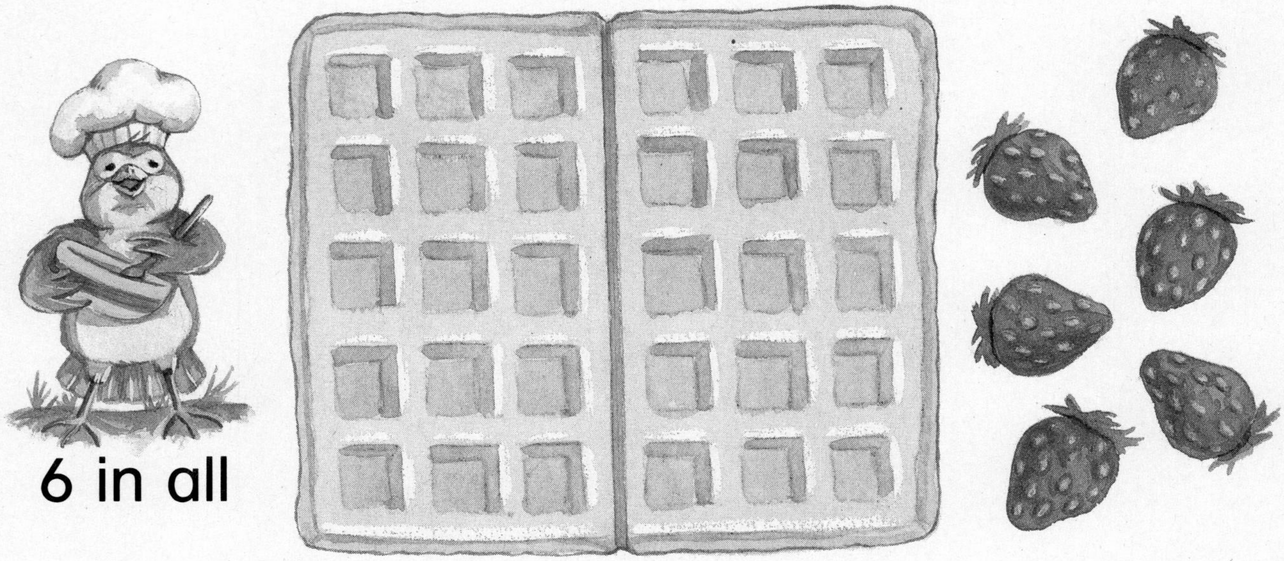

6 in all

☐ + ☐	☐ + ☐
☐ + ☐	☐ + ☐

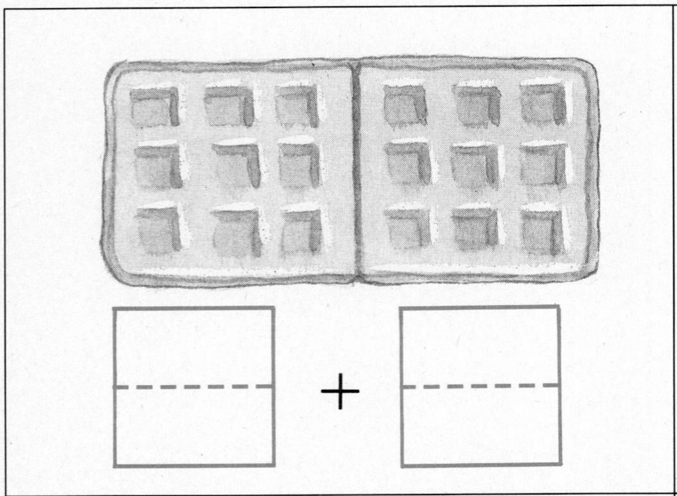

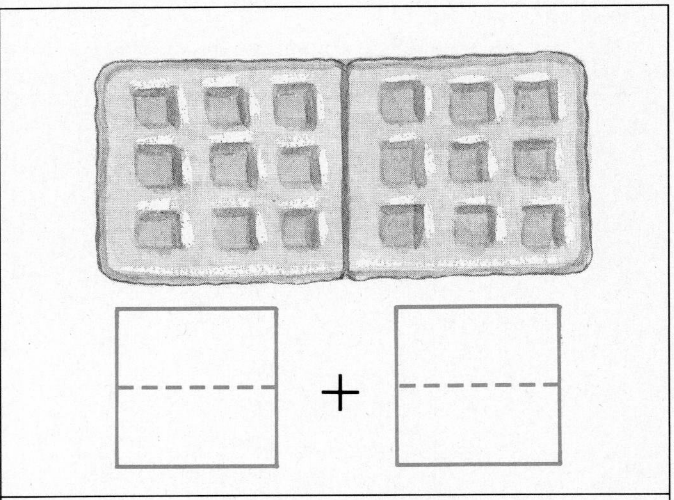

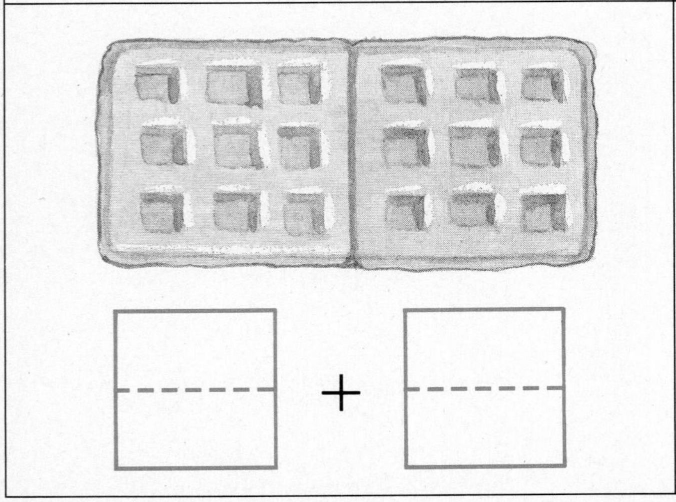

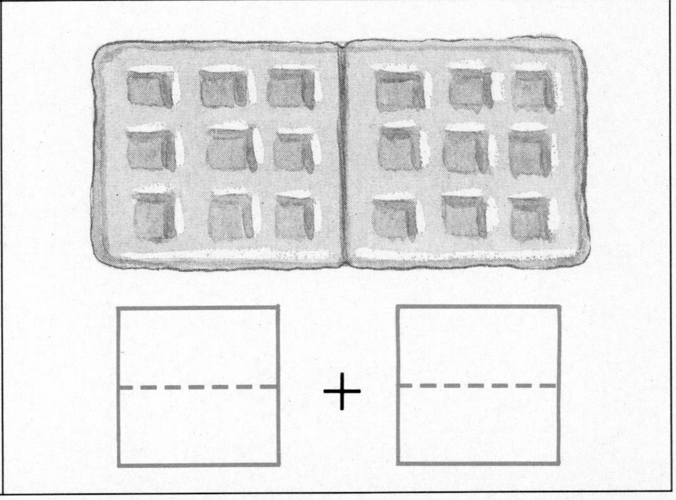

Name ______________________________

I can show the action.
I can tell how many in all.

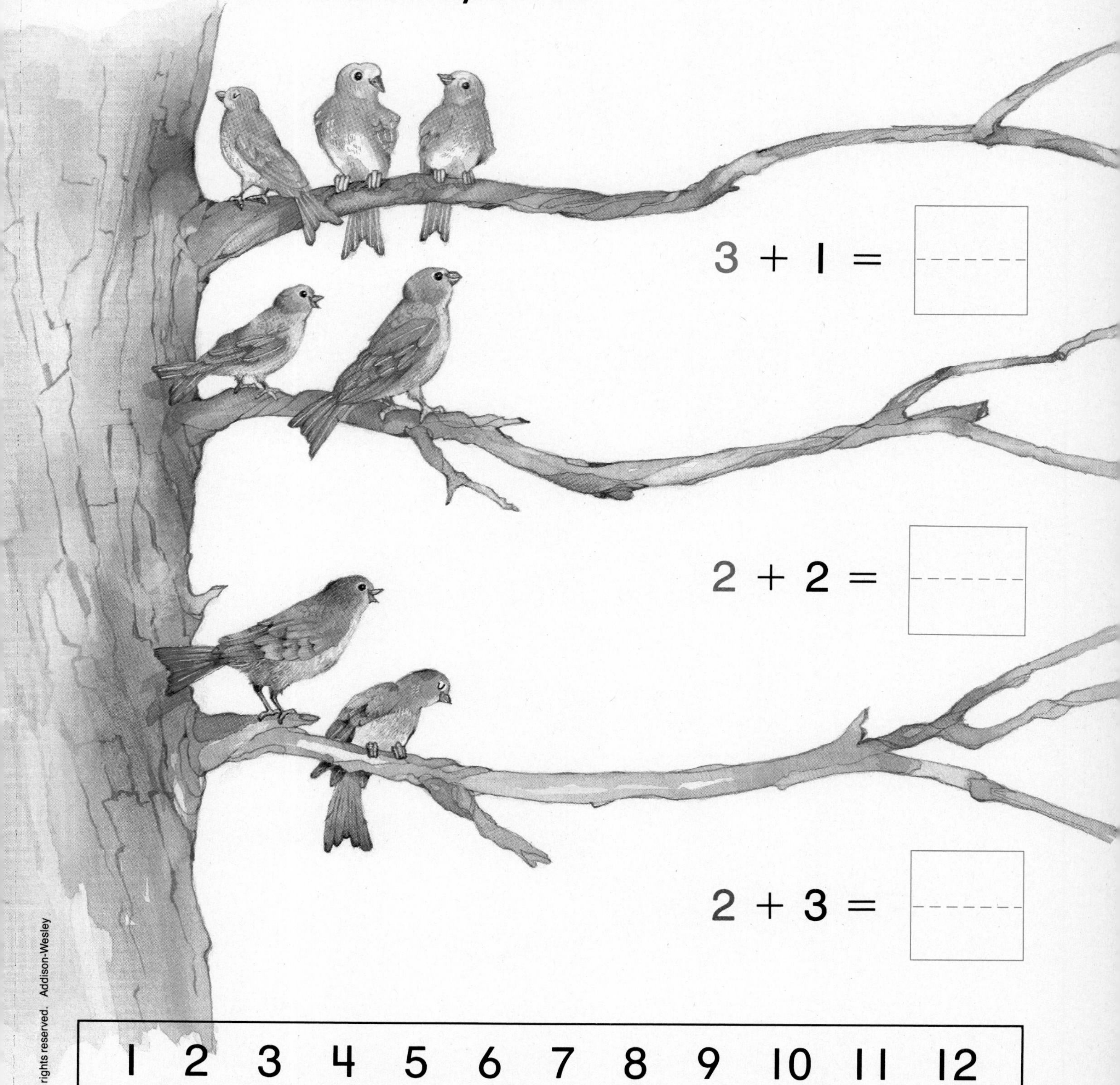

$3 + 1 =$ ☐

$2 + 2 =$ ☐

$2 + 3 =$ ☐

1	2	3	4	5	6	7	8	9	10	11	12

I can show the action.
I can tell how many in all.

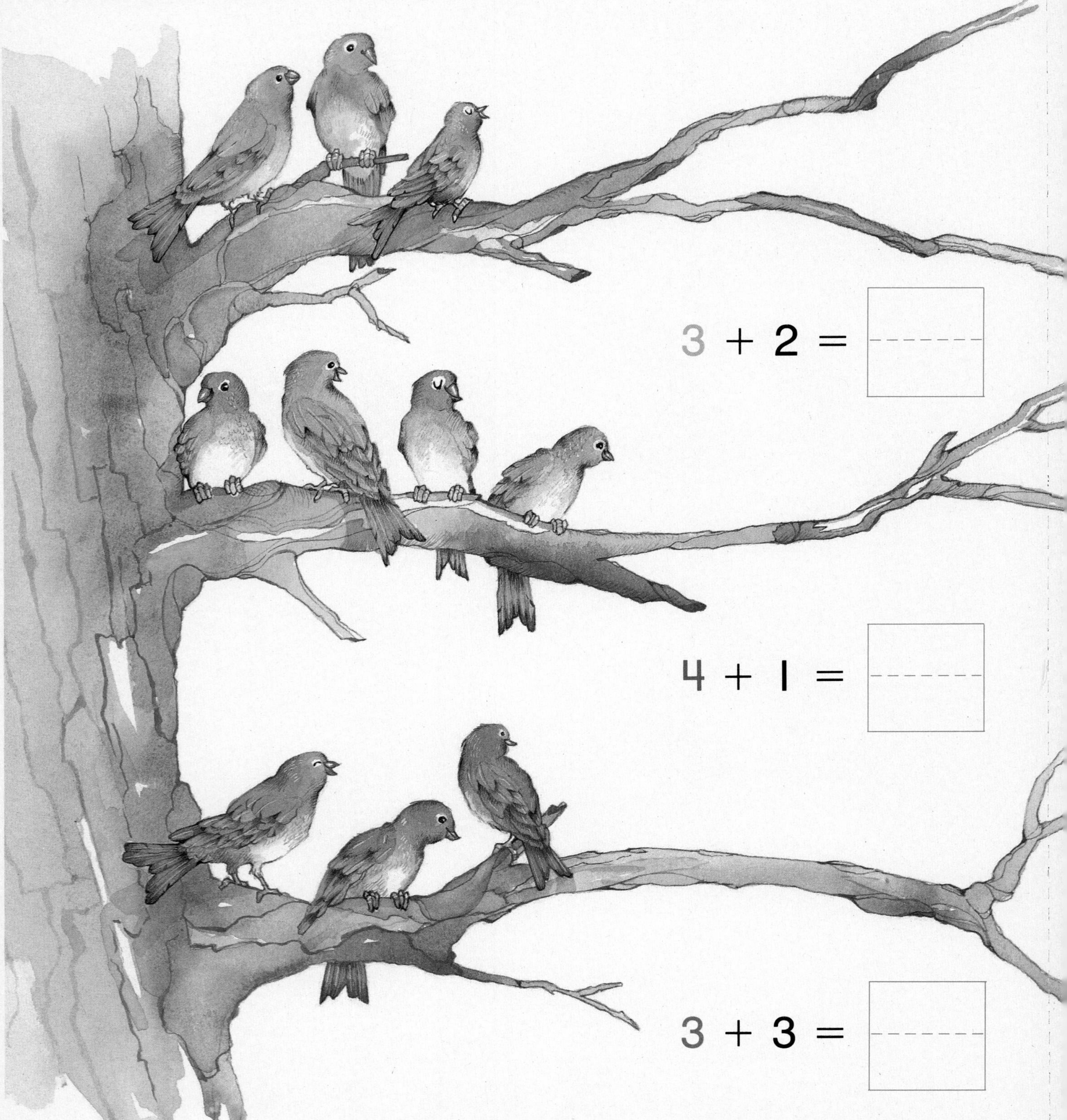

3 + 2 = ____

4 + 1 = ____

3 + 3 = ____

Name ______________________________

I can tell how many are in each car. I can tell how many in all.

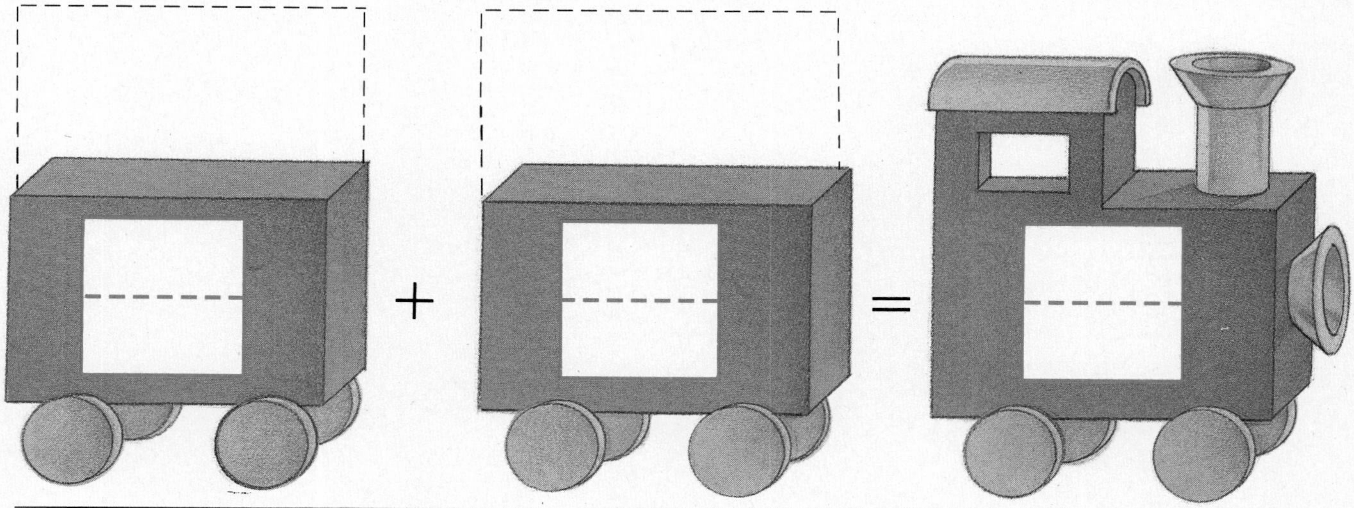

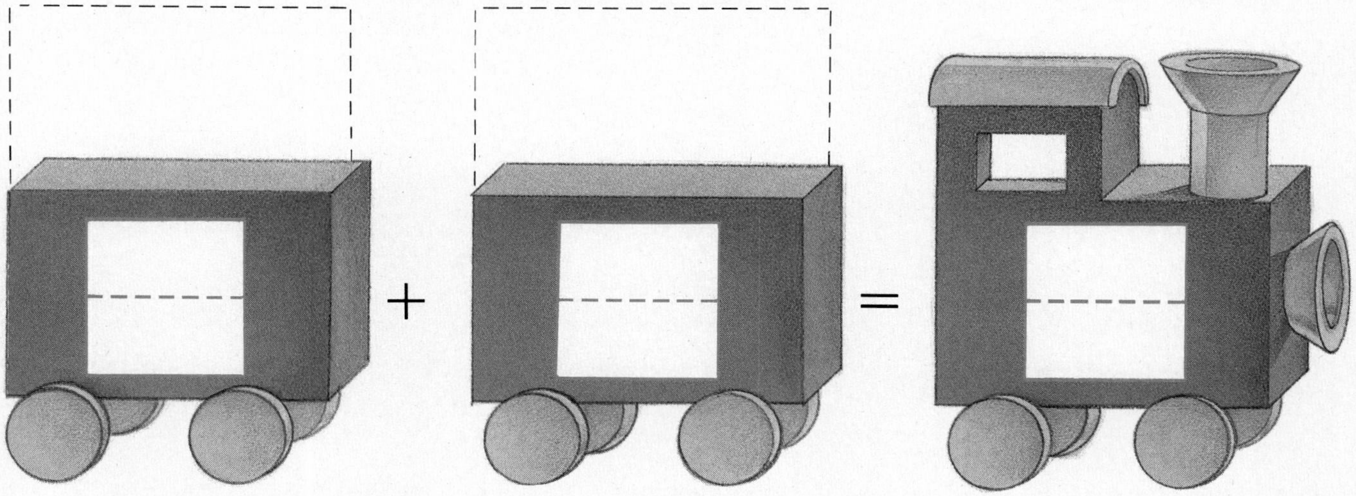

1 2 3 4 5 6 7 8 9 10 11 12

I can tell how many are in each car.
I can tell how many in all.

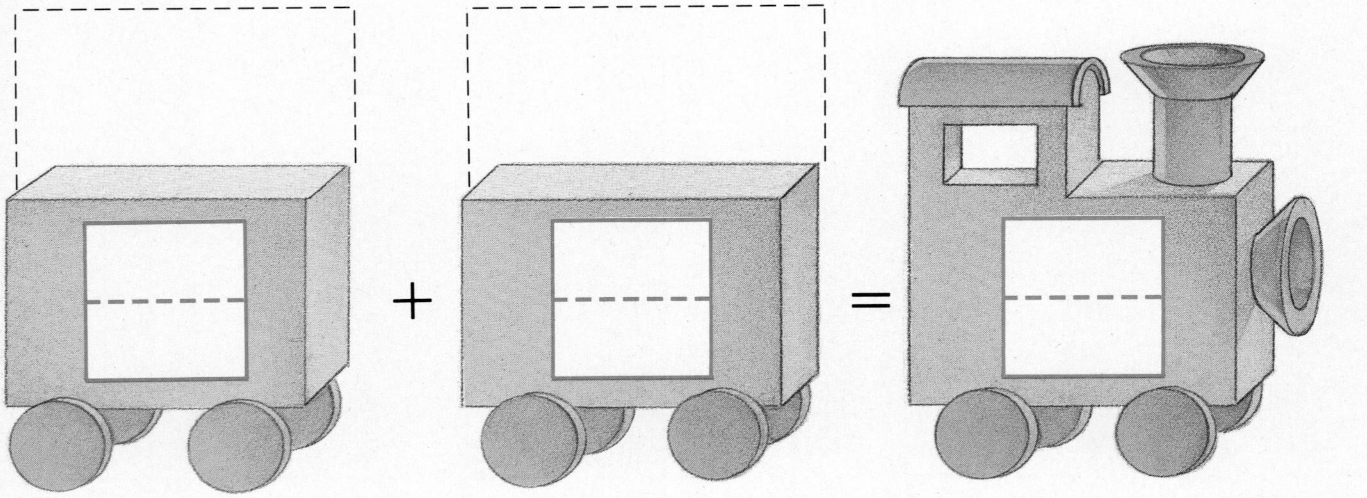

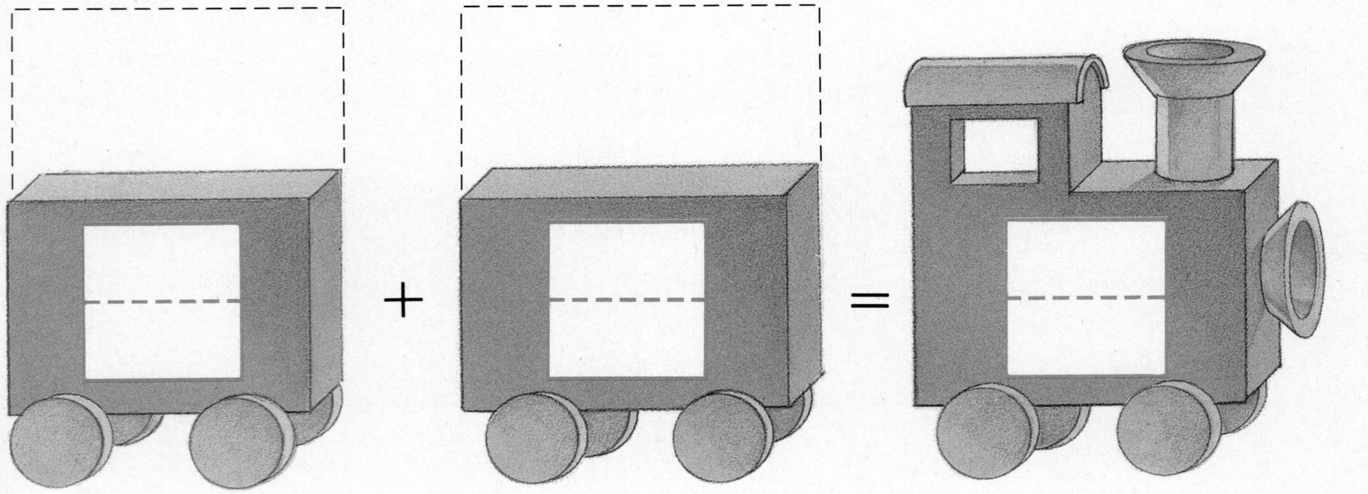

Name ______________________________

I can use pennies to show prices.
I can tell the total cost.

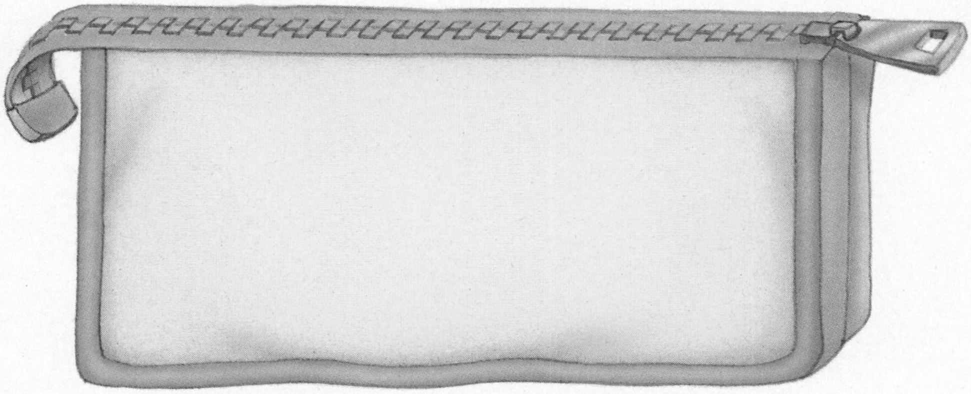

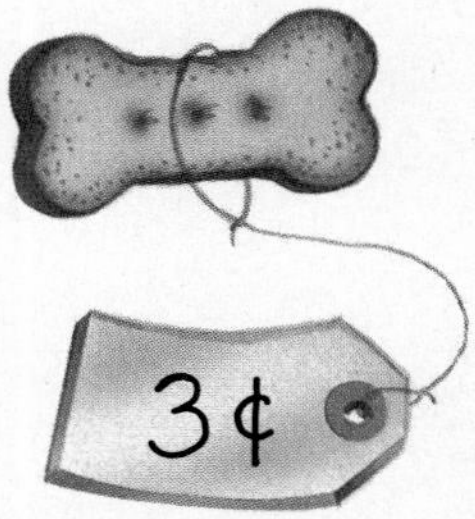

+

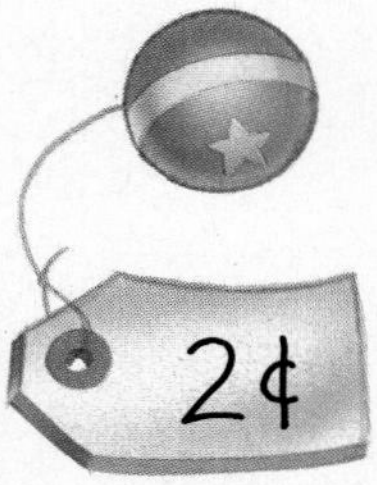

= ☐ ¢

+

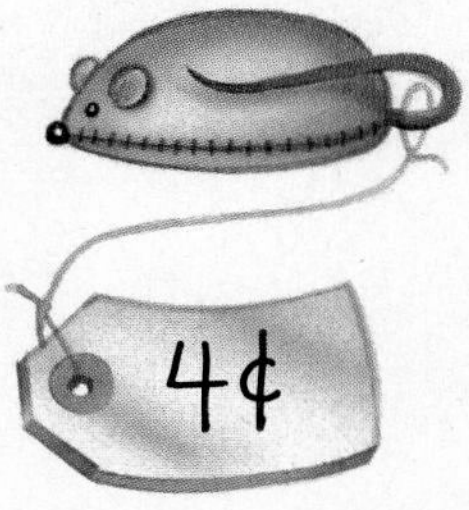

= ☐ ¢

+

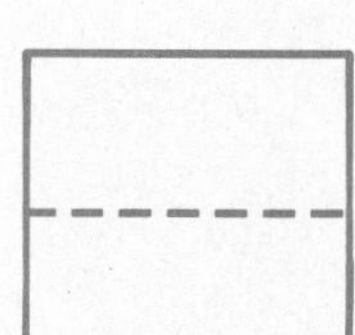

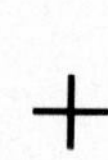

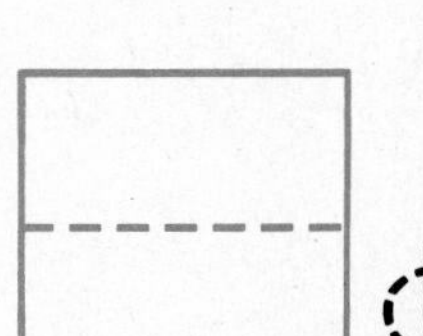

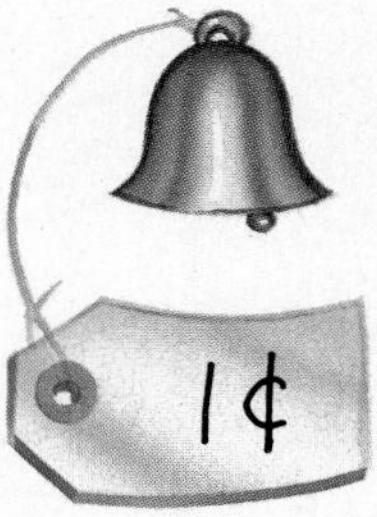

= ☐ ¢

1	2	3	4	5	6	7	8	9	10	11	12

I can tell how much in all.

1¢ + 2¢ = ____ ¢

2¢ + 2¢ = ____ ¢

2¢ + 4¢ = ____ ¢

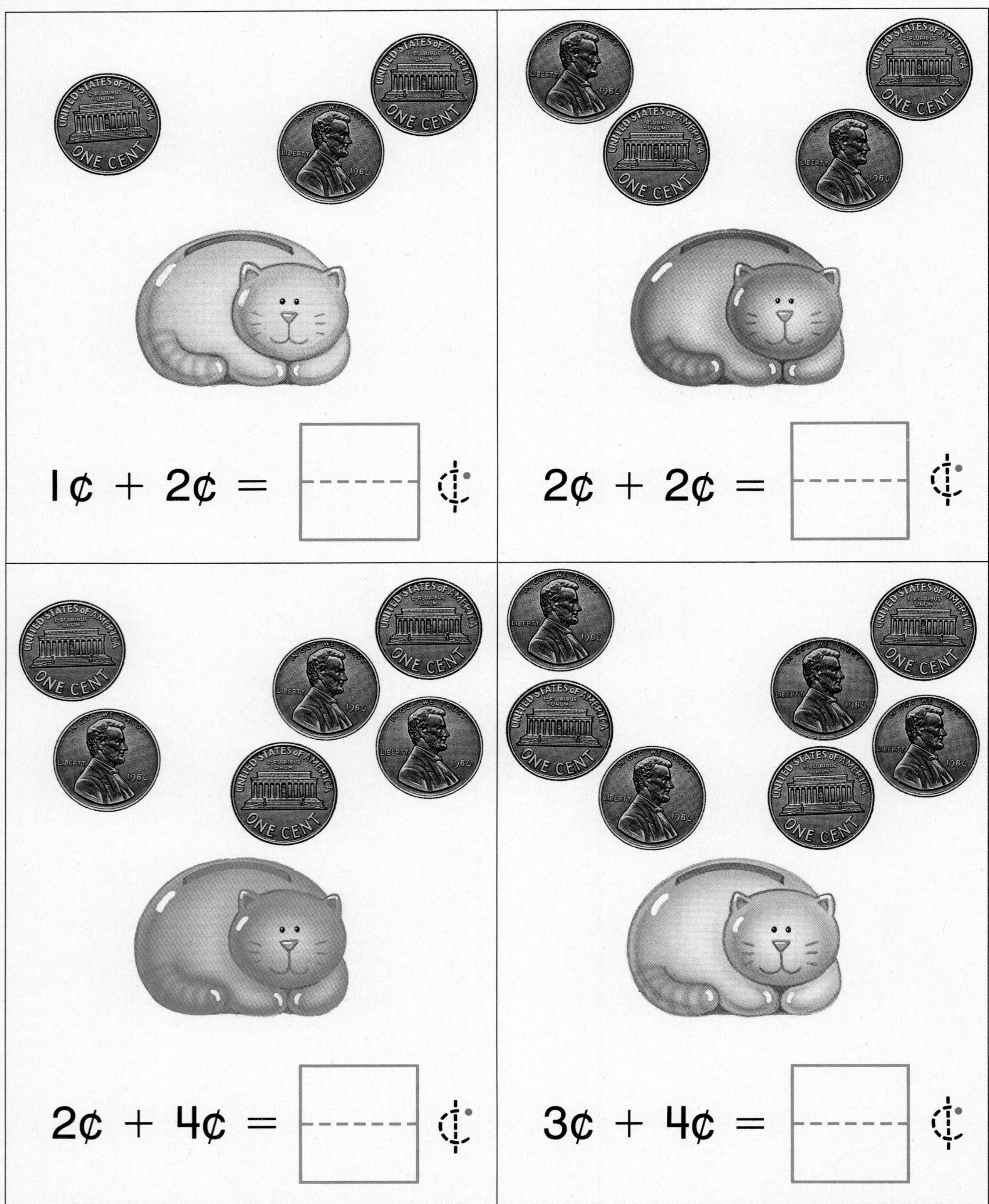

3¢ + 4¢ = ____ ¢

Name ____________________

the  story

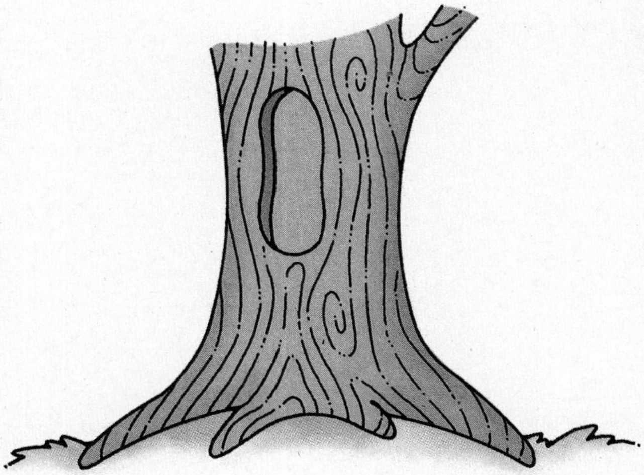

☐ acorns

2 + 3 = ☐

1 + 2 = ☐

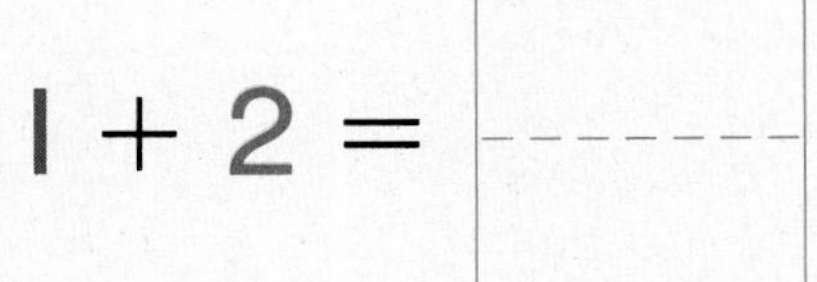

2¢ + 2¢ = ☐ ¢

Name ____________________

I can show how many go in the empty wagon.

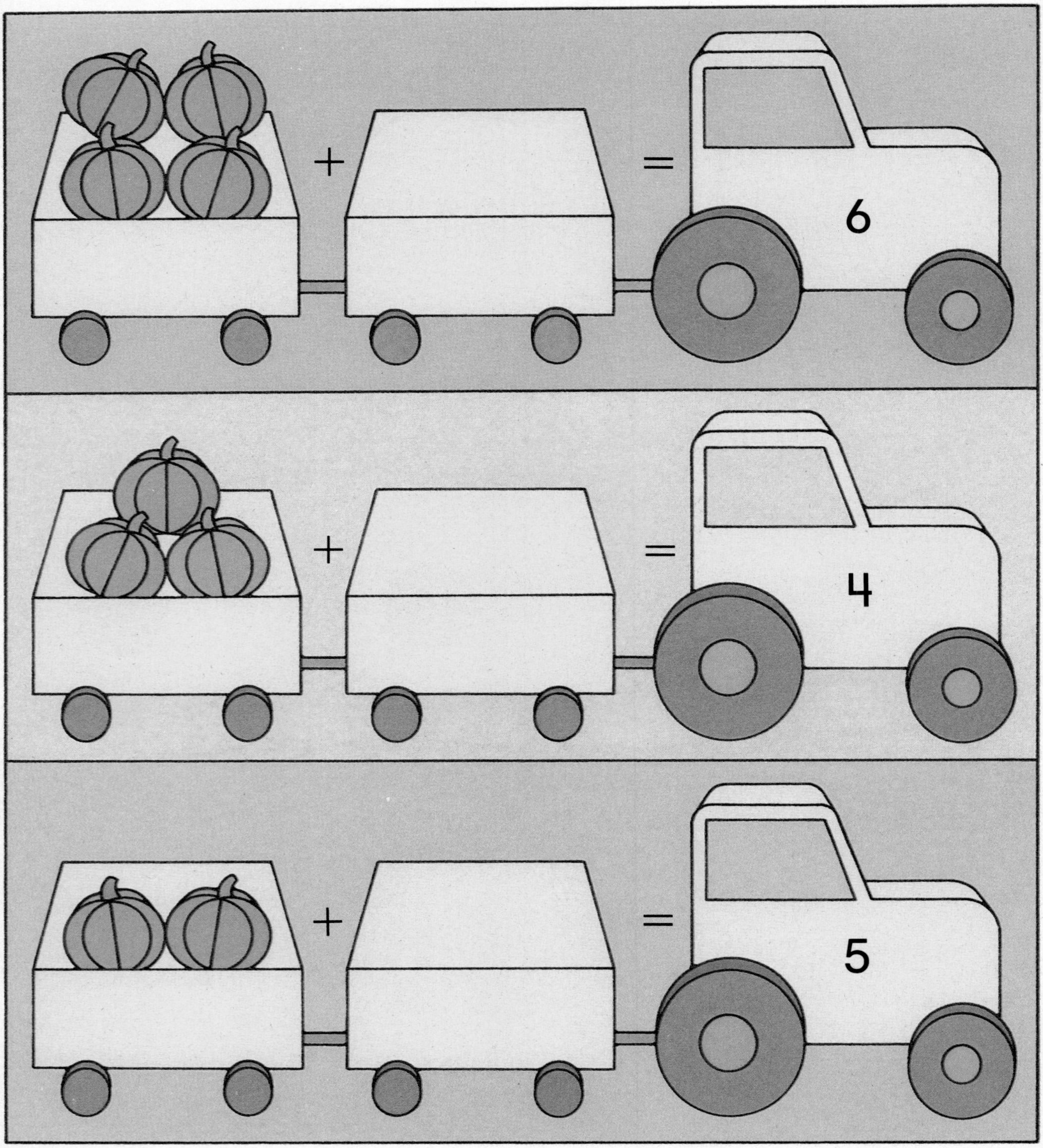

12 Taking Away

Workmat

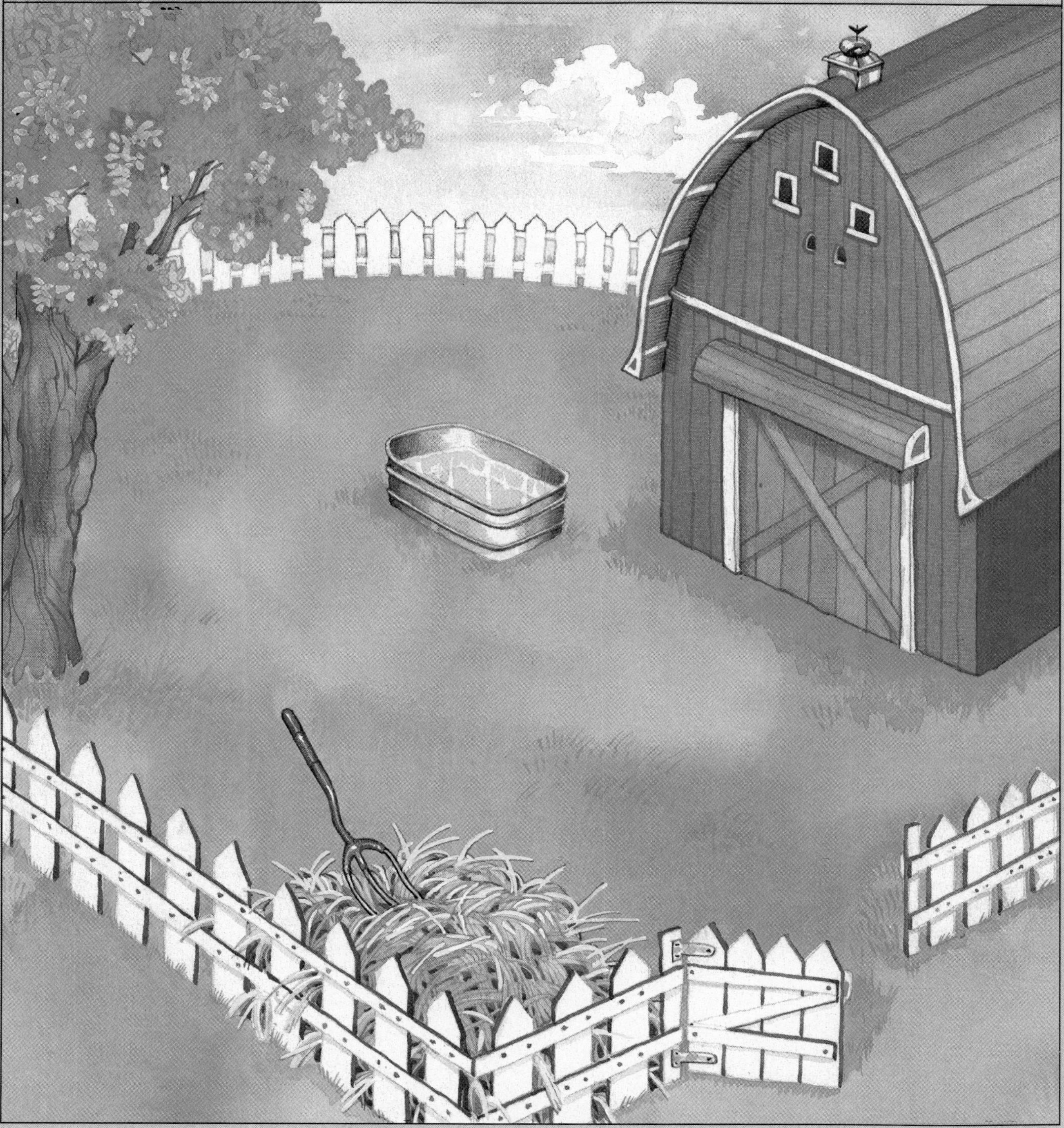

Theme: At the Farm

Name ______________________________

I can take some away.
I can show how many are left.

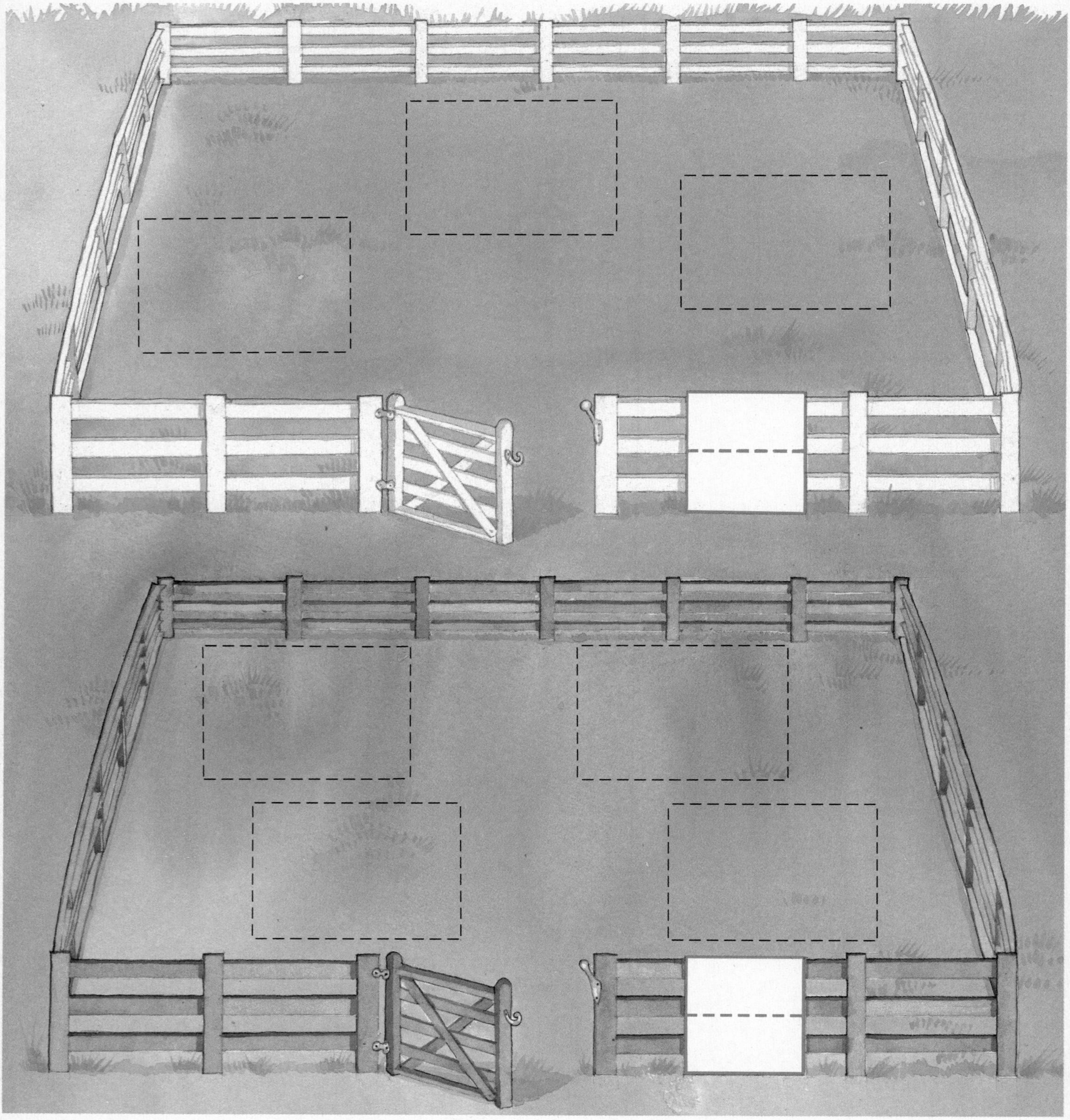

Name ______________________________

I can act out a story.
I can tell how many are left.

the  story

☐ hats

the  story

☐ egg

the  story

☐ apples

the  story

☐ pails

UNDERSTAND
FIND DATA
PLAN
ESTIMATE
SOLVE
CHECK

I can listen to a story.
I can tell how many are left.

apples

flowers

carrot

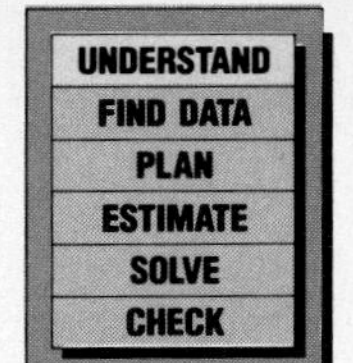

eggs

Name ______________________________

I can show the action.
I can tell how many were picked.

4 − [ ]

3 − [ ]

5 − [ ]

I can show the action.
I can tell how many were picked.

5 − ☐

3 − ☐

4 − ☐

Name ____________________

I can show ways to take away from 4.

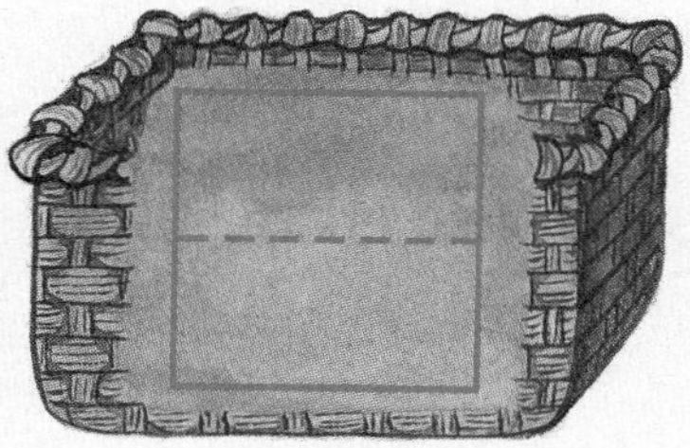

4 −

4 −

4 −

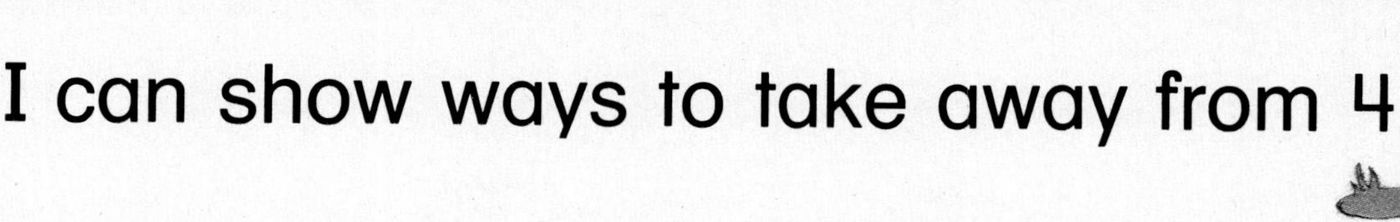

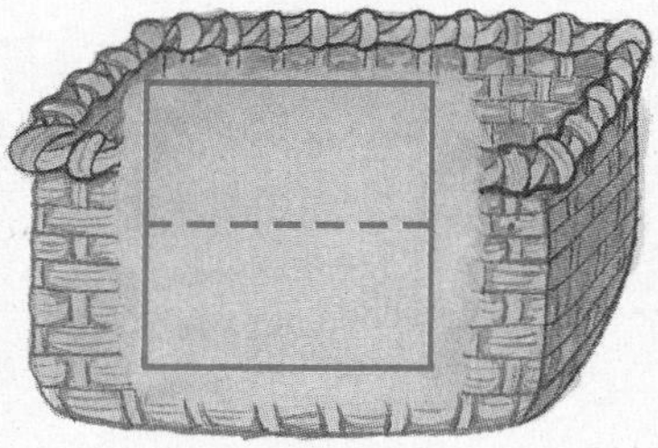

4 −

I can show ways to take away from 5.

5 − 

5 − 

5 − 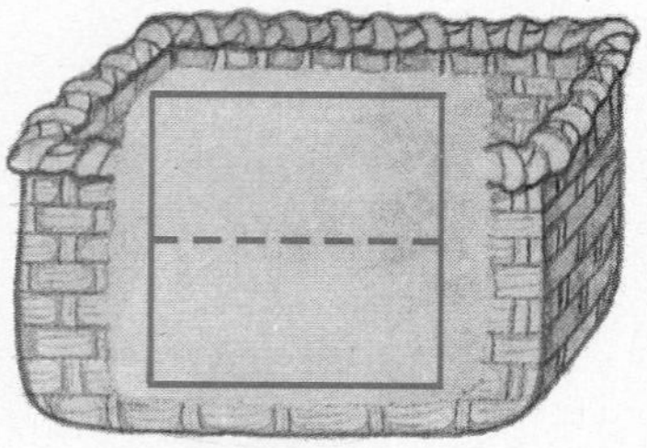

5 − 

Name ____________________

I can show the action.
I can tell how many are left.

3 − 2 = ☐

4 − 3 = ☐

I can show the action.
I can tell how many are left.

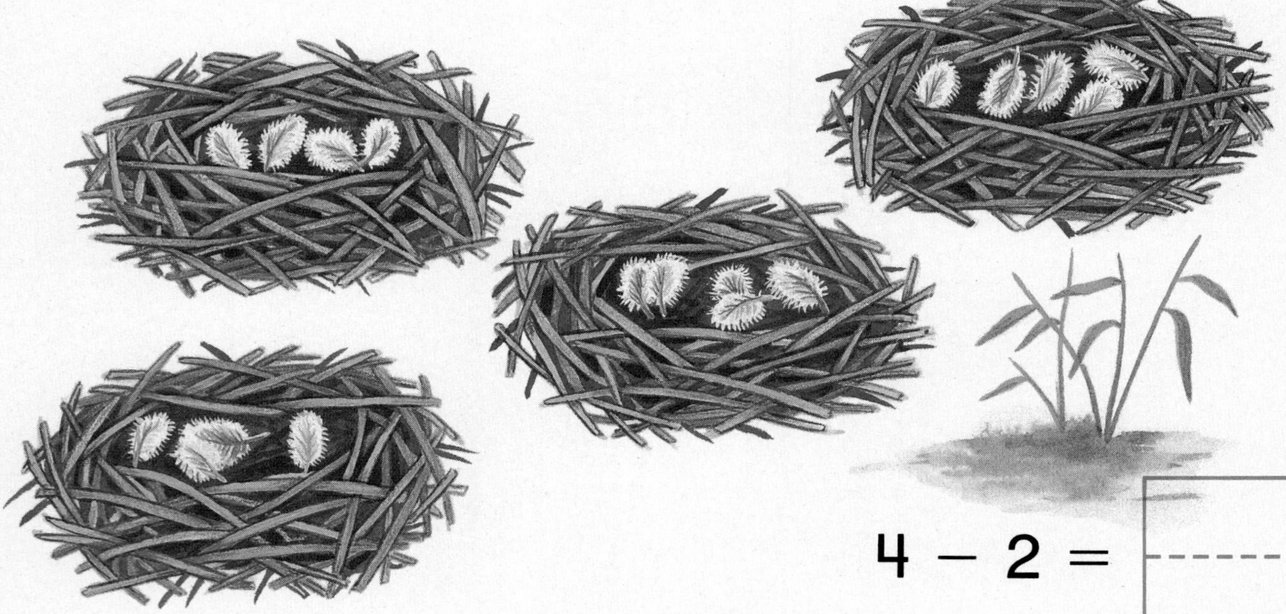

4 − 2 = ☐

2 − 1 = ☐

Name ____________________

I can use pennies to show prices.
I can tell how much money is left.

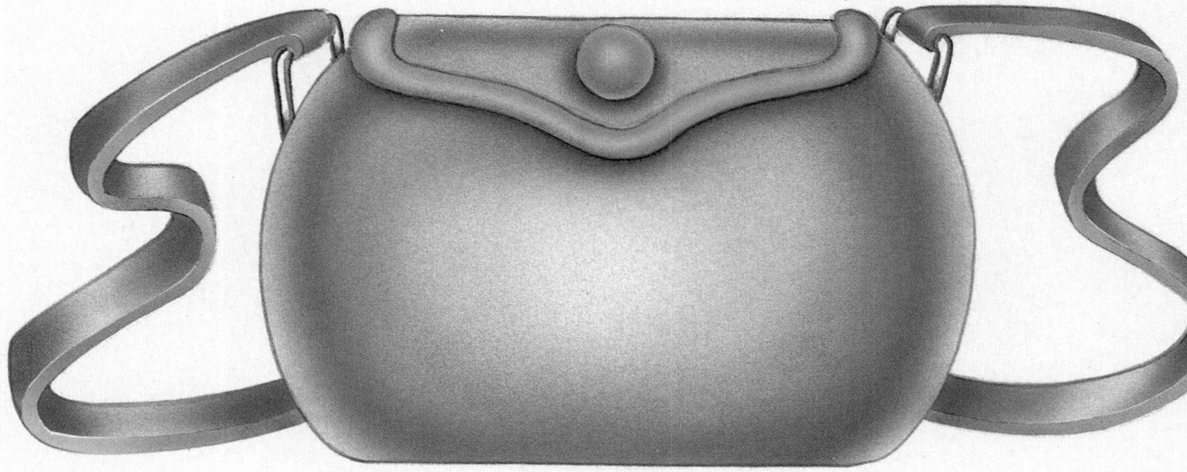

6¢ − 3¢ = ___ ¢

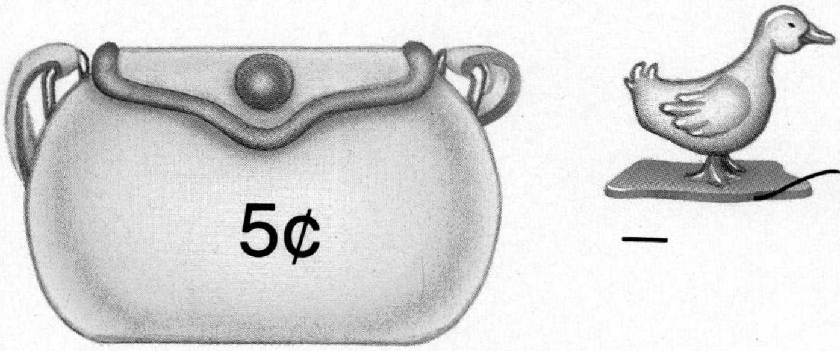

5¢ − 4¢ = ___ ¢

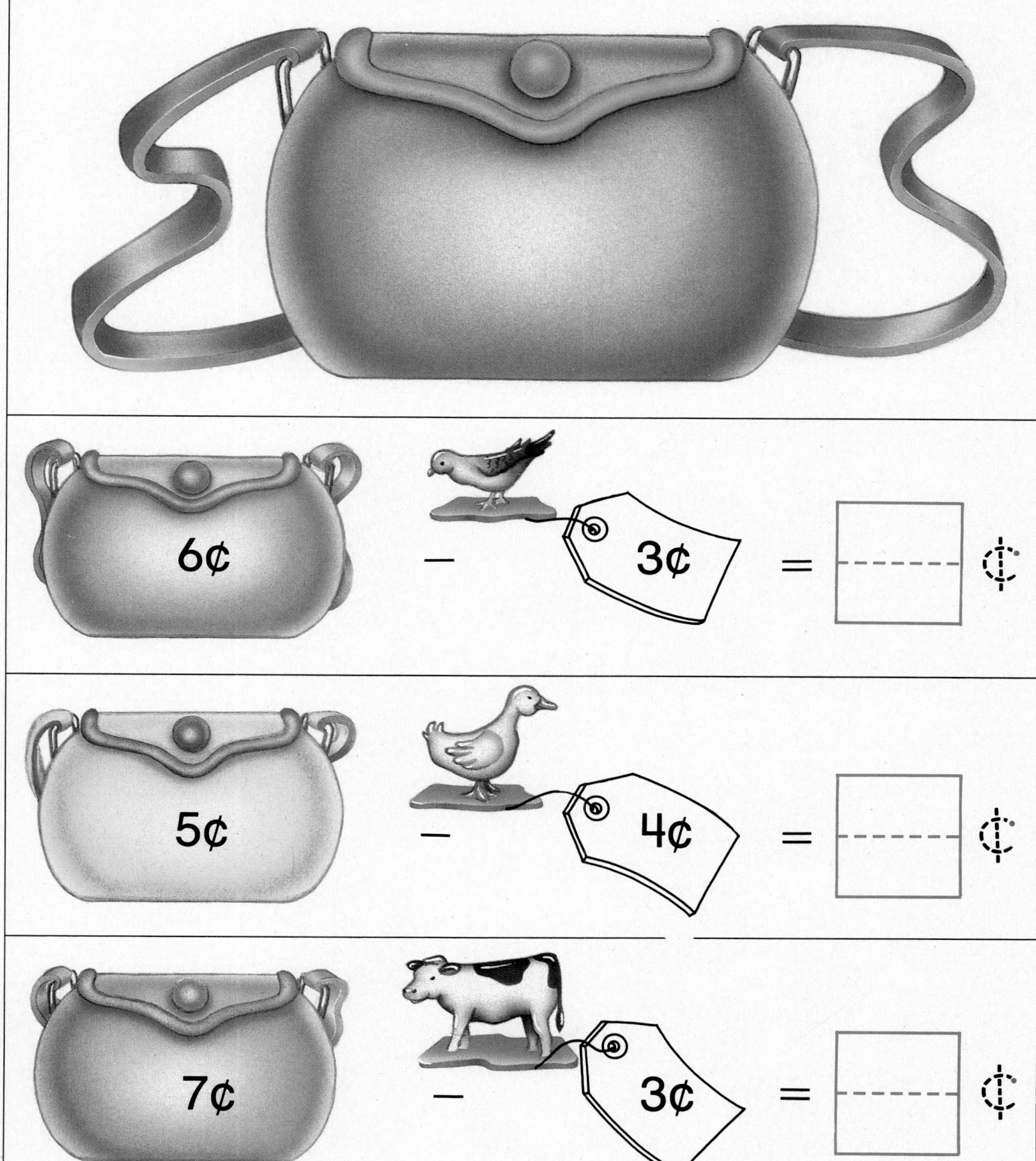

7¢ − 3¢ = ___ ¢

I can tell how much money is left.

5¢ − 2¢ = ☐ ¢

6¢ − 1¢ = ☐ ¢

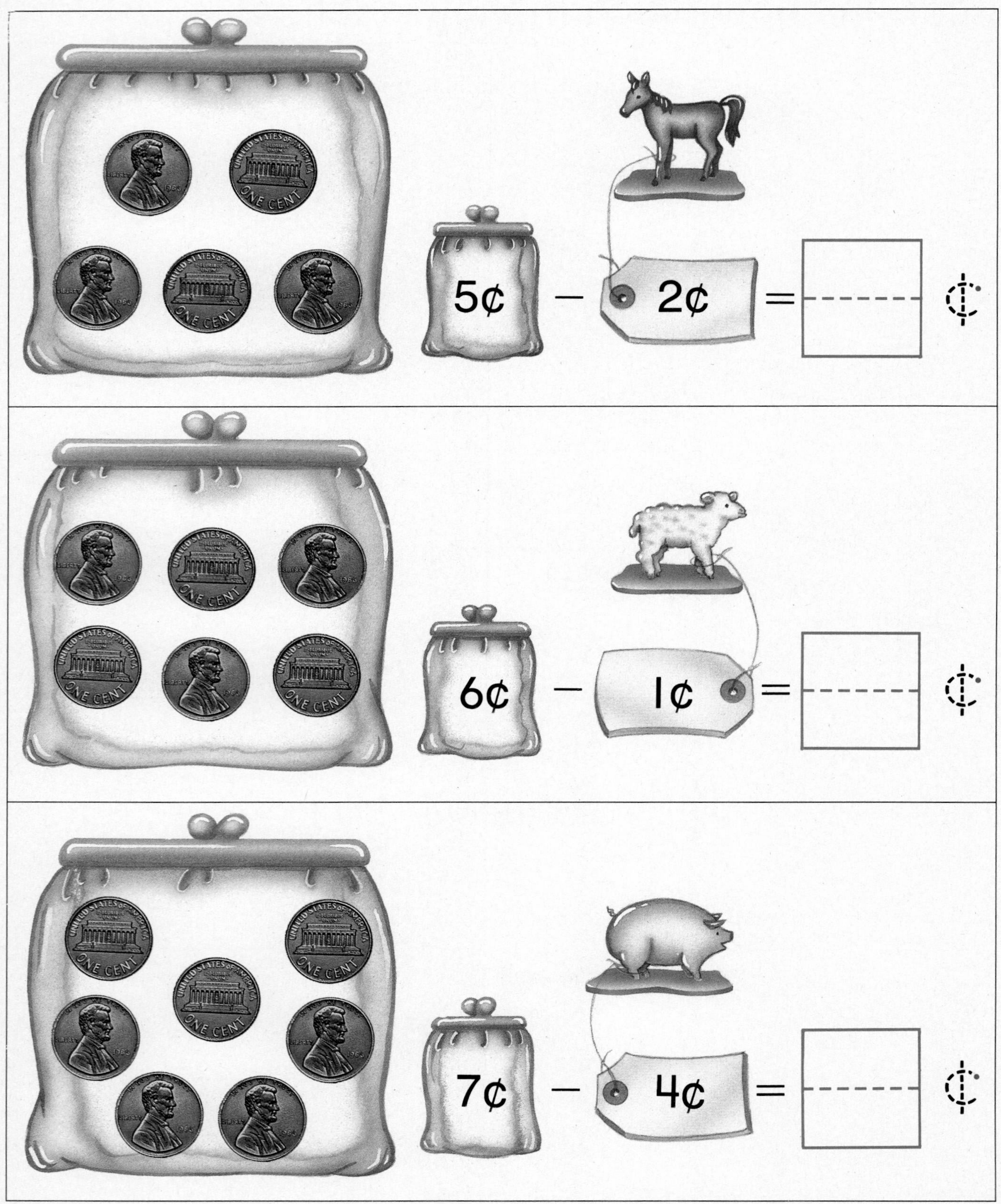

7¢ − 4¢ = ☐ ¢

Name ____________________

UNDERSTAND
FIND DATA
PLAN
ESTIMATE
SOLVE
CHECK

I can listen to a story.
I can show what happened.

the  story

$4 - 1 =$ ☐

the  story

$3 + 2 =$ ☐

the  story

$3 + 1 =$ ☐

the  story

$4 - 2 =$ ☐

UNDERSTAND
FIND DATA
PLAN
ESTIMATE
SOLVE
CHECK

I can listen to a story.
I can show what happened.

3 − 1 = ☐

2 + 1 = ☐

2 + 2 = ☐

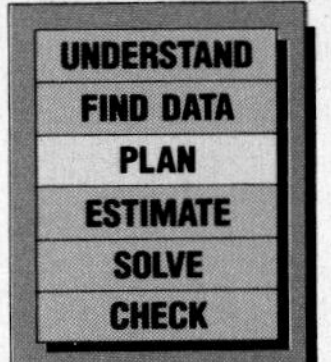

3 − 2 = ☐

Name ______________________________

I can show how many.

I can show how many.

Name ______________________________

the  story

☐ apples

3 − 1 = ☐

4 − 2 = ☐

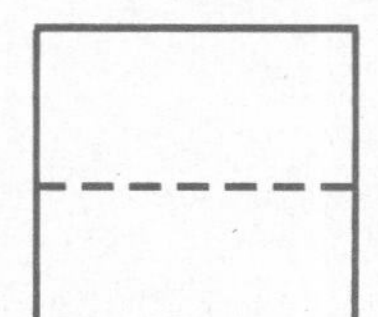

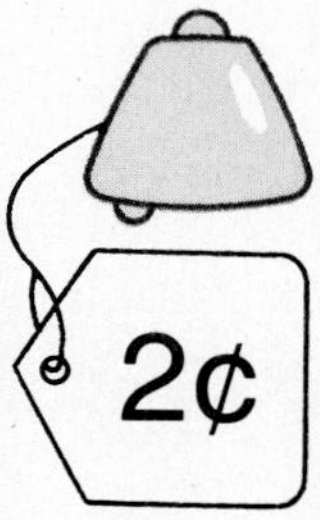

5¢ − 2¢ = ☐ ¢

Name ____

I can play a number game.

13
Sharing

Workmat

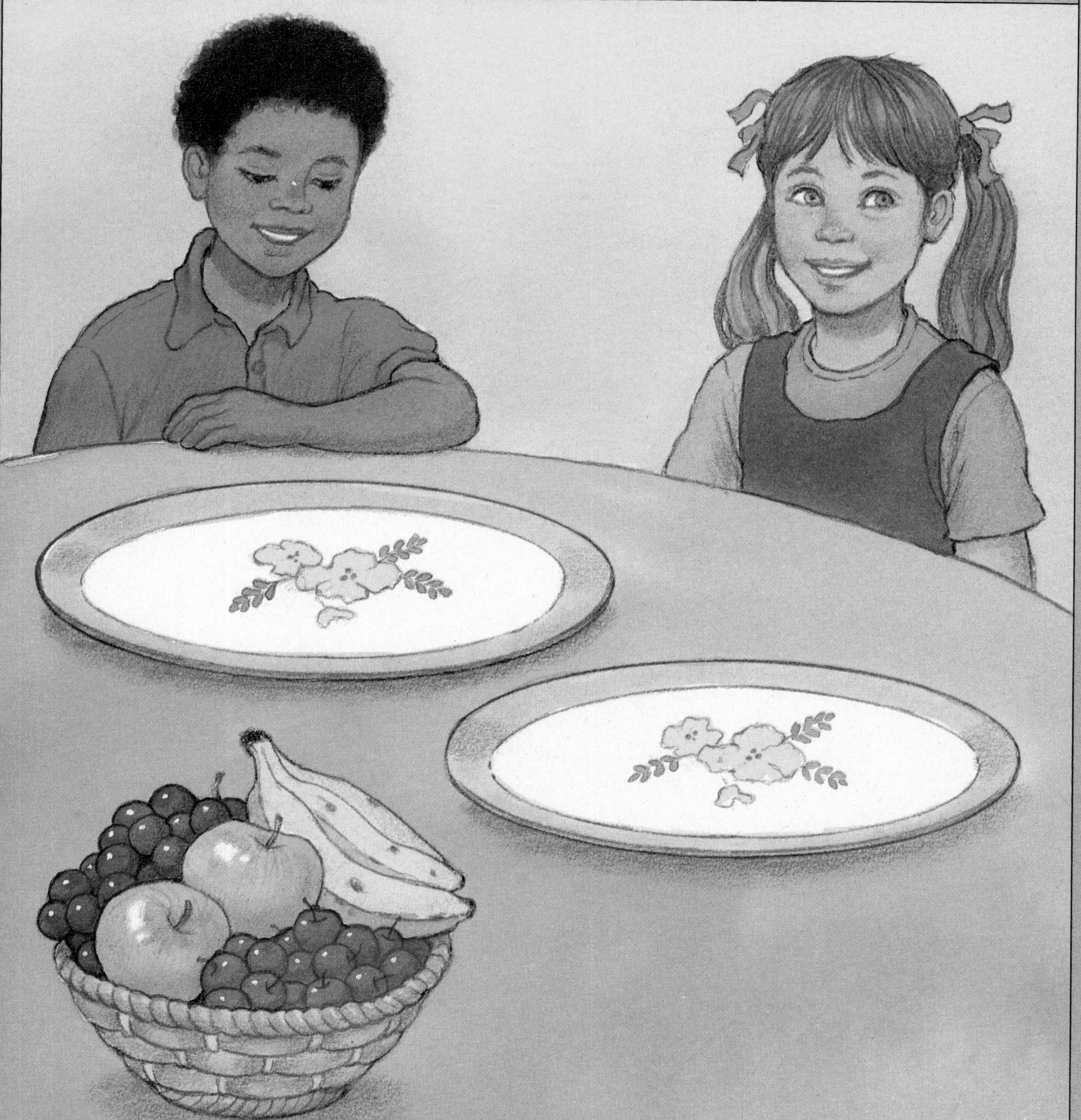

Theme: Food

Name ______________________________

I can show fair shares.

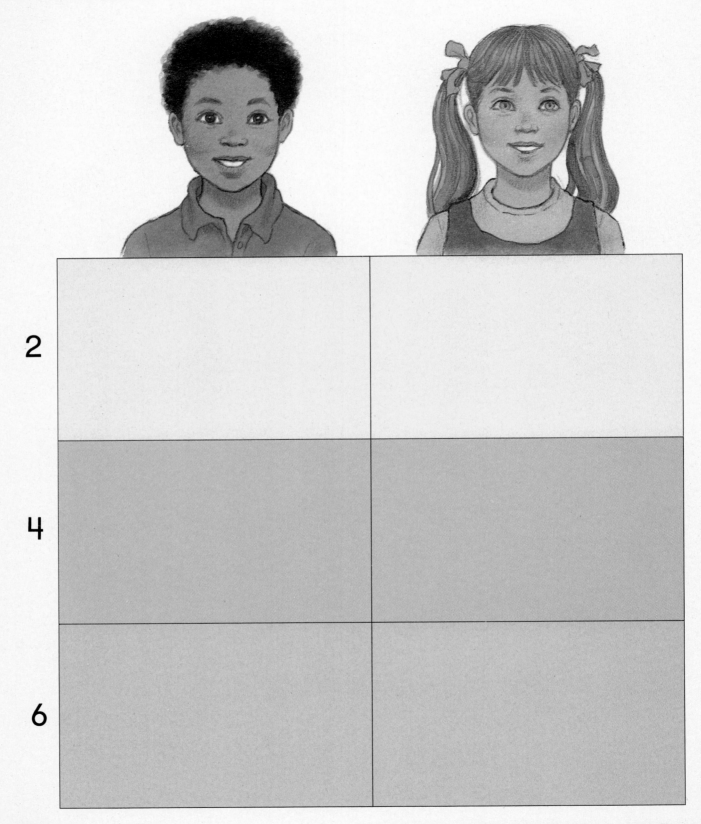

2		
4		
6		

Name ______________________

I can show fair shares.

I can show fair shares.

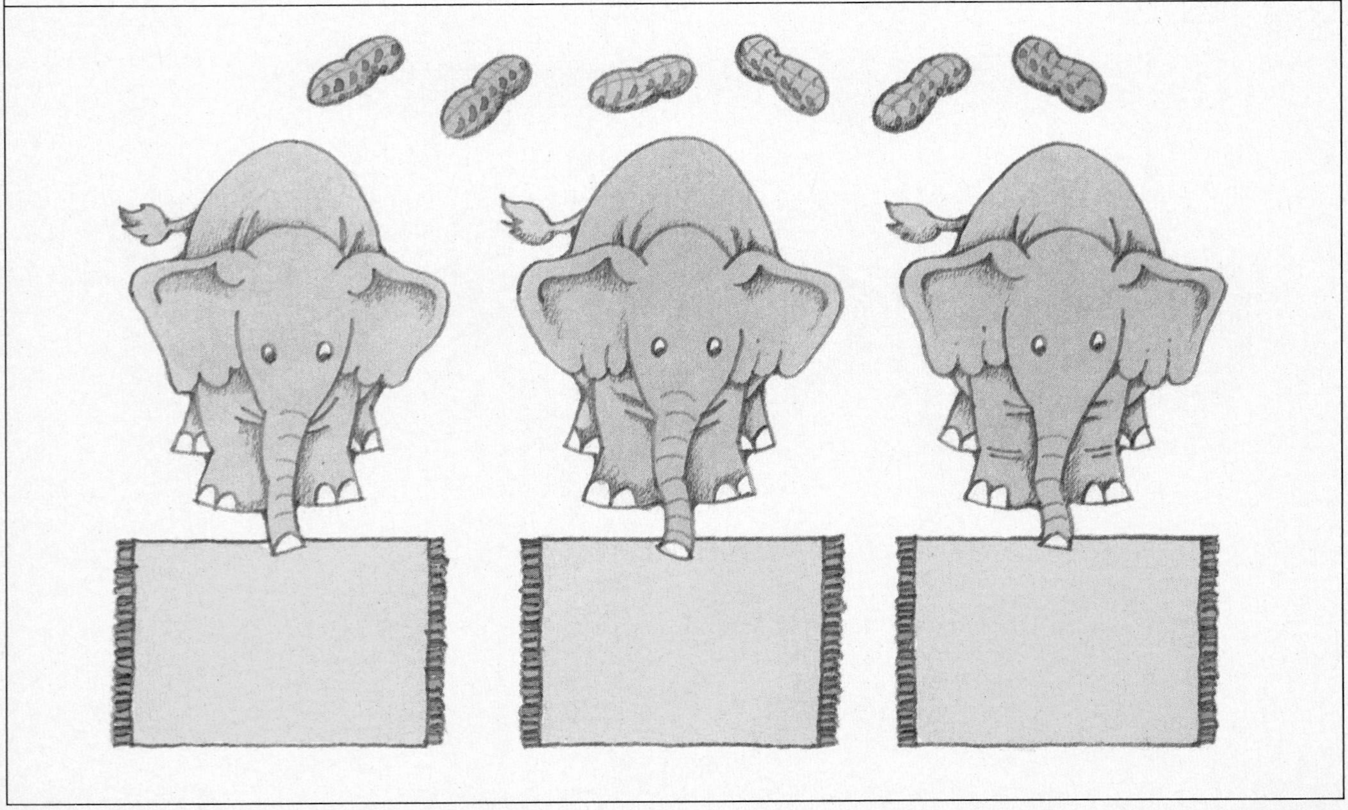

Name ______________________________

I can make fair shares.
I can show what is left over.

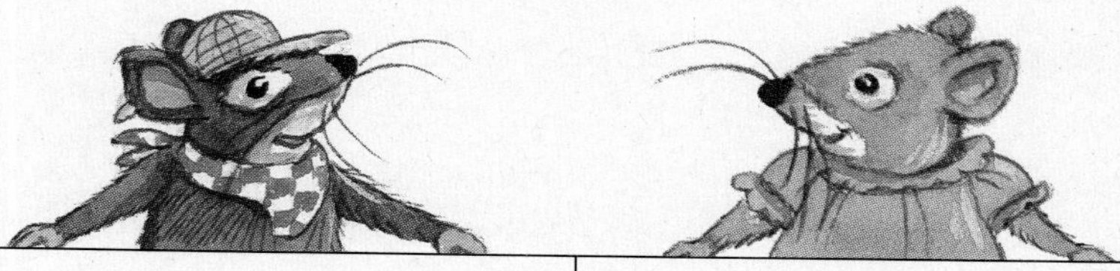

3				
4				
5				
6				

I can make fair shares.
I can show what is left over.

4

5

6

7

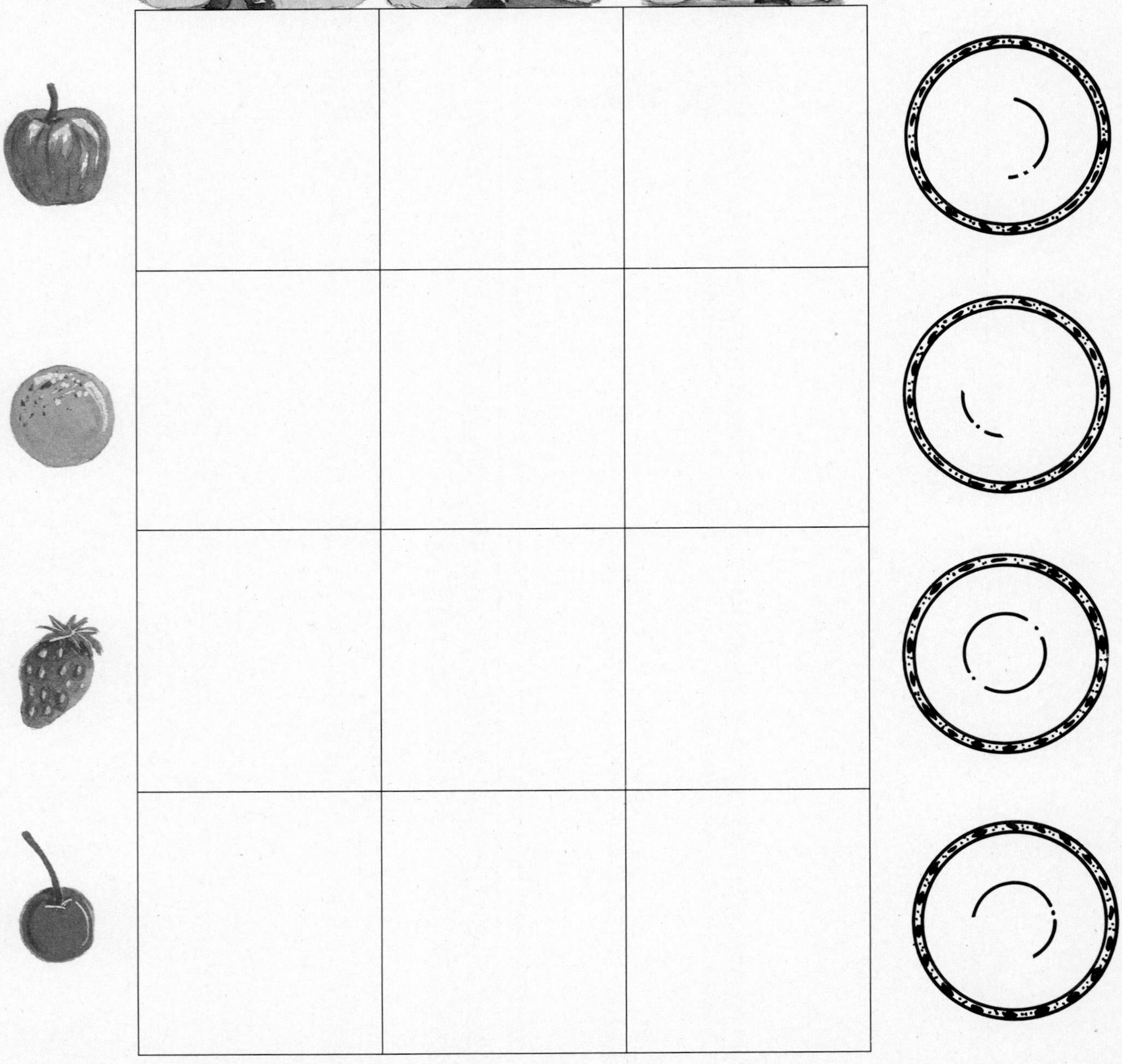

Name ______________________________

I can tell if the shares are fair.

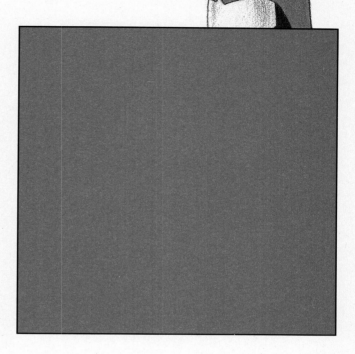

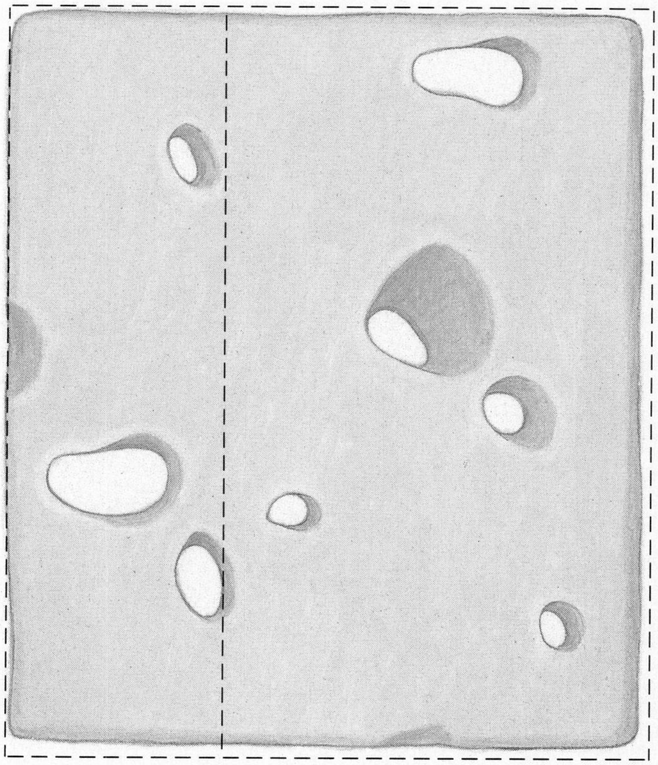

I can tell if the shares are fair.

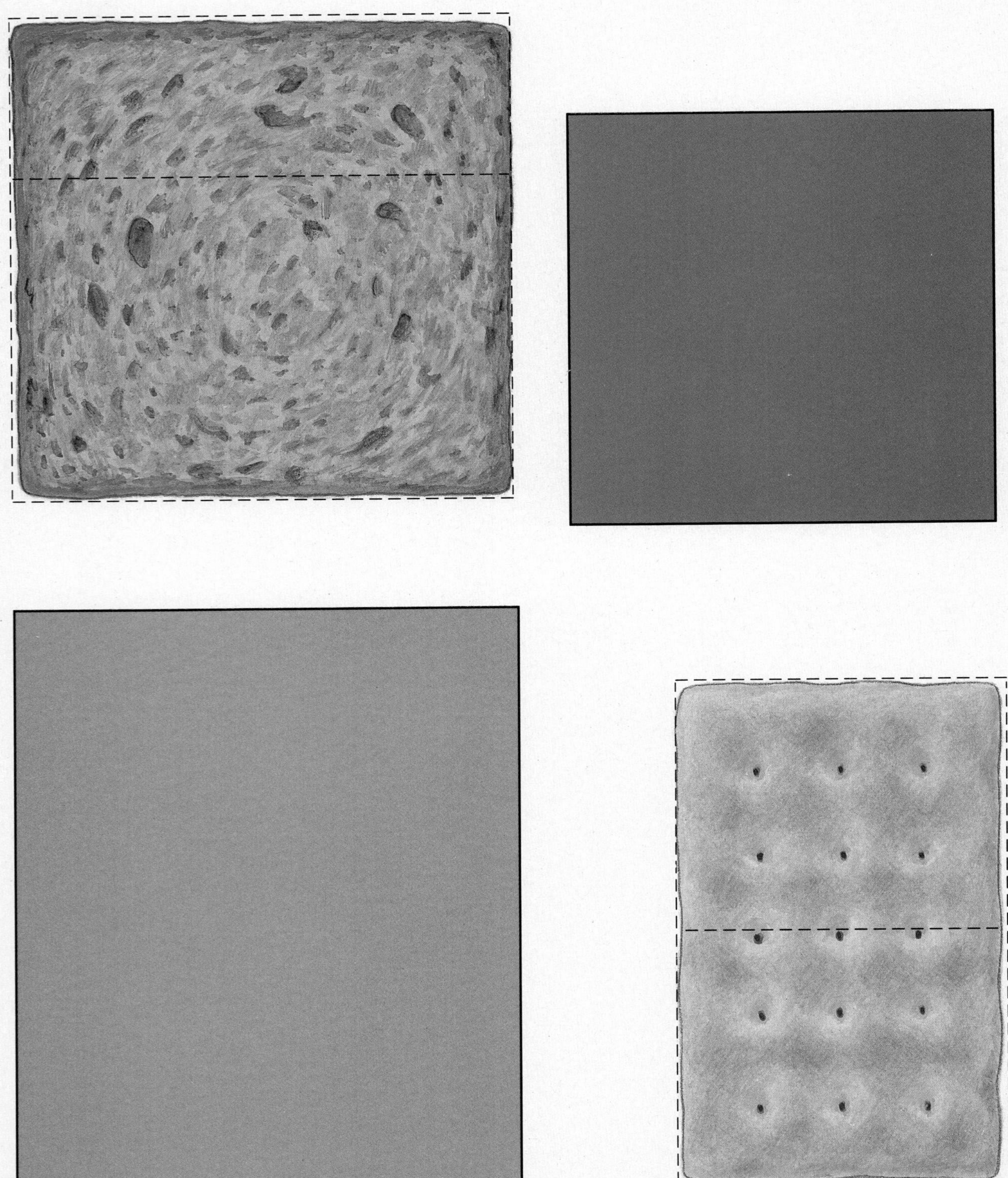

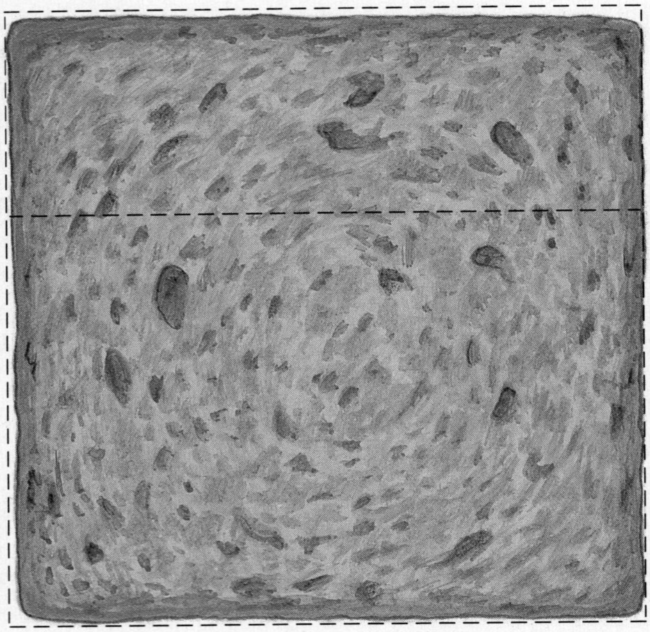

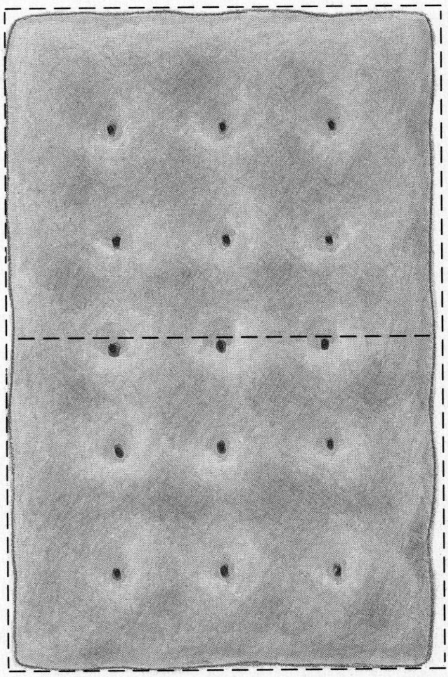

Name ______________________________

I can estimate.
I can show about half.

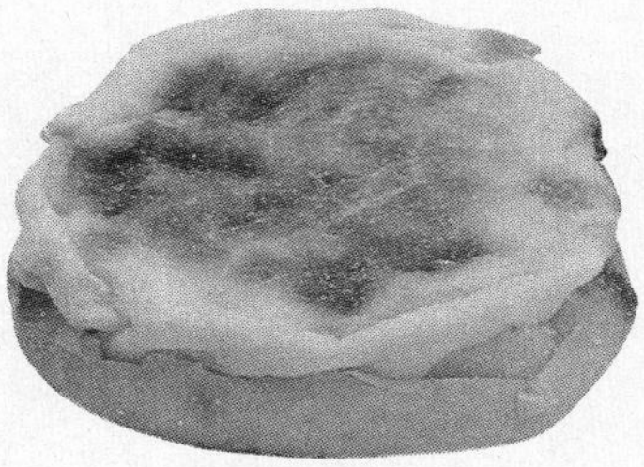

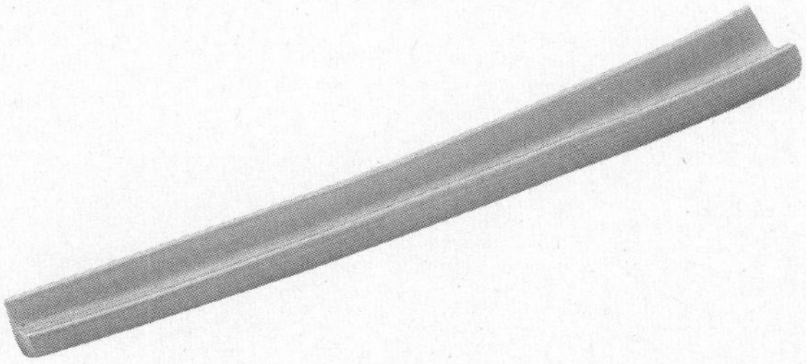

I can tell if the shares are fair.

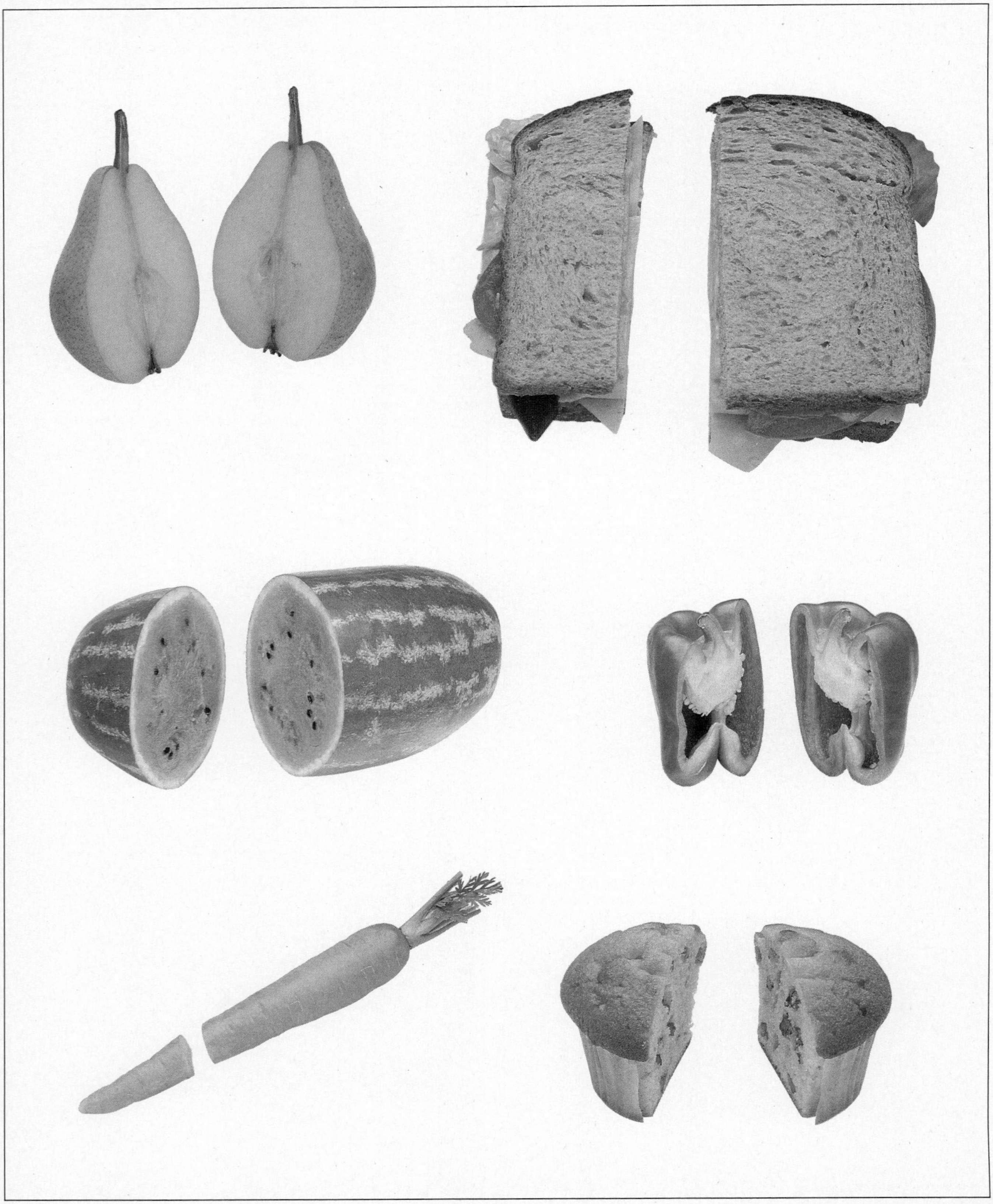

Name ______________________________

UNDERSTAND
FIND DATA
PLAN
ESTIMATE
SOLVE
CHECK

I can show all the ways.

UNDERSTAND
FIND DATA
PLAN
ESTIMATE
SOLVE
CHECK

I can tell which spinner spins more blues.

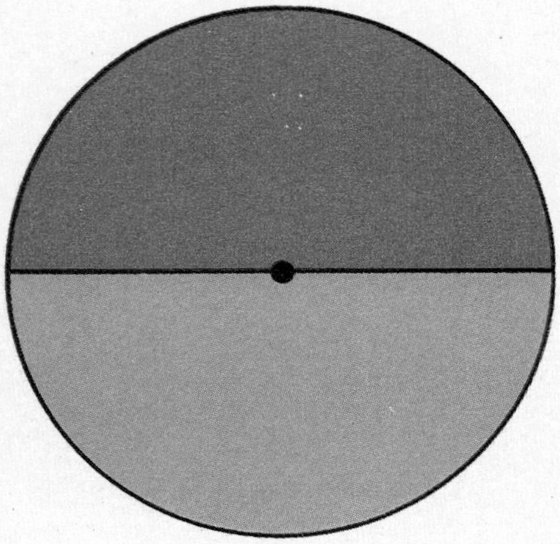

reds

blues

1	2	3	4	5	6	7	8	9	10

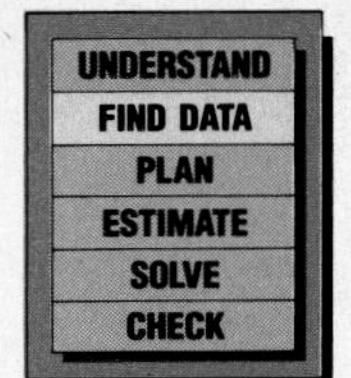

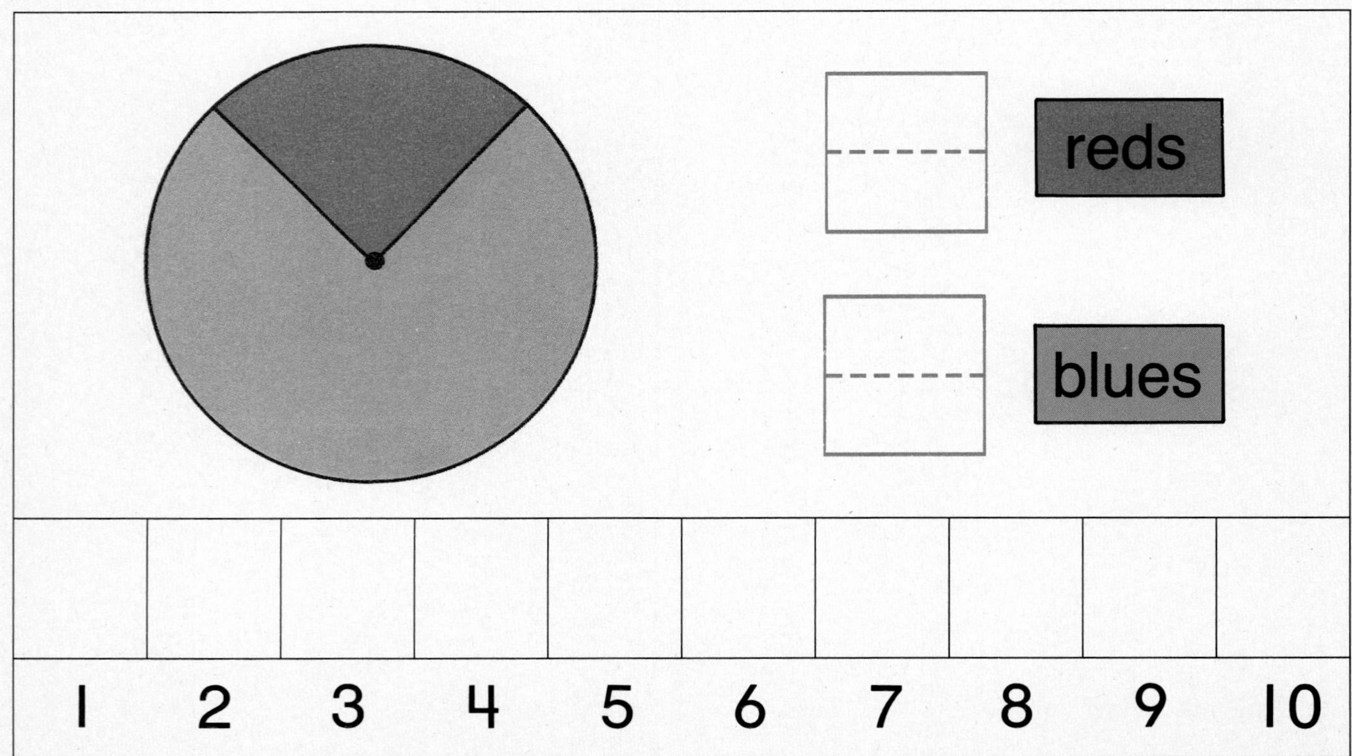

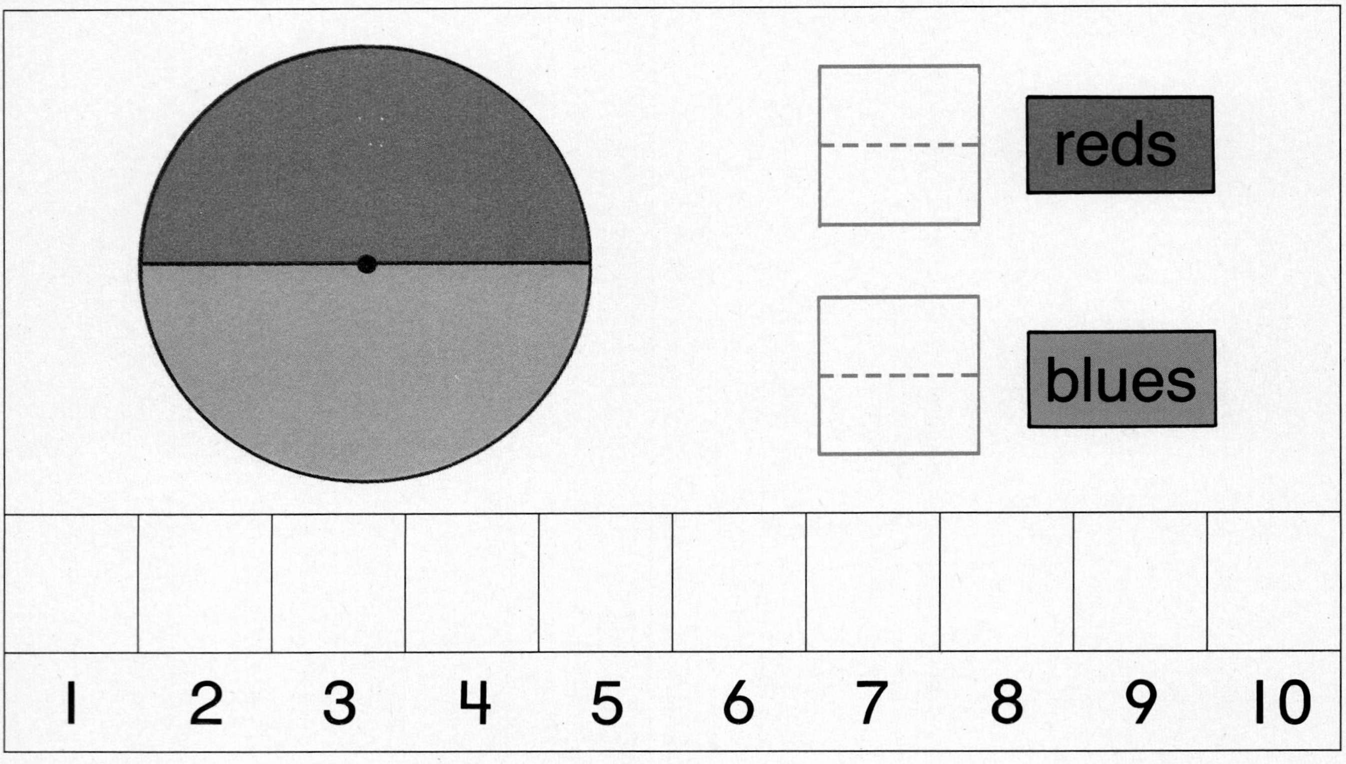

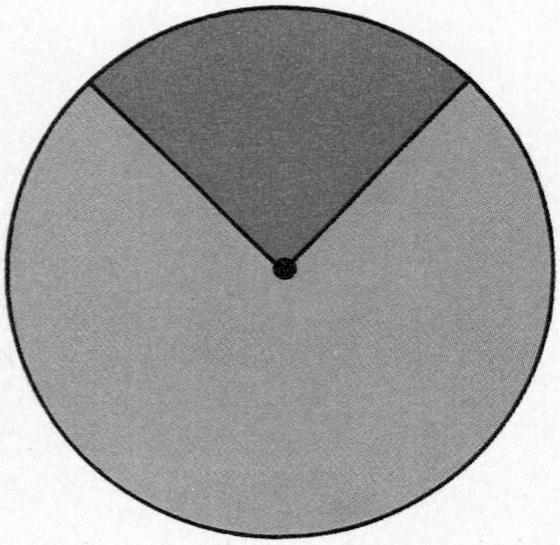

reds

blues

1	2	3	4	5	6	7	8	9	10

Name ______________________________

4 

6 

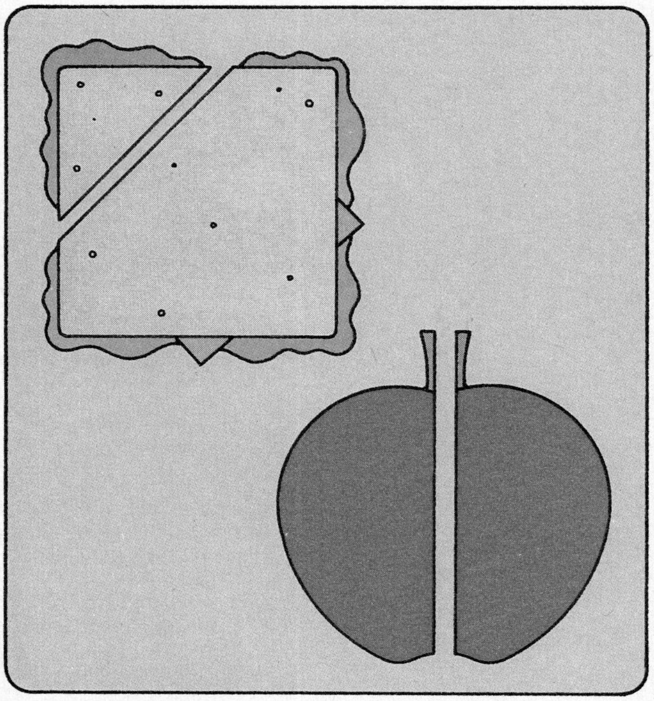

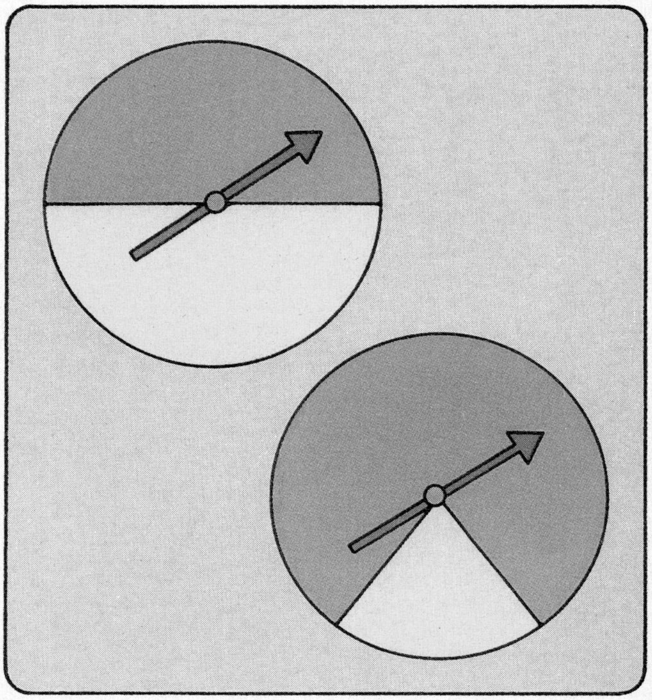

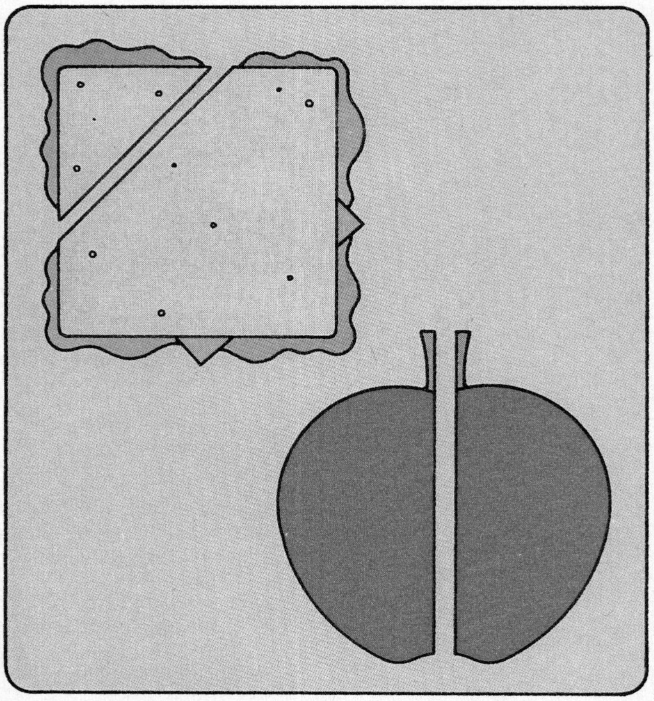

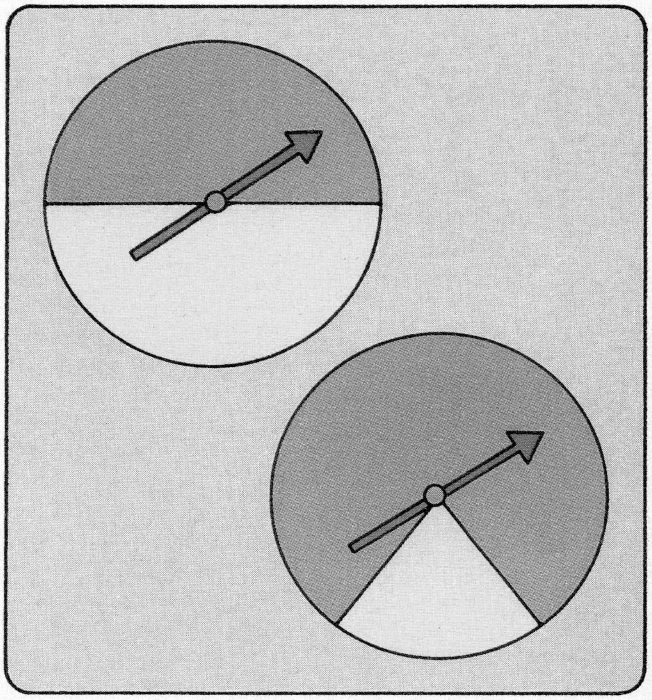

Name ________________________________

I can match right and left.

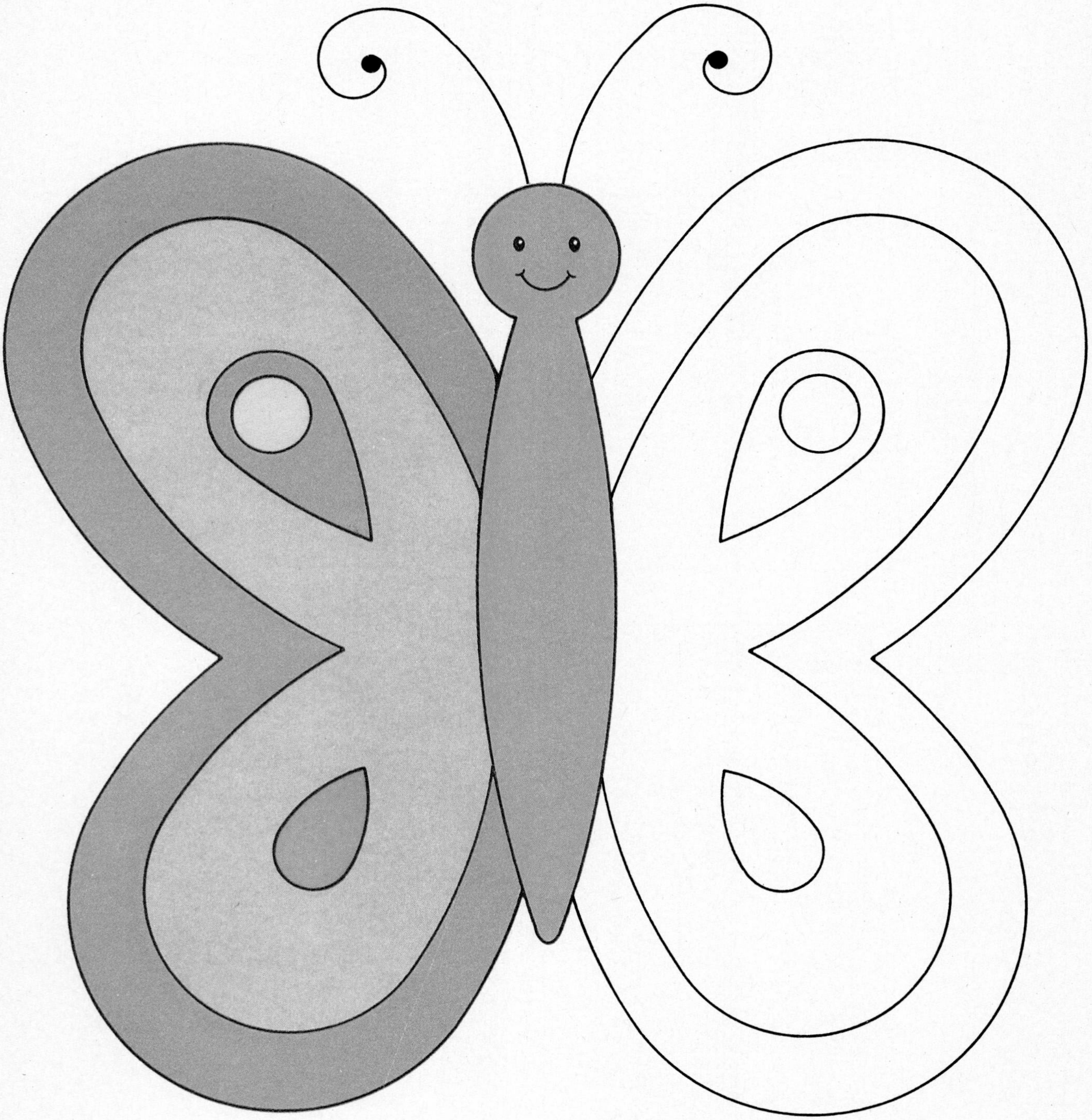

14
Numbers to 31

Workmat

Theme: At the Seashore

Name ______________________________

I can show tens and extras.
I can write the number.

11

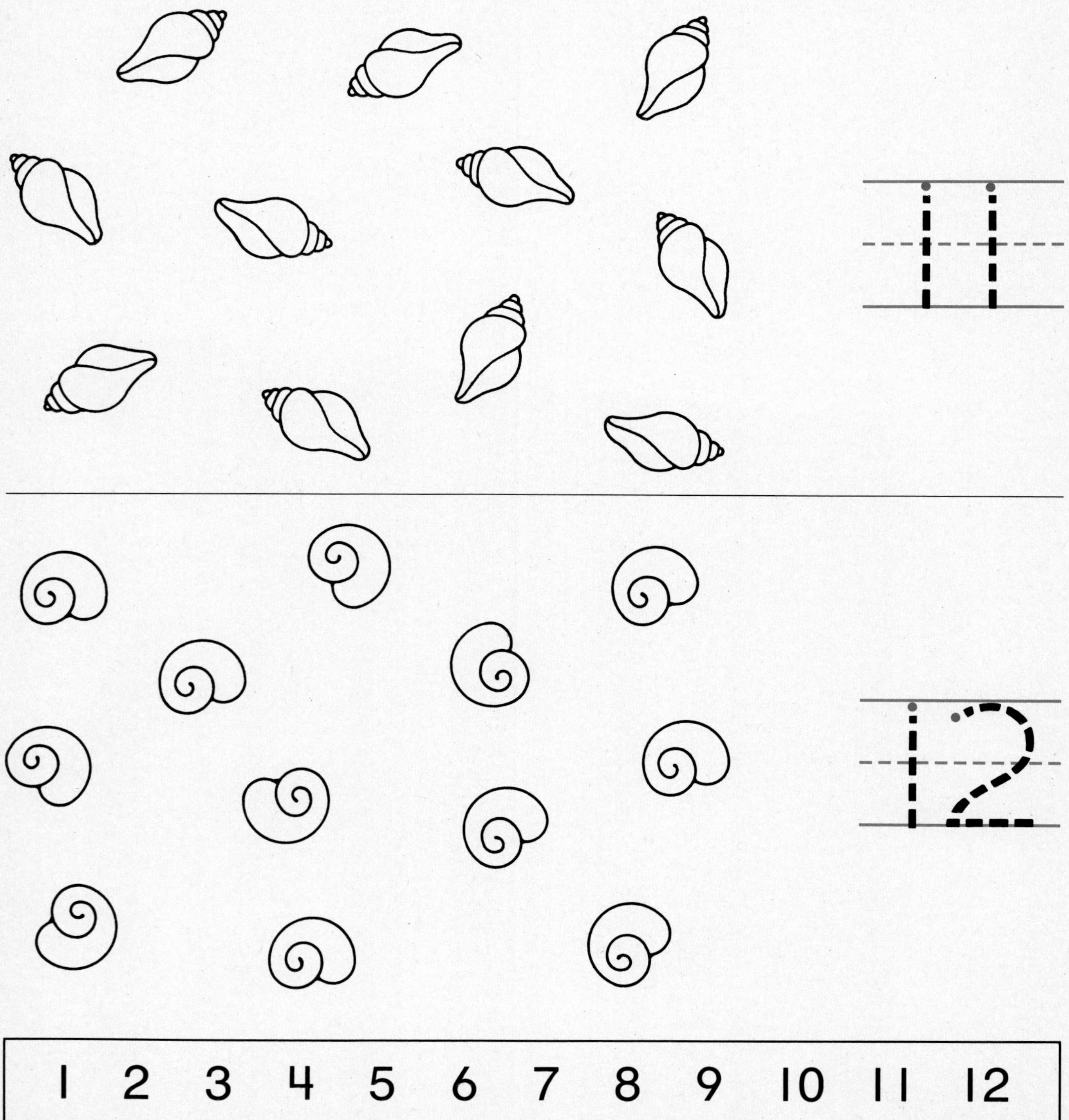

12

1	2	3	4	5	6	7	8	9	10	11	12

Name ____________________

I can show tens and extras.
I can write the number.

13

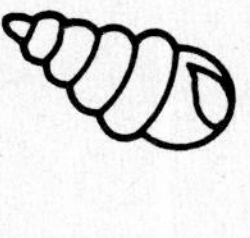

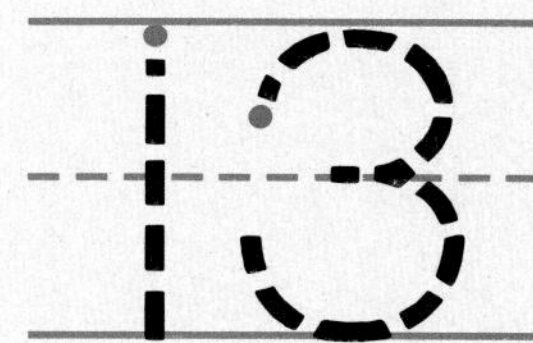

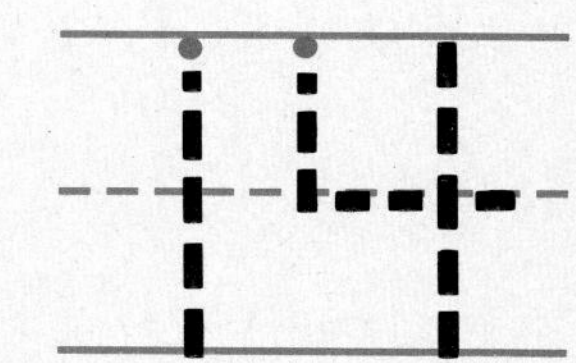

14

I can show tens and extras.
I can write the number.

15

16

Name ____________________

I can show tens and extras.
I can write the number.

17

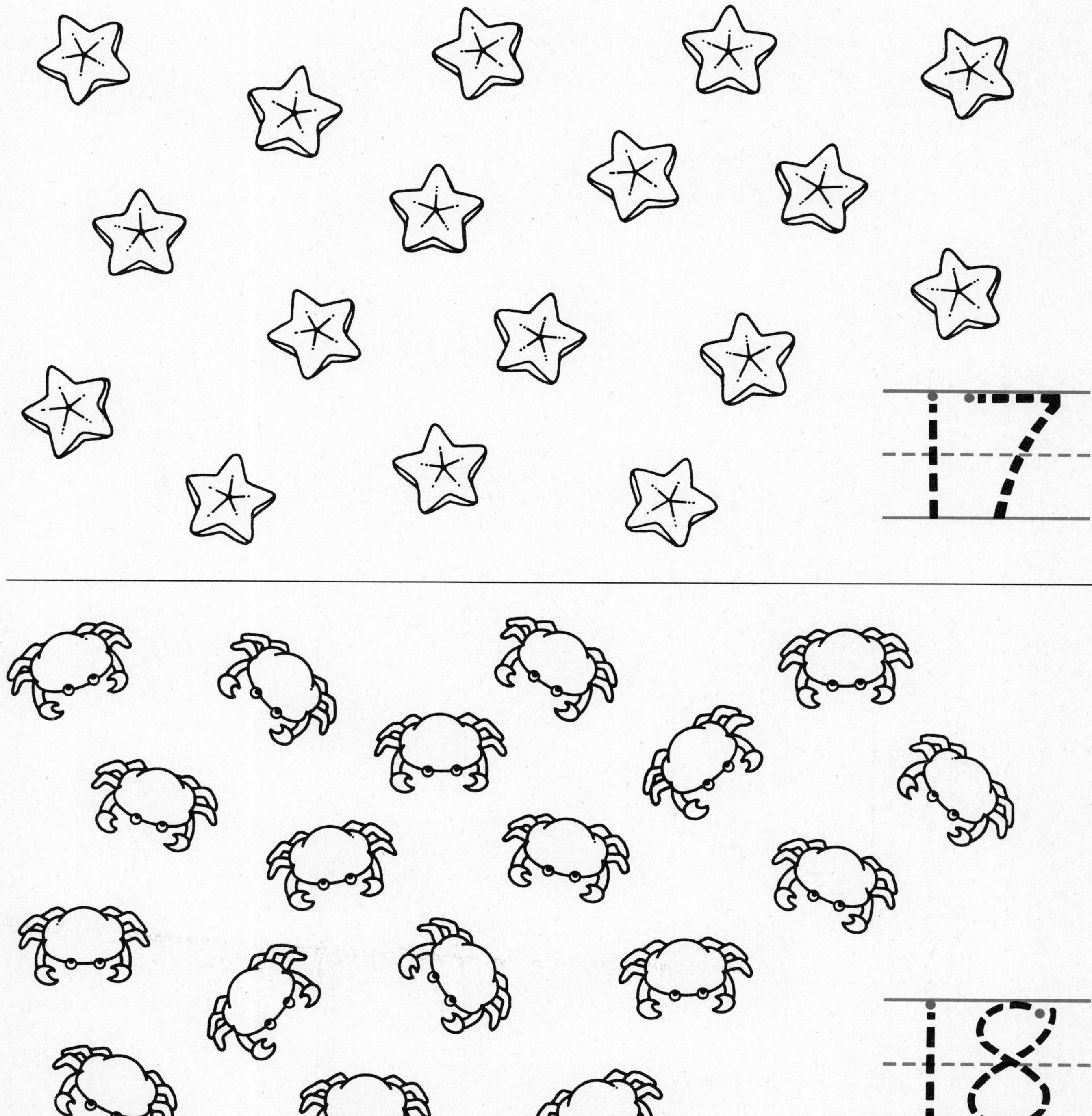

18

I can show tens and extras.
I can write the number.

19

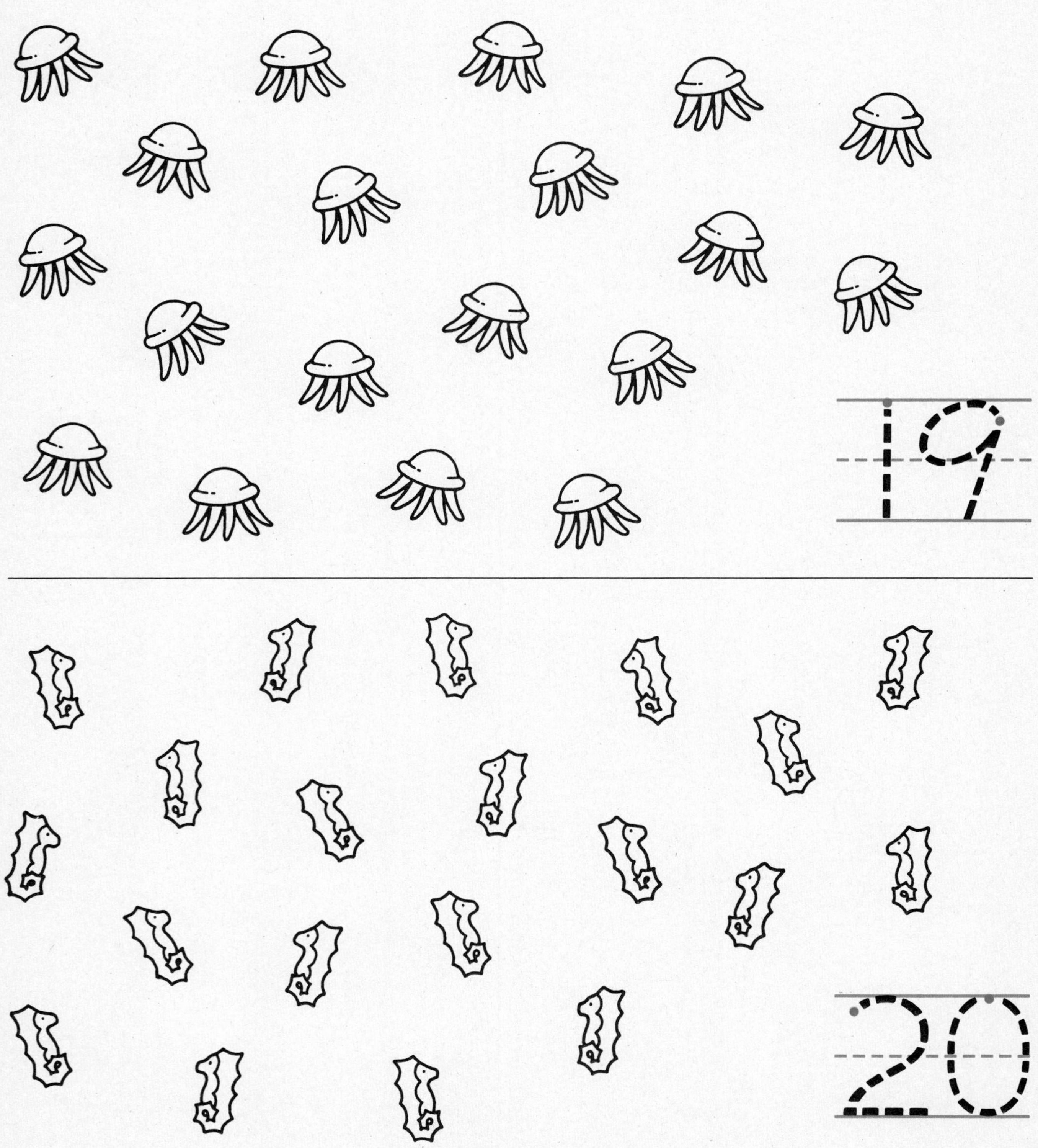

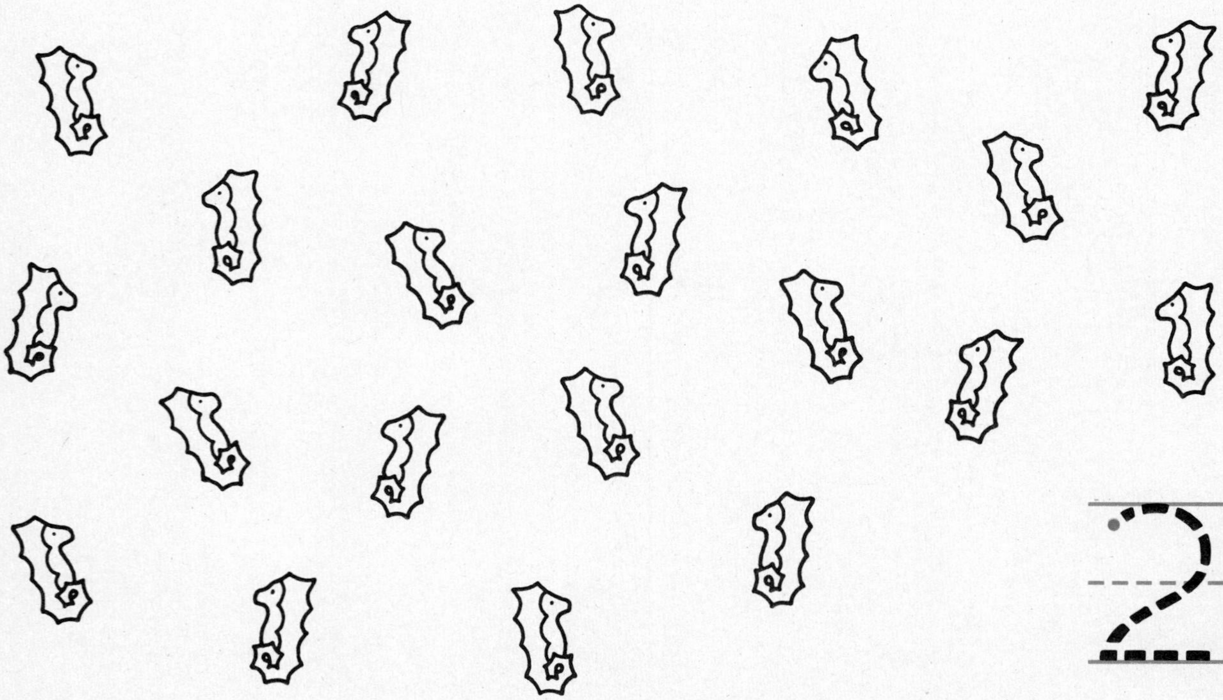

20

Name ______________________________

UNDERSTAND
FIND DATA
PLAN
ESTIMATE
SOLVE
CHECK

I can act out a story.
I can tell how many there are.

the  story

[ ] turtles

the  story

[ ] birds

the 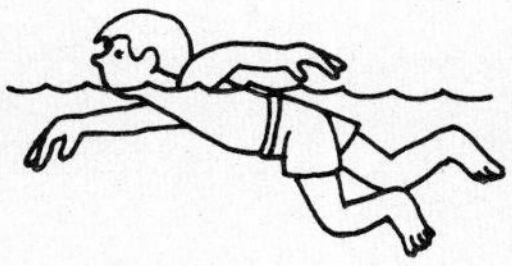 story

[ ] swimmers

the  story

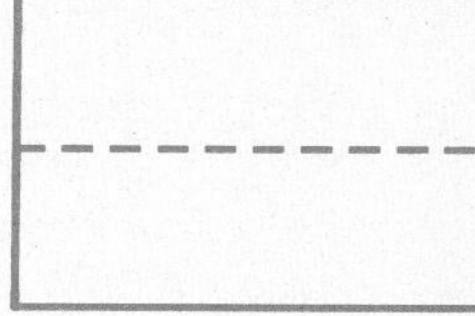

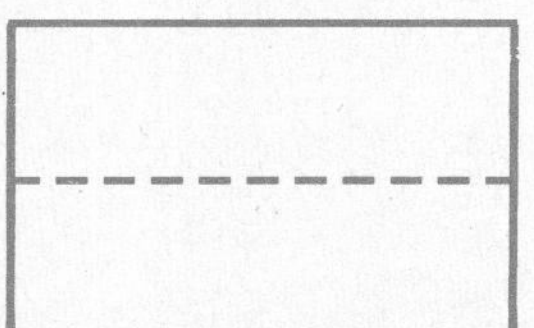

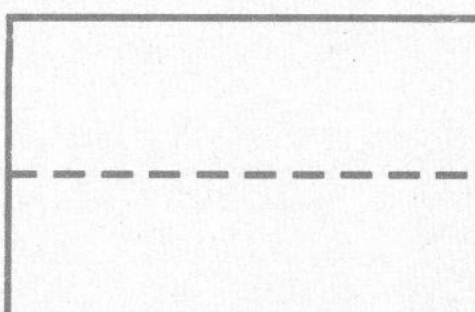

[ ] crabs

1	2	3	4	5	6	7	8	9	10
11	12	13	14	15	16	17	18	19	20

I can listen to a story.
I can tell how many there are.

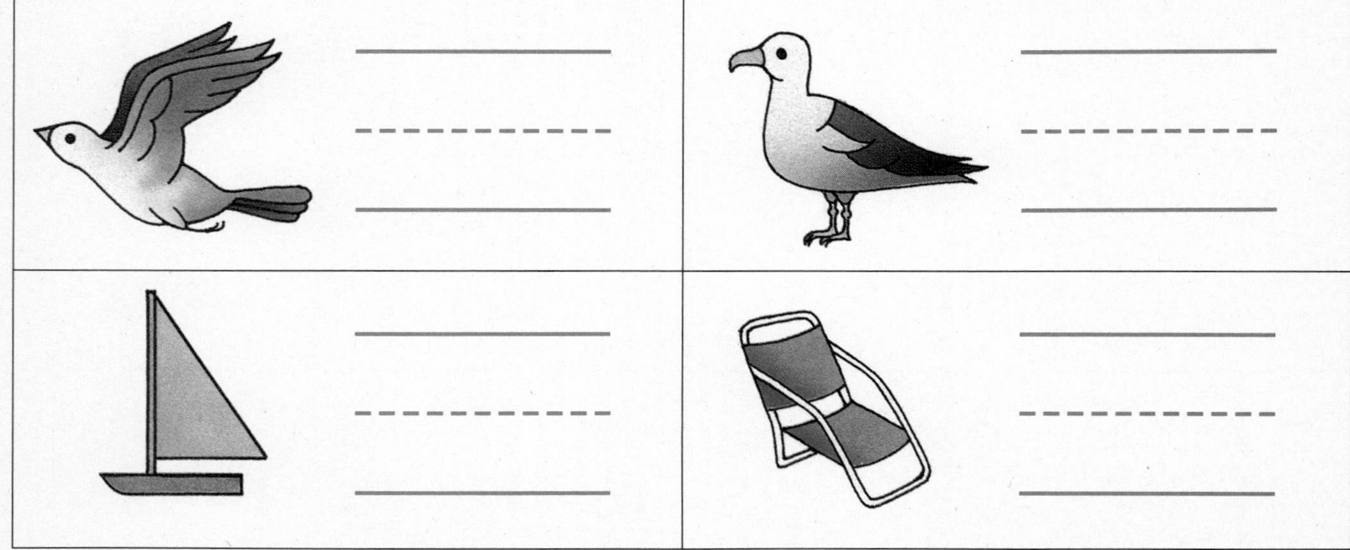

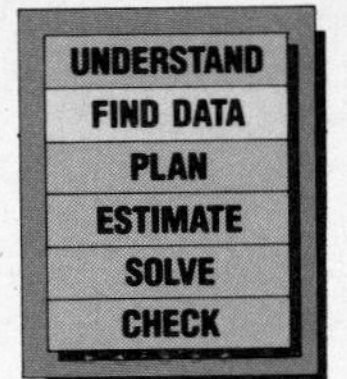

Name ______________________________

I can tell about how many cover the shape.

about ______

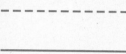

about ______

1	2	3	4	5	6	7	8	9	10
11	12	13	14	15	16	17	18	19	20

I can tell about how many cover the shape.

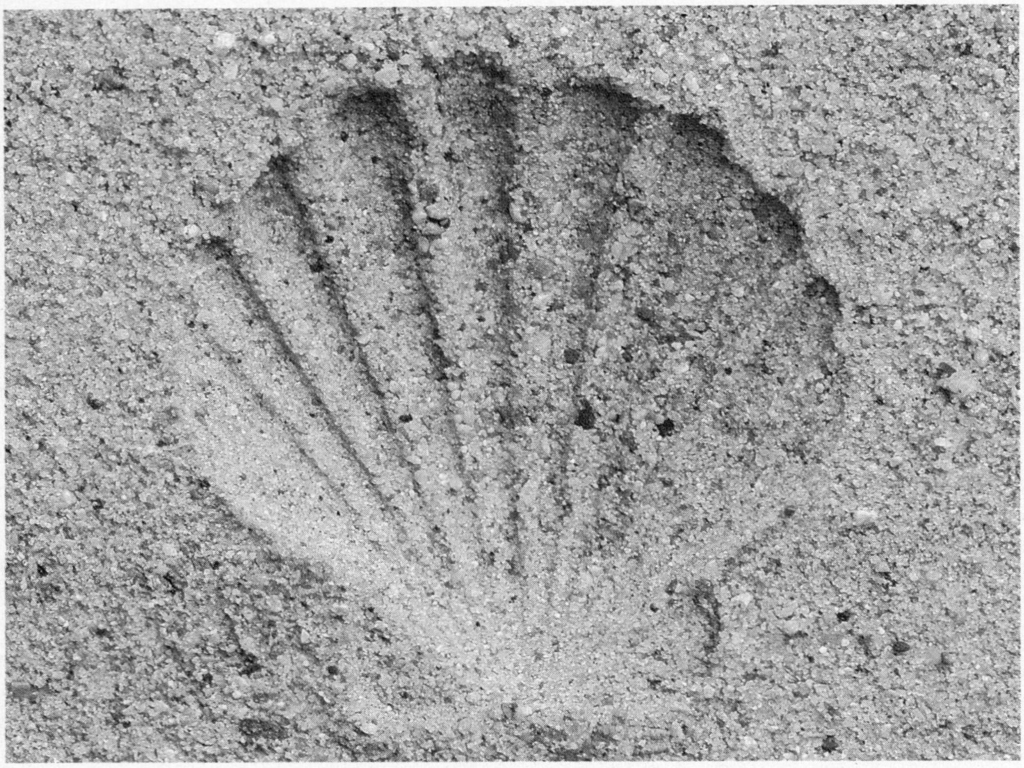

about

about

Name ______________________

I can make a graph.
I can compare the numbers.

14 limpets	12 scallops	13 mussels	15 clams

Shells We Found

limpets	scallops	mussels	clams

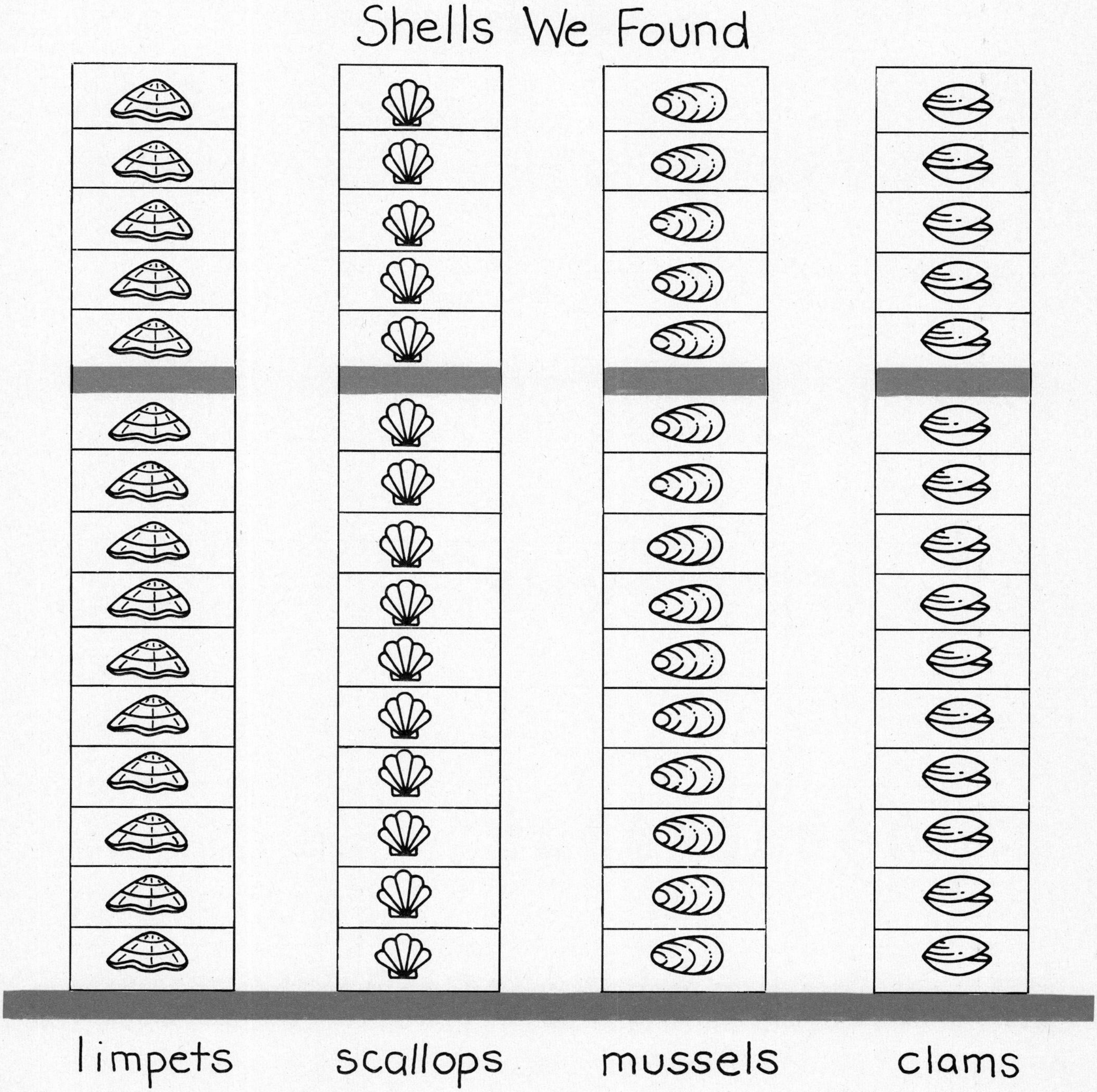

I can compare numbers.
I can tell which one is less.

14 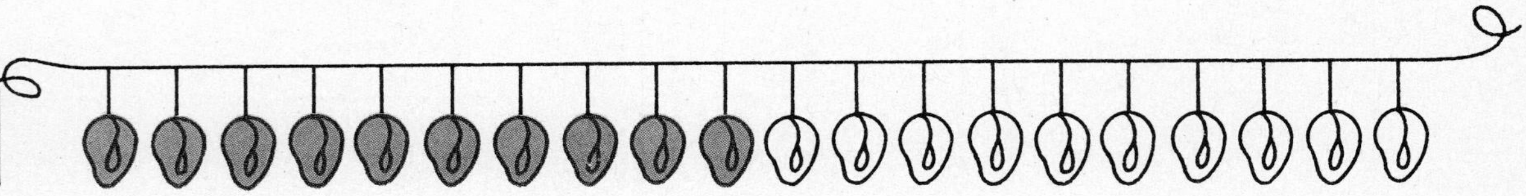

18 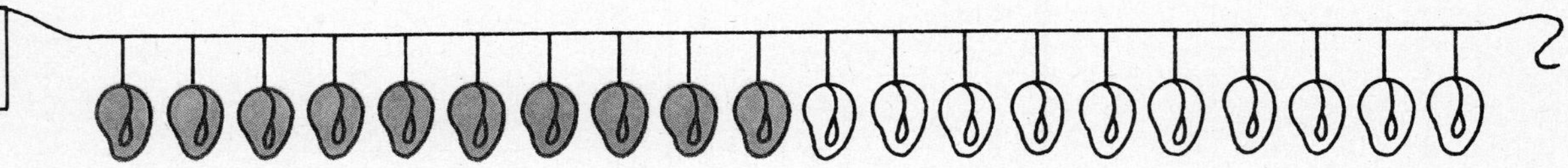

19 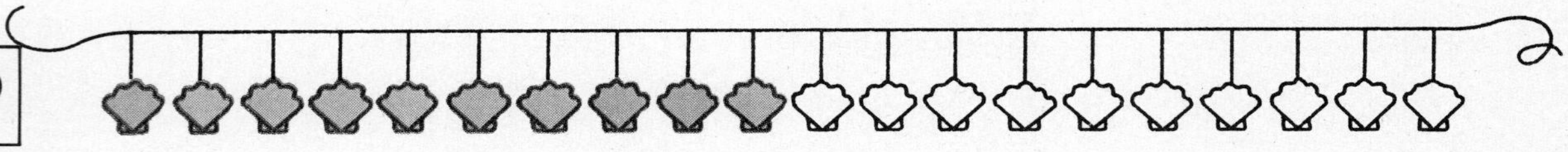

16 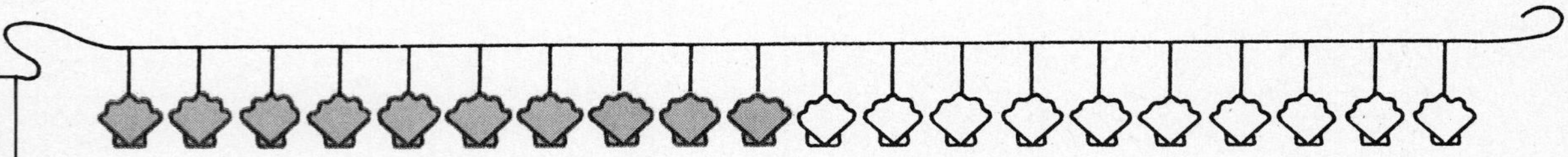

20 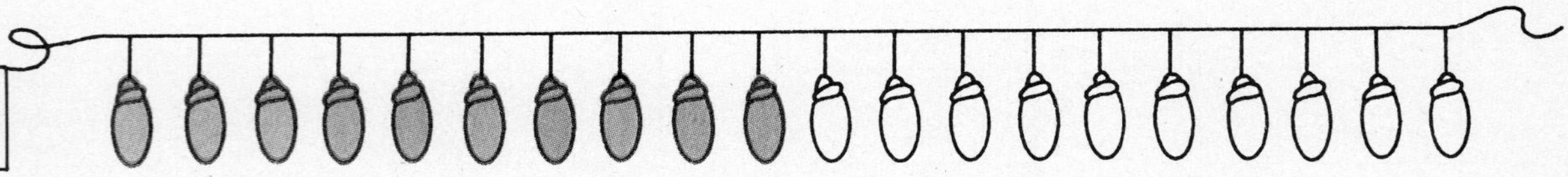

17 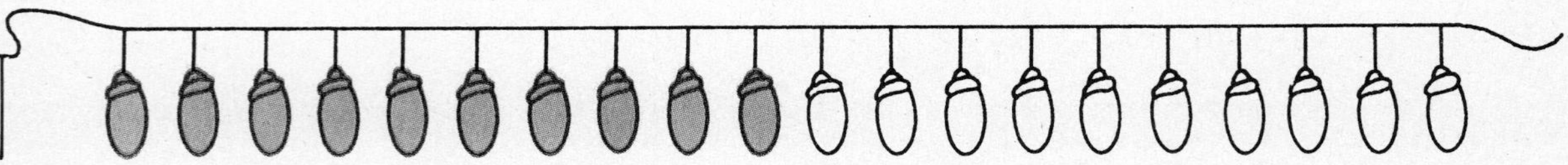

Name ______________________________

I can put numbers in order.

I can connect dots in order.

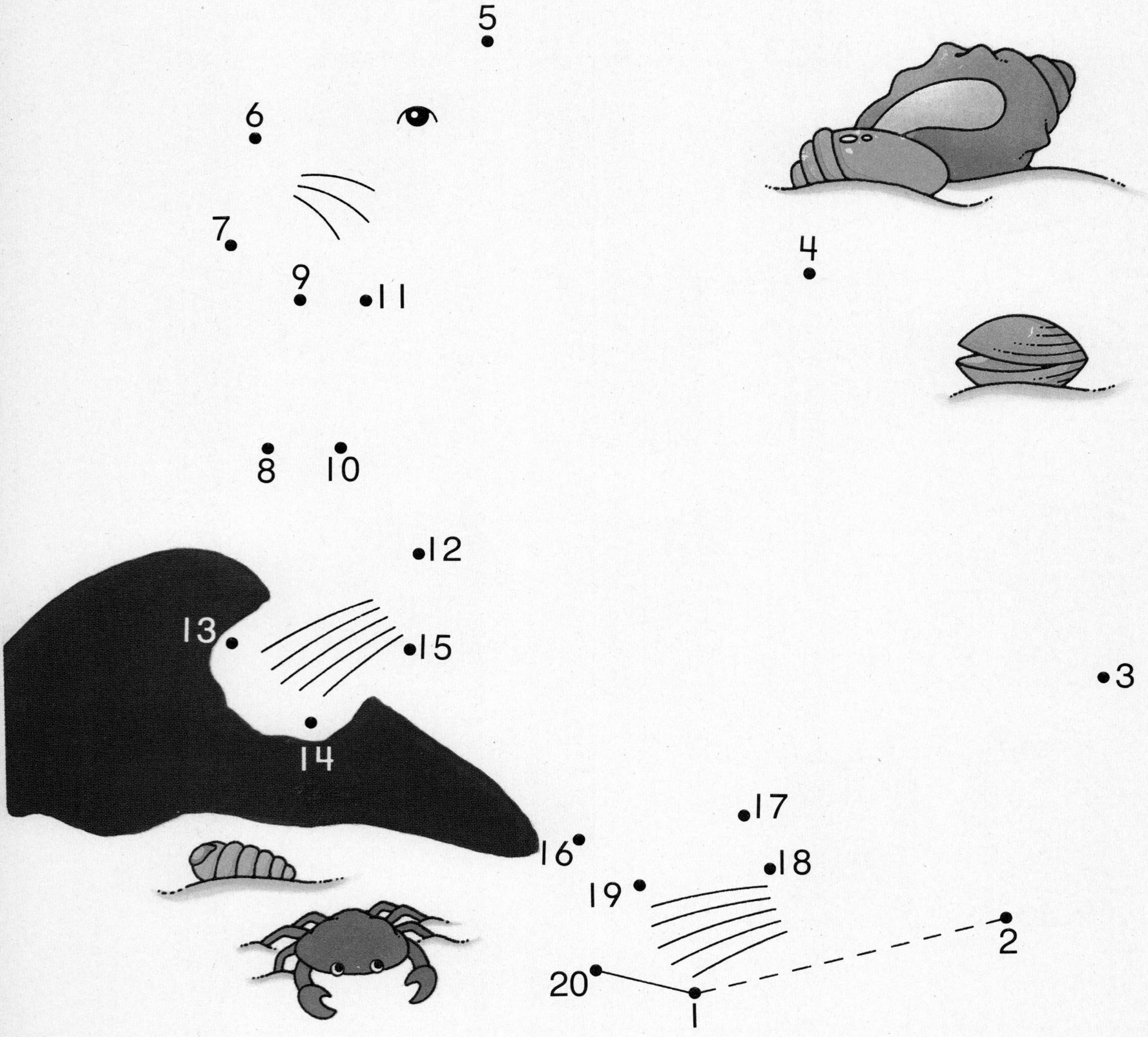

Name ______________________________

I can show tens and extras.

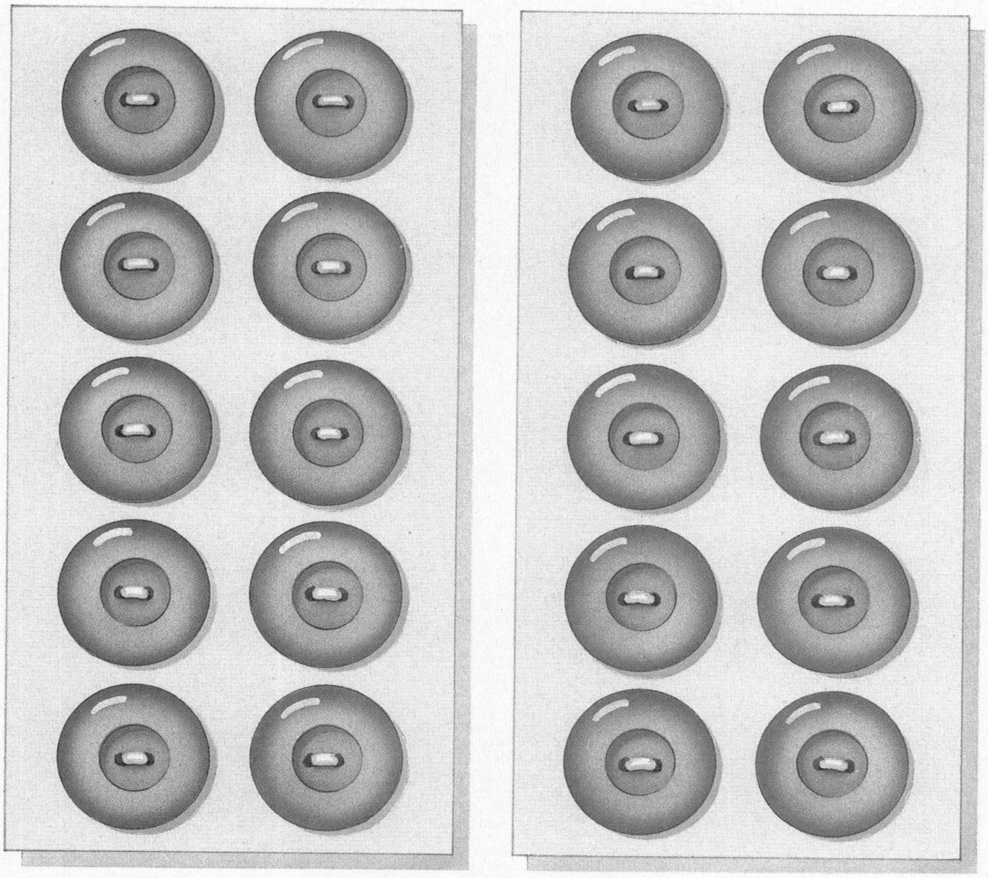

20 — 21 — 22 — 23 — 24 — 25 — 26 — 27 — 28 — 29

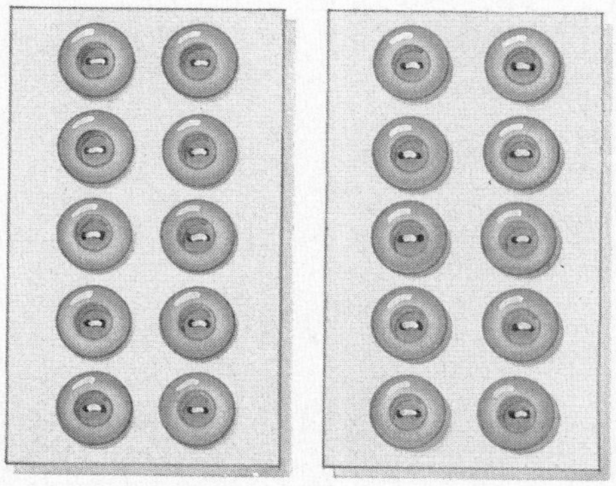 21	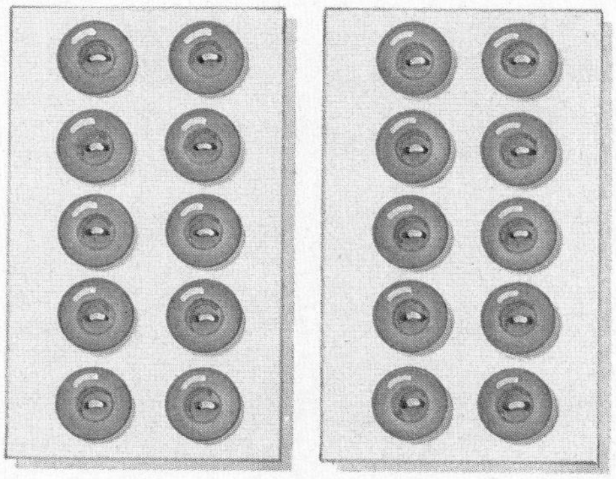 22

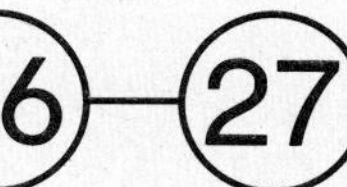

I can show tens and extras.

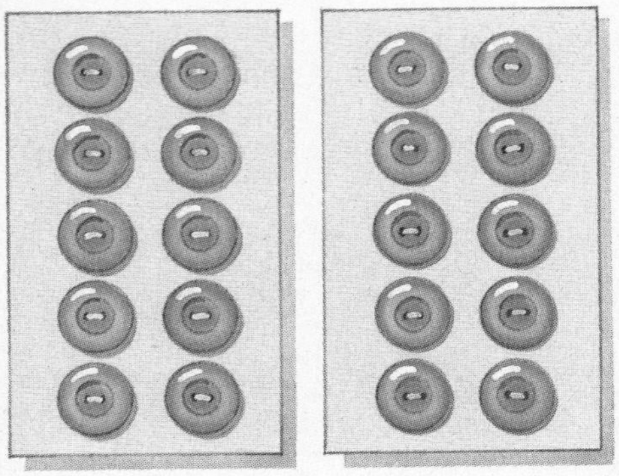

23

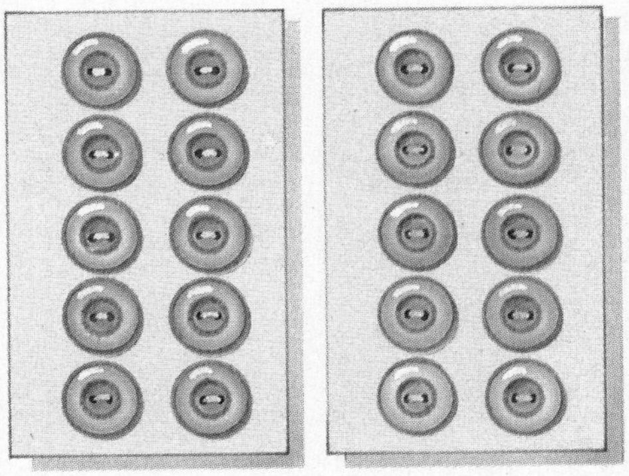

24

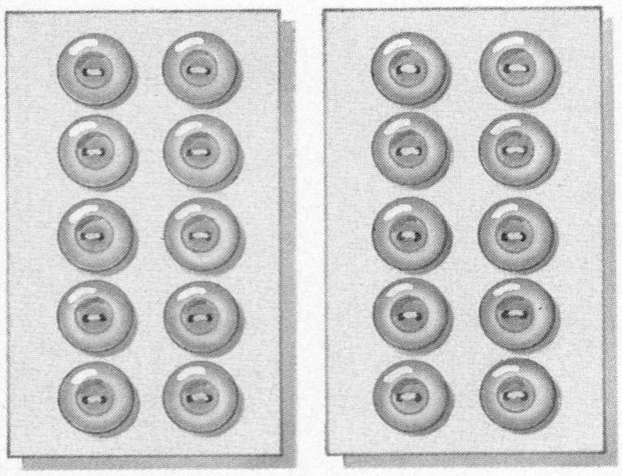

25

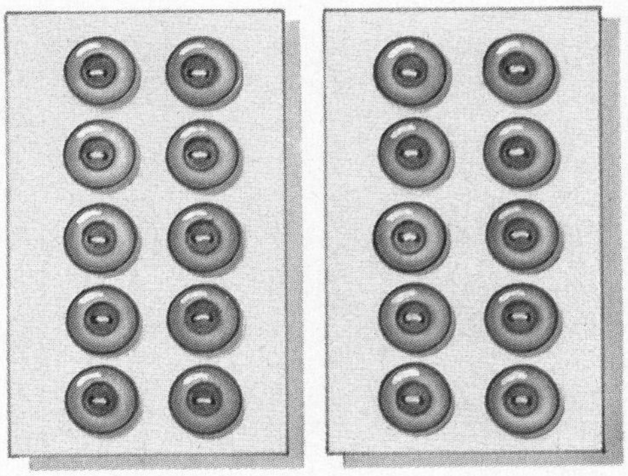

26

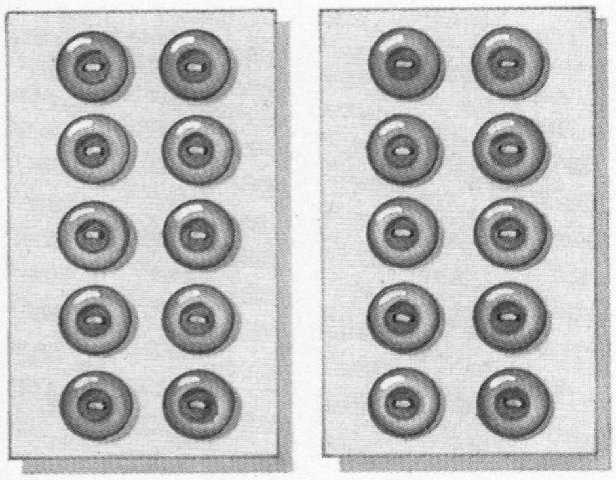

27

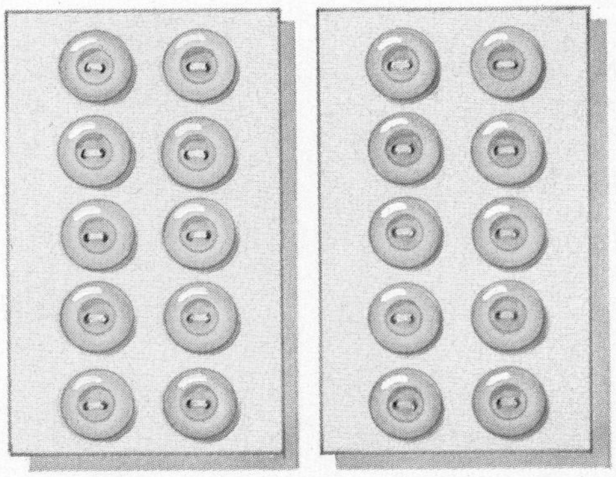

28

Name ______________________________

I can write calendar numbers.
I can find dates on the calendar.

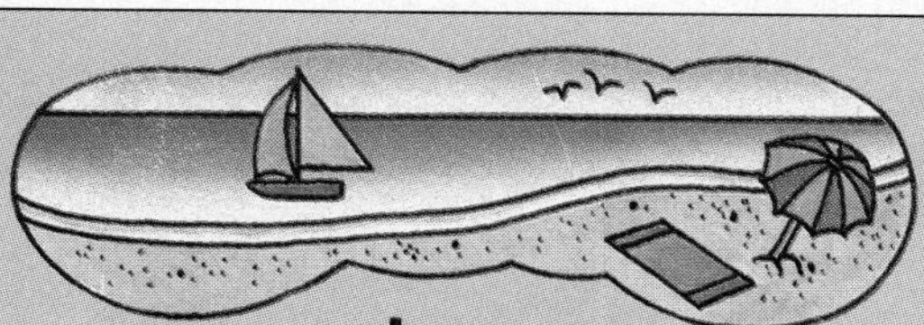

June

Sunday	Monday	Tuesday	Wednesday	Thursday	Friday	Saturday
	1	2	3	4	5	6
7	8	9	10	11	12	13
14	15	16	17	18	19	20
21	22	23	24	25	26	27
28	29	30				

I can find dates on the calendar.

July						
Sunday	Monday	Tuesday	Wednesday	Thursday	Friday	Saturday
			1	2	3	
5	6		8	9	10	11
12	13	14	15		17	18
	20	21	22	23	24	25
26	27	28	29	30	31	

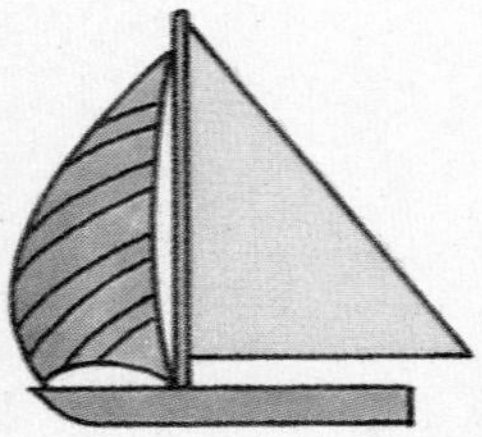	July ______		July ______
	July ______		July ______

Name ______________________________

16 12 17

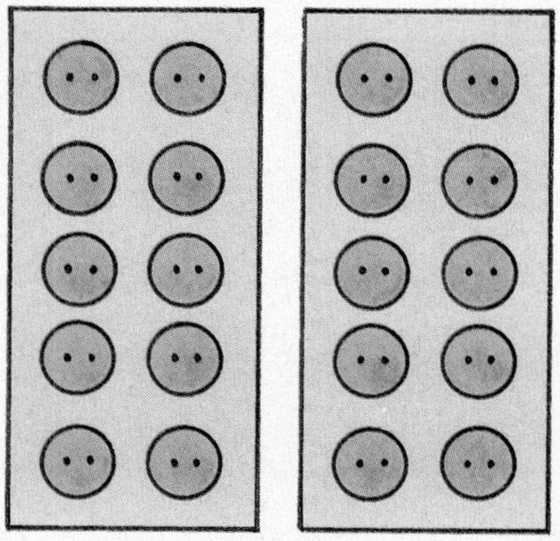

23

1	2	3	4	5	6	7	8	9	10
11	12	13	14	15	16	17	18	19	20

Name ______________________________

quarter

25¢

1¢ 1¢ 1¢ 1¢ 1¢

5¢ 5¢ 10¢

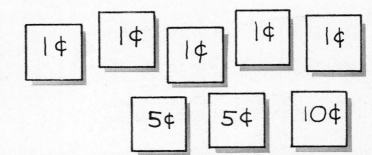

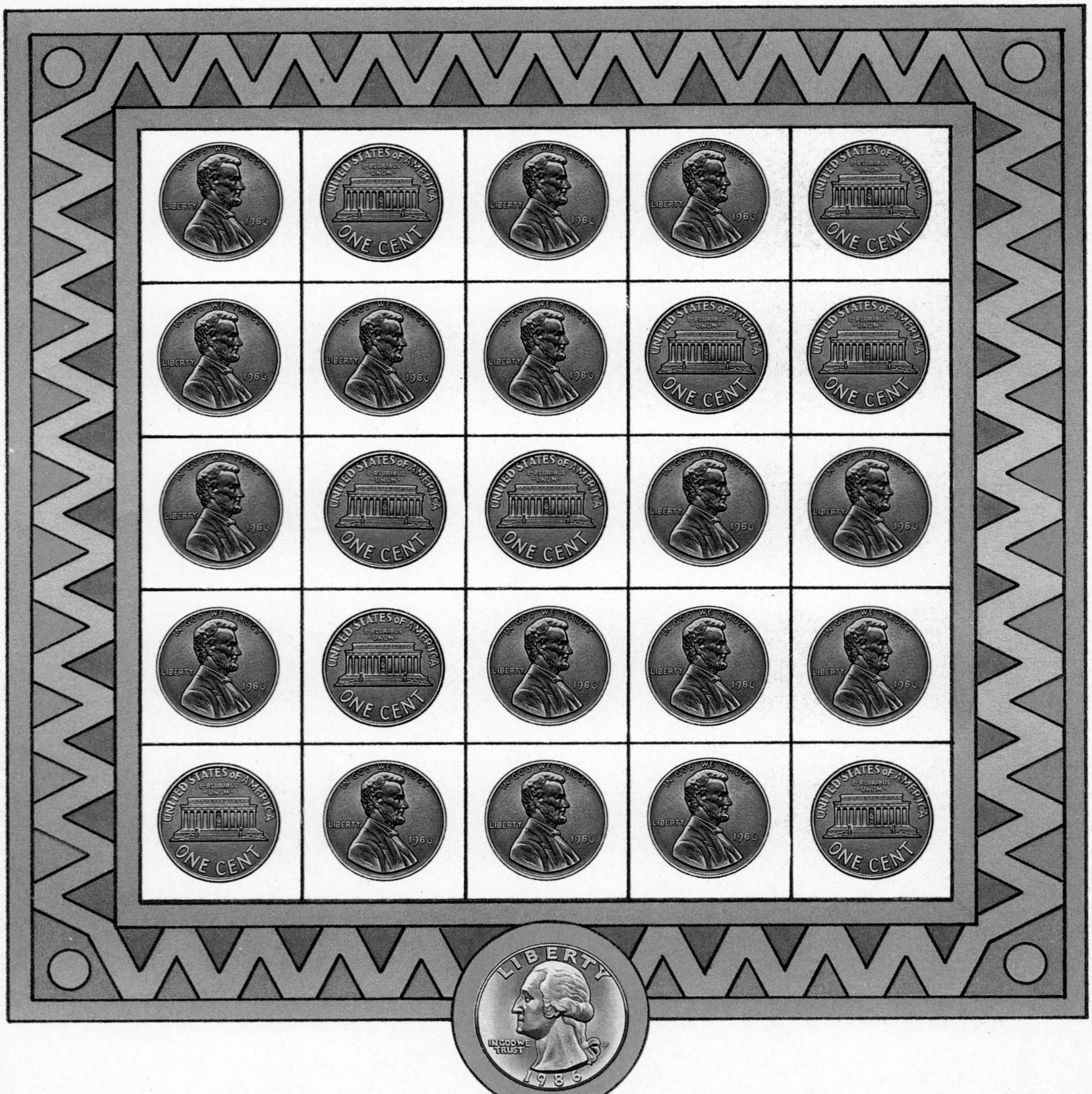

15
Counting Patterns

Workmat

Theme: Patterns

Name

I can record counting patterns.
I can count by 1 and 2.

1	2	3	4	5	6	7	8	9	10
11	12	13	14	15	16	17	18	19	20

Name ______________________________

I can record counting patterns.
I can count by 3.

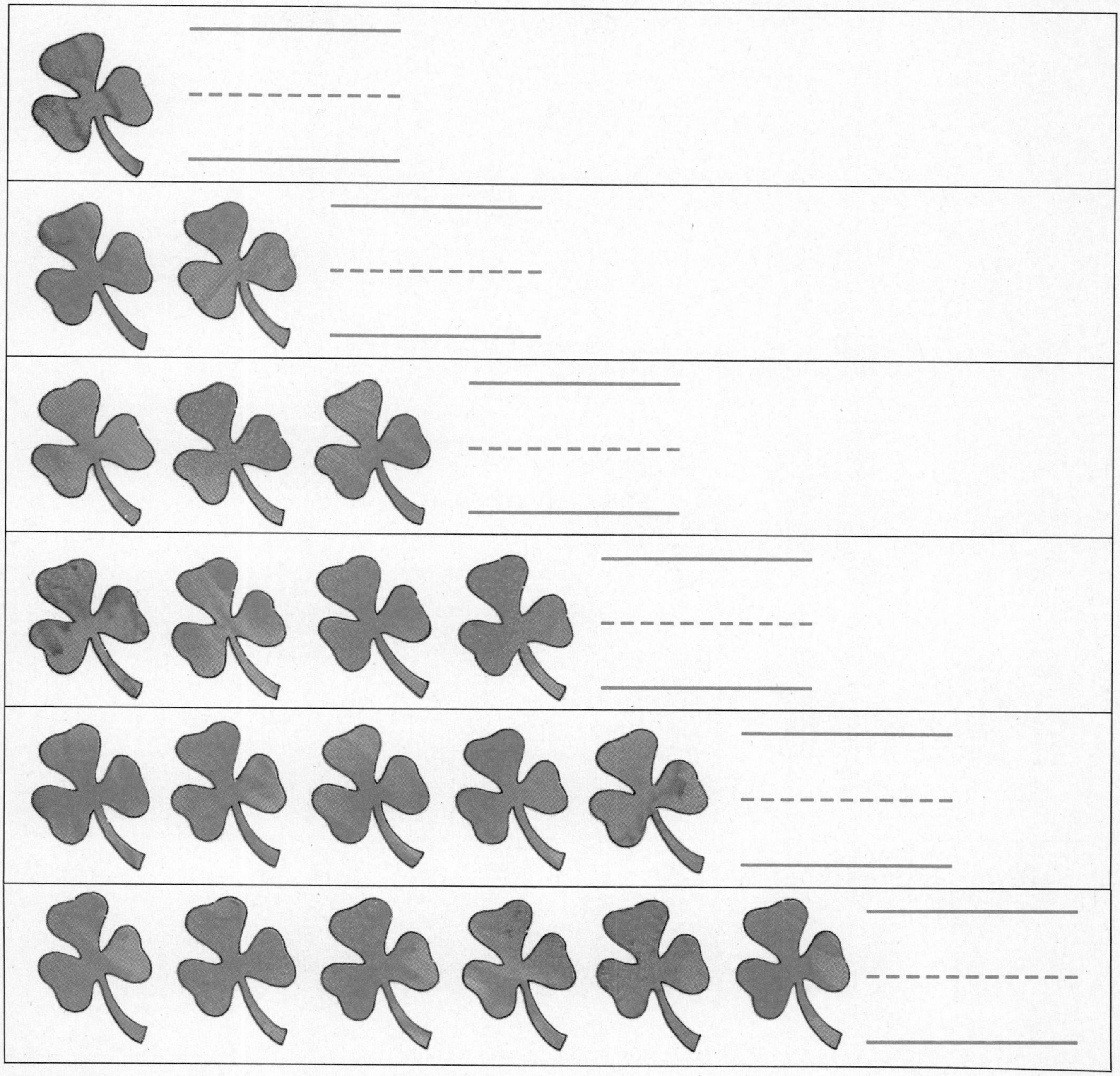

1	2	3	4	5	6	7	8	9	10
11	12	13	14	15	16	17	18	19	20

I can record counting patterns.
I can count by 4.

1 2 3 4 5 6 7 8 9 10
11 12 13 14 15 16 17 18 19 20

Name ______________________________

I can record counting patterns.
I can count by 5.

1	2	3	4	5	6	7	8	9	10
11	12	13	14	15	16	17	18	19	20

I can record counting patterns.
I can count by 5.

¢

¢

¢

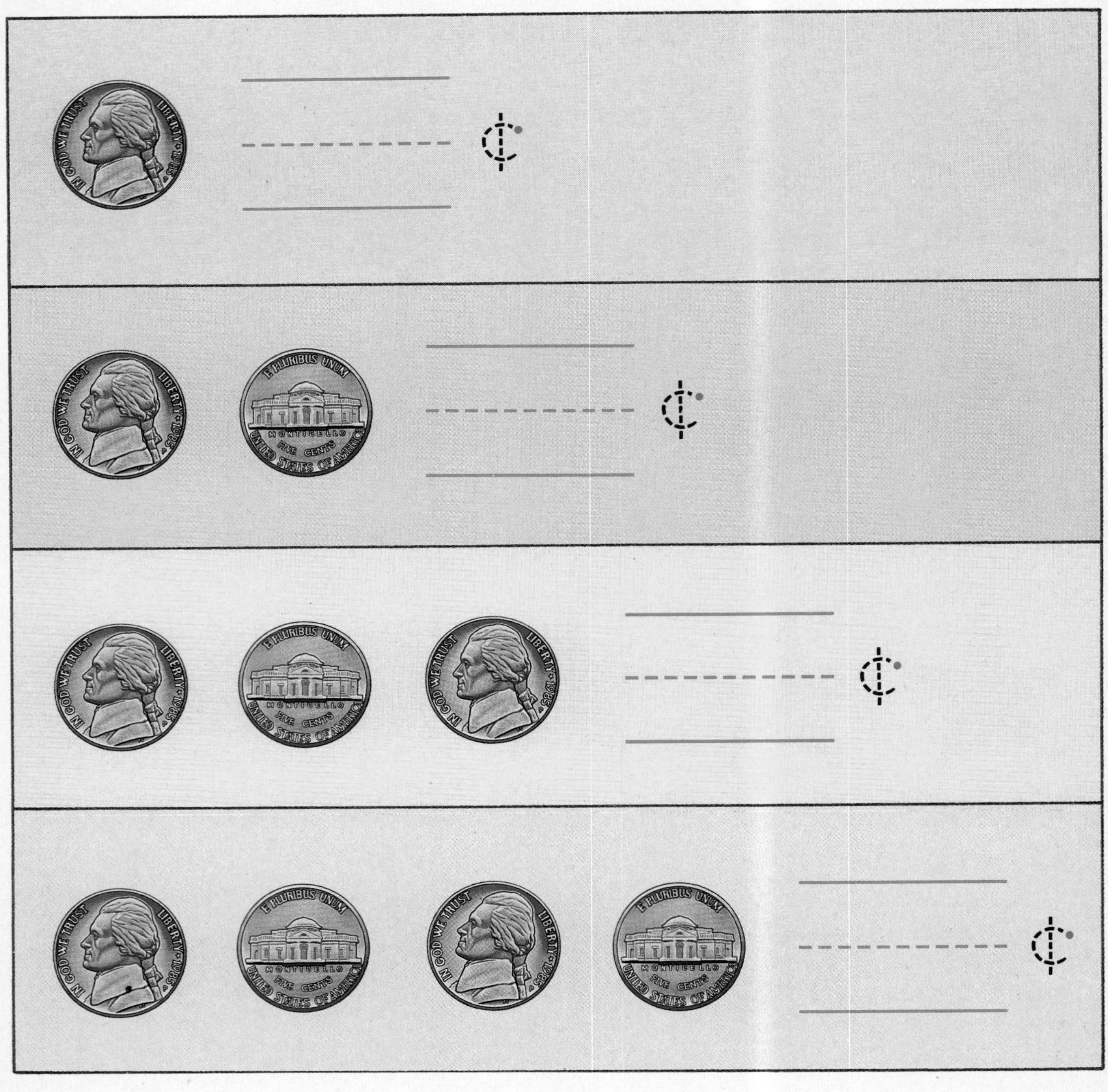

¢

1	2	3	4	5	6	7	8	9	10
11	12	13	14	15	16	17	18	19	20

Name ______________________________

I can record calculator patterns.

ON/C	0	+	1	=	=	=	=

1	2	3	4	5	6	7	8	9	10
11	12	13	14	15	16	17	18	19	20

ON/C	0	+	2	=	=	=	=

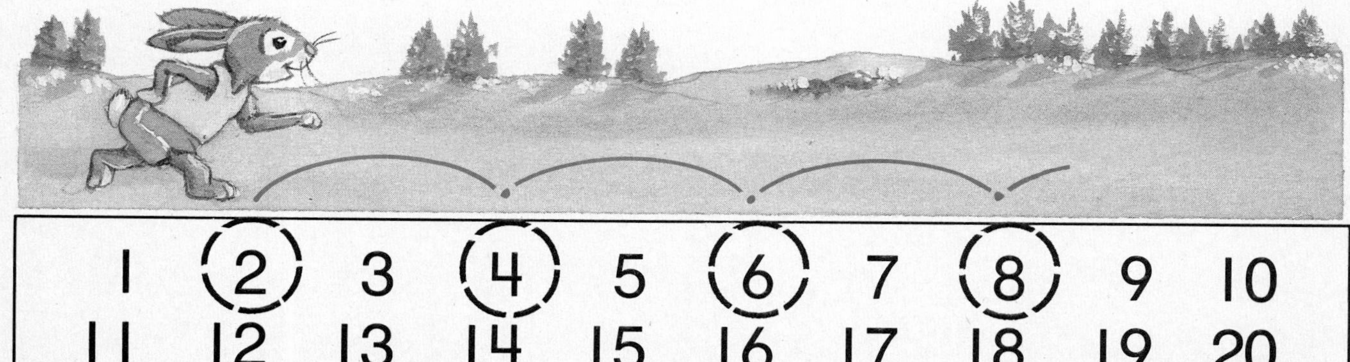

1	2	3	4	5	6	7	8	9	10
11	12	13	14	15	16	17	18	19	20

I can record calculator patterns.

ON/C | 0 | + | 3 | = | = | = | =

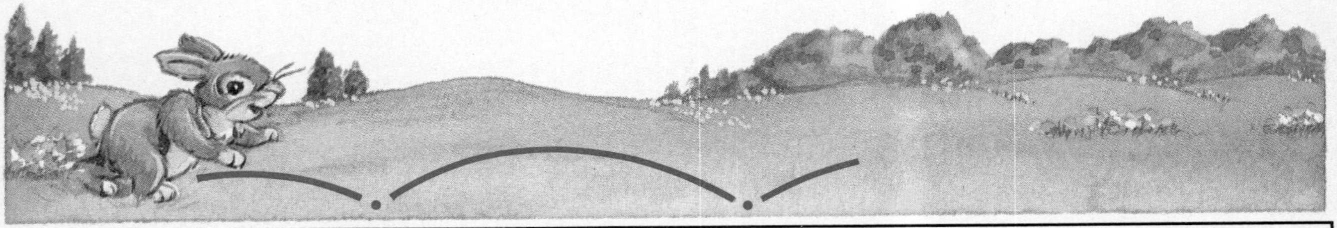

1	2	3	4	5	6	7	8	9	10
11	12	13	14	15	16	17	18	19	20

ON/C | 0 | + | 4 | = | = | = | =

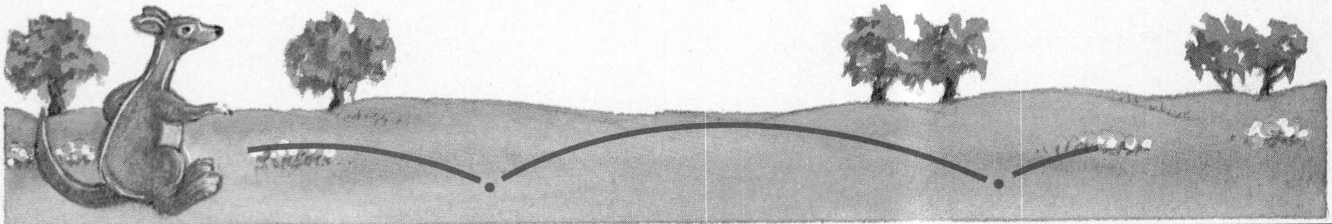

1	2	3	4	5	6	7	8	9	10
11	12	13	14	15	16	17	18	19	20

ON/C | 0 | + | 5 | = | = | = | =

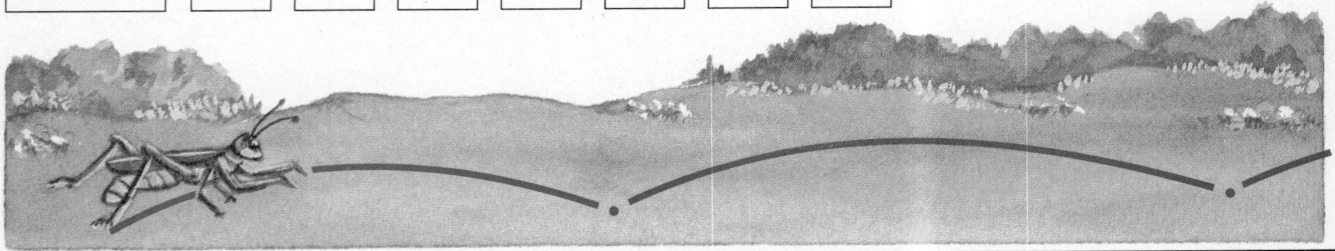

1	2	3	4	5	6	7	8	9	10
11	12	13	14	15	16	17	18	19	20

Name ________________________________

I can count on from a number.

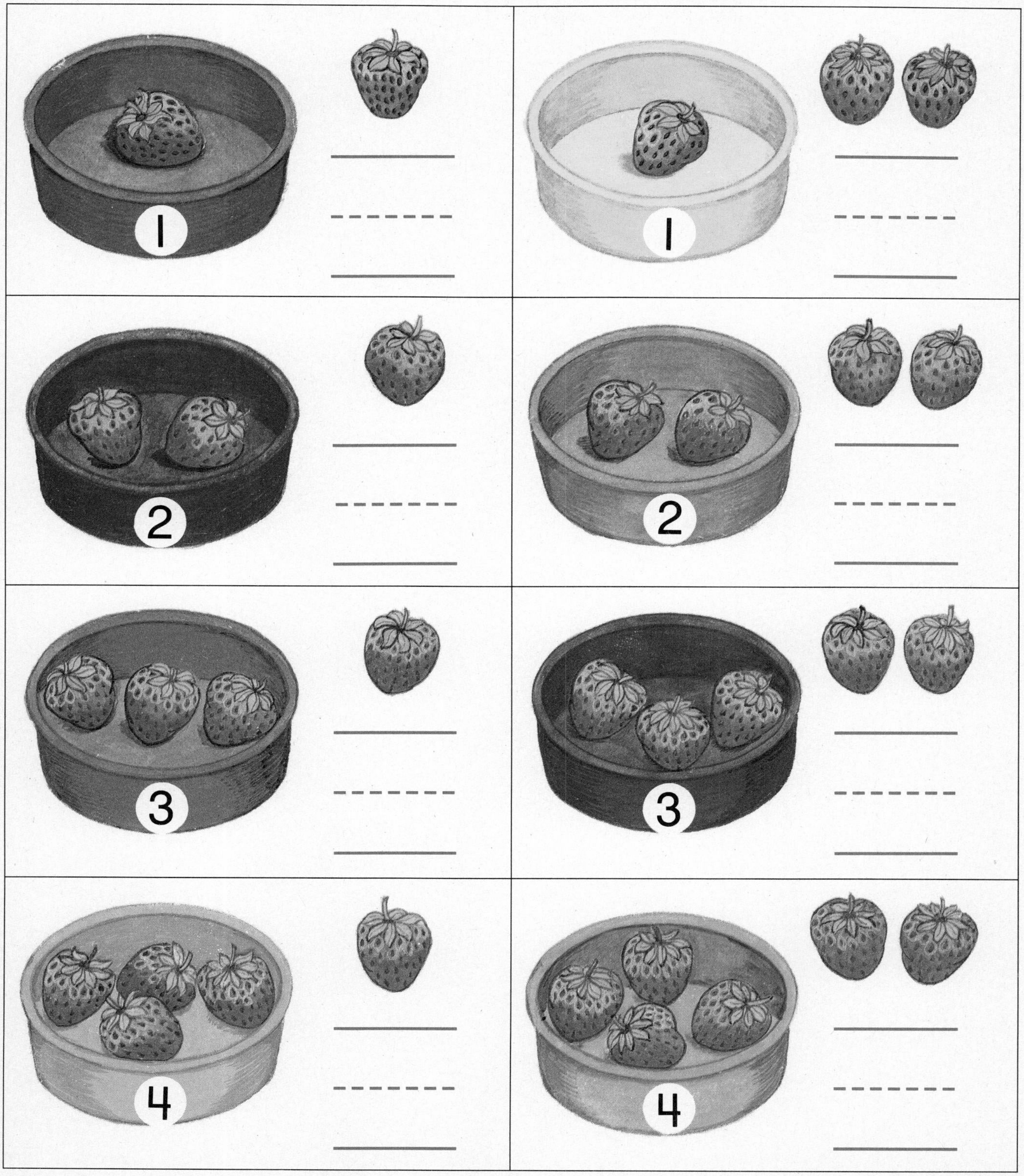

I can count on from a number.

Name ____________________

I can count on from a nickel.

____ ¢

____ ¢

____ ¢

____ ¢

____ ¢

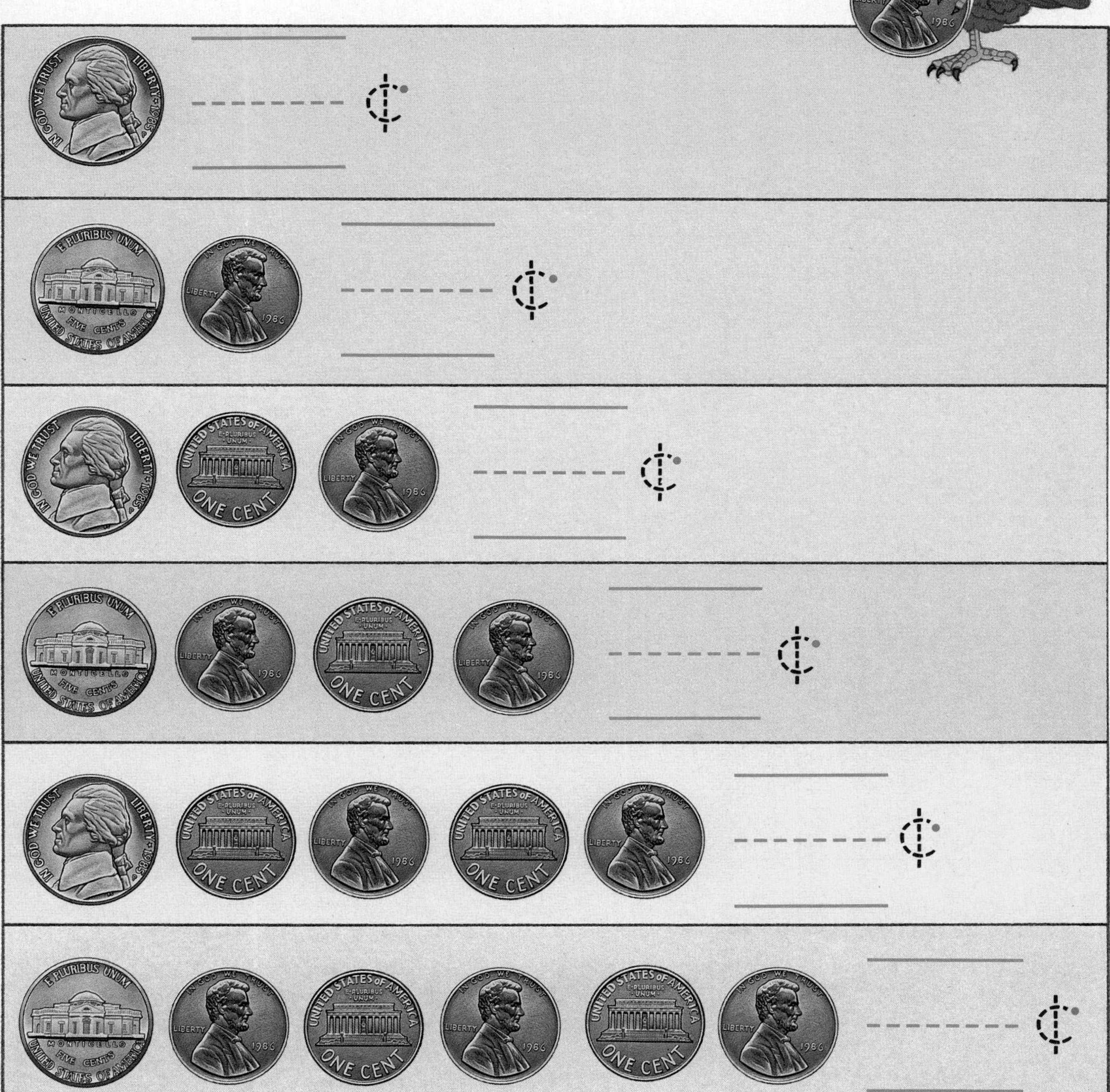

____ ¢

1	2	3	4	5	6	7	8	9	10
11	12	13	14	15	16	17	18	19	20

I can count on from a dime.

______ ¢

______ ¢

______ ¢

______ ¢

______ ¢

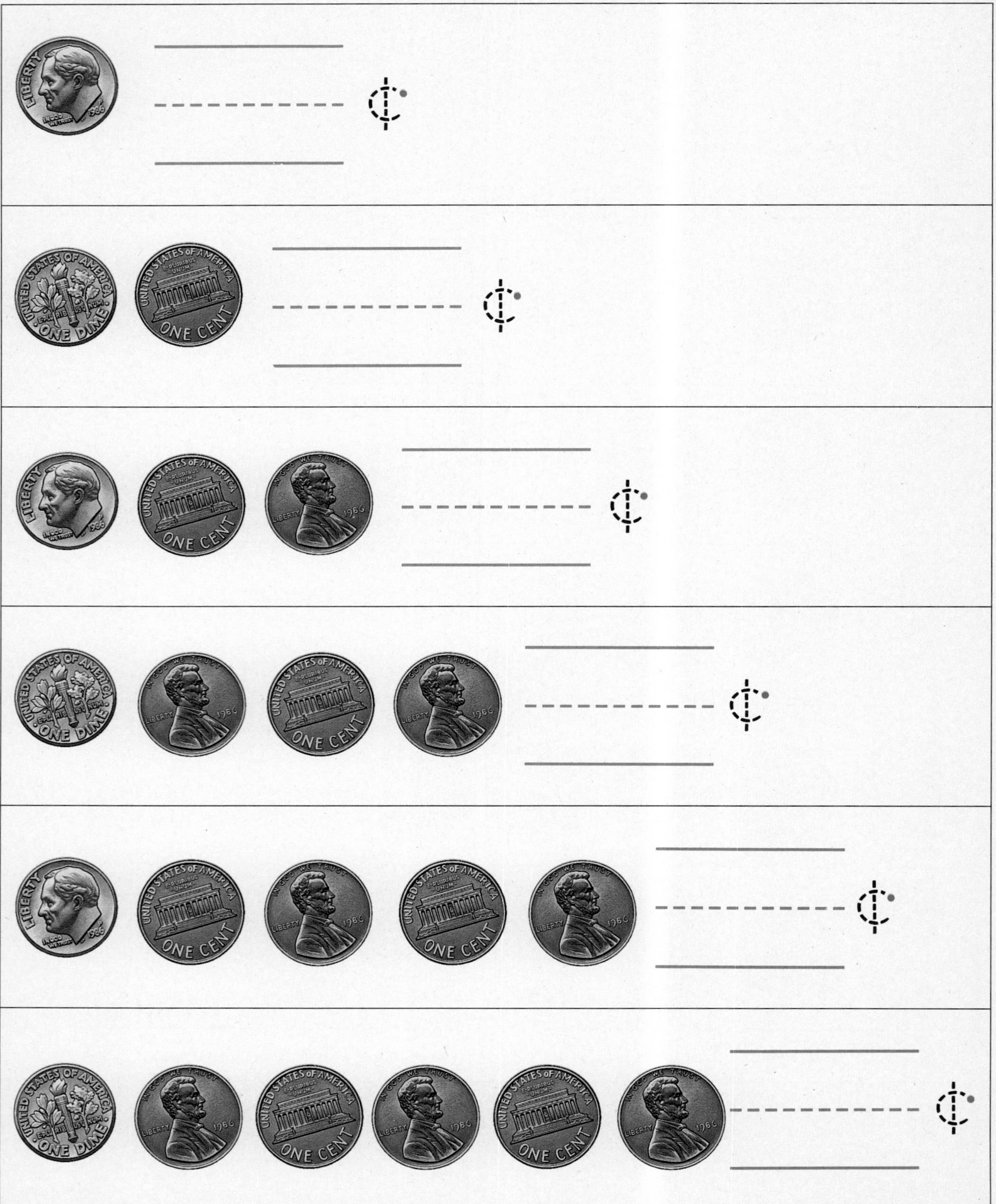

______ ¢

Name ______________________________

UNDERSTAND
FIND DATA
PLAN
ESTIMATE
SOLVE
CHECK

I can listen to a story.
I can tell how many there are.

the  story

☐ nuts

the  story

☐ birds

the  story

☐ fish

the  story

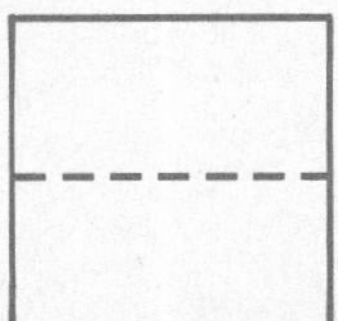

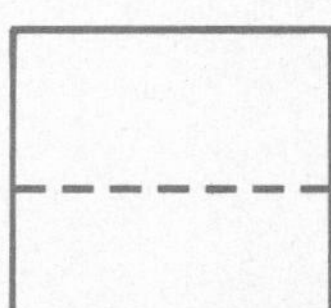

☐ rocks

I can listen for clues in a story.

UNDERSTAND
FIND DATA
PLAN
ESTIMATE
SOLVE
CHECK

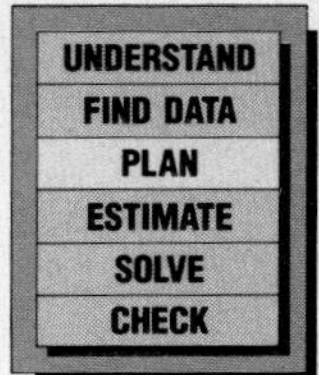

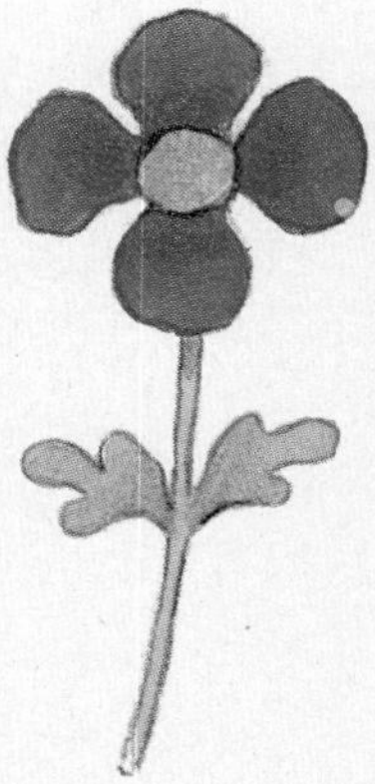

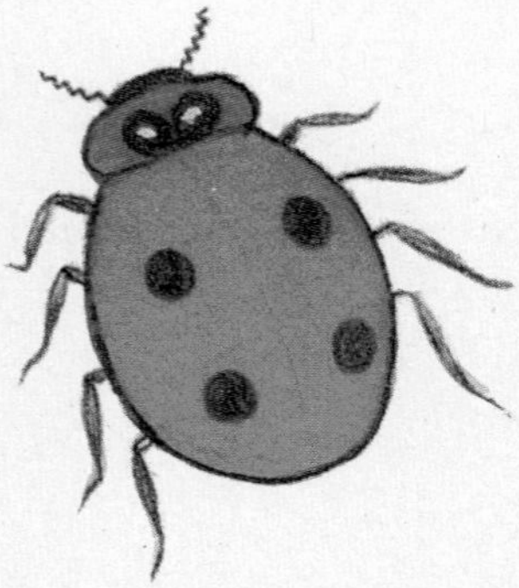
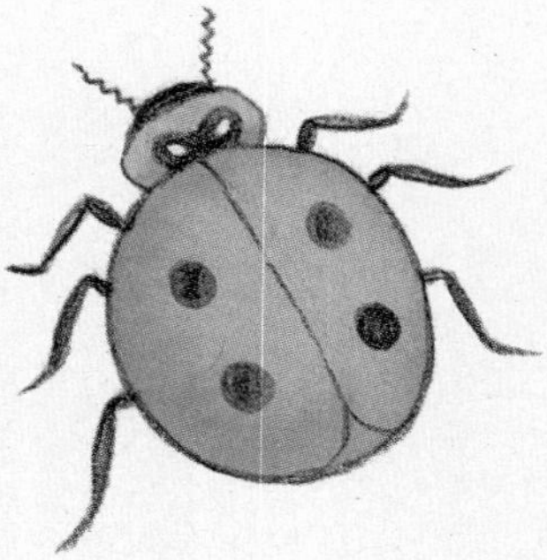
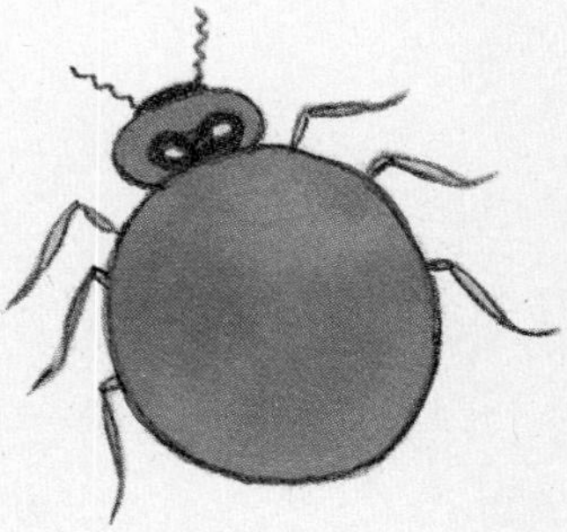

Name ______________________

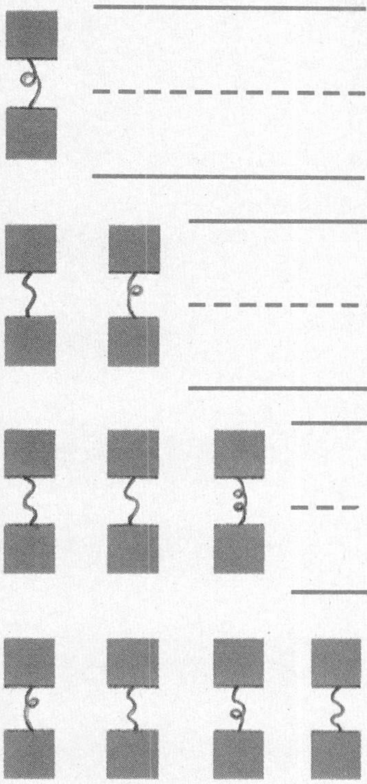

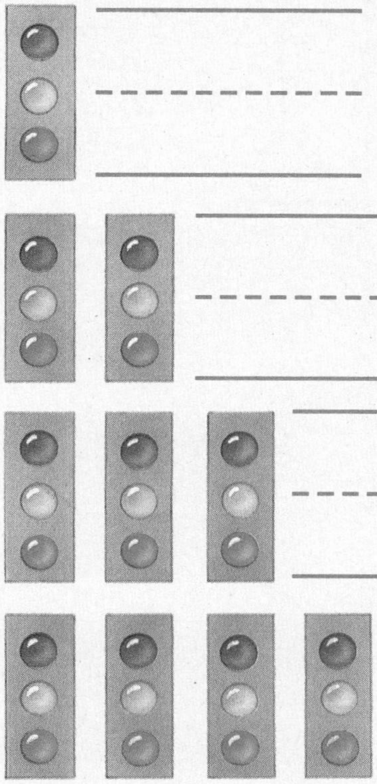

LIBERTY
IN GOD WE TRUST
E PLURIBUS UNUM
MONTICELLO
FIVE CENTS
UNITED STATES OF AMERICA

¢

3

LIBERTY
IN GOD WE TRUST
UNITED STATES OF AMERICA
E PLURIBUS UNUM
ONE CENT
UNITED STATES OF AMERICA
E PLURIBUS UNUM
ONE CENT

¢

Name ______________________________

I can find a pattern.

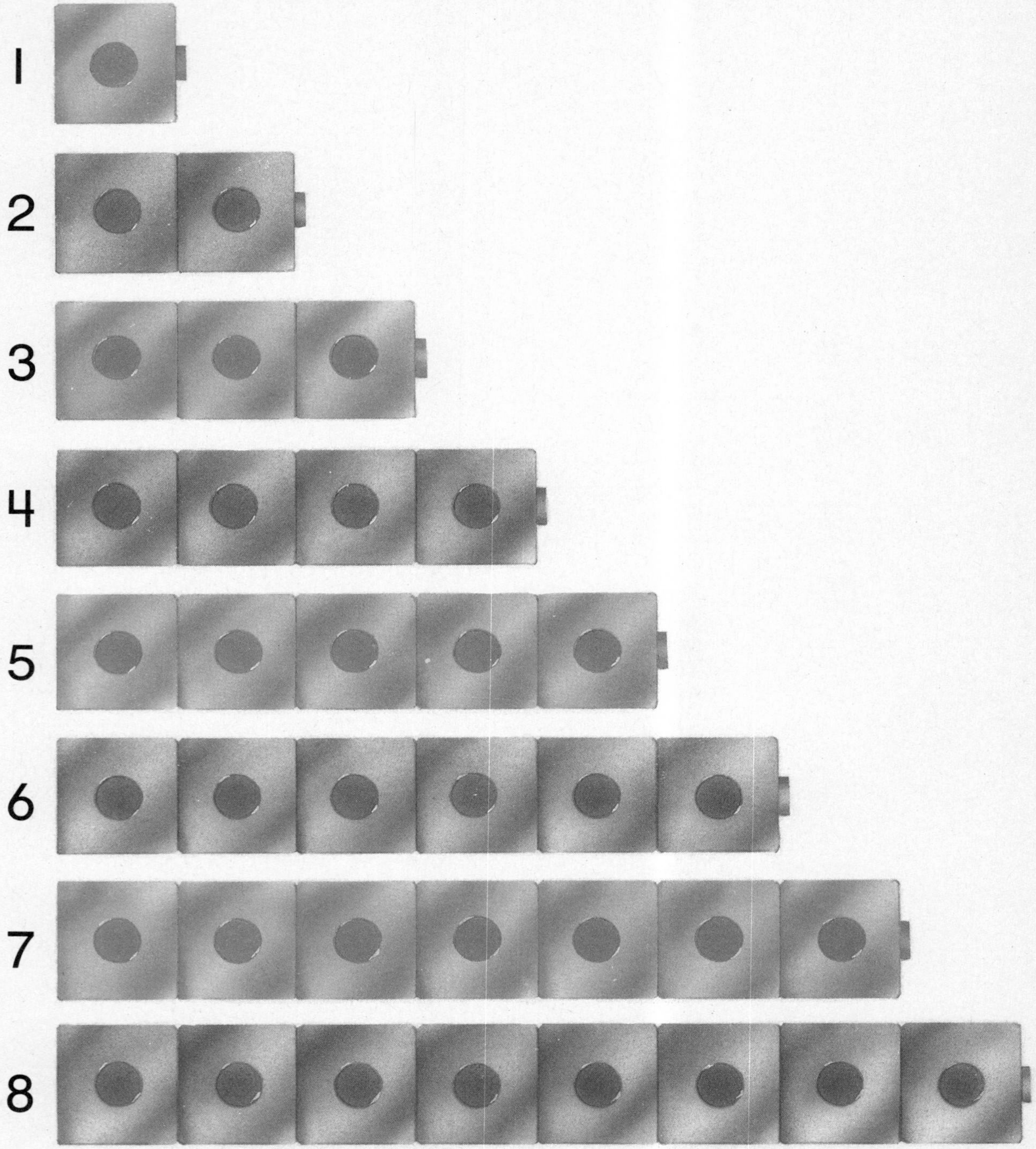

1	2	3	4	5	6	7	8	9	10
11	12	13	14	15	16	17	18	19	20

Name ______________________________

PERFORMANCE ASSESSMENT

I can find circles, squares, and triangles in solid shapes.

Directions:

Find an object that has a circle face. Put it on the circle. Repeat finding objects with squares and finally triangle faces.

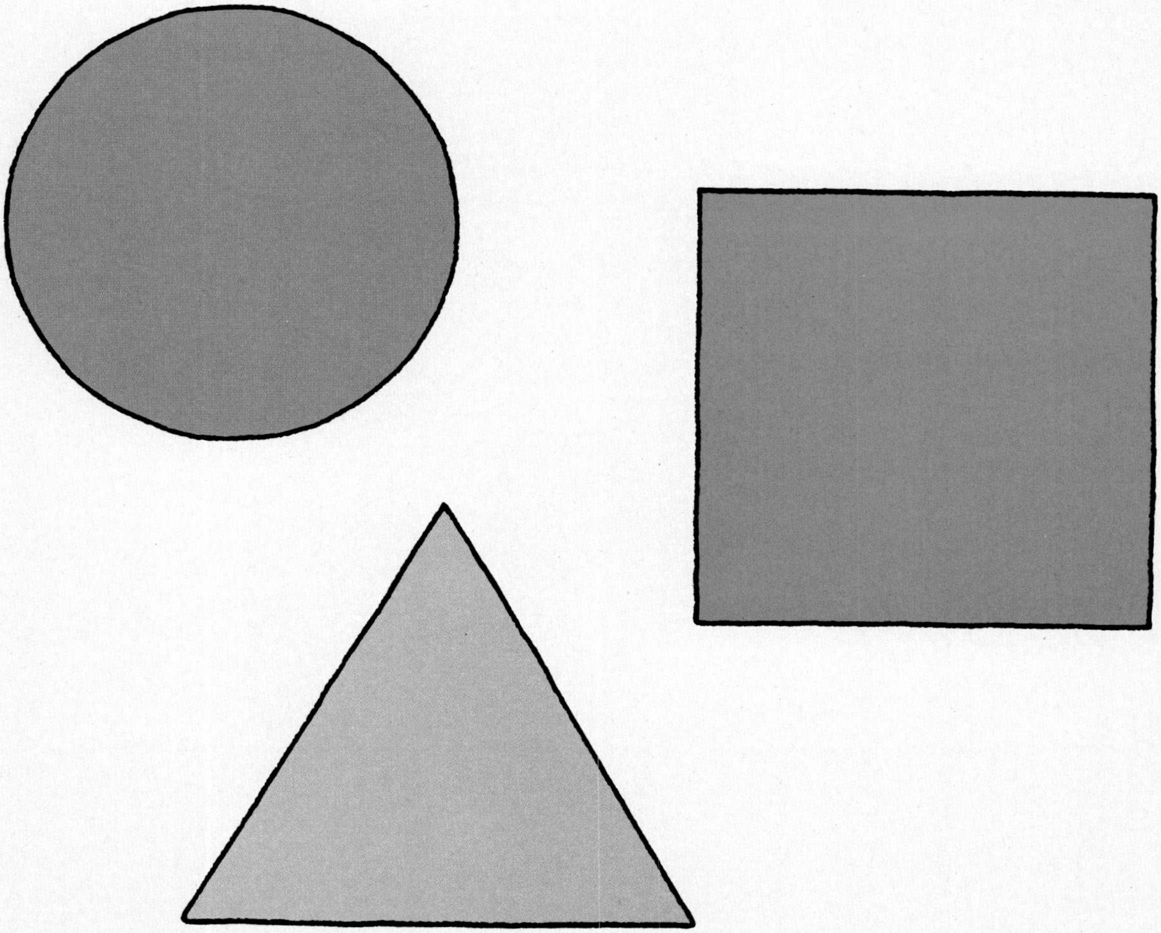

Name ____________________

Performance Assessment

Directions:
Put things shorter than the elf in the short box. Put things longer than the elf in the long box.

I can find things longer and shorter than the elf.

Name ______________________________

PERFORMANCE ASSESSMENT

I can make groups and write how many.

Directions:

Put some cubes on the page for the clown to juggle. Count and write how many. Do again with different numbers.

0 1 2 3 4

Name ______________________

Performance Assessment

I can make groups and write how many.

Directions:

(Teacher shows 5 or 6 fingers.) Use cubes as boxes. Count my fingers and put the same number of cubes on the truck. Do again with a different number.

0 1 2 3 4 5 6 7 8

Name ________________________________

Performance Assessment

I can make groups and write how many.

Directions:

(Teacher shows 5 or 6 fingers.) Use cubes as boxes. Count my fingers and put the same number of cubes in the picnic basket. Do again with a different number.

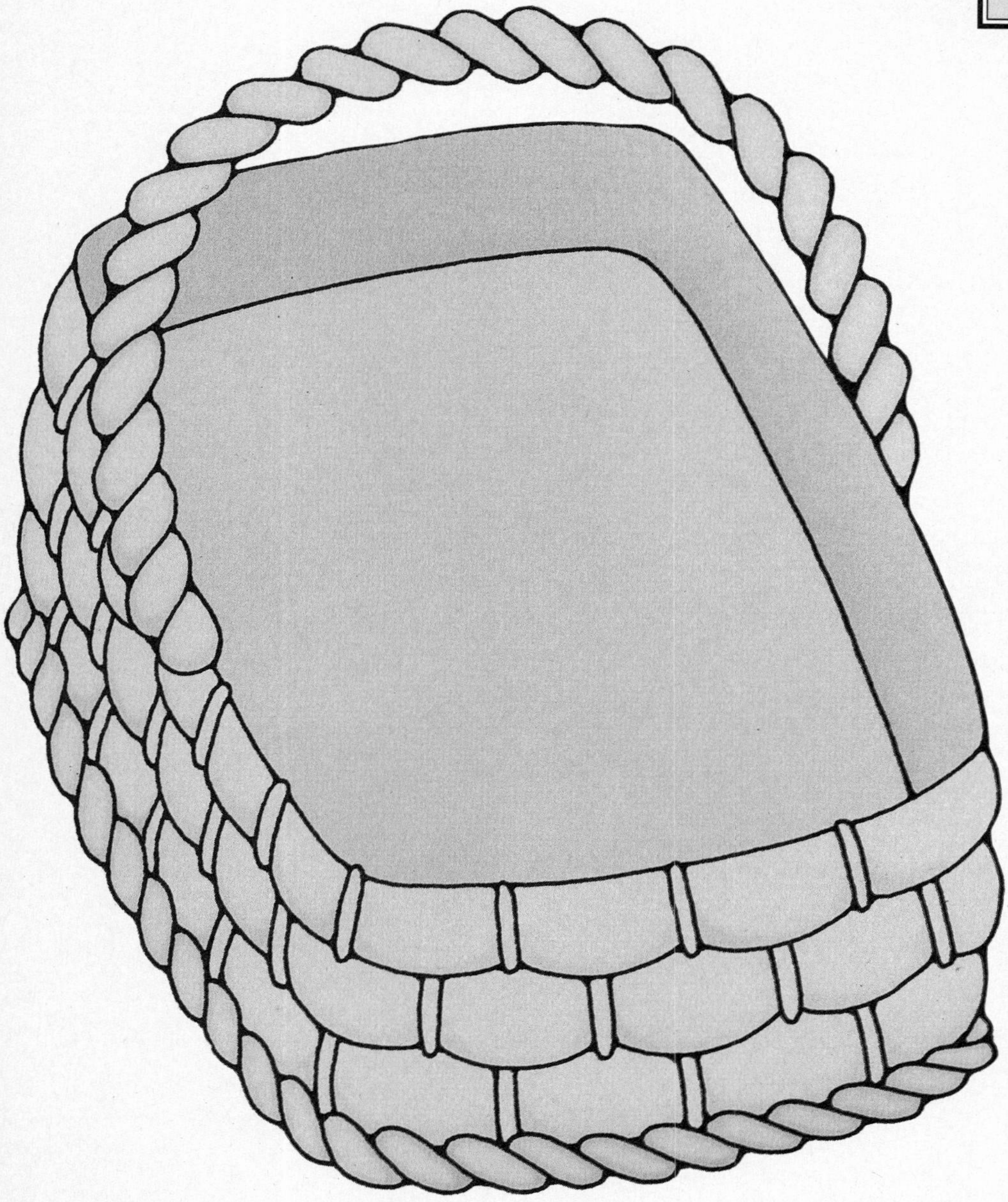

0 1 2 3 4 5 6 7 8 9 10 11 12

Name ______________________________

PERFORMANCE ASSESSMENT

Directions:

Find out how many cubes long these objects are.

I can measure things. I can tell how many cubes long they are.

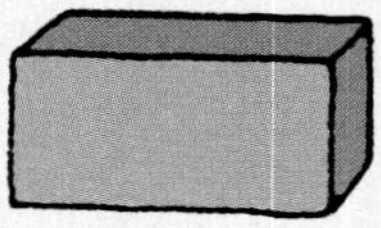

____

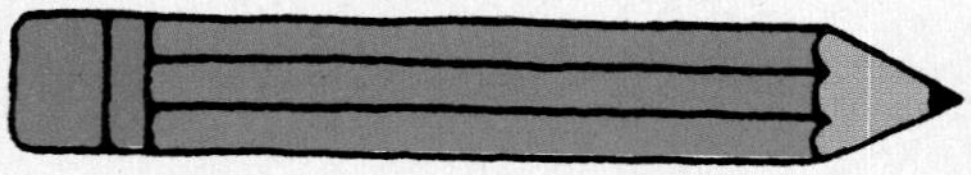

____

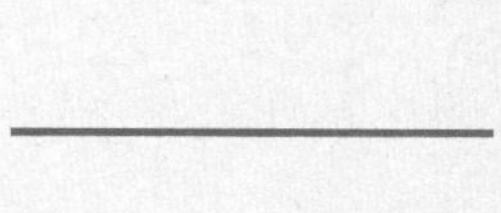

____

Name ____________________

Performance Assessment

I can show the action.
I can write how many in all.

Directions:
Use cubes as dog biscuits. Put in cubes to match the first number. Add more cubes to match the second number. Write how many in all.

3 + 1 = ______

2 + 2 = ______

4 + 3 = ______

1 + 5 = ______

Name ______________________________

PERFORMANCE ASSESSMENT

I can show the action.
I can write how many are left.

Directions:
Use cubes as ducks. Put cubes in to show the number to start. Then take away the number of cubes given. Write how many are left.

4 - 1 = ______

6 - 2 = ______

5 - 3 = ______

7 - 4 = ______

For use with Chapter 1

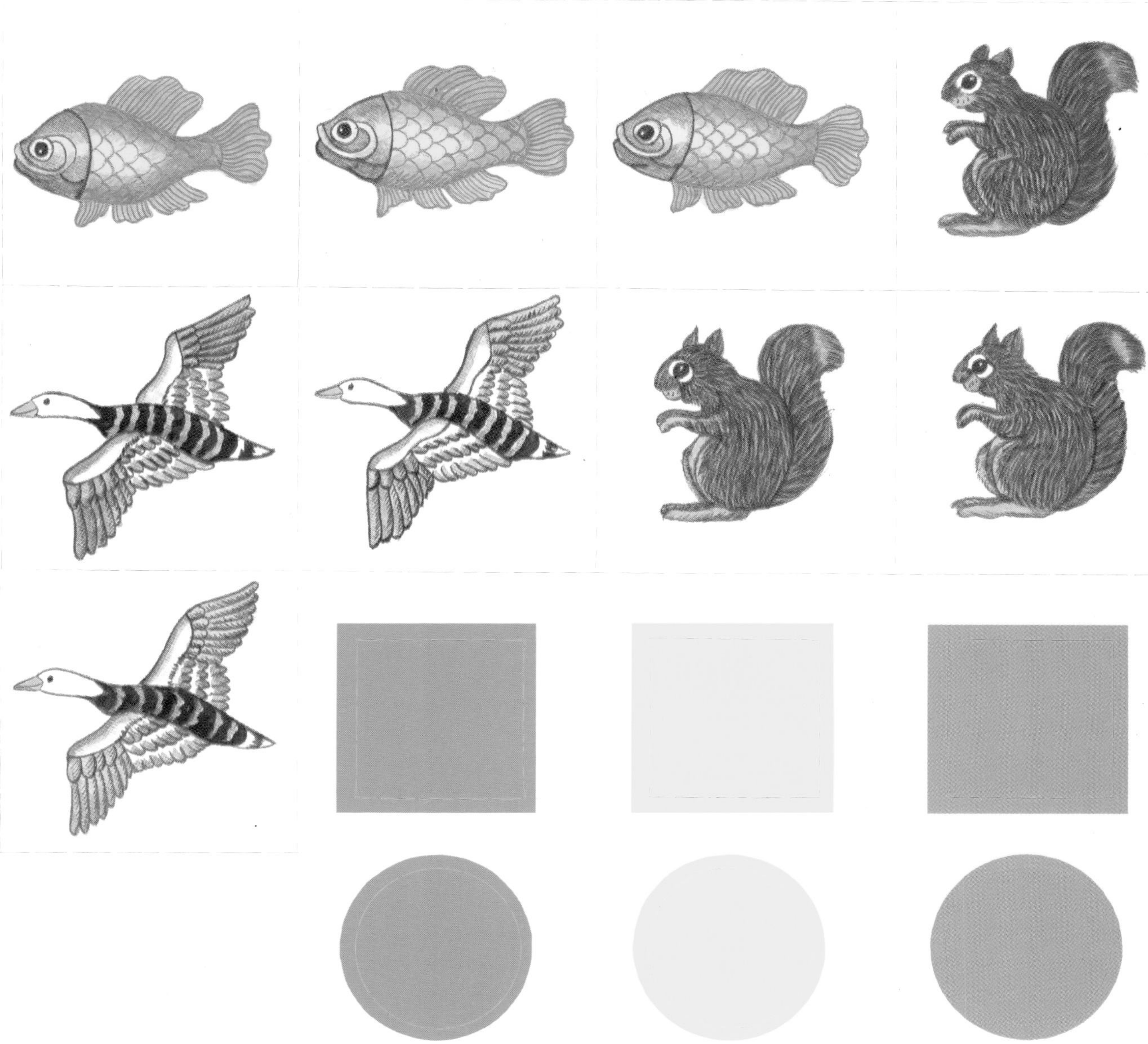

For use with Chapter 2 and Chapter 4

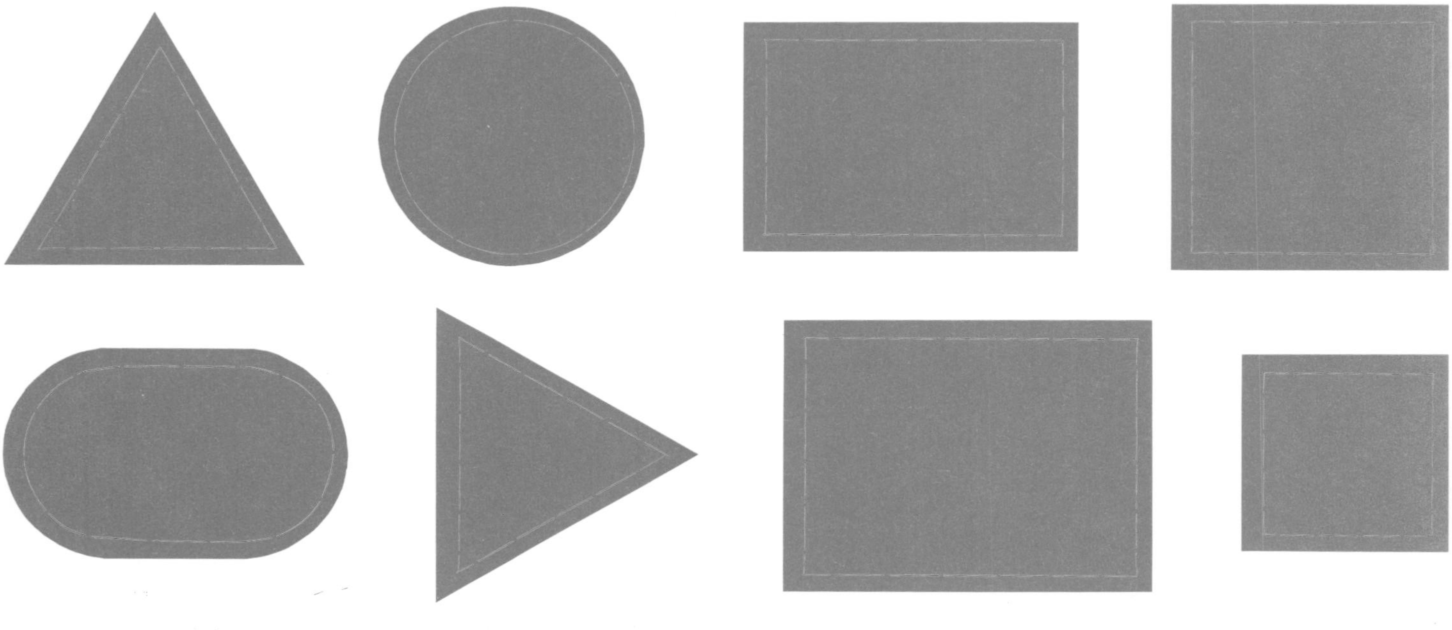

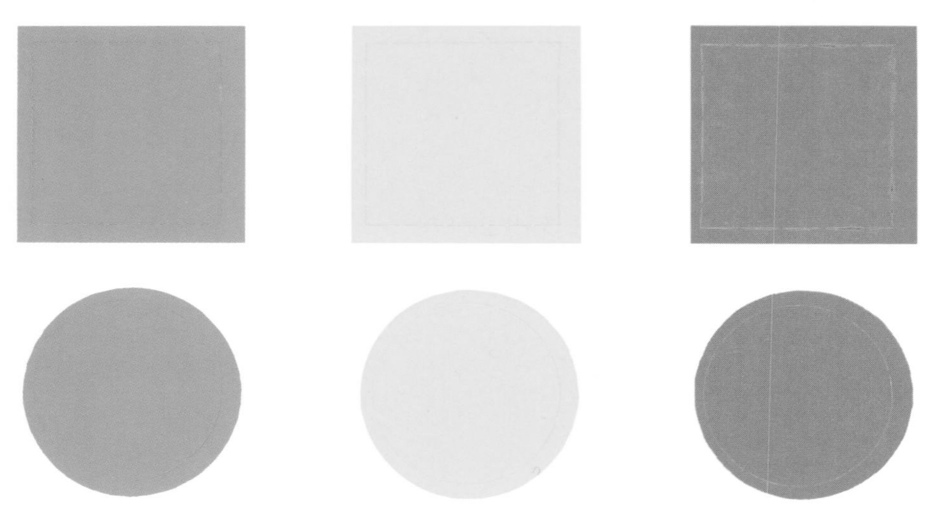

For use with Chapter 2 and throughout

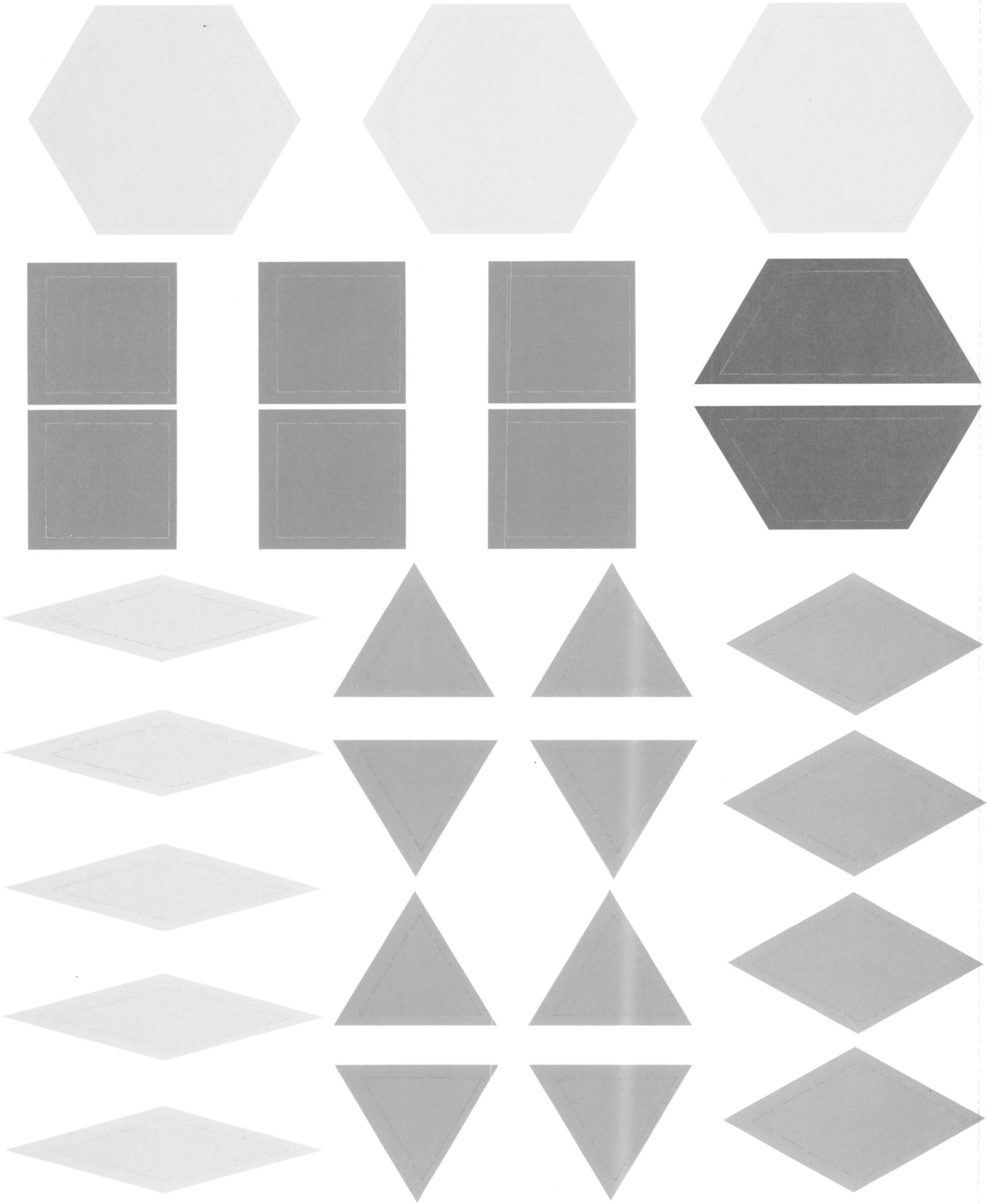

For use with Chapter 3

For use with Chapter 4

For use with Chapter 4

For use with Chapter 5

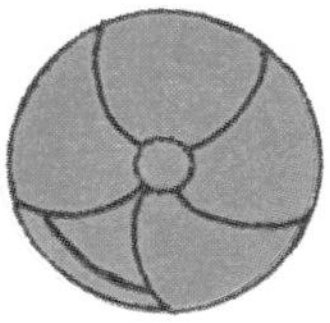
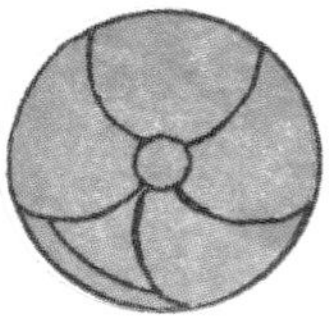
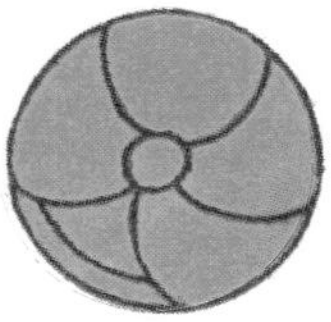
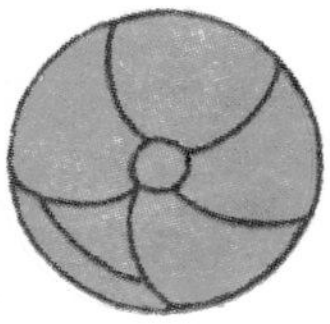
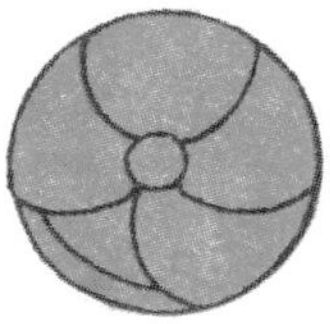
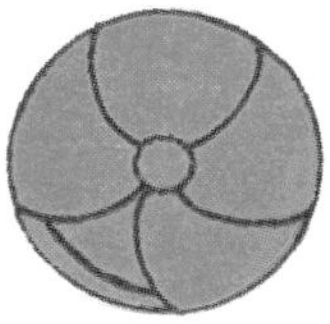
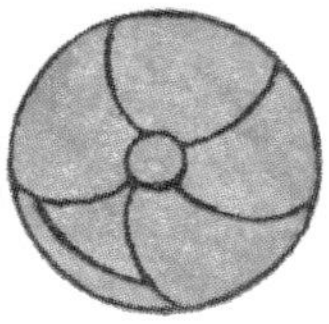

For use with Chapter 6

For use with Chapter 6

For use with Chapter 7

For use with Chapter 9

For use with Chapter 10

1¢ 2¢

1¢ 2¢

1¢ 2¢

1¢ 2¢

For use with Chapter 11

For use with Chapter 11

For use with Chapter 12

For use with Chapter 12

For use with Chapter 13

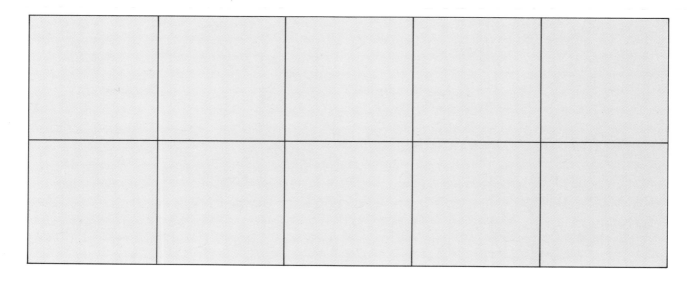

For use with Chapter 14

0	1	2
3	4	5
6	7	8
9	10	11
12	13	14

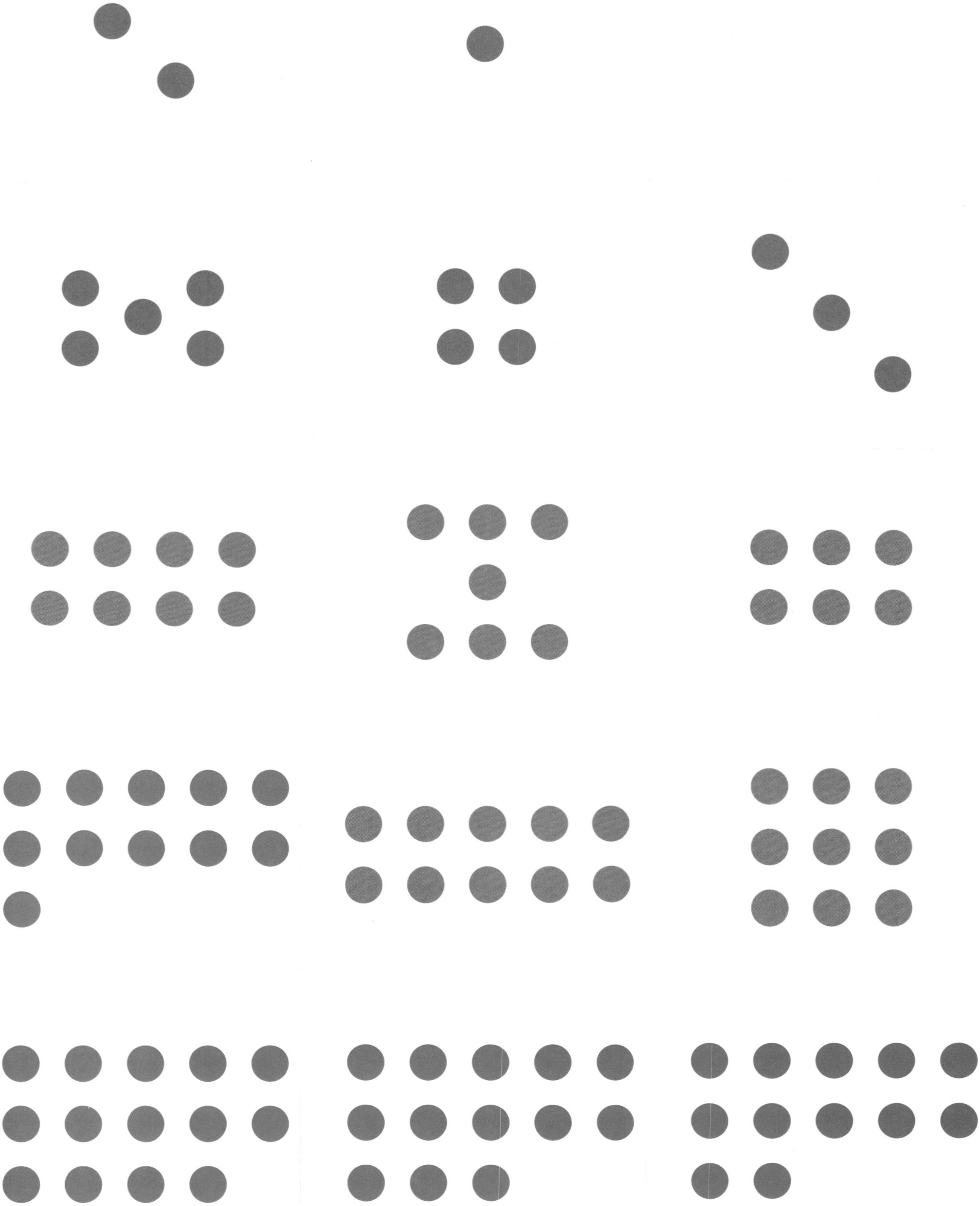

15 16 17

18 19 20

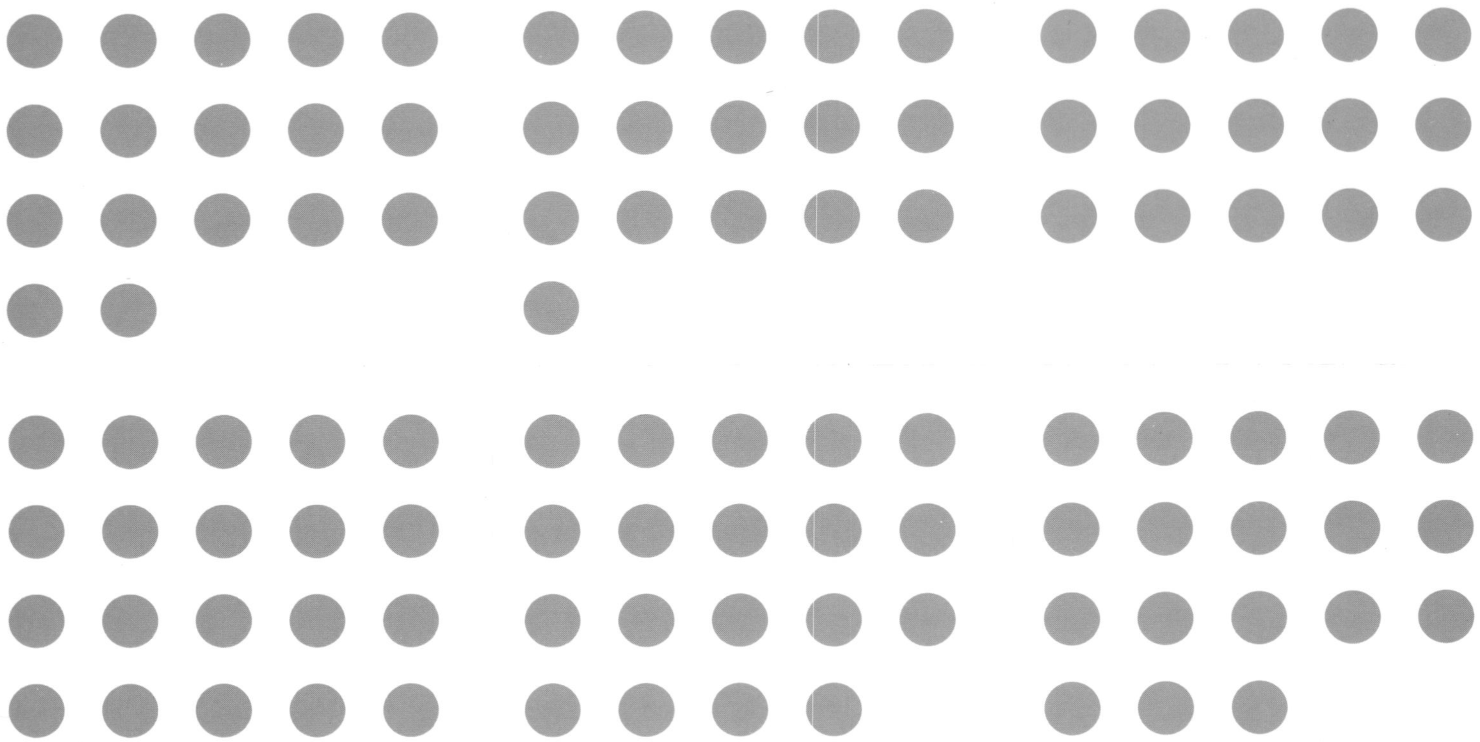

UNITED STATES OF AMERICA
ONE DIME
LIBERTY
ONE CENT
FIVE CENTS
MONTICELLO
QUARTER DOLLAR